HUMAN SERVICES for older adults: CONCEPTS & skills

Lifetime Series in Aging

Available now from Wadsworth:

Available now from Brooks/Cole:

Available now from Duxbury:

Forthcoming titles from Wadsworth:

HUMAN SERVICES for older adults: CONCEPTS & skills

ANITA S. HARBERT
West Virginia University

LEON H. GINSBERG
West Virginia University

Wadsworth Publishing Company
Belmont, California
A Division of Wadsworth, Inc.

Gerontology Editor: Stephen D. Rutter
Production Editor: Kathie Head
Designer: Cynthia Bassett
Copy Editor: Susan Weisberg
Technical Illustrator: Don Felich

The chapter opening photographs are from the following sources.

Chapter 1: © Marc Riboud/Magnum. Chapter 2: © Richard Kalvar/Magnum. Chapter 3: © Ken Heyman. Chapter 4: C. Huber/World Health Organization. Chapter 5: © Owen Franken/Stock, Boston. Chapter 6: E. Mundelmann/World Health Organization. Chapter 7: © Mimi Forsyth. Chapter 8: © Karen Preuss/Jeroboam. Chapter 9: © Mimi Forsyth. Chapter 10: © Ken Heyman. Chapter 11: © Gilles Peress/Magnum. Chapter 12: © Liane Enkelis/Jeroboam. Chapter 13: © James Motlow/Jeroboam. Chapter 14: Interphoto/World Health Organization.

Printed in the United States of America

2 3 4 5 6 7 8 9 10   83 82 81 80

Library of Congress Cataloging in Publication Data

Harbert, Anita S   1937–
    Human services for older adults.

    Bibliography: p.
    Includes index.
    1. Social work with the aged—United States.
2. Aging.   3. Old age.   I. Ginsberg, Leon H., joint
author.   II. Title.
HV1461.H36   362.6'0973   78-13958
ISBN 0-534-00607-8

To our children,
Robert, Michael, and Meryl Sue Ginsberg
and Roberta Harbert.

CONTENTS

pREfACE

This book was written to provide educators and human-service workers with a text that deals with the fundamental principles of working with older adults. In the past few years the market has been flooded with textbooks on gerontology. However, few of these texts address themselves to how one can successfully provide services to older adults. Our book focuses on methods for helping older people directly through services such as outreach; individual, group, and family counseling; and aid to the chronically and terminally ill aged. It also reviews how older adults can be helped indirectly through program planning and development and advocacy. As social workers who have worked with older people and conducted numerous continuing education workshops for others working with the elderly, we have attempted to put our experiences and knowledge into a text that should have broad applications in the field of aging.

Two types of information, theoretical and practical, are available in the book. There is a growing knowledge base in gerontology that stems from a limited amount of research and study conducted on the later phase of life called old age. Moreover, awareness of the broad range of problems that confront people as they move into this phase of life is growing, too. We strongly believe that this knowledge base should be the starting point for all those who plan to work with older people.

The text also covers various services workers are asked to make available to older people. These are presented from a "how-to" perspective, including discussions on the specific steps necessary. We emphasize how older people themselves can learn to resolve their own difficulties.

The book is divided into four parts. Part One considers the implication of growing old in our modern society. It covers the development of aging as a social problem in this country; the physical, psychological, and social aspects of the aging process; and the problems experienced by old people as they move into the last phase of life. This part of the book also includes a discussion of the special problems of minority and ethnic elderly.

Part Two addresses the provision of direct services to older adults. The various methods and techniques of helping through outreach, individual and group counseling, working with the families of older people, and the problems of chronically and terminally ill older people are reviewed.

Part Three focuses on planning and development of programs to meet the needs of older adults. On the whole, more programs are needed to aid older people. This section provides some guidance on the character these programs should take and suggestions for support services and advocacy.

Part Four deals with the various resources available to deal with the problems of older adults, giving case examples of how these resources are used to resolve individual and group problems.

Each chapter in the book contains readings that further illustrate the implications of the material discussed. Study questions following the readings will assist the instructor in stimulating students' thinking about working with older people.

We believe this text will be of use to college instructors in a variety of helping professions. It will also be useful for agency staff development purposes.

We would like to take this opportunity to thank all those who assisted us in the writing of this book: Vivian Wood, University of Wisconsin; Eugene Dawson, Syracuse University; Graham D. Rowles, West Virginia University; Jacqueline Ridley, Riverside City College; Judith Altholz, Florida State University; Greta Singer, Monmouth College; Don Miller, University of Pittsburgh; and Jacqueline Driver, James Madison University, reviewed early drafts of the book. Judy Starr and Joyce Lehrer, social work graduate students at West Virginia University, were responsible for preparation of the readings used in the book, and Vilma Peary and Viola Smith typed the manuscript. Finally, we are indebted to our families, especially Elaine Ginsberg, Dr. Ginsberg's wife, who is Chairwoman of the English Department at West Virginia University.

Anita S. Harbert
Morgantown, West Virginia

Leon H. Ginsberg
Morgantown, West Virginia

HUMAN SERVICES
for
older adults:
CONCEPTS
& skills

PART ONE

THE ELDERLY
IN CONTEMPORARY
AMERICAN SOCIETY

*In Part One we discuss what it means to grow old in the United States. The many people reaching old age today constitute a social problem in our society. A **social problem** is defined as a situation affecting a large number of people that they or others believe to be a source of difficulty or unhappiness (Atchley, 1975). Some gerontologists believe old age should not be classified as a social problem, but for older adults movement into old age is not generally viewed as a joyous occasion, and individuals or groups certainly experience difficulties when they reach this stage of life.*

How old people have come to be identified as a social problem is discussed in this part of the book. In addition, through a general overview of the aging process and its varying physical, social, and psychological characteristics, we review the adaptive capacities available to older adults for coping with the difficulties that confront them in later life. The various problems experienced by old people are reviewed in three broad categories: economic, physical and mental health, and leisure time. Finally, attention is given to the plight of specific subgroups, such as minority, ethnic, women, and rural elderly, who experience specific problems when they reach old age.

CHAPTER 1
THE IMPACT OF AGING ON SOCIETY AND THE INDIVIDUAL

At the turn of the century people 65 and older composed only 1.2 percent of the total U.S. population; today they are the fastest growing age group in the country. Government documents indicate that between 1900 and 1974 the percentage of people aged 65 and over in the United States more than doubled, going from 4.1 percent in 1900 to 10.3 percent in 1974 (*Facts about Older Americans*, 1975). Their number increased about seven times, from 3 million to 22 million. The same documents predict that by the year 2000 older people will represent approximately 11.7 percent of a national population of about 262 million, and their numbers will have reached approximately 31 million (see Figure 1.1).

The increased number of older people in the United States represents a paradox. On the one hand, improvement in health care and the quality of life have made it possible for people to live longer. On the other hand, for many older people survival into old age is not a blessing, as many suffer from poverty, isolation, and unproductivity, and for society their large number has become a problem, as we have not created channels for productive use of leisure time and means for old people to successfully meet their own needs. On the whole, our society is ill prepared to cope with the increasing number of older people.

Increased services and programs have been created because older people have become more visible to society as a whole. To work successfully with older people, it is important to understand their social status today in relation to changes that have occurred in this century. In addition, it is important to understand the aging process and the strengths and weaknesses of people in the later phase of life in coping with their status and problems. In this chapter we will examine the factors that have

caused old age to emerge as a social problem and the effects of the aging process on the individual.

Changing Population Patterns
in the United States

The increase of the elderly in the population can be attributed to several factors, the most important being a dramatic increase in **life expectancy** in this century (Atchley, 1977). This change does not mean that the average human life span has increased dramatically; we have not substantially increased longevity, that is, the total number of *years* we can expect to survive, so much as the total number of *individuals* who live to old age (see Table 1.1). For example, people born between 1929 and 1931 who reach age 65 can expect to live about 12 additional years; those born in 1971 can expect to live an additional 15 years beyond 65. The increase in longevity is only about 3 years in a 40-year period.

We can see a more dramatic increase, however, when we look at the growing number of older individuals in the population over the last century. Modern technology and improved health care have decreased the risks of pregnancy and childbirth and reduced deaths among infants and young adults. As a result more individuals survive infancy and young adulthood and live to reach old age. In 1900, for example, the life expectancy for an infant was approximately 48 years; a child born today can expect to live approximately 71 years. Thus in this century we have increased life expectancy at birth by approximately 24 years.

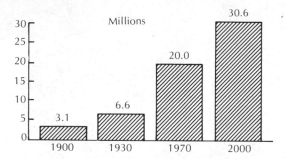

The Older Population in the Twentieth Century

Figure 1.1   Growth of the Older Population in the Twentieth Century. (Source: *Facts about Older Americans*, 1975)

Although the increase in life expectancy was dramatic, such a marked rate of increase has not continued into the 1970s. Between 1959 and 1971, for example, an infant's life expectancy increased only two years, as compared to an increase of 10 years between 1929 and 1959 (see Table 1.1). However, scientific advances in contraceptive measures and social concerns over population growth have caused a decrease in the birthrate in the United States over the 1960s and 1970s. The resulting decline in the growth of the younger segment of the population means that in the future older people will make up a larger part of the population. Although this growth

Table 1.1   Life Expectancy in the United States 1930-1976

| Year | Estimated Average Number of Years of Life Remaining (both sexes) | | |
	At Birth	At 45	At 65
1900– 1902	48.2		11.9
1929– 1931	59.2	25.8	12.2
1959– 1961	69.9	29.5	14.4
1967	70.5	29.9	14.8
1969 male	66.8 }70.4	27.1 }29.9	13.0 }14.8
female	74.3	32.9	16.5
1971 male	67.4 }71.0	27.4 }30.3	13.2 }15.3
female	74.8	33.2	16.9
1972 male	67.4 }71.2		13.1 }15.3
female	75.2		17.2
1973 male	67.6 }71.5		
female	75.3		
1974 male	68.2 }71.9		13.4 }15.6
female	75.9		17.5
1975 male	68.7 }72.5		13.7 }16.0
female	76.5		18.0
1976 male	69.0 }72.8	28.4 }31.5	13.7 }16.0
female	76.7	35.5	18.0

Source: Ruth B. Weg, *Who, What of Aging.* Reprinted by permission.

will not be as dramatic in the latter half of this century as it was in the first half, we can expect older people as a group to become an increasing concern of the society.

Perhaps the most clearcut issue raised by the change in the **demographic** makeup of this country is an economic one: How will the nation bear the cost of caring for so many older people? In a sense, the number of people each productive worker has to support won't have changed much, since the number of children is destined to shrink, but the elderly are considerably more expensive to maintain, living mainly in households of their own, having high medical costs, and needing more services. Maintaining a population made up largely of older adults requires more services on the whole and a new supply of labor to provide those services. We are just now beginning to make efforts to prepare those who will deliver the services.

The Changing American Lifestyle

The rapid industrialization of the past century and its impact on family life have also had major effects on the lives of older adults. As our nation shifted from an agrarian to an industrial society, the American family changed considerably. In our early agrarian economy every family member was needed to produce the essential goods for life. Fathers, mothers, sons, daughters, grandparents, and sometimes aunts and uncles all worked together tilling, planting, hoeing, harvesting, weaving, cooking, and putting up preserves to support the family as an economic unit. Thus the extended family was important to survival, and elderly people tended to live out their years cared for by their families and contributing to the family group.

With industrialization and the mass production of goods came a gradual change from the extended to the nuclear family. Rapid urbanization opened up many new jobs in the cities, and many young people migrated from rural areas in search of good pay and a higher standard of living than they had known on the farm. At the same time there was a great influx of immigrants from central and southern Europe into American cities, further swelling the urban population. As families grew and the cost of land increased, it became more difficult to support all members of the family on the farm. As younger people found jobs and became established in the cities, other family members followed, until eventually only parents and grandparents remained behind. Extended families began to split up into smaller units, and older people no longer had their original family roles. Today a disproportionately high number of elderly live in rural areas.

The urban elderly were experiencing a different kind of problem created by immigration. Because of inadequate housing in the early part of the century, two- or three-generation urban families, especially immigrant families, usually shared a single dwelling. The cities developed, and as younger members of immigrant urban families became more affluent, they followed industry and the housing industry to single-family units in the suburbs. Again the elderly family members were left behind, this time in the deteriorating inner-city neighborhoods. In both shifts—from country to city and from city to suburbs—a precedent was set for older family members to maintain separate households and to function as economically independent units.

The problem created by the shift from the extended to the nuclear family is that although older people are expected to be independent economic units, in reality this is an impossibility. Too frequently independent older people are unable to live alone because of failing health or the problems of isolation, immobility, and poverty. Consequently, if the elderly are to survive, society must provide services or programs to subsidize them as an independent economic unit.

Establishing Economic Independence for Older Adults

Prior to the turn of the century, the ability of older people to maintain economic independence was relatively unimportant, since few people survived into old age, and those who did played a significant part in the economic survival of the entire family. Today neither situation is true. We no longer consider it the responsibility of the family to maintain its elder parents, grandparents, aunts, and uncles. We now think it desirable for the elderly to maintain their economic independence both for the good of the society and the good of the individuals themselves.

As our values and customs now stand, however, the means to this end are blocked. In our industrial society we aim at keeping everyone employed while maintaining a stable wage structure in which everyone can make enough money to live on. In recent times we have stabilized wage structures by reducing the number in the work force (i.e., supply of labor) and redefining what we mean by *employable*. In effect, we have kept two groups out of the labor market: the young and the old. The young are kept out by increasing the number of years of prework education required; the old are removed through mandatory retirement.

Once workers reach retirement age and leave the work force, it is virtually impossible for them to reenter; few employers want to hire older workers. Retired people generally have income from Social Security and private pensions. Increasingly, these sources of income are too small to meet the elderly's needs, however, and older people are stuck in the middle: The income they have is insufficient, yet they are blocked from obtaining additional income. Because of this double bind elderly people are increasing their demand on society to help them meet their needs. Their economic welfare has now become a social problem for which we have not yet developed solutions. Nor have we developed ways that older adults can enjoy their nonproductive years in our society, although by removing older people from the work force, we have created the problem for them of finding satisfactory uses of their leisure time.

We can see from the above discussion that, as it now stands, older people present very demanding problems for the country as a whole. We are trying to find ways of dealing with this group, but to date we have not been successful. One of the reasons we are not successful is that we do not understand old age as a process or as a phase of life. If we are to successfully serve older people, we must have a clear understanding of what it means to grow old: What are the social, physical, and psychological implications of the aging process? How do these factors affect the behavior of older people as they relate to the constantly changing environment? In the next part of this chapter we will examine the aging process and highlight its significance for those working with aging individuals.

What It Means to Grow Old

Aging is difficult to define. We generally associate increasing age with physical changes, such as graying hair, wrinkles, a bent back, a slow gait, and perhaps absentmindedness. These changes certainly occur, but they represent only a part of a complex process marked by physical, psychological, and social effects. Although we can discuss these three aspects of aging separately, they all interact and influence one another throughout the aging process. Similarly, although we can generalize about older people for the purpose of our discussion, keep in mind that the processes we discuss are characteristic of *most* older people but may not be true of specific individuals. One person may age faster than another physically or psychologically.

Physical Aging and
Uneven Decline

We don't yet know when the aging process actually begins and what factors contribute to or control it. We know more about what creates life than we do about what causes it to cease. Researchers believe that **physical aging** begins when we reach middle age, since the physical changes that occur with advancing years are increasingly noticeable at this stage of life. Recently, however, researchers have begun to redefine aging as a continuing process that begins with conception and is distinct from chronological age.

One theory of physical aging suggests that changes in the body's retention of fluid and production of energy are the keys to physical changes (Calloway, 1974). Proponents of this theory point out that at conception the percentage of water found in the human fetus and the amount of heat produced are much greater than those found in later stages of life (see Figure 1.2). As we grow older, our bodies progressively retain less water and generate less heat. The theory suggests that the faster we lose fluid and body heat, the faster we age.

There are various other theories of aging. The "wear and tear" theory, based on a mechanical analogy (Atchley, 1977), sees the body as a machine; eventually its parts wear out and the machine breaks down. The "waste product" theory gives accumu-

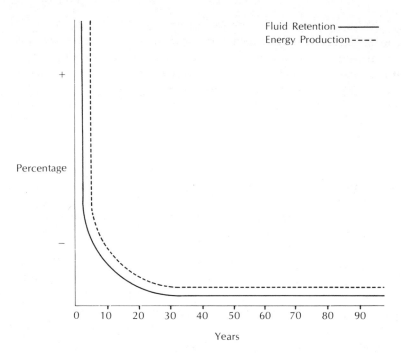

Figure 1.2   Age, Fluid Retention, and Energy Production. (Source: Nathaniel Calloway, Symposia II, Washington, D.C. Reprinted by permission of the American Geriatric Society, Inc., and the author.)

lated waste products in the body a key role in the process of physiological aging. So far, however, we have no conclusive explanation for physical aging.

Although we do not understand why physical aging occurs, we do know that all parts of the body do not age at the same rate. In those parts of the body where cells are regenerated, for example, skin and stomach lining, the aging process is slower than in those parts of the body in which the cells are not regenerated, for example, the nervous system and muscle. We assume that the wrinkled skin of old age is due to the aging of the skin, but, in fact, the skin ages at a slower rate than other parts of the body. Wrinkling of the skin is due to the degeneration of the muscular system that supports the skin.

The pattern of physical aging is a linear decline that begins at about age 30 and continues throughout the life span. Figure 1.3 shows that certain body functions, including metabolic rate, percentage of body water, cardiac output, and breathing capacity, reach their peak at age 30 and decline from there on. Muscle tone and strength seem to peak between 20 and 30 years of age and then decrease. This fact is exemplified by the professional athletes who are at the peak of their careers in their mid-20s and are seen as has-beens in their late 30s. All of the senses (vision, smell, hearing, taste, and touch) decrease in function with time. Hearing loss, for example,

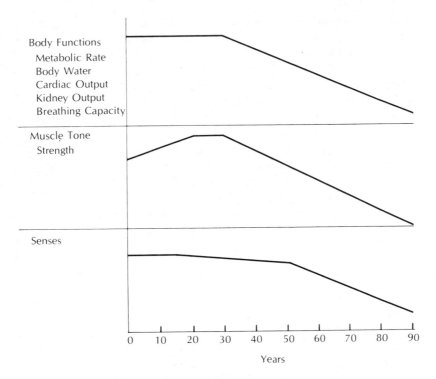

Figure 1.3   Rate of Physical Changes with Age.

begins in adolescence, but there are significant losses between the ages of 40 and 50. What these facts tell us is that the physical characteristics of aging involve a gradual process beginning earlier than most people assume. Various body functions have their own characteristic pattern of change.

When we look at total body function over time, the speed of return to normal levels of functioning generally decreases after exposure to stress, such as extensive exercise or extreme fear. Blood sugar, pH factor, blood volume, perhaps even heart rate and blood pressure, of young and old subjects at rest may be quite close. This could lead to the assumption that homeostatic equilibria are not modified with age. However, significant differences in body functions are revealed during stress. For the older person the magnitude of displacement is greater, and the rate of recovery is slower. When reactions to stress are measured, for example by oxygen consumption, we find a decrease in the maximum breathing capacity and a decrease in the residual lung volume. In addition, a decrease in vital capacity, such as blood pressure and heart rates, is revealed in older adults under stress.

Although the body changes, we should emphasize that aging is not a disease (Weg, 1974): People do not die of old age. Death occurs because, over time, the body becomes more vulnerable to outside assault, less adaptable to the environment, and more subject to stress and crisis. Scientists predict that the major diseases affecting the aged will no doubt be significantly reduced if not eliminated by the beginning of the twenty-first century as a result of current medical and technical revolutions. With improved sanitation, nutrition, and antibiotic therapy, morbidity and mortality from infectious disease will be virtually eliminated from our society.

The knowledge we gain about the physical aspect of aging that is most significant for those working with older people is the fact that the physical deterioration that occurs with age is not an irreversible process. Research studies support the belief that some body functions can be restored with proper treatment or care. Muscle strength and muscle tone can be regained with an exercise regime of six to eight weeks for 60- to 90-year-old men. It is also possible to reverse some confusion, fatigue, irritability, and insomnia with changes in diet. Treatment in the form of correcting vitamin and protein deficiency and hormone balance and tender loving care will reverse many conditions of physical aging that were once thought to be irreversible.

Psychological Implications
of Old Age

The psychological characteristics of the aging process can be viewed in the context of the life cycle (Birren, 1974). Individuals pass through various phases in life: infancy, childhood, adolescence, adulthood, middle age, and old age. We generally attach approximate years to these phases, but chronological age is only a clue to where one stands in relation to the phases of life. There are experiences characteristic of each phase of development; as we move through life, we successively make choices regarding education, career, marriage, children, and retirement. Although it is difficult to avoid viewing these events as problems, from a developmental perspective they are part of a normal **life cycle;** we become differentiated individuals depending on our characteristic pattern of coping with these challenging events. Old age is one phase in the life cycle, and the changes individuals experience at this time of life are thought by some to be characteristic of this stage of development.

Until recently old age was not given much attention in the study of human development, but now more emphasis is being placed on understanding this phase of life. It was once believed that old age began at 65 and continued until death. Psychologists assumed a 65-year-old person experienced the same developmental events as an 85-year-old person. This is no longer considered true. We now believe that 65- and 75-year-old individuals must learn to cope with different experiences in the later part of life. To reflect this belief, the later years of life are divided into three stages: **middle age, later maturity,** and **old age,** and a series of developmental events are identified for each. Figure 1.4 identifies the significant events for each phase of later life (Manney, 1975).

Middle Age	Later Maturity	Old Age
40 50	60 70	80 90

Events	Events	Events
Job Stabilization	Loss of Spouse	Major Loss of Health
Loss of Parenthood	and Friends	Increased Dependence
Minor Loss of Health	Chronic Health Problems	Loss of Life
	Loss of Status	
	Considerable Leisure Time	
	Increased Independence	
	Retirement	
	Reduced Income	

Figure 1.4   Significant Events in Later Life.

Psychological Capacities of Older People   Psychological age relates to the various adaptive capacities individuals use to cope with problems confronting them throughout life. So far, psychologists studying older people have occasionally found contradictions in their research because of differences in the educational levels or health status of those studied. Certain diseases, such as cerebral, vascular, and primary brain disease, can seriously impair mental functioning and limit effective behavior in later life. The presence of people with these conditions in a research sample often distorts what can be generally regarded as the developmental or normative changes of later life.

The adaptive capacities studied by psychologists include sensory and perceptual functioning, speed and timing, psychomotor skills, learning abilities, problem-solving abilities, and personality traits. How these capacities change with advancing years is our concern in understanding **psychological aging.**

Sensory and Perceptual Functions   The senses are the way we experience the world both outside and inside the body. In order to respond to our environment, we must be able to learn something about it; we depend upon our senses—vision, hearing, taste, smell, touch—to gather the information. The function of the sensory organs is to pick up information about changes in the internal or external environment and pass this information on to the brain. Research in both the physiological and psychological aspects of aging has demonstrated that there is a decline in functioning of the sensory organs with increasing age (Kalish, 1975).

The senses provide the means for assembling and classifying information, but they do not evaluate it. The process of evaluating the information gathered by the senses and giving it meaning is called *perception*. As for perception in later life, people appear to suffer, with age, a decline in the general speed with which they can organize and evaluate stimuli. The available evidence concerning perceptual processes, however, is far less conclusive than that concerning sensory processes.

Speed and Timing   Whereas young adults generally behave quickly or slowly in accord with the demands of the situation, older adults exhibit generally slower behavior. This generalized slowness is seen as most likely an expression of a primary process of general neural aging (Birren, 1974). One consequence of the slowing-down process is that aged individuals are limited in the number of behaviors they can emit at a given time.

Older people adapt to their slowness by avoiding situations with unusual time pressures. Slowness itself can be partly a manifestation of adaptation. If the individual becomes less confident in walking, fearing the consequences of a fall, he or she may tend to slow movements considerably. In addition, psychomotor slowness of older people may be affected by depressive mood. However, depression is not an adequate explanation for the slowness of advancing age, although it can be a factor that amplifies its consequence. As we can see, there is no single explanation for slowness in older people's behavior; several related factors may be at work. We do not know much about modifying conditions that would maintain an alert organism with a potential for precise and rapid responses. We do not know whether continuous high-level stimulation in later life will retard or advance psychomotor slowness.

Psychomotor Skills   **Psychomotor performance** refers to a complex chain of activity beginning with a sensory response and ending with some sort of reaction, usually through a muscle. In the ideal situation psychomotor performance involves taking sensory input, attaching meaning to it through perception, incorporating the perceived information into the mind alongside other ideas, making a decision concerning the act if one is required by the new information, and then sending instructions to the appropriate nerve and activating a nerve–muscle response. In lay terms we might refer to this behavior as hand–eye coordination.

Studies of psychomotor functioning in later life have shown changes in the central nervous system and in the peripheral sensory receptions that result in a reduced sensory input with age (Woodruff and Birren, 1975). The reduced sensory input of older people affects their level of activity. On the whole, older people have less muscular strength, take longer to react to many forms of stimuli, take longer to make a motion, and are generally less capable of performing athletic tasks such as running and swimming.

Psychomotor functioning is extremely important to certain types of employment, especially assembly-line work. Much of the evidence from industrial studies indicates that little change in worker performance is found up to about age 60–65 (Birren, 1974). It is believed that individual limits are not often taxed in occupational performance and tend to be well counterbalanced by experience and better work methods. Workers' capacities change so generally that adaptation is an almost unconscious process. When dramatic changes in skills do occur, they are likely to be the result of injury or disease with accompanying neurological damage. It is perhaps only after age 70 that a worker seems old, primarily because of the slowness of action and the tendency to work according to an internal tempo rather than an external pace.

Mental Capacity   Learning ability is another adaptive capacity examined by psychologists. Evidence in the study of both animal and human learning suggests that, counter to general belief, learning ability does not diminish with age. Learning continues throughout life, although the rate of learning is slower for the old than for the young. Because of the many sensory changes that occur with age, methods of teaching may need to be different, but advancing age is not a hindrance to learning.

Studies suggest there is no simple answer to the question of whether problem-solving abilities increase or decrease with age. Some evidence suggests that as people age, their knowledge increases, and this strengthens their problem-solving ability. Furthermore, how effectively older people solve problems is determined by whether the problem contains familiar or unfamiliar elements. Problems containing familiar elements are frequently solved more quickly by older people than by young people. Other evidence suggests that older individuals do not function as effectively where speed or pressure are concerned. Over the life span older people develop ready-made solutions to most problems and apply these in later life. The model of problem solving characteristic of old age is to search within the existing repertoire of responses to problems rather than to generate new or creative approaches.

Whether intelligence declines with age has been a subject of study for some time. It was once thought that intelligence declined with age, but recent research suggests that it does not (Baltes and Schaie, 1974). This research maintains that decline in intelligence in older adults is related to their state of health; there appears to be a direct relationship between poor health and decline in an older person's mental capacity.

Personality Traits   There is much evidence to substantiate the stability and con-tinuity of certain personality traits or underlying disposition into old age. Some evidence does suggest age-related changes in traits, motivational patterns, and ego energy. For example, the individual's drive and spontaneous physical and sexual behavior may be reduced. In general, personality traits may vary more than mental capacity over the adult years. Personal value and vocational interests remain stable into old age, but other traits such as self-regard or self-identity may change markedly with age. However, studies of personality traits in relation to age and intelligence indicate that age is less important than intelligence in adaptation over adult life. Adaptive people modify their behavior over time and age successfully. The internal habit system of the individual personality that promotes adaptation is not fully un-derstood, and successful adaptation in old age can occur in quite different and almost opposite types of personalities.

Although a great deal of research has been conducted into the psychosocial aspects of aging, psychologists are still not sure which coping capacities contribute most to successful aging. Those working with older people must keep in mind that each individual takes into old age an individual coping pattern, and some can adjust better than others. On the whole, old people adapt better than we believe; perhaps with modification in the external factors influencing their lives, they would be able to age more successfully.

Social Aspects of Aging

The third set of characteristics of concern in examining the aging process are those related to social aging. **Social aging** refers to the habits and roles of aging individuals as they relate to groups or society. Sociologists are interested in determining the extent to which older people continue to interact socially. **Social interaction** refers to the behavior exhibited in groups or by classes of people without reference to specific individuals.

Socialization in Later Life   Sociologists are also interested in the process by which individuals learn to negotiate the social changes experienced throughout life (Bengtson, 1973). The term most often used to characterize this adaptation to change is **socialization,** which may be defined as the learning of new behaviors and orientations as one moves into new positions in the social structure.

Usually socialization is most obvious during childhood. One must learn to say *please* and *thank you,* to talk only at specific instances in school, to comb one's hair in a certain way, and to wear certain types of clothing. The list is endless. It is equally true but not as apparent that socialization occurs throughout the life cycle. Whenever people move into different social positions, they must learn many new behaviors in order to fill the position acceptably. In childhood one is helped—even forced—to learn the new behavior by institutions of socialization like the family and the school; in adulthood one finds few institutions to program individual behavior into ways acceptable to new positions. The Army or college are exceptions to this, but they pertain to very specialized positions and very specific periods of life. This is what makes the normal transition of adulthood, that is, the role changes, so difficult in our society. How does one learn the behaviors necessary to become a good mother? A happy retiree? A valued grandmother? A graceful widow?

Such questions reflect some of the fundamental problems in the natural course of adulthood and aging. For those working with older people, these problems are translated into more general terms: How does the social system change for individuals as they move into the later phase of the life cycle, and how may socialization into the roles associated with old age be characterized?

Social Age and Age Grading   Aging in the everyday interactional world is socially defined (Riley, 1971). To be "old" or "elderly" is to have reached some social milestone. The term **age-grading** refers to age positions and the system developed by a culture to give order and predictability to the individual's life course. Students entering college define themselves and behave differently than they did earlier as seniors in high school, because they now occupy a different position. Different things are expected of them, and their behavior is judged accordingly.

The points along the life cycle at which a person moves from "child" to "adolescent" to "adult" to "older adult" are socially defined but closely related to biological development. After physical maturity is reached, social age continues to be marked off by relatively clearcut biological or social events in the life cycle. For example, marriage marks the end of one social age period and the beginning of another; so does the appearance of the first child, the departure of children from the home, and the birth of grandchildren (Riley, 1971). At each stage we take on new roles, and our prestige is altered in relation to other family members. At each of these points we may be said to occupy a new position within the family.

Age Norms   **Age norms** and age expectation operate as probes and brakes to behavior, in some instances hastening and in others delaying it. Men and women are aware of their own timing and readily describe themselves as early, late, or on time with regard to family and occupation events—for example, "He married late," or "He is too young to marry." Age norms also operate in many less clearcut ways and in more peripheral areas of adult life, as illustrated by phrases such as, "He's too old to be working so hard," "She's too young to wear that style of clothes," or "That's a strange thing for a man his age to say."

Norms are defined simply as expectations of behavior (Bengtson, 1973). They are rules that socially define what is appropriate or inappropriate in a situation. Norms are enforced by sanction, and a person is generally rewarded for conformity and punished for nonconformity.

One study suggests that there are few norms specifically related to old age (Bengtson, 1972). Those things that are norms for older people apply as appropriately to adults of all age groups; for instance, religion, interest in grandchildren, maintaining contact with children, and maintaining financial independence as long as possible. Behaviors disapproved for older people were related to social isolation and inactivity, solitude, and inattention to religion. The evidence confirms that there are few norms regarding appropriate or inappropriate behavior in old age.

Sociologists suggest that, in old age, there are positive as well as negative consequences to a lack of norms (Bengtson, 1972). Lack of norms allows a greater range of personal choice in structuring one's life. In addition, lack of norms permits old people to be inwardly directed, expending all their energies on themselves. On the other hand, the lack of norms creates an environment without expectation, making it difficult to structure one's life.

Stereotypes   In this society the young people's attitudes about the old are often stereotypic. Aging individuals frequently accept such **stereotypes,** so that their own expectations concerning aging are inaccurate. On the basis of information about the small percentage of institutionalized elderly, for example, the erroneous generalization may be made that most old people are "senile." Similarly, it is often assumed that older people are politically conservative, lacking in sexual interest and motivation, and more religious than younger people, or that they dread death. Other stereotypes are that old people are rigid, narrow-minded, old fashioned, and crabby; that they do not care about their physical appearance; that they are always sick; and that they are generally neglected by their families. These attitudes about the elderly in general are false, but they encourage stereotypic thinking.

Role Loss in Old Age   **Roles** are defined as special positions for the division of labor within groups. Roles are generally derived from the various tasks an individual performs in a social system. For example, if a man works to support his family, he assumes the role of "breadwinner." There are expectations of behavior that are associated with certain positions or roles. Over time the social world of the aging person changes. In some instances he or she can no longer assume the roles of friend, parent, spouse, and worker. The number and kind of social contacts diminish, and various roles are lost through retirement, death of friends and relatives, and decreased mobility.

There are two significant aspects of role change associated with old age. One is role confusion: Many older adults are confused about the role they play in society. The other is related to the shrinking range of roles possible in old age. Fewer and fewer roles exist for individuals with advancing age. Role loss in later life may have severe emotional ramifications for older adults; for instance, the high incidence of suicide among older men is generally attributed to the effects of role loss.

Status   **Status** refers to one's position in the social order. Sociologists suggest that in most societies there are age status systems that determine how individuals are to behave in various age groups. For example, in many Eastern societies old age is a time when individuals are given a great deal of status within society. For the most part, status is given to the extent that an individual possesses something that is of value to the group. Status is generally obtained through two means: It is achieved or earned, that is, gained on the basis of something accomplished; or it is ascribed, that is, given on the basis of one's position. For example, a war hero may achieve status through his deeds; a princess has ascribed status on the basis of her position of high rank in the social order.

As we stated earlier, individuals are prepared for new positions and change in status in a society through the process called socialization. The goal of socialization is to assist the individual to personally reorganize the internal effects created by new positions and a change in status. Passage from childhood to adulthood is marked by many institutional arrangements—legal, interpersonal, and occupational—that prepare the individual for this transition. The transformation from middle age to old age is not characterized by similar socialization experiences. With retirement and the consequent change in status associated with it, for example, there is no formal process that prepares the individual for the role of nonworker.

Essentially, old age has a devalued status in our society. Being old has less value than being middle aged or young, and consequently no gain of status accompanies movement into old age. This devaluation is exemplified by the fact that, when speaking of themselves to others, older people often do not identify themselves as "old." Rather, they might say they are "senior citizens."

When people reach old age they are relegated to a position in society in which their skills are not demanded, and they are left to their own devices to survive. As Robert Atchley (1975) suggests, the old, like most expendable elements in society, are subject to poverty, illness, idleness, and social isolation. Those working with older people should be aware that society has institutionalized means of systematically limiting the roles of older people, and, in many instances, the service programs provided for them are an effort to compensate for this fact. The consequence of their status in society is discussed in more detail in Chapter 2.

Summary

In the past decade the United States has been confronted with a tremendous increase in the number and proportion of older people in the population. The increased number of older people and the need to provide services for them have resulted in a greater attempt to understand the aging process as it affects individuals. We know that old age is not characterized by physical changes alone. As individuals move into old age, they are confronted with physical, psychological, and social changes that they may or may not be able to cope with.

As a nation we are not prepared to deal with the increased number of older people. Since older people are viewed by society as unproductive, they are not seen as an essential segment of our population, and their status in society reflects this. The lives of older people are plagued with three major problems: poverty, illness, and idle time. These problems will be discussed in Chapter 2.

READING 1.1

We've Come a Long Way, Baby! / Sarah Fitzjarrald

*Aging has been characterized as a "slowing down" process, while American society has been
characterized as one of mobility and rapid change. One perspective from which to observe the
tension that arises from this dichotomy is the place of impact, where the aged individual meets
change. Sarah Fitzjarrald illustrates this perspective in the following article.*

That is not intended as a "glowing tribute" to my father. "That stuff is for heroes and
politicians," he would have said and meant it.

But progress, like old age, creeps up on us, the perverse creatures that we are, we tend to
adjust slowly and take our advantages (or disadvantages) for granted. My father died in 1949
and it is at those times when I think about how far we have come in the last quarter of a century
that I wonder how he would react to the world as it is today—not that he would react differently
from us or make any great philosophical observations. To say the least, he would enjoy life to
its fullest and his comments would be interesting.

Income tax was just getting really under way in 1949 and he had said, "I don't mind
paying the government money—it shows that I'm making some."

But the rate has gone up considerably since then and average taxpayers get audited. My
father never heard of anybody getting audited except the local bank and the postoffice, and
that as a matter of routine once a year.

He would be aghast at any man's having his private bank account opened by a government agent for inspection. But he'd take it in stride. He used to say, "That's the thing about
being truthful and honest, you don't have to remember what you said and you don't have to
make explanations."

Anybody is liable to have to make explanations in our time, just because he's a taxpayer.

He would have enjoyed central heat and air conditioning but he would have laughed
about putting an air conditioner in his old Ford. "She couldn't take it," he'd have said. "Too
fancy." And he'd probably still be driving that old Ford to this day.

He'd have liked television and been entertained by Gunsmoke, The Waltons, Walt Disney
and Hee-Haw. He heard most of the current jokes of the Hee-Haw. (He [had] the radio's
Grand Ole Opry.)

The first moon walk would have had him glued to the set, and the political conventions
would have kept him up past ten o'clock. But if Jane Russell had come on with one of her
uplifting commercials and one of his daughters had been present, he'd have left the room.

He would have liked baseball, football, and the Indy 500.

(The family's only speed demon was my Uncle John in his Chrysler.)

My father would have been a poor credit risk because he never had any. The only thing he
ever bought on time was a house and lot. His motto would have been, "pay now or cry later."
And a credit card would have been as welcome as a case of the plague.

From *Golden Times*, Fort Smith, Arkansas. Reprinted by permission of the author.

Any confrontation between my father and a computer would have been something to watch. Never mechanically minded, he dreaded to replace a blown fuse. And any instructions not to spindle, fold, or mutilate would have filled him with determination, just once, to try it.

The instant foods and all the convenient contraptions I have around the house to help me get my work done would have caused a very pointed question. "Well now, what are you doing with all the extra time that these things have saved you?"

"Just this." I would say to my father. "I'm writing. Writing about you."

Questions 1.1

1. Fitzjarrald focuses on the impact of technological changes. Changing population patterns have also had a profound impact on the life of the aged individual. Discuss some of these various changes, giving examples wherever possible. (Note: Even if an aged individual has never moved, has lived throughout life in the same rural area, for instance, where his or her parents lived all their lives, these population shifts would still have an effect.)

2. Changes in the American lifestyle, especially from the extended to the nuclear family pattern, have had many ramifications for the aged. Discuss these ramifications.

3. If you were 70 years old today, you would have been born in the first decade of the twentieth century, your work life would have begun sometime in the 1920s, and probably you would have retired recently. Keeping in mind that individual coping patterns help to differentiate individuals, discuss how you think you would respond to the various physiological and psychological changes that occur in old age.

4. Discuss the coping patterns of Fitzjarrald's father.

READING 1.2

The Long Life Diet / Ronald E. Gots, M.D.
People who live in the Caucasian region of the Soviet Union have about 50 chances in 100,000 to live to be 100 years old; the odds for a person who lives in the United States are 3 in 100,000. Dr. Gots suggests some answers to the question of longevity in this article.

You've probably seen the commercial: An 89-year-old man is eating, with great gusto, a container of yogurt. His mother, 114 years old, pats her "little boy" fondly on the back and gives him an approving smile. We can't help marveling at the extraordinary scene. Are these people for real, we wonder, or are they actors in old-age makeup? Our skepticism is understandable. For who, after all, lives that long? Yet, the mother and son in this remarkable commercial come from Soviet Georgia and they are playing themselves!

Reprinted by permission of the author from the August 23, 1977 issue of *Family Circle* magazine. Copyright © 1977 by Ronald E. Gots, M.D.

Tales of very old people aren't new. Adam, the Bible tells us, lived a venerable 930 years. His son Seth was born when he was 130. Seth fathered Enos at age 105 and lived on for 807 more years! But these are Bible stories, and few people today take them as literal fact. Nine hundred years of life is still beyond our comprehension but perhaps the limits of our concept of human life expectancy need a fresh look, for several groups of 20th-century people have already broken the 100-year barrier.

The Republics of Georgia, Azerbaijan and Armenia in the Caucasus region of the Soviet Union boast scores of these oldsters: an estimated 4,500 to 5,000 over-100-year-old folk. Nearly 50 out of every 100,000 people in that part of the world live to celebrate their 100th birthday, and many don't stop at 100! The oldest Russian, Shirali Mislimov, is reported to be a hale-and-hearty 168 years old. By comparison, we Americans are lightweights at growing old. Only three in 100,000 of us reach 100, and very few go much beyond.

But these Soviet centenarians aren't alone. Two other out-of-the-way societies are also blessed by the miracle of long, vigorous life. The Pakistani Hunzas live high in the sky in the Karakoram Range of the Himalayas. There, villagers speak of many friends and relatives who have celebrated their 100th birthdays, but the true number of centenarians in the Hunzan society remains a mystery. Exact birth records are hard to find. However, there is one well-substantiated fact about the Hunzas. According to UNESCO, they are the only totally cancer-free people in the world.

The Vilcabambans of the Ecuadorian Andes live thousands of miles from the Pakistani Hunzas and the Soviet Georgians; yet they too seem to share the secret of long life. Their population is small, only 819, but at last count at least nine of their number exceeded 100 years of age. And we're quite certain of their ages, since detailed birth records, kept in the local church, provide written proof.

If these oldsters were ailing and decrepit, their longevity would lose its appeal. What value is there in merely existing for a long time? But their story is so intriguing because they seem to have stumbled, if not on the fountain of youth, at least on the fountain of perpetual middle age! They remain vigorous in body and spirit despite the passage of time. Often many Americans in their 60's or 70's stare blankly from chairs and beds in convalescent homes, bodies twisted by arthritis and vascular diseases, minds blurred by senility. By contrast, Soviet Georgians aged 110 to 140 work in fields beside their great-grandchildren.

Even the concept of aging is foreign to them. When asked "At what age does youth end?" most Soviet oldsters had no ready answer. Several replied, "Well, perhaps at age 80." The very youngest estimate was age 60.

As a scientist I am intrigued by these long-lived peoples. Although they may be unsophisticated by our standards and relatively untouched by our "modern medical miracles," they have stumbled onto something that has eluded our most probing searches. A number of nature's secrets have combined to bless them with long, healthful lives. What specifically accounts for their ability to survive, and to survive so well?

First of all, vigorous, physically demanding work is a way of life for all of these long-lived peoples. They begin their long days of physical labor as children and never seem to stop.

For instance, Khfaf Lasuria, who is at least 130 years old, worked on a collective farm for 40 years. At age 100 she was rewarded with the title, "Farm's Fastest Tea Picker." Finally, in

1970, at age 124, she hung up her tea-collecting burlap bag and retired from the fields—not because she had to or because she could no longer handle the work, but because she was ready for a change. Now she can be found early in the morning in her garden tending tomatoes or feeding the pigs and chickens. Every week or two she hikes down the unpaved road to the bus stop to visit relatives in a distant village. The thought of idly watching time pass is as foreign to her as her ways seem to us.

Rustam Mamedov, 142 years of age, puffs calmly on his pipe as he recounts life's experiences: the Crimean War of 1854; the Turkish War of 1878; the Bolshevik Revolution in 1917. By his side sits his wife, 119 years old, his bride of 90 years. Their youngest son is only 35. He was born when Rustam Mamedov was 107 and his wife 84—a reproductive feat never equalled in the Western World! Mr. Mamedov has no intention of retiring from his life as a farmer. "Why? What else would I do?" he asks. Oh, he's slowed down a bit. Now he might quit for the day after six hours in the field instead of 10.

High-Altitude Living

These people don't need to don warm-up suits for a morning jog. Obviously, their work is a natural conditioner. What's more, they reap healthful rewards from the environment in which they work. It is interesting to note that all these long-lived peoples come from mountainous regions. They carry out their chores at elevations of 5,000 to 12,000 feet above sea level. Oxygen-poor and, of course, pollution-free air—the kind these mountain people breathe—is a known tonic for the cardiovascular system. Blood vessels that feed the heart widen and become more efficient in a reduced-oxygen environment. Hearts and blood vessels conditioned this way have back-up power to respond, when necessary, to an emergency call.

Another factor that may contribute to the good health of these long-lived peoples is their isolation. To a great extent, they are separated from the pressures and worries of civilization, but all of these societies are not equally remote. The Soviet Union is one of the world's leading technological societies, and the trappings of modern civilization are available to the residents of the Caucasus. For instance, Seliab Butba from the village of Ataro regularly mounts his horse for the 24-mile journey to his sister's home. But, if he wanted to, he could go by bus or car. Yet he has ridden horseback for 120 years and has no intention of stopping now.

One-hundred-and-six-year-old Markhti Tarkil from Soviet Duripsh has a modern bathroom with a tub. But a day wouldn't be complete without his two-mile hike to an icy stream.

In fact, these Russians are very tuned-in to the ways of the modern world. The crew who went to the Caucasus to film those yogurt commercials found that even without being told, villagers always turned the Dannon label toward the camera!

The other long-lived peoples are farther removed from modern life. But it won't be long before they, too, will have the machinery to make their lives easier and softer, if they want it.

Inherited factors undoubtedly play some role in these peoples' longevity. Part of this may be due to the inbreeding of their populations, but that doesn't tell the whole story either. The genes of the Vilcabambans and Hunzas have not been diluted by outsiders for thousands of years. But the Soviet oldsters come from a wide mix of different racial and genetic groups:

Mongolians, Caucasians, Armenians, Russians, Georgian Jews—all contribute to the over-100 population.

One thing is certain: Most of the longest-lived peoples had parents and grandparents who also reached ripe old ages. Good family genes may, therefore, be one factor in living longer.

It is clear that insulation from urban pressures and pollution, clean mountain air, daily hard work, good genes and a youthful approach to life all contribute to the vigor and remarkable longevity of all these peoples. Yet, there is another common bond that is so striking it deserves special attention. The foods that all these people eat is a common link that may be the single most important secret to their long, healthful lives. [This diet consists of vegetables and fruits they grow, goat and sheep dairy products, and occasionally meat.]

Questions 1.2

1. **Compare and contrast the way the Georgians relate to their environment to the way we Americans relate to ours.**

2. **Environment and genetics are two dimensions of Gots's discussion. What are some other factors that he suggests may be related to long life?**

3. **A child born in the United States today can expect to live approximately 71 years. If that average life expectancy were to rise to 100 years, what would be some effects on society (assuming all else remains the same)?**

READING 1.3

Joie de Vivre / Simone de Beauvoir

Socialization is the process through which we learn new behavior and orientations. Age norms are rules, which vary from culture to culture, for those behaviors that are appropriate and those that are inappropriate at a given age. In this excerpt Simone de Beauvoir takes issue with restrictive norms regarding sexuality among aged people, and she concludes that "sexuality, vitality, and activity are indissolubly linked."

We have one most remarkable piece of evidence concerning an old man's relationship with his body, his image, and his sex: this is Paul Leautaud's *Journal*.[1] He provides us with a living synthesis of the various points of view that we have considered in this study.

Leautaud always looked at himself with a certain approval. It was from the outside that he learned he was aging, and it made him very angry. In 1923, when he was fifty-three, a railway official referred to him as "a little old gentleman." Furious, Leautaud wrote in his Journal, "Little old man! Old gentleman? What the devil—am I as blind as all that? I cannot see that I

Reprinted by permission of G. P. Putnam's Sons from *The Coming of Age* by Simone de Beauvoir. Copyright © 1972 by Andre Deutsch, Weidenfeld and Nicolson and G. P. Putnam's Sons.
[1] Leautaud was a critic and an editor of *Mercure de France*, a literary journal.

am either a little or an old gentleman. I see myself as a fifty-year-old, certainly, but an exceedingly well preserved fifty-year-old. I am slim and I move easily. Just let them show me an old gentleman in such good shape!'' At fifty-nine he looked at himself with a critical eye: ''Mentally and physically I am a man of forty. What a pity my face does not match! Above all my lack of teeth! I really am remarkable for my age: slim, supple, quick, active. It is my lack of teeth that spoils everything; I shall never dare to make love to a woman again.''

In him we see with remarkable clarity how impossible it is for an old man to realize his age. On his birthday he wrote, ''Today I begin my sixty-fourth year. In no way do I feel an old man.'' The old man is Another, and this Other belongs to a certain category that is objectively defined; in his inner experience Leautaud found no such person. There were moments, however, when his age weighed upon him. On April 12, 1936, he wrote, ''I do not feel happy about my health nor about my state of mind: and then there is the sorrow of aging, too. Aging above all!'' But at sixty-nine he wrote, ''During my seventieth year I am still as lively, active, nimble and alert as a man can be.''

Leautaud had every reason to be pleased with himself: he looked after his house and cared for his animals: he did all the shopping on foot, carrying heavy baskets of provisions; wrote his *Journal:* and he did not know what it was to be tired. ''It is only my sight that is failing. I am exactly as I was at twenty. My memory is as good as ever and my mind as quick and sharp.''

This made him all the more irritable when other people's reactions brought the truth home to him. He was seventy when a young woman lost her balance as an underground train started off with a jerk: she cried out. ''I'm so sorry, Grandpa, I nearly fell on you.'' He wrote angrily, ''Damm it all! My age must show clearly in my face. How impossible it is to see oneself as one really is!''

The paradox lies in the fact that he did not really dislike being old. He was one of those exceptional cases I have mentioned, where old age coincides with childhood fantasy: he had always been interested in old people. On March 7, 1942, when he was seventy-two, he wrote, ''A kind of vanity comes over you when you reach old age—you take a pride in remaining healthy, slim, supple and alert, with an unaltered complexion, your joints in good order, no illness and no diminution in your physical and mental powers.''

But his vanity demanded that his age be invisible to others: he liked to imagine that he had stayed young in spite of the burden of his years.

He only gave way to discouragement at the very end of his life, when his health failed. On February 25, 1945, he wrote, ''I am very low indeed. My eyesight. The horrible marks of age I see on my face. My *Journal* behind-hand. The mediocrity of my life. I have lost my energy and all my illusions. Pleasure, even five minutes of pleasure, is over for me.'' He was then seventy-five, and his sexual life had come to an end. But except in his very last years one of the reasons for his pride was that he still felt desire and was still capable of satisfying it. We can follow his sexual evolution in his *Journal*.

Leautaud only became fully aware of women when he was approaching his fiftieth year. At thirty-five he wrote, ''I am beginning to regret that my temperament allows me to enjoy women so little.'' He lacked the ''sacred fire.'' ''I always think too much of other things—of myself, for example.'' He was afraid of impotence and his lovemaking was over very quickly:

"I give women no pleasure since I have finished in five minutes and can never start again. . . .
Shamelessness is all I really like in love. . . . There are some things not every woman can be
asked to do." He had a lasting affair with a woman called Bl——. He says he loved her very
much, but he also says that living with her was hell. When he was about forty, although he was
still rather indifferent, since he could give his partner no pleasure, he delighted in looking at
pictures of naked women. Yet a few years later he speaks sadly of the "rare love-scenes in my
life which I really enjoyed." He reproaches himself for being "timid, awkward, brusque,
oversensitive, always hesitant, never able to take advantage of even the best opportunities"
with women. All this changed when at fifty he met "a really passionate woman, wonderfully
equipped for pleasure and exactly to my taste in these matters," and he showed himself to be
"almost brilliant," although up until then he had thought that he was not very good—as he had
only known women who did not suit him. From this time on, sex became an obsession to him:
on December 1, 1923, he wrote, "Perhaps Madame (one of the names he gave to his mistress)
is right: my perpetual desire to make love may be somewhat pathological. . . . I put it down to
a lifetime's moderation—it lasted until I was over forty—and also to my intense feeling for her,
which makes me want to make love to her when I see so much as a square inch of her body.
. . . I think it is also because I have been deprived of so many things, such as that female
nakedness for which I acquired such a liking. I am quite amazed when I think of what has
happened to me in all this. . . . Never have I caressed any other woman as I caress Madame."
In the summer they parted, and abstinence lay heavy upon him: he masturbated, thinking of
her. "Of course I am delighted to be such an ardent lover at my age, but God knows it can be
troublesome."

Madame was a little older than he: all his life he had loved only mature women. A
twenty-three-year-old virgin threw herself at his head, and he agreed to have an affair with her:
but it did not give him the least pleasure and he broke immediately. Except for this one fling he
was faithful to Madame for years. He liked watching himself and her in a mirror during their
lovemaking. From 1927—age fifty-seven—on, he was forced to take care not to make love too
often; he found consolation in bawdy talk with the Panther (another name he gave to his
mistress). He did not get on well with her; "we are attached to each other only by our
senses—by vice—and what remains is so utterly tenous!" But in 1938 he did recall with great
satisfaction the "seventeen years of pleasure between two creatures, the one as passionate and
daring as the other in amorous words and deeds." When he was fifty-nine his affair with the
Scourge, as he now called her, was still going on, though she was already sixty-four. He was
shocked by couples where the woman was much younger than the man. "I myself at fifty-nine
would never dare to make any sort of advance to a woman of thirty."

He was still very much attracted to the Scourge, and he took great pleasure in his
"sessions" with her. Yet he did complain, "What a feeble ejaculation when I make love: little
better than water!" Later he wrote, "I am certainly better when I do not make love at all. Not
that it comes hard—far from it—but it is always a great effort, and I do not get over it as quickly
as I did a few years ago. . . . What I miss most is female nakedness, licentious attitudes, and
playing amorous games."

"Until I was sixty-six or sixty-seven I could make love two or three times a week." Now he complained that his brain was tired for three or four days after love, but he still went on, and he corresponded with three of his former mistresses.

When he was seventy Leautaud wrote, "I miss women and love terribly." He remembered how he used to make passionate love to the Scourge from the age of forty-seven to sixty-three, and then for two years with CN (another mistress).

"It was only three years ago that I noticed I was slowing down. I can still make love, and indeed I quite often feel sad at being deprived of it: though at the same time I tell myself that it is certainly much better for me to abstain."

At seventy-two he was still planning idylls that never came to anything, and he had erotic dreams that gave him an erection. "At night I still feel ready for anything." But that same year he observed that his sexual powers were declining. "It is no use giving yourself over to lovemaking when the physical side is dead or nearly so. Even the pleasure of seeing and fondling is soon over, and there is not the least eagerness to begin again. For a real appreciation of all these things, there must be the heat of physical passion." It is clear that Leautaud's greatest pleasure was visual. He retained it longer than any other form of sensual enjoyment, and after the age of forty he prized it very highly indeed. When he lost it he considered that his sexual life was over. It is also clear how a man's image of himself is bound up with sexual activity. He was "in the depths of sorrow" when he could no longer experience these pleasures. Still, his narcissism did survive his sexual decline at least for some time.

The Feminine Disadvantage

Biologically women's sexuality is less affected by age than men's. Brantome bears this out in the chapter of his *Vies des dames galantes* that he dedicates to "certain old ladies who take as much pleasure in love as the young ones." Whereas a man of a certain age is no longer capable of erection, a woman "at no matter what age is endowed with as it were a furnace . . . all fire and fuel within." Popular tradition bears witness to this contrast. In one of the songs in the Merry Muses of Caledonia[2] an old woman laments her elderly husband's impotence. She longs for "the wild embraces of their younger days" that are now no more than a ghostly memory, since he no longer thinks of doing anything in bed except sleeping, while she is eaten up with desire. Today scientific research confirms the validity of this evidence. According to Kinsey, throughout their lives women are sexually more stable than men: when they are sixty their potential for pleasure and desire is the same as it was at thirty. According to Masters and Johnson, the strength of the sexual reaction diminishes with age: yet a woman can still reach orgasm, above all if she is regularly and properly stimulated. Those who do not often have physical relations sometimes find coition painful, either during the act or after, and sometimes suffer from dyspareunia or dysuria: it is not known whether these troubles are physical or psychological in origin. I may add that a woman can take great pleasure in making love even though she may not reach orgasm. The "preliminary pleasures" count even more perhaps for her than they do for a man. She is usually less sensitive to the appearance of her partner and therefore less worried by his growing old. Even though her part in lovemaking is not

[2] Popular Scottish songs collected in the eighteenth century.

as passive as people sometimes make out, she has no fear of a particular failure. There is nothing to prevent her from going on with her sexual activities until the end of her life.

Still, all research shows that women have a less active sexual life than men. Kinsey says that at fifty, 97 percent of men are still sexually active compared with 93 percent of women. At sixty it is 94 percent of men and only 80 percent of women. This comes from the fact that socially men, whatever their age, are subjects, and women are objects, relative beings. When she marries, a woman's future is determined by her husband's; he is usually about four years older than she, and his desire progressively lessens. Or if it does continue to exist, he takes to younger women. An old woman, on the other hand, finds it extremely difficult to have extramarital relations. She is even less attractive to men than old men are to women. And in her case gerontophilia does not exist. A young man may desire a woman old enough to be his mother but not his grandmother. A woman of seventy is no longer regarded by anyone as an erotic object. Venal love is very difficult for her to find. It would be most exceptional for an old woman to have both the means and the opportunity of getting herself a partner: and then again shame and fear of what people might say would generally prevent her from doing so. This frustration is painful to many old women, for they are still tormented by desire. They usually find their relief in masturbation: a gynecologist told me of the case of one woman of seventy who begged him to cure her of this practice—she was indulging in it night and day.

When Andree Martinerie was conducting an inquiry for *Elle* magazine (March 1969) she gathered some interesting confidences from elderly women. Madame F., a rich middle-class sixty-eight-year-old, a militant Catholic, mother of five and grandmother of ten, told her, "I was already sixty-four. . . . Now just listen: four months after my husband's death I went down into the street just like someone who is going to commit suicide. I had made up my mind to give myself to the very first man who would have me. Nobody wanted me. So I went home again." When she was asked whether she had thought of remarrying, she answered, "That is all I ever do think of. If I dared I would put an advertisement in *Le Chasseur francais*. . . . I would rather have a decrepit invalid of a man than no man at all!" Talking of desire, Madame R., sixty years old and living with her sick husband, said, "It is quite true that you don't get over it." She sometimes felt like beating her head against the wall. A woman reader of this inquiry wrote to the magazine, "I must tell you that a woman remains a woman for a very long time in spite of growing older. I know what I am talking about, because I am seventy-one. I was a widow at sixty; my husband died suddenly and it took me at least two years to realize fully what had happened. Then I started to answer advertisements in the matrimonial column. I admit that I did miss having a man—or rather I should say I do miss it: this aimless existence is terrifying, without affection or any outlet for one's own feelings. I even began wondering whether I was quite normal. Your inquiry was a great relief. . . ." This correspondent speaks modestly of "affection," an "outlet for one's feelings." But the context shows that her frustration had a sexual dimension. The reaction of a young woman who wrote to *Elle* is typical: "In our group of young people we laughed heartily about the passionate widow (the member of the Action Catholique) who cannot 'get over it.' I wish you would now hold an inquiry on love as it appears to the fourth age of women, in other words those between eighty and a hundred and twenty." Young people are very shocked if the old, especially old women, are still sexually active.

A woman, then, continues in her state as erotic object right up to the end. Chastity is not imposed upon her by a physiological destiny but by her position as a relative being. Nevertheless it may happen that women condemn themselves to chastity because of the "psychological barriers" that I have mentioned, which are even more inhibiting for them than for men. A woman is usually more narcissistic in love than a man; her narcissism is directed at her body as a whole. She has a delightful awareness of her body as something desirable, and this awareness comes to her through her partner's caresses and his gaze. If he goes on desiring her she easily puts up with her body's aging. But at the first sign of coldness she feels her ugliness in all its horror; she is disgusted with her image and cannot bear to expose her poor person to others. This lack of assurance strengthens her fear of other people's opinions: she knows how censorious they are toward old women who do not play their proper role of serene and passion-free grandmothers.

Even if her husband wants to make love with her again later, a deeply rooted feeling of shame may make her refuse him. Women make less use of diversion than men. Those who enjoyed a very active and uninhibited sexual life before do sometimes compensate for their enforced abstinence by extreme freedom in conversation and the use of obscene words. They become something very like bawds, or at least they spy upon the sexual life of their young women friends with a most unhealthy curiosity, and do all they can to make them confide their secrets. But generally speaking their language is as repressed as their lovemaking. Elderly women like to appear as restrained in their conversation as they are in their way of life. Their sexuality now shows only in their dress, their jewelry and ornaments, and in the pleasure they take in male society. They like to flirt discreetly with men younger than themselves and they are touched by attentions that show they are still women in men's eyes.

However, it is clear from pathology that in women, too, the sexual drive is repressed but not extinguished. Psychiatrists have observed that in asylums female patients' eroticism often increases with age. Senile dementia brings with it a state of erotic delirium arising from lack of cerebral control. Repressions are also discarded in some other forms of psychosis. Dr. Georges Mahe recorded twenty cases of extreme eroticism out of 110 sixty-year-old female patients in an institution: the symptoms included public masturbation, make-believe coition, obscene talk, and exhibitionism. Unfortunately he gives no idea of the meaning of these displays: he puts them into no context and we do not know who the patients were who indulged in these practices. Many of the inmates suffer from genital hallucinations such as rape and physical contact. Women of over seventy-one are convinced that they are pregnant. Madame C., seventy and a grandmother, sings barrackroom songs and walks about the hospital half-naked, looking for a man. Eroticism is the most important factor in many delirious states; it also triggers off some cases of melancholia. E. Gehu speaks of an eighty-three-year-old grandmother who was looked after in a convent. She was an exhibitionist, showing both homosexual and heterosexual tendencies. She fell upon the younger nuns who brought her meals: during these crises she was perfectly lucid. Later she became mentally confused. She ended up by regaining her mental health and behaving normally once more. Here again, we should like a more exact detailed account of her case. All the observations that I have just quoted are most inadequate: but at least they do show that old women are no more "purified of their bodies" than old men.

Neither history nor literature has left us any worthwhile evidence on the sexuality of old women. It is an even more strictly forbidden subject than the sexuality of old men.

There are many cases of the libido disappearing entirely in old people. Ought they to rejoice in it, as the moralists say? Nothing is less certain. It is a mutilation that brings other mutilations with it: sexuality, vitality, and activity are indissolubly linked. When desire is completely dead, emotional response itself may grow loose at its edge. At sixty-three Retif de La Bretonne wrote, ''My heart died at the same time as my senses, and if sometimes a tender impulse stirs me, it is as erroneous as that of a savage or a eunuch: it leaves me with a profound feeling of sorrow.'' It seemed to Bernard Shaw that when he lost interest in women he lost interest in living. ''I am ageing very quickly. I have lost all interest in women, and the interest they have in me is greater than ever and it bores me. The time has probably come for me to die.''

Even Schopenhauer admitted, ''It could be said that once the sexual urge is over life's true centre is burnt out, leaving a mere shell.'' Or again, ''life is like a play acted at first by live actors and then finished by automata wearing the same costumes.'' Yet at the same time he says that the sexual instinct produces a ''benign dementia.'' The only choice left to men is that between madness and sclerosis. In fact what he calls ''dementia'' is the spring of life itself. When it is broken or destroyed a man is no longer truly alive.

The link that exists between sexuality and creativity is striking: it is obvious in Hugo and Picasso and in many others. In order to create there must be some degree of aggression—''a certain readiness,'' says Flaubert and this aggressivity has its biological source in the libido. It is also necessary to feel united with the world by an emotional warmth: this disappears at the same time as carnal desire, as Gide understood very clearly when on April 10, 1942, he wrote. ''There was a time when I was cruelly tormented, indeed obsessed by desire, and I prayed 'Oh let the moment come when my subjugated flesh will allow me to give myself entirely to. . . .' But to what? To art? To pure thought? To God? How ignorant I was! How mad! It was the same as believing that the flame would burn brighter in a lamp with no oil left. If it were abstract, my thought would go out; even today it is my carnal self that feeds the flame and now I pray that I may retain carnal desire until I die.''

It would not be truthful to state that sexual indifference necessarily brings inertia and impotence. There are many examples to prove the contrary. Let us merely say there is one dimension of life that disappears when there is no more carnal relationship with the world: those who keep this treasure to an advanced age are privileged indeed.

Questions 1.3

1. Discuss to what extent our norms regarding sexuality coincide with what we know about the physiology of aging.

2. Discuss how the problem of sexuality differs for aged men and aged women.

3. de Beauvoir obviously believes that age norms are in operation in our attitudes toward sexuality. Others have demonstrated that age norms are not a factor with the elderly. Argue for either position, giving examples to support your point of view.

4. Sexuality is one dimension of age stereotyping (''dirty old men,'' ''old maids''). Discuss other dimensions of age stereotyping.

CHAPTER 2
THE SOCIAL PROBLEMS
OF LATER LIFE

Those working with or planning to work with older people should be aware of the many problems that confront individuals as they move into old age. To gain insight into these problems one must first delve into the factors that create them. Human-service workers should understand the influence social attitudes have on the prevailing condition for older people in a society. Attitudes have a far-reaching effect on the status of the elderly, as they determine the magnitude of resources made available to people in this stage of life. In addition, they determine the resources available to human-service workers who attempt to help older people with their problems. In this chapter we will discuss various cultural perspectives on aging and how the different views contribute to social conditions for older people. We will also review the major problems the elderly experience.

Old Age: A Time of
Growth and Wisdom

The history of human development has shown two dominant beliefs about old age (de Beauvoir, 1972). One belief is that old age is a time of growth and reflection; the other focuses on old age as a time of decline. Some social attitudes toward aging are deeply rooted in religious beliefs. For example, Confucius set forth the tenet of absolute obedience to the head of the household, and in prerevolutionary China respect for the eldest male reached far beyond the limits of the family to embrace all the elderly of the community. In the intensive agrarian society of ancient China, experi-

ence and wisdom were seen as greater virtues than strength. Confucius provided a moral justification for the patriarchal system by giving old age and wisdom the same status:

At fifteen, I applied myself to the study of wisdom: At thirty, I grew stronger in it: At forty, I no longer have doubts: At sixty, there was nothing on earth that could shake me: At seventy I could follow the dictates of my heart without disobeying the moral law (Manney, 1975).

Another Chinese religion, Taoism, also depicted old age as a virtue. The doctrines of this religion set the age of 60 as the moment when a man can free himself from his body by esthetic experience and become a holy being. The "neotaoism" man's supreme aim was the quest for the long life. Accordingly, ecstasy could lead to a holiness that would protect the adept from death itself. Old age was therefore seen as life in its very highest form.

Because of Eastern culture's respect for old age, the elderly were given status and power of life and death over the young; perhaps old age was a better time of life than young adulthood. Many of these ancient values have transcended time and exist today in Eastern cultures, where the elderly are generally revered and, therefore, are well cared for by the society as a whole. Simone de Beauvoir (1972) maintains that in Chinese literature people may deplore the oppression of which they are the victims, but they never cry out against old age as a curse.

The Western Perspective:
The Old Gray Mare Syndrome

Reverence for old age does not exist in Western societies. One of the earliest Western writings depicts old age as a curse:

How hard and painful are the lonely days of an ancient man; he grows weaker every day; his eyes grow dim; his ears deaf; his strength fades; his heart knows peace no longer. . . . The power of his mind lessens and today he cannot remember what yesterday was like: All his bones hurt. . . . Old age is the worst misfortune that can afflict man (de Beauvoir, 1972).

This perspective continues throughout the history of Western civilization. It is called to mind by Michel Philibert (Manney, 1975), a French gerontologist and philosopher, in his characterization of the Western perspective on aging, which suggests that four main themes run through the Western attitudes. We will discuss these themes below.[1]

Aging Is Biological

In Western societies the biological concept of age governs our attitude toward what is clearly a complex and ambiguous collection of gains and losses. Our mental images of age are primarily images of unfavorable physical change. A problematic social institution such as mandatory retirement is justified as a necessary response to this biological decline. Old people's social isolation is similarly explained as an appropriate response to people whose physical conditions are rendering them socially, economically, and spiritually obsolete. The biological concept of aging even governs much of academic gerontology, which itself developed from the biological sciences. On the other hand, as we noted above, many historical non-Western and primitive cultures conceive of aging as a process in which biological, spiritual, and psychological forces have at least equal weight. For some, aging is a time of growth and learning, of continuing maturity, and of accomplishments.

Aging Is Unfavorable

The Western biological model of aging largely skirts the possibility of fulfillment in old age, a possibility that other cultures have allowed and enjoyed. If one conceives of aging as mainly a biological process, an unfavorable attitude is invariable in relation to this process, because the dominant physical experience in later life is one of loss and decline. However, a perspective on aging that foresees the possibility of

[1] This material is excerpted from Manney, 1975.

spiritual growth outweighing physical decline is a more favorable view. All major cultures in history record examples of contempt for the old. However, past societies have tended to view this contempt as a feature of their own culture, usually one they perceive as inhumane. Our society views the devaluation of old age as a law of nature.

Aging Is Universal

Our biological perspectives, the social and economic isolation of the elderly, and their increased number combine to separate the old from everyone else. Since we believe aging is governed by irreversible biological processes, we perceive aging as happening the same way in all times and in all places, and our chronological age expectations govern social and economic isolation of the elderly. Although we must often think about the social problem of aging, we do so at the cost of obscuring the fact that aging is a differential and variable process.

Aging Is Unmanageable

The final aspect of the Western perspective as characterized by Philibert is ironic. We see aging as an essentially unmanageable process, precisely at the time when medical science has brought biological aging under control to a large degree. We isolate and worry about older people at a time when the number of older people is increasing, and they are much healthier and more alert than older people at any other time in history. Yet our conception of aging includes the notion that there is nothing we can do about this process.

These four aspects of the Western perspective on aging are somewhat loosely defined, but they exert a powerful influence on the way we view older people and treat them. These attitudes toward the elderly in our society also have an effect on how the elderly view themselves.

Society versus Older Adults

The most important indication of society's attitude toward older adults is how well it provides for them. One would assume that in a society of affluence all would benefit. In a capitalist society, however, the rules of the game are that you reap what you put into the system in the way of production. Consequently, for many older people old age is a tragedy, a period of quiet despair, deprivation, desolation, and muted rage.

Such a fate can be the consequence of the kind of life a person led in younger years and of problems in relationships with others. There are also inevitable personal and physical losses to be sustained, some of which can become overwhelming and unbearable. But age is frequently a tragedy even when the early years have been fulfilling and people seemingly had everything going for them. The American dream promises old people that if they work hard enough all their lives, things will turn out well for them. Today's older adults were brought up to believe in pride, self reliance, and independence. Many are tough, determined individuals who manage to survive against adversity, but even the toughest reach a point where they need help. Herein, maintains Dr. Robert Butler, Director of the National Institute on Aging, lies the tragedy of old age in the United States. The tragedy is not that each of us must grow old and die but that the process of doing so has been made unnecessarily, and at times excruciatingly, painful, humiliating, and debilitating. We have shaped a society that is externally harsh to live in when one is old. For the most part, the elderly struggle to exist in a hostile environment.

The Economic Crisis of Old Age

Poverty

Poverty or dramatically lowered income and old age seem to go hand in hand. Insufficient income is by far the most serious problem for most older people, for it affects every aspect of their lives (Chen, 1970). Financial needs can lead directly to serious medical and social problems. To conserve finances, old people may visit the doctor infrequently, permitting minor difficulties to develop into serious illness. They may sell their cars, shop less, eat starchy but filling foods, see less of friends, and perhaps withdraw into a kind of aimless half-existence in order to conserve income so that there are sufficient funds to pay rent and utility bills (Butler, 1975). In an era when the annual rate of inflation has reached major proportions, few middle-age workers can escape anxiety as they consider the prospects of possibly 20 years or more in retirement. Although public and private programs have substantially improved the financial situation of most old people, economic issues will continue to be the primary concern of older people in the years to come.

It is generally well known that people who have been poor all their lives remain poor as they grow old, but what most of us do not realize is that these poor are joined by a multitude of others who became poor only upon growing old. When Social Security becomes the sole or primary source of income, it means a subsistence-level lifestyle. Recent increases in Social Security do not keep up with the soaring cost of living. Private pension plans often do not pay off, and pension payments that do come in are not tied to inflationary decreases in buying power. Savings can be wiped out by a single, unexpected catastrophic illness.

In 1970 one in every four older individuals had less income than the official, very conservative, poverty estimate based on the government's own emergency food budget (Butler, 1975) (see Table 2.1). In January 1971 half of the elderly, or over 10

Table 2.1   Poverty Levels

Organizations Which Have Defined Poverty	Point Below Which Poverty Occurs	
	Couple	Individual
Official poverty level, 1970	$2,328	$1,852
Retired couple's budget (Bureau of Labor Statistics, 1971)		
Intermediate budget, "Modest but adequate"	4,776	2,627*
Higher budget	7,443	4,094
National Welfare Rights Organization, 1971	**	2,250
Chairman, National Caucus on Black Aged, 1971	9,000	6,000

* Estimated as 55 percent of couples.
** No "guideline" available.
Source: Robert N. Butler, *Why Survive? Being Old in America*, p. 28. Copyright © 1975 by Robert N. Butler, M.D. Reprinted by permission of Harper & Row, Publishers, Inc.

million older adults, lived on less than $75 a week, or $10 a day, and many others lived on far less.

Over half of our elderly population live in deprivation. This means that they lack food, essential drugs, a telephone in the house to call for help in emergencies. Some must take desperate means to make ends meet. One frequently hears on the national media incidences of older people being arrested for shoplifting such things as a can of soup or a package of wieners. There has also been much notoriety about the fact that many older people purchase pet foods as a means of subsisting.

In his book *The Other America*, Michael Harrington (1960) shows that the millions of older people who live in poverty are the victims of a downward spiral. Poor people are ill more often than others because they live in unhealthy and poorly heated slum housing and feed themselves badly. The problem is circular, for they are too poor to take care of themselves, so their illnesses grow worse, preventing them from working and making their poverty even more acute. These older people are ashamed of their destitute conditions and may avoid all social contacts. They attempt to hide from others the fact that they live on public assistance and may deprive themselves of the little help available. A witness testifying before a United States Senate commission set up to inquire into problems of old age stated that "these outcasts of society were the victims of a three-fold set of causes: bad health, poverty, and solitude" (de Beauvoir, 1972). Some join the ranks of poverty after a relatively rewarding life. Their abilities diminish as they grow old: They could no longer find jobs because their techniques were out-of-date. For those who had earned a reasonable amount, retirement meant a precipitous drop in income.

But most of the very poor have always been poor (de Beauvoir, 1972). They came from the country when they were young and they did not thrive in the cities. Moreover, Social Security does not cover farm laborers. The mass of these very poor people, the retired with inadequate incomes or workers with no retirement pensions, have to turn to social agencies in order to survive.

Only an affluent society, Butler maintains, can have so many old people; but it refuses them the fruits of abundance and grants them mere survival and no more. Such is the economic plight of a large proportion of the elderly in America.

Unemployment

Major contributors to the economic and social plight of older people are mandatory retirement and discriminatory employment practices. Age discrimination in employment persists, taking the form of arbitrary retirement practices and biases against hiring older people. For a variety of reasons, unemployed workers over age 45 have difficulty reentering the work force. About 15 percent of all workers age 45 and over are unemployed at any one time. For many early retirement means permanent unemployment. Along with technological changes, factors contributing to this situation are the unwillingness of older workers to relocate, the concentration of older workers in dying industries such as railroad transportation, and age discrimination by employers (Manney, 1975).

The greatest constraint to employment flexibility is the compulsory retirement age. The concept of compulsory retirement age is largely a creation of the Social Security system, which in 1935 established 65 as the minimum age for receiving full retirement benefits. Thousands of businesspeople have adopted 65 as their own mandatory retirement age. Although data on the subject are incomplete, Manney (1975) suggests at least two-thirds of all private employers demand retirement at 65, regardless of the individual's ability to handle work assignments satisfactorily. The effects of this requirement are dramatic. Male labor-force participation dropped from about 90 percent from ages 55 to 59, to about 80 percent for ages 60 to 64, to about 35 percent for ages 65 to 69.

The compulsory retirement trend is bolstered by both subtle and overt pressures on older workers to leave their jobs (Sobel, 1970). Here again, data are hard to obtain, but there are indications that both employers and unions are interested in getting older workers out of the labor force to make way for younger workers. Employers believe that younger workers are more capable, and unions want older workers removed so that young members can move up in seniority. Studies show that about 20 percent of employers directly encourage retirement prior to age 65. A majority of employers are officially neutral but nevertheless encouraged early retirement through financial incentives, mainly in the form of supplementary pension benefits until full Social Security benefits take effect at age 65. In 1977 the Supreme Court ruled that mandatory retirement at age 65 is unconstitutional, and Congress raised the mandatory retirement age to 70 in 1978. We still do not know what effects these actions will have on age discrimination in employment practices.

Mandatory retirement is a way of reducing the size of the work force, particularly in the hard-pressed dying industries where older people tend to be concentrated.

Another major constraint on work-force participation among older people is the Social Security retirement test. Retiree benefits are reduced one dollar for every two of earnings over $2,400 a year. However, retirees receive benefits every month in which they do not work, regardless of total annual income from other sources.

The right to work is basic to the right to survive. Denying older people the right to work, by practice or by attitudes, is often denying them the right to earn a living or gain personal satisfaction. In his book *Why Survive Old Age,* Dr. Robert Butler (1975) states that the oldest volunteer for the National Institute of Mental Health Study of Human Aging was a 92-year-old man who complained, "I want a job and no one will hire me." This man was a vest maker who became unemployed during World War II because of the fabric shortage. By the time vests came back into style he was in his 80s, and no one would hire him. This man detested having nothing to do and being forced to live with his daughter, who was in her 60s and who was annoyed with having him around the house.

Some older workers, however, look forward to not working, but the price of retirement leisure for older people is a loss of about one-fourth to one-half of their former annual income.

Shelter

Housing is the number-one expenditure for most older Americans. They spend about 34 percent of their total income for shelter, in contrast to about 23 percent for younger people. A home is also the only major asset for most older individuals. Approximately 80 percent of the elderly own homes that are free and clear of mortgage. Home ownership does not guarantee satisfaction and comfort, however. Rapidly rising property taxes and maintenance costs are driving older people from their homes, yet suitable alternative rental quarters at prices they can afford are scarce or nonexistent. Since January 1969 property taxes have increased for most older people by 39 percent, and maintenance costs have jumped by one-third. The net impact is that millions of older people are finding themselves in an impossible situation.

On the basis of crude estimates, it is projected that about 6 million older adults live in substandard or unsatisfactory housing (Robbins, 1970). Older people, for the most part, tend to live in older, less valuable, and more dilapidated housing. An estimated 30 percent of all older Americans live in substandard housing. Among poor older people the situation is significantly worse: 40 percent live in housing with major defects. Fifty percent of those dwellings lack running water, 30 percent lack inside toilets, 40 percent lack hot water, and 50 percent lack central heating. Substandard housing is commonest in rural areas in the South; the 11 southern states have 68 percent of all the substandard housing in the United States.

Another problem is that the supply of housing designed for older people is severely limited. In particular, there is very little congregate or group housing that would provide frail old people with an alternative to completely independent living or institutional placement in a nursing home or other long-term care facility.

Consequently, very few people are entirely free from at least some housing difficulty in later life. They are caught between a desire to stay put and the need to adjust to changing physical and social circumstances. Most older adults desire to live independently and have strong feelings against moving. Studies indicate that the factors reflecting a poor living situation, such as high living costs, loneliness, and distance from relatives and friends, are not likely to motivate older people to move unless their situation becomes very serious. Neither is the availability of good housing elsewhere likely to cause older people to look more favorably on relocation, even though a move may be inevitable.

Most living arrangements become less adequate as people advance in age. House furnishings are incompatible with physical limitations; for instance, high shelves, heavy doors, bathtubs and showers that are difficult to enter, and inadequate lighting all become troublesome and often quite hazardous for an older person. Children leave and spouses die, leaving the surviving old person with more house and more responsibility than is necessary or possible to maintain. The neighborhood changes, scattering a former network of friends and activities. The conflict between a desire to remain independent and the changing housing needs of older people places them under great tension.

A Crisis in Mobility

Many older people identify transportation as their most serious problem after income and health, and a surprisingly large number name transportation as their number-one problem (Revis, 1970). Without adequate transportation, many other problems of the elderly are intensified. Transportation, like income, is a compounding factor for old people. If older people are mobile, they frequently find it easier to adjust to new problems that come with age; without mobility they are likely to experience a syndrome of deprivation.

The transportation problems of older people stem from four major factors: (1) The U.S. transportation system is based on use of the private auto; (2) many older people cannot afford the cost of transportation; (3) many live in areas poorly served by public transportation; and (4) many have difficulty using public transportation. The factors are interrelated. For example, because many older people live in areas not well served by public transportation, they do not have easy access to health care and other services (Manney, 1975).

Private Car Economy   The root of the transportation problem for older people as well as other groups is a dominance in this country of the privately owned automobile. The automobile influences lane use, zoning patterns, highway construction, and all but a small fraction of public transportation funds. Even traffic signals, traffic markings, street signs, and other pedestrian helpers are geared toward the smooth flow of automobile traffic, which is one reason older people constitute a disproportionate number of pedestrian fatalities. The private auto, with the economic and social change it has produced, has destroyed public transit systems in many cities. When people can afford cars they stop riding buses, reducing the income of transit systems. Fares go up to cover expenses, further discouraging additional riders. Routes are curtailed, quality of service declines, and equipment deteriorates. The poor, the young, and the old cannot support a transit system caught in this circular dilemma.

Cost   One-fourth of all older people live in poverty or on severely squeezed incomes. They must spend most of their money on food, housing, and medical care, leaving little money for luxuries such as private cars, or even for public transportation. Those who drive must cope with an even greater problem because of the high cost of gasoline, insurance, and auto maintenance. Thus by virtue of their low income, older people have trouble obtaining any kind of transportation.

Access   Even if older people have enough money to use public transportation, services are usually only minimally available in the areas where they live. The private automobile rules supreme outside central cities, and the rural and suburban elderly are often totally without public transportation. Within cities the public transportation system is geared to the rush hour needs of commuters, not to the pace or needs of older residents.

Barriers to Use   Many older people cannot overcome physical and psychological barriers to the use of public transportation. To ride buses and subways requires a high degree of speed, agility, and quick reactions. Printed schedules are often largely incomprehensible, and it is frequently impossible to obtain information over the telephone from transit companies. According to some studies the most serious obstacle to better transportation for the elderly is their psychological reluctance. Older people are simply unwilling to face the uncertainty, terrors, and dangers of riding on public buses and subways. Muggings, purse snatchings, and pickpocketing are common crimes committed against older people using public transit systems. These dangers are real; much of the public transportation in the United States seems to be designed for the strongest, heartiest, and most agile riders. High bus steps, hard-to-open exit doors, poorly placed handrails, and open-air bus stops without benches constitute formidable physical barriers for older people who must rely heavily on public transit.

Insufficient Support Services

Although inadequate income is the most serious problem confronting older people, we must keep in mind that many older individuals need certain **support services** as much as they need adequate income (Morris, 1970). In some cases, such as a friendly visiting service for the homebound, the service may be as important as money, because it enables the older person to remain in familiar surroundings rather than in an institution. The denial of services on the basis of age is common among both governmental and voluntary agencies and reflects institutional discrimination (Butler, 1975). The absence of services is a fundamental indicator of a general unwillingness to provide for the disadvantaged. Many of the old must become totally impoverished or so ill as to require hospitalization or institutionalization before they are regarded as eligible for even minimal services. They do not have access to preventive services, early diagnosis and treatment, or routine services that could prevent the emergence of new problems. In general, old people have had to wait for services essential to survival and imperative to a decent and pleasurable old age (Butler, 1975). They need facilities, programs, and services to enable them to survive short-term crises and meet long-term needs. Without these services many lose their capacity to live independently or semi-independently in their own homes. They often wait through agonizing intervals for the doctor to visit, the homemaker to come, and the Meals on Wheels to arrive. They also wait in vain for needed services that may be totally unavailable.

Health, Mental Health, and Security

Health Care for Older Adults

In our society those most in need of health care are least likely to have access to it. Health care for the elderly, because of the various chronic health problems characteristic of later life, represents about one-fourth of the expenditure for health services in the United States (Manney, 1975). Older adults frequently experience primitive health problems like malnutrition as a result of their inability to purchase food because of disability, loneliness, depression, and even fear of crime. Older people require more care, see doctors more frequently than people of other age groups, spend more time and longer periods in hospitals, and are more likely to need care upon release from the hospital. Older people consume approximately 25 percent of the drugs used in the United States.

Although older adults are the major consumers of health care, the medical and auxiliary health professions are not sensitive to the unique problems and needs of this group. Older patients are viewed by the health profession as difficult and complaining; consideration is seldom given to the likely association between mental and physical health problems. The plight of older people in the United States with respect to health care seems almost insurmountable. Some of the problems are discussed below.

The Dilemma of Chronic Illness   Management of older adults' chronic health problems presents a unique challenge in the health-care field. The health-care professions are readily able to deal with short-term or acute care problems. They clearly understand the cause of and treatment for chronic medical conditions. But they have not yet effectively dealt with the social and psychological ramifications of chronic illness on older patients and their families.

Anselm Strauss (1973), a noted sociologist, maintains that the major concern of a chronically ill person is not just to stay alive or to keep the symptoms under control, but to live as normally as possible despite symptoms and disease. Many older people have evolved adaptive measures that enable them to cope effectively with the difficulties chronic illnesses present. Others, however, are not successful in carrying out normal life functions. They experience diseases that are just too serious and demanding for a normal home environment. Older people very often find it impossible to manage a treatment plan; for example, they get confused about taking medication and frequently either overmedicate or discontinue taking medicine altogether. Many older people give in to the limitations of chronic illness because they lack the necessary support to resist them. Without the assistance of trained personnel or proper resources, many chronically ill individuals become depressed or isolated. Those who cannot live alone generally must enter nursing homes or other institutions that provide extended care.

Very often children of chronically ill elderly attempt to care for them in the home. Such efforts are usually unsuccessful because of the psychological strains created by the demands of the chronically ill patient. Families must ultimately institutionalize parents, grandparents, aunts, or uncles and suffer subsequent intense feelings of guilt. The dilemma of the chronically ill presents a challenge that demands social as well as medical considerations.

High Cost   At the time of its passage in 1965, the Medicare program was heralded as the answer to the medical cost problems of older people, but it has not lived up to these expectations. The cost of health care is still a major problem and creates barriers to proper health care for older adults. The Medicare program provides assistance for those older adults with acute conditions and in need of limited hospitalization and covers about 75 percent of costs under these circumstances. Medicare is not as helpful, however, in the more common case of the older person with a long-term chronic illness. Medicare pays only two-fifths of an older person's annual medical bill that averages about $1,000 (Manney, 1975).

A major reason medical costs persist as a problem for older adults is that many of the day-to-day or long-term care needs of the older adult are not covered by Medicare. The program excludes such items as prescriptions and other drugs, dental care, foot and eye care, and prosthetics. Many other health services, such as long-term care, nursing home care without prior hospitalization, and most psychiatric care are excluded as well. The increasing cost of participation in a program like Medicare is another cause of high medical expenses. The fees and deductibles have doubled since the passage of the program in 1965.

Perhaps most important, however, is the fact that medical costs have skyrocketed for the population as a whole. Manney (1975) indicates that between 1967 and the fall of 1973, all medical costs rose 30 percent. The cost for a semi-private hospital room increased 82 percent, operating room fees increased 79 percent, and physician fees increased by more than one-third.

The overall effects of increased health care costs in the United States are frightening. Total expenditures for health care increased by 500 percent between 1950 and 1970; and between 1960 and 1970 hospital costs increased about 500 percent (Manney, 1975). Medical costs have increased twice as fast as the cost of living in general. The government has recognized this trend and is taking steps to curtail it, but how long it will take for medical costs to stabilize is uncertain at this time.

The Health Nonsystem   Still another aspect of the overall health problem for older people is a health-care system that is not responsive to their needs. A major weakness of the system is its fragmented or piecemeal nature. By all standard definitions our system should probably be called a nonsystem. A health-care system generally consists of a comprehensive and well-coordinated continuum of service. Such a system follows a path of health education, diagnostic screening, and preventive medicine; and includes acute health-care facilities, flexible alternatives for chronic care, and rehabilitation of the chronically ill. Many of the vital components of a health-care system, such as rehabilitation and alternatives for chronic care, are not provided systematically in this country. Generally, many of these services are available only to those who are financially well-off and can purchase them privately.

Another problem in the health-care system is the shortage of medical personnel. There are not enough physicians, nurses, dentists, medical social workers, therapists, psychologists, nutritionists, paraprofessionals, and other medical specialists to meet our national health-care needs. Rural areas in particular suffer the effects of this shortage.

Problems of Institutionalization   A major problem in this country is the lack of facilities that would provide a continuum of care for older people who cannot care for themselves. Currently, if older people cannot care for themselves at home, the only alternative is institutionalization in a nursing home or other chronic care facility.

Some years ago a special Congressional hearing called national attention to the abuse of old people by the nursing home industry in the United States. Even today, however, we have not begun to deal with this problem effectively. As a matter of fact, as the industry has grown, the problems have become even more complex. Of major concern is the fact that the nursing home industry appears to have attracted unethical proprietors connected with dishonest businesspeople intending to make a "fast buck" on the elderly. The industry has grown so fast that even well-intended nursing homes are rarely staffed with trained personnel. Butler (1975) maintains that only in the United States does such extensive commercialization of facilities for the old exist. In this country nursing homes are often described as human junkyards and warehouses.

The words *nursing home* have stereotypic meaning for older people in the United States. Such institutions are viewed as places to await death and to be mistreated. They also symbolize the replacement of independent living with an existence of boredom and total dependence. No matter how well-intended a family's motives, giving permission for placement in such a home connotes rejection to the older person.

Nursing homes create a painful dilemma for families. A decision to move older parents or relatives into a nursing home, even when other alternatives do not exist, frequently causes guilt and ambivalence about the decision. To many families removal from the home to an institution is synonymous with death. Nursing homes are viewed as "preburial storehouses," for it is extremely uncommon for an individual, once admitted, to return (Butler, 1975).

Because we as a nation do not openly like to discuss or deal with death, the trend has been to remove people from their own homes to die. When a family or physician feels that death is near, immediate measures are taken to remove the person either to a nursing home or to a hospital setting so that the individual will not die at home in the presence of family members. For the older person this is probably the most uncomfortable way to die—that is, away from familiar surroundings. Many believe it would be much more desirable to permit older people to die with dignity in their own homes. This problem will be discussed in more detail in Chapter 8.

Mental Health in Old Age

Public awareness of the needlessly high risk of mental disorder among older people has emerged gradually in recent years (Butler and Lewis, 1973). Acknowledgement of the psychosocial toil of growing old has stimulated concern and activities toward determining and meeting the mental-health needs of the aged.

Among the factors that contribute most to the development of the elderly's emotional problems are the social ostracism to which they are subjected, the shrinking of their circle of friends, their intense loneliness, the reduction and loss of human respect, and their feelings of disgust. Such feelings are instilled in older people through a number of means that basically involve a systematic effort on the part of this society to deny the elderly or remove them from positions, resources, and associations that might provide them satisfaction. Some of the means that result in the demoralization of older people include various types of changes and losses that occur in later life.

Butler (1975) maintains that old age has the potential for being an immensely interesting and emotionally satisfying period of life, but this potential is endangered by many forces. Changes are frequent, and loss of physical health and the death of important individuals, such as spouse, close friends, colleagues, and relatives, place enormous stress on human emotions. Older adults meet crises of all kinds, sometimes one after another, sometimes simultaneously—retirement, widowhood, major and minor illness, changes in body appearance, sensory loss, decreasing social status, a dramatically lowered standard of living, and so on. Much energy is expended as old people go through the process of mourning for their losses, adjusting to the changes involved, and recovering from stresses. Exposure to multiple crises leaves people emotionally and physically drained.

A range of emotional problems may also be produced by the stresses of everyday living. For example, struggling with financial and medical needs without adequate support from family and friends can be an overwhelming experience for some. Normal reactions, such as grief, guilt, depression, and helplessness under these circumstances do not in themselves constitute mental problems. If such feelings remain unresolved, however, and fester, outside assistance may be needed to resolve them.

Crimes against Older Adults

Another stress that must be faced by older adults is the fear of victimization by rapists and robbers (see "Prisoners of Fear," 1976). In recent years individuals over 50 have been seen as easy targets for vandals and criminals. Because of a dramatic increase in crimes against older people in many metropolitan areas, they are often afraid to walk the streets alone. Television and newspaper stories report that in these areas older people remain virtually barricaded within their own homes. They are afraid to answer the door or leave the security of the home for any reason.

In some low-income neighborhoods younger people, either as individuals or in groups, vandalize and even terrorize older citizens. Purse snatching and personal assaults are not uncommon. Property destruction, such as broken windows, torn-down fences, and trampled gardens, are frequent occurrences. Even the telephone and mail have been used as means of terrorizing or extorting older people.

In addition, in some areas the elderly are systematically preyed upon by thieves and con artists. High-pressure sales tactics are used to obtain signatures on contracts for nonexistent services. Many older people are subject to robberies that involve either forceful entry or breaking and entry. In addition, income checks are regularly stolen. Approximately 20,000 Social Security checks are stolen each year by direct looting of mailboxes (Butler, 1975). Besides the tremendous material loss, the psychological strain of living under these circumstances can affect physical health and result in driving older people deeper into a world of isolation.

Leisure Time

Besides the status problems retirement poses for older people, it also creates another difficulty: We have a whole generation of people with about 20 years of leisure time (Streib, 1970). The transition from work to retirement is one of the major changes occurring in the later years. Kalish (1975) reminds us that although in the past retirement has been primarily a concern for men, increasing numbers of women have entered the labor force during the past decade, and in the future, retirement will be a vital consideration for women as well.

Retirement is a new institution in our society. Until fairly recently the rich could retire, but others had to work until poor health and physical disabilities removed them from the labor force. In 1900, 68 percent of American men 65 years of age and older were working; by 1960 the proportion was reduced to 32 percent; and by 1975 it had dropped to 23 percent (Kalish, 1975). The percentage of older women who are working has remained roughly the same over the 60-year period, although the proportion of all adult women working increased substantially.

Leisure and Work

Like many concepts that defy precise definition, leisure and work can be approached in various ways. Kalish (1975) suggests that one possibility is to differentiate leisure and work activities by whether or not they are income producing; another consideration is whether or not the activity is sought for pleasure. On the whole, however, we need to recognize that the concepts are blurred. If a person dislikes gardening it becomes work, whereas it may be pleasurable for other people. Many older people find gardening very relaxing and seek the opportunity to garden many hours each week. If someone gardens for other people, should this be considered work? Is it work even if the individual thoroughly enjoys gardening and would rather be doing that than anything else?

Retirement and Use of Leisure Time

Old people in Denmark, Great Britain, and other European countries view retirement as essentially a time of rest (Manney, 1975). Perhaps typically, Americans speak of retirement in terms of leisure *activities;* retired people in this country feel they must be doing things. Even passive leisure activities are seen as opportunities to accomplish something or to improve oneself. For example, retired people prefer "serious content" in their television shows, such as documentaries and news programs. The kinds of leisure activity available are numerous, depending on the income, health, mobility, and preference of the individual.

In general, however, the leisure activities of older Americans do not reflect great enthusiasm for the cultural opportunities of a leisure society. Manney (1975) reports the most popular leisure pursuit for old people, as for Americans of all ages, is watching television. On the average, retired people spend just under three hours a day in front of the television. The next most frequent activities are visiting, reading, gardening, walking, and handy work. Older people also spend some time just sitting, but pure idleness is not common until very advanced years. Older people do not frequently engage in creative activities, such as playing music, painting, sculpting, or writing. Neither do many attend concerts or plays.

In fact, patterns of leisure tend to remain extremely stable over the life span. While people will drop some interests, such as participating in sports, as they grow older, most retired people do the same thing for relaxation that they have done all their lives. Significant changes toward more effective use of leisure time will probably come slowly, as young people learn the skills necessary for more creative activity. Whether this is happening yet is questionable. Social critics observe that mass higher education, including widespread exposure to liberal arts education, has not led to a wide range of leisure pursuits. Both college graduates and those with little education tend to pursue the same activities for relaxation—television foremost among them. Our educational system is still primarily oriented toward preparing young people to fill instrumental work roles not toward showing them how to enjoy themselves while not working. As Norman Cousins put it, "Science tends to lengthen life and education tends to shorten it. . . . Education has the effect of deflecting men from the enjoyment of living" (Manney, 1975).

Differential Concepts
of Leisure by Class

The low-income elderly men or women in the inner cities may spend much of their time sitting on a park bench visiting and talking with friends or neighbors (Kalish, 1975). This lifestyle may appear unsatisfactory or lonely, and indeed the old person may feel lonely and isolated. On the other hand, this behavior may represent the continuation of a lifelong pattern as a "loner."

Middle-income elderly couples living in suburban areas may be socially involved with friends, participating in political activities, doing volunteer work, or taking courses in painting or ceramics. Their lives may appear full and rich on the surface, but they also express feelings of loneliness, especially after a spouse dies.

Throughout life, time is structured for us by the various institutions of which we are a part. For example, when we work, our life is structured by a time clock; when we were children and went to school, our time was structured by the school bus and the school schedule. In retirement the days, the weeks, and the years may be without external structure, so individuals must structure their own time. The task of structuring one's own time can be very difficult, and very disconcerting for those who feel that time must be used in a constructive way, however that may be defined (Kalish, 1975). Others may take pleasure in unstructured time, whiling it away in casual pursuits. But in general, there are very few choices for how the older person can make use of leisure time. Many times individuals can use their leisure through volunteer activities, but on the whole they are left to their own resources to plan for how they spend the retirement years.

Summary

The problems discussed above are the types of difficulties experienced by older people that have called for the creation of many new service programs. Those working with older individuals must keep in mind that, at any given time, an elderly person is probably trying to cope with several of these problems simultaneously. Although we may first deal with an acute crisis, we must be sensitive to the fact that the difficulty may be accompanied or caused by several other underlying problems or conditions. The problems of older people are complex, and the solutions are complex as well. One of the most difficult aspects of helping older people deal with their problems and concerns is that there are many barriers preventing the helping person from providing the kind of assistance that is actually needed.

Social attitudes and prejudice toward the elderly in this society have created a world for them and those who attempt to help them that lacks adequate resources. This is not to say that what does exist is not good. But compared to other industrialized countries like England and Sweden, the United States allocates a small proportion of its resources to its elderly population.

READING 2.1

Growing Old in America / Grace Hechinger

At age 75 Margaret Mead remains an active participant in and observer of life. In the following interview she shares her reflections on American values and the status accorded older people.

Margaret Mead celebrates her 75th birthday this year. We went to see her in her office, tucked away in a Victorian turret of New York City's Museum of Natural History. It is the same place she began her work 50 years ago—cozy, comfortable and cluttered with books and memorabilia. To get there, we had to take a large museum elevator, walk down long, dimly lit corridors lined with fossil specimens and finally climb a tiny winding staircase. Few with her fame could resist the temptation to move to grander and more accessible quarters. But one secret of Margaret Mead's long and productive life is her ability to know instinctively what is right for her.

She has been acclaimed "one of the greatest women alive" and is known throughout the world as a pioneer in her chosen field of anthropology. She is the author of nearly two dozen books and countless articles on primitive peoples and all aspects of family life.

A petite and lively woman, she's seated behind her large desk, which overflows with papers and other evidence of work in progress, and beams her famous smile as she talks. Dr. Mead's energy and unflagging interest in life pervade her own unique and inspiring perspective on old age in America.

Family Circle: America has a bad reputation for our treatment of the elderly. Do you think it is warranted?

Dr. Mead: America is pretty negligent in this respect. As a nation of immigrants, we have always put a tremendous premium on youth. The young people, the first generation born here, understood American life better than their parents, who had come from other countries. In the more uprooted families, grandparents became a source of embarrassment. Though children whose grandparents were not English-speaking might learn to understand their grandparent's language, they would refuse to speak it.

But at least older people used to stay in the family. Homes were big, and there was room for extra aunts and grandparents. Families lived close together in communities. Today we have many more old people than in the past. And we have changed our whole life-style. The flight to the suburbs in the last 25 years has done a great deal of harm. In these age-segregated, class-segregated communities, there is no place for old people to live near the young people they care about. So the poor ones are stacked away in nursing homes, which are sometimes called "warehouses for the old." The more affluent ones move into golden ghettos or go to Florida, but they too are segregated and lonely.

FC: How were the elderly treated in some of the primitive cultures you have studied?

Dr. Mead: You don't find many early or primitive societies that treat old people as badly as the civilized societies do. The very earliest civilizations, of course, had to let their older people die, very often because they weren't strong enough to walk the necessary distance to find food. But as soon as there were ways of storing food, older people were looked after.

FC: Do you see any parallel in the way America treats its older people and the way we treat our children?

Dr. Mead: Our treatment of both reflects the value we place on independence and autonomy. We do our best to make our children independent from birth. We leave them all alone in rooms with the lights out and tell them, "Go to sleep by yourselves." And the old people we respect most are the ones who will fight for their independence, who would sooner starve to death than ask for help.

We in America have very little sense of interdependence. The real issue is whether a society keeps its older people close to children and young people. If old people are separated from family life, there is real tragedy both for them and the young.

FC: How could we structure our society to help bring older people back into the lives of their families?

Dr. Mead: It is primarily a question of replanning, of building communities where older people are welcome—not necessarily your own grandmother, but somebody's grandmother. Older people need to live within walking distance of shops and friends and family. They need younger people to help with the heavy chores, to shovel the snow and cut the grass so they can continue to live on their own.

FC: What do you think about the way we approach retirement?

Dr. Mead: The practice of early retirement is terribly wasteful. We are wasting millions of good years of good people by forcing them into retirement. The men especially suffer. Whether or not women work, they've always had to do the housekeeping and the shopping and the planning. So when they retire, they still have some continuity in their lives. But the men are admirals without a fleet. They don't know what else to do but die.

FC: What can we do to keep older people active in community life?

Dr. Mead: We can do many things. Some universities are building alumnae housing on campuses so that graduates will be able to move back near the universities. Some can teach, and all can enjoy the lectures, the intellectual stimulation and being near young people.

We shouldn't drop people from the PTA when their last child leaves school. We should have a grandparents' association that works for the local schools. At present, older people vote against school issues for schools their children once attended. They get selfish because they're no longer involved.

FC: It has been a fond American myth that in the good old days—whenever those were—we treated old people much better. Did the elderly really have fewer problems?

Dr. Mead: For one thing, there weren't a great many older people, and the ones that lived long lives were very, very tough.

Older people are more frail today. Many are the kind who would have died during infancy in earlier times and have had uncertain health all their lives. I had never seen an older person lying around like a vegetable, taking up the energy of doctors and nurses, until I was 28 years old. Every old person I knew as a child was somebody I could admire and listen to and enjoy.

When we're involved with old people whose hearing and eyesight go and who have to be cared for, we don't treat them like people, and that is frightening to old and young alike.

FC: When you were a child, grandparents had a much more active role in child-rearing than they do today. Do you believe that grandparents can educate their grandchildren?

Dr. Mead: If only today's grandparents would realize that they have seen more social change than any other generation in the history of the world! There is so much they could pass on!

In the small towns of earlier times, one good grandmother went a long way with her stories, her store of old-fashioned songs and her skills in the vanishing arts. From her, children absorbed a sense of the past and learned to measure time in meaningful biological terms— when grandmother was young, when mother was young, when I was young. Dates became real instead of mere numbers in a history book.

When my grandmother died in 1928 at the age of 82, she had seen the entire development of the horseless carriage, the flying machine, the telephone, the telegraph and Atlantic cables, radio and silent films.

Today, telephoning has largely replaced the family correspondence of two generations ago. I still treasure a letter that ends: "You are always in the thoughts of your grandmother by the sea. P.S. 'Apartment' is spelled with one 'P'."

FC: Was your grandmother very important to you when you were growing up?

Dr. Mead: One of my grandmothers, who always lived with us, was the most decisive influence on my life. She sat at the center of our household. Her room was the place we immediately went when we came home from school. We did our lessons on the cherry-wood table with which she had started housekeeping. Later it was my dining room table for 25 years.

I think my grandmother was the one who gave me my ease in being a woman. I had my father's mind, which he had inherited from her. Without my grandmother's presence—small, dainty and pretty—I might have thought having my father's mind would make me masculine. Though she was wholly without feminist leanings, she taught me that the mind is not sex-typed.

You know, one reason grandparents and grandchildren get along so well is that they can help each other out. First-person accounts of the parents when *they* were children reduces parental fury over disorders and fads of "the younger generation" and does away with such pronouncements as: "My father would never have permitted me to. . . ."

In small-town schools, there used to be teachers who taught two generations of children and mellowed in the process. They were there to remind the children that their parents had once been young, played hooky and passed forbidden notes in school. They were also able to moderate the zeal and balance the inexperience of young teachers.

FC: It is a popular belief that the way people were treated as children influences the way they treat older people. Do you agree?

Dr. Mead: There is a story that I like about a father bird who was carrying a little bird in its beak over the river. The little bird was completely in the power of the father bird. The older bird said, "My son, when I am old, will you care for me?"

The little bird said, "No, father, but I will care for my children the way you have cared for me."

The story shows something of the way affection is passed down through the generations. But it also reveals a fear of aging. In this country, some people start being miserable about growing old while they are still young, not even middle-aged. They buy cosmetics and clothes that promise them a young look.

A concomitance to the fear of aging is a fear of the aged. There are far too many children in America who are badly afraid of older people because they never see any. Old people are not a regular part of their everyday lives. Also, children are aware that their middle-aged parents cling to youth.

FC: It's true. We Americans are obsessed with staying young. There are not enough models like you, Dr. Mead, to show younger people goals to grow toward.

Dr. Mead: We have always had a good number of lively old people—it is just the proportions that are changing. We had Bernie Baruch sitting on his park bench, advising one president after another. We have many physicians who go on practicing late in life. Writers, too, and justices of the Supreme Court.

FC: How can middle-aged and young people lessen the fear of growing old?

Dr. Mead: It's very important to prepare yourself. One useful thing is to change all your doctors, opticians and dentists when you reach 50. You start out when you are young with everybody who looks after you older than you are. When you get to be 50, most of these people are 65 or older. Change them all and get young ones. Then, as you grow older, you'll have people who are still alive and active taking care of you. You won't be desolate because every one of your doctors is dead.

Another thing is to consider what you want to do later in life while you are still young. If you think of your whole life-span and what you are going to do at one stage and then at another, and incorporate these plans in your life picture, you can look forward confidently to old age. If you associate enough with older people who do enjoy their lives, who are not stored away in any golden ghettos, you will gain a sense of continuity and of the possibilities for a full life.

FC: How did you plan for your life when you were young?

Dr. Mead: I went to work at the Museum of Natural History as a young girl, and of course I had no idea how long I'd stay. You don't when you are 24. Then I saw a doddering old man walking around the corridors, and I asked, "What is he doing here?" I was told, "He is working on a book. He retired 20 years ago." I discovered that at the Museum they keep you until you die. And so I decided to stay right there.

FC: How do you think people can learn to appreciate the past?

Dr. Mead: I frequently have my students interview older people. For the Bicentennial, we developed a model book called *How to Interview Your Grandfather.* It is the reverse of a baby book. The students made up the questions simply by thinking of what they wanted to know about the past. The older people adore being asked. They stop complaining that nobody is interested in them or that "nobody listens to me anymore. . . ." And the young people find that what they have to say is fascinating.

FC: It's so important for children to sense the treasure of memory, both personal and national.

Dr. Mead: Another thing we are doing with students is to tell them to write an autobiography for their as-yet-unborn-grandchildren. What would you like your grandson or granddaughter to know about you? Thinking like this gives young people a new perspective about the future: They begin to realize that someday they themselves will be old.

My mother was very fond of Robert Browning. She used to quote these lines from Rabbi Ben Ezra. They are favorites of mine:

> Grow old along with me!
> The best is yet to be,
> The last of life, for which the first was made:
> Our times are in His hand
> Who saith 'A whole I planned,
> Youth shows but half; trust God; see all, nor be afraid!'

Questions 2.1

1. Americans place a high value on independence and autonomy. Discuss how we express this value, through our institutions and personal attitudes, in relation to older people.

2. Mead suggests that interdependence is related to family life. Discuss the meaning of interdependence, especially for older people.

3. Discuss the potentially positive functions of open communication between the elderly and children.

4. To whom is Mead referring when she speaks of older people who are "stored away" in "golden ghettos"?

READING 2.2

The Company Tells Me I'm Old / James A. McCracken

The author was a Reader's Digest *editor for 26 years. As he approaches his own retirement, he reflects on some of its meanings.*

I was a young man, once. Now I'm not. Now I'm an old man. Leastwise, the company I work for tells me I'm old. I'm almost sixty-five. In a couple of months they're going to retire me. Put me out to pasture.

What's old? Folks sixty-five don't think sixty-five's old. It's the young people who think sixty-five's creaking age. Once I thought anybody sixty-five was ready for the grim reaper. Now? Well, now I'm hoping I've got a few years left, anyway. I find that life doesn't become less precious as you get older. I keep jumping out of the way of cars just as keenly as I did twenty, thirty years ago. And when lightning's flashing around in the sky, I don't go outside looking at it, thinking, Well, if it hits me, it hits.

There was a time, a long time ago, when I used to watch my old man when he was sixty-five or so. He'd sit in his chair just thinking about getting up. He'd run his hands up the arms of the chair a little way, brace, and push. And he'd stand up. Well, he was up. He'd stand for a moment, put his hands on the back of his hips. He'd still be bent over a little bit. But then he'd straighten up and be off about his business. Maybe his business was going to the bathroom or into the kitchen to ask my mother what was for supper. My old man had a belly. And jowls. They hung down from his cheeks like his face was made of soft wax that was beginning to melt and run down.

I can remember. Maybe I'd be sitting in a chair, too. I'd watch my old man get himself started. Then I'd get up. Quick. No creaks or grunts. I was young. I had a young man's body. My hair was dark and thick. Plenty of it. I tried to picture myself old, like my old man. No way.

I wasn't ever going to look like that. No soft belly for me. I was good-looking. I knew I'd always be good-looking. Even when I was old. No wrinkles. No soft white wax running down to my collar. Maybe my hair would turn white. But I wouldn't go bald. I wouldn't sag. I wouldn't groan when I sat down. Or when I got up. I'd do it quick. Sit down. Get up.

I always thought it was my old man's fault for getting old. He could have run a mile or two every day. He could have lifted weights or played tennis or worked out at a gym.

I look back now. My old man's gone, of course. And in a sense I'm him. I wake up in the morning. I lie there. Well, I haven't got a headache. My toes work. My fingers move. So I didn't have a stroke or nothing during the night. Friend of mine, my age, he woke up one morning. Felt same as usual. Only his left leg didn't work. He didn't know it didn't work. He didn't find out until he got out of bed. Left leg didn't work. Left arm didn't work, either. He wondered, What the hell. Tried to call his wife. Mouth didn't work. Well, in the hospital they told him he'd had a stroke. Right there in bed. While he was sleeping. It just crept up on him.

Now I get up from a chair like my old man did. And then I stand there. Got a little crick in my back. Just a little one. So. There's some grass to cut. And I ought to fix that venetian blind. My wife's been after me for two weeks to fix it. Aw, I've been cutting grass and fixing things all my life, it seems. Something's always got to be fixed or moved or trimmed or hauled. That's what keeps you young, they say. That doesn't keep you young. Always doing things. That gets you old. I stand and think about things like that. My wife's in the kitchen, clattering around. I hear the pots and pans banging. I go in. "What's for supper?" I say. Just like my old man used to.

Now, though, I'm going to get retired. It's like I've been in a corral, fenced in with all the other working horses. Along comes a man and he slips a halter over my head. He takes ahold of the halter and he leads me out of the corral toward a long white fence. I've seen that fence many a time. I've glanced over there at a couple of old horses off there in the pasture. They move slow. They raise their heads slow, then lower them and go back to grazing. Old horses. Old folks' home. A condo in Florida, maybe St. Petersburg. Sit on a green bench in the sunshine. So the man leads me over to the white fence. He opens the gate and pats me on the rump. "It's green pastures for you, old fella," he says. He takes the halter off, walks back to the gate. Closes it. And there I am.

That's what my company says. They hold a little party. Not much. I'm not a big shot. All the younger ones, they say, "Boy, are you lucky. No more getting up early to rush to work. Play golf, work at hobbies. Don't do nothing if you don't want to." They laugh and clap me on the back. They sort of look at me. Yeah. It would be nice to have some time off, all right. But they sure wouldn't want to be old. What can you do when you're old? Striving's gone, ambition's gone. Competition's gone. Challenge's gone. This old man here, his road's all downhill now. Down and out.

So I'm a Golden Ager now. The golden years, they say. Maybe they mistake rust for gold. The hinges get rusty. The bones creak, but there isn't any oil that's going to fix them. Do I mind? Well, it'd be nice to move around quick again. It'd be nice to shed this fat and these jowls. And grow a little more hair. I don't much like being bald. I got a few hairs left on top. So I massage them and comb them around a little bit. There aren't many, but they're all I got. And do I hate to sort of creak and groan a little? Well, I guess so. But you know something? As long as my joints creak, they're still moving. It's when they stop that I'll have me some problems.

I been reading some about how you should prepare for old age. For retirement. Prepare for the golden years. Develop hobbies. Take up woodworking or arts and crafts. Get yourself a little corner of the house where you can set yourself up a shop and do something. Well, what? I collected postage stamps when I was a kid. I collected them for about six months.

I didn't have enough money to buy an album, so I kept the stamps in an old shoe box. Well, one day I was home from school, sick. My old man was at work and my mother had to go down the street to buy some groceries. I didn't have anything to do but be sick, so I was looking at my stamps. They weren't doing any good lying around in the shoe box. I wanted to display them. We had a big sort of picture window. I got busy and mixed up some paste—flour-and-water paste. My mother was proud of that picture window. It looked out on a little garden she kept. I figured I'd pretty things up even more.

I guess I had three, maybe four hundred stamps. I pasted up the back of every one of those stamps one at a time, and one at a time, I stuck them onto that picture window. It was some sight. You couldn't see anything but postage stamps. I got the whole job done before my mother came home. I knew it would surprise her, but I didn't know it would surprise her so much.

I rushed off to bed and was lying there, sick, when she came home. Downstairs. I was upstairs. I could hear her humming around the kitchen while she put things away. The window was in the parlor (we didn't call them living rooms in those days). I heard her walking from the kitchen into the hall. First the footsteps stopped. Then the humming. There was silence. I was chuckling and laughing to myself, lying there in bed.

Suddenly there was a scream, then a sort of yelp. Then my name came up. "James!" (I was usually "Jimmy" around the place, but when somebody became angry, I became "James!") "James!" my mother hollered. I stopped laughing and giggling. She wasn't happy with what I had done? Where she got the hairbrush so fast I'll never know, but she did. First she got it, then I got it.

I spent the next month scraping stamps and paste off that window. I never collected stamps again.

I tried woodworking. I bought a long pine board and cut it down to about four foot long. Foot or fourteen inches wide. I shaped it by planing and sanding. It was going to be a nice table for before the fireplace. And I made legs. I had me quite a time fitting them into the board, but I finally did it. Then I sanded everything until I thought I had a pretty nice table. Then I stained it. And I varnished it. Then I set it up. And you know what? The legs weren't even. I thought I'd got them even, but I hadn't. So I sawed a mite off one leg. It still wobbled. I guess I'd sawed a mite too much. I sawed another one off a touch. That didn't do it, either. That table was about a foot and a half high when I started. I got her down to about six inches, and she still wasn't even. Well, she got to look sort of funny. This table, about four foot long, a little over a foot wide. And six inches high. And still not even. My wife snickered a good bit about it. I was half mad and the other half determined. But sometimes I could see that it did look sort of odd. Finally those legs got down to little nubbins. Like about an inch and a half high. She just barely cleared the carpet. And she still wobbled.

We ended up with a nice big fire in the fireplace one night. The stain and the varnish sort of smelled up the house for a while. But I got that table down to even. When she was all burned out and down to ashes, I spread them out on the hearth. Spread them out all nice and smooth. Now she lay level. She didn't wobble anymore. I never tried woodworking anymore, either.

So now I been sort of practicing up for retirement. I sit around the house on weekends, pretending I'm retired. What'll I do this morning? Well, now. There's grass to be cut. Hell, there's always grass to be cut. Something new is what I want. A project. My wife says, "Well, then, how about washing the windows?" I've washed those windows. My wife's washed those windows. That glass started out years ago being about a quarter of an inch thick. It's been washed so many times, one more washing and you're likely to be washing air. No more glass.

One Wednesday morning we had a hard snowstorm. I couldn't get to work. Maybe twenty years ago I could have. But back then I was racing. I was competing. But I'm not now. The race is run. I didn't win. I didn't lose, either. Just came out sort of even, I guess. Anyhow, toward noon the snow began to melt, and my wife, she says, "How about taking me shopping? I got shopping to do." That'd be a project. She's always telling me about seeing other old fellows down to the supermarket with their wives. So we got into the car, spun the wheels around for a while, and drove down to the village. We got a cart and went shopping. I looked around. Because of the snowstorm, there weren't many people in the store. Just some old wives and their old men. I looked at the old men. Not so old. Maybe like me. The old men, they generally shoved the cart around while their wives studied the shelves. They'd pick up a can of soup, study the label, and either put the can back or put it in the cart. The old men, they'd follow their wives with their eyes. They'd stand and stare. Like tired old horses. Their eyes sort of looked blank. Like there wasn't much going on inside. The wheels had almost stopped turning.

We wheeled around a corner. My wife was going to attack a new aisle. I looked over to one side. There was an old man with his cart. But he was bent way over the handle. He was standing on the ground but his head was darn near in the food. I looked at him and I thought, Thank God I'm not him. That old man—he wasn't much older than me—he had arthritis of the back so bad he was bent double. That shopping trip hadn't been much up to that point, but now it was important. It made me mighty thankful. I might be pretty old but I could still stand up straight. The old man swiveled his head out of the food. His eye caught mine. I sort of shook my head in sympathy. You sure got a bad break, friend, I seemed to say. All of a sudden he got embarrassed. And he straightened up! He straightened right up. As straight as I was standing. You know something? There wasn't a thing wrong with him. He was just so bored and fed up he couldn't think of anything else to do but lean over something. That's what that old man was doing. I got hold of my wife and we finished up that shopping trip in a hurry, checked out, and I haven't been back shopping since.

So what am I going to do in retirement? Well, like I said, the Golden Age advisers, they say plan ahead. I'm not going to do woodworking, that's for sure. And I won't collect stamps. I can cut grass. Maybe I could cut fancy patterns and designs in it. Just for something to do. The neighbors might not like it, the front lawn looking sort of funny with pictures and things sculpted in it. I don't know yet. I could polish and wax the car. I haven't done that much. The old bus could stand some cleaning. I could work on the engine. But if I did that, I'd sure fix it so she'd never run right again. I'm just not mechanical inclined.

Speaking of mechanical. Once a friend of mine thought he'd teach me how to do my own engine work. My wife and I didn't have much money and we sure had an old car. Always something busting in it. So, to begin, my friend took a carburetor apart. With me watching, of course. And he put it back together again. With me still watching every move. It was the carburetor out of my car. So I learned how to do that. He put the thing back in the car, hooked her up, and she ran perfect. I didn't want to lose my new talent, so the next Saturday, I took the carburetor apart myself. I had a little trouble, of course. That was only natural. But not too much. But then I started to put it back together. That was sure one bad mistake. I should have left it apart. I worked all Saturday morning and well into the afternoon. I'd get her together and have three parts left over. I'd take her down, put her together, and have five parts left. And not the same parts as the first time. I could have made two carburetors with all the things I had lying around. Finally, I sort of stuffed everything inside the case and shoved it all together. Something sort of gave. I left it all lying there on the bench and hustled to the telephone to call my friend.

His telephone rang. My friend's daughter answered. She was about eighteen. She was nice and sweet as she could be. "Mommy and Daddy," she said, "have gone away for a week's vacation." I started to cuss out my friend for abandoning me. The girl started to cry. I had to take that carburetor down to a garage on Monday morning for them to fix it. I had to walk down, about two miles, because the car sure couldn't run. A smart-aleck mechanic asked me what fool kid had been playing with the auto engine. I told him it was my wife. I missed a day's work and a day's pay. I had to bum a ride the next day while the mechanic came up to the house and put the carburetor back in the car. My wife missed shopping and a bridge game. Neither of us was speaking happy for a couple of days. And it cost me nine bucks! Mechanical inclined? Not me. I never let my friend touch the engine in my car again. I never touched it again, either.

You know how I look at planning for retirement? I look at it, forget it! I didn't plan my career when I was working my way through life. It just happened and I went along with it. I figure, things come up. You got to cut the grass. It always grew while I was working. It's not going to stop now. Things bust. Maybe I can learn to fix them. Maybe not. I have to be careful about that, though. In retirement I'm sure not going to be able to afford a group of auto mechanics and plumbers and carpenters falling over each other fixing what I mess up. But I'll try. Like fixing a leaking faucet. Trouble is, my wife always could fix leaking faucets better than I could. Well, I'll watch her and sort of supervise. If it isn't right, I'll make her fix it over again. That'll kill some time.

And blue jays! I'll chase blue jays. We got a bird feeder, and those big, blustery birds are always chasing the little ones away so they can glutton themselves on our sunflower seeds. And I'll throw rocks at the neighbor's dog. He always comes over onto our lawn to do his morning business. He does it while I'm at work. Now I'll be home. That dog's going to find some other lawn. Like his own, maybe.

My wife says she'll find things for me to do. She says she's got to. She says it sort of franticlike. She says if she doesn't—well, she's got a cousin in California she hasn't seen in years. She never did like that cousin, but she says maybe she's just misjudged her. She says she'll go visit her cousin for a couple of years. She'll get to like that cousin, maybe even learn to love her—that's what my wife says—even if it kills her. My wife's kidding, of course. She wouldn't do that. But if she does, she's got a surprise coming. I'm going with her. It's a man's place to protect his wife. Whether she needs protecting or not.

Questions 2.2

1. How did McCracken decide that he was old?

2. One area that often presents problems in retirement is the change in the relationship between husband and wife. In what ways would this be a difficult adjustment?

3. In your opinion, what is the prognosis for McCracken's retirement? Will it be especially problematic? Give reasons for your answer.

4. Discuss McCracken's individual coping pattern.

CHAPTER 3
THE SPECIAL PROblEMS of MINORITY, ETHNIC, WOMEN, ANd RURAL ELDERLY

We stated in Chapter 1 that most older people go through a similar process of aging and experience many of the same kinds of problems. However, minority, ethnic, women, and rural elderly may suffer more intensely from the overall effects of growing old in the United States. We believe those working with older people should be intensely aware of the plight and special problems of these subgroups among the elderly population and keep their special needs in mind when planning and providing services.

Minority Elderly

On the whole, the **minority elderly** are the most disadvantaged of the elderly population (Stanford, 1974). Elderly members of minority groups vary considerably in their social situations and cultural characteristics. One should use caution in comparing the conditions of an elderly black living in New York, an elderly Native American on a reservation, and an elderly Chicano in a small Texas town. Yet these minority elderly share a common vulnerability in their old age. They are vulnerable because they are poor and because they have minority group status in a predominantly white culture. They are stigmatized by their race and are the victims of prejudice and discrimination.

Older blacks, native Americans, Latinos, Asians, and other minority group members share other characteristics. They are not as numerous as one might expect. As a group they constitute only about 10 percent of all Americans age 65 and over. When

minority groups are considered independently, this percentage declines sharply. For instance, elderly blacks constitute only 7 percent; native Americans, 5.7 percent; Chicanos, 3.2 percent; and Puerto Ricans 2 percent of the total elderly population. Educational levels reveal a similar pattern of deprivation. The percentage of older Chicanos, for example, who have completed five years or less of formal schooling is six times greater than the percentage for the total population over age 65.

The major common characteristic of older minority individuals is their poverty. The Social Security increase that lifted 1.5 million of the white elderly from poverty between 1967 and 1972 had a relatively modest impact on minority elderly. This is due to the fact that a much higher proportion of minority elderly never acquired an employment record that would entitle them to Social Security benefits. Minority elderly have suffered not only from high ratios of unemployment but also from the types of jobs available to them. Menial jobs, such as migrant work and domestic and day work, have only recently been included under Social Security benefits. In addition, across-the-board benefits have less significance for those at the lower levels. For example, a 10 percent increase in Social Security benefits means $30 more to a white couple receiving $300 a month, but only $9.60 to a black widow receiving $96 a month. Social Security benefits, as a consequence, are generally about 26 percent higher for whites than they are for blacks and other minority retirees.

Still another similarity among minority elderly is their general state of health. The minority population in America has always experienced higher mortality rates (measured by prevalence of disease) than the white population. Mortality rates among minorities from diseases such as cancer and diabetes are increasing rapidly, while the mortality rates for whites from similar conditions are stabilizing or declining. Life expectancy for minority groups on the whole is lower than for whites. For white males and females, life expectancy is 67 and 71 years, respectively; for black males and females it is only 60.1 and 65 years, respectively. The life expectancy rate for native Americans and Chicanos is even more dramatic—about 44 to 48 years of age.

The issue of leisure time is virtually nonexistent for minority elderly, as they seldom retire because of the dire poverty that requires them to maintain employment as long as health permits in order to subsist.

The discussion of the particular cultural and ethnic aspects of each minority group is beyond the scope of this book and, to a great extent, beyond the scope of gerontologists. Sociologists and other researchers know more about minority cultures as a whole than they do about minority elderly. Perhaps those working directly with older people, rather than academicians, will enlighten us in this area. However, we will try to identify here some of the special needs and problems of the various minority groups and their implications for service workers.

Black Elderly

Older black people are fighting a losing struggle against poverty. During 1972, 500,000 white elderly left the poverty rolls, but poverty among older blacks increased by 17,000 people. The percentage of black elderly living in poverty grew from 39.3 percent in 1971 to 39.9 percent in 1972. This increase occurred while the poverty level among the total over-65 population dropped from 19.9 percent to 16.8 percent.

For the black elderly, poverty is concentrated among women and those living alone. A stunning 68 percent of black women living alone subsist on less than $2,000 annually. The figure for males is only slightly lower—54.7 percent. One-quarter of all elderly black families headed by a man survive on less than $40 a week; the comparable percentage for white households is 9.5 percent. The magnitude of this poverty both overshadows and leads to other deprivations. As with other poor old people, the poverty of black elderly brings substandard housing, chronic illness, malnutrition, and immobility.

Jacquelyn Jackson of Duke University, one of the leading advocates for the black elderly, urges social service systems to become more responsive to the needs of black elderly. However, she cautions well-meaning planners and social workers not to interfere with the effective extended family system that surrounds many older blacks. It is common for black elderly to be important and supportive resources for their children and grandchildren, helping with food, housing, income, baby-sitting, and other essential functions. Jackson (1973) suggests that black elderly may suffer significant family role losses if society intervenes in black family life carelessly. Rather than undermining these strengths, those who serve black elderly should attempt to build on them.

Spanish-speaking Elderly

The Spanish-speaking elderly include the Mexican-American (or Chicano), Puerto Rican, Cuban, and other Latin elderly (Manney, 1975). The Spanish-speaking elderly, particularly Mexican-Americans, are not ordinarily connected to Social Security or to any part of the social service system. The language barrier is a particularly serious problem for these people, most of whom speak English poorly, if at all.

To serve Spanish-speaking old people effectively, social agencies must have bilingual personnel available. In most instances federal offices and other Anglo-dominated agencies have improved their services to Spanish-speaking people when they supply bilingual personnel. What seems to be needed is a strong commitment to broaden and sustain such efforts.

Like blacks, Spanish-speaking elderly are usually part of a protective extended family and seek social agencies only as a last resort. In addition, many are reluctant to approach public agencies because they are concerned about their citizenship status and are fearful of being deported. Bilingual human-service workers should be used to serve this elderly group to facilitate their use of social service programs.

Native American Elderly

The problems of Native Americans are in many ways the most serious facing any minority group. Tribes and families have great difficulty meeting their fundamental needs. The vast majority of old Native Americans live as wards of the federal government on reservations located on some of the poorest land in the country.

The Native American elderly in particular could very well be the most deprived identified group of Americans. For most English is a second language, if it is spoken at all. Most live on little or no income in housing that is the worst for any population group in the country. Most have no formal education. Since unemployment rates on reservations average 50 percent, few have ever worked steadily. Only one of every three Native Americans and Alaskan natives will reach age 65, exactly half the rate for the U.S. population as a whole.

As with many Eastern cultures, Native American elderly are revered for their wisdom and experience. They are the educators who perpetuate the folklore and culture of the tribes. This position within the tribe should be supported and sustained if at all possible.

Asian-American Elderly

Data regarding elderly Asian-Americans are sparse. Most surveys indicate, however, that traditional close kinship ties in Asian-American families are beginning to erode in the urban cities. Language barriers and the traditional reluctance to rely on outside help are obstacles to the use of services by Asians.

Ethnic-Group Elderly

A large segment of the elderly population is comprised of individuals who immigrated to this country as children or young adults. The first-generation immigrants are now older adults, but they still practice old-world customs and beliefs. In many regions of the country there are enclaves of ethnic older Americans, for example, the French Canadians of New England. Many of our large metropolitan areas still have neighborhoods with strong ethnic identities, such as the North End of Boston. Those who came here as immigrants were a very independent and self-reliant breed. Because of the existence of ethnic neighborhoods and towns in this country, many found it unnecessary to learn English. Women who did not work outside the home relied upon their bilingual husbands and children to interact with the English-speaking community. In addition, these ethnic neighborhoods and towns had very strong informal social systems, including brothers, sisters, aunts, uncles, nieces, nephews, godparents, and friends, who would always come forth during any crisis. The existence of this system made it unnecessary to go outside the ethnic community for almost any type of service. Even social and recreational needs were met within the community through ethnic social clubs such as the Sons of Italy.

Many of these communities still exist in large cities. The non-English-speaking elderly in them often live alone but retain close ties with family and friends of similar ethnic origin. Because of their origin in this country, they are usually part of the "blue collar" culture and generally are not subject to extreme poverty. In some ethnic communities many of the elderly's needs are met through agencies set up by the ethnic community, for instance, Jewish homes for the elderly.

In some cases, however, out-migration of the middle aged and young have dissolved the ethnic community, and the non-English-speaking elderly who remain there may be subject to a form of cultural deprivation. The older immigrants' ethnic origins were kept alive in this country because they continued to practice old-world customs here. Marriages, christenings, and holiday celebrations were all occasions for continuing established old-world traditions.

Second- third-, and fourth-generation immigrant families are now assimilated into the American culture, and they neither speak a second language nor identify with ethnic origins. They do not carry out the old tradition of parents or grandparents. Very often old, non-English-speaking immigrants can rely only on other older individuals to help maintain ties with their ethnic origin. As the older immigrants' peers or cohorts die off, however, they have fewer and fewer avenues through which to maintain these ties.

As it now stands, when older, non-English-speaking elderly find they need assistance, they must deal with an unfamiliar English-speaking world. Consequently, due to language barriers, the ethnic elderly often may not avail themselves of much-needed services. In addition, many service programs for older people do not take into consideration the dietary or religious traditions that are an integral part of the ethnic elderly person's life. Because of an earlier need to maintain ethnic ties, ethnic individuals frequently find themselves socially isolated in later life due to language barriers and others' lack of concern for their special needs.

Older Women

Some gerontologists have begun to suggest that the 6.1 million older women in the United States constitute a technical minority group (Butler, 1975). Dr. Juanita Kreps, Secretary of Commerce, maintains that widows, single women, and female members of minority groups are particularly disadvantaged. Older women are generally the poorest individuals in our society today. In 1970, 51 percent of elderly women living alone lived below the poverty level. Many are isolated from family, friends, and community.

Women have an average life expectancy seven years longer than men and tend to marry men older than themselves. Consequently, 20 percent of American women are widowed by age 60, 50 percent by age 65, and about 67 percent by age 75. The income of a retired couple is generally based on the husband's work history, and upon his death the wife's benefits are dramatically reduced. Until 1973 housewives who were widowed received only 82.5 percent of their husbands' Social Security benefits, even though they were full-time housewives.

The older widow or single woman also suffers from social ostracism. Older women do not have the same social prerogatives as older men to date and marry those who are younger. Since the ratio of older women to older men is three to one, the likelihood of remarrying an elderly cohort is slim. As a result, older women end up alone. This is an ironic state of affairs, since most of them were raised from childhood to consider marriage as the only fulfilling role in life for a woman. In addition, older women alone are subject to the prejudice that exists in this country against single and divorced individuals. The adult world of couples has little place for a single older woman. Even older friends avoid the widow, because her state of widowhood makes very vivid the unbearable thought of death as the ultimate end to this stage of life.

The income levels of older working women are generally lower than those of men. This is due to employment practices that discriminate against women and the job opportunities available to women in the United States. It was not until World War II that employment in this country was seen as appropriate for women. Of the current generation of older women, most never worked outside the home until their children were grown, and then only at unskilled, low-paying jobs. Others who worked all their lives typically received lower wages, with lower Social Security and private pension benefits as a result.

Because of the high proportion of older women in the elderly population, when we speak of the plight of the elderly, we are to a large degree speaking of the plight of the poor older woman. The social norms set for women by the society, which have been challenged only recently, are now taking their toll on older women. The woman who conformed to the norms of a male-dominated society and was economically totally dependent on her husband must pay tremendous social costs in old age.

The Rural Elderly

The rural elderly, for the most part, are older, are more isolated, have greater transportation problems, live in the same place longer, have lower incomes, and reside in poorer houses for longer periods of time than do their urban counterparts (Auerbach, 1976). On the other hand, they appear to be healthier, live longer, complain less, and are freer from fear of crime and confusion of city streets. However, the attitude of the rural aged emphasizes the singularity, independence, isolation, xenophobia, and individualism that is a reflection of the psychology of rural living. Whatever the reason, rural aged are apt to be less knowledgeable about available social services, more indifferent or hostile to government-supported programs, more difficult to mobilize for participation in social programs, and less receptive to community action that supports social legislation.

The problems of growing old in the rural United States presents special and unique problems. Sheer distance between people and between people and services is the most obvious aspect in which rural areas differ from urban ones. Distance complicates the delivery of any services to rural older people; the expense of maintaining private cars and lack of public transportation bar older people from coming to the services. Many people in rural areas are isolated by a basic lack of roads.

One of the biggest problems of the rural elderly is that programs established to meet their needs are often not designed to fit their way of life. Most rural older people have been very self-reliant all their lives. They were their own mechanics, plumbers, carpenters, and doctors because often others were not available. When crises arose, neighbors quietly chipped in, often without being asked. Age has now stripped these people of all their resources but not their traditions. Many refuse to take advantage of the few services that are available because they don't know how to take the initiative in dealing with government officials, and they feel a strong sense of shame and failure if they must.

Programs for rural older people must be designed in a way that is not foreign to their lifestyle. Given that their needs are greater than those of their urban counterparts, greater energy and resources should be deployed to help meet the needs of the rural elderly.

Summary

In this chapter we have called to your attention the fact that programs and services developed for the elderly frequently do not take into consideration the special needs of the minority, ethnic, women, and rural elderly. Consequently, these groups of individuals either cannot or do not receive services they need badly. Very often special outreach efforts must be conducted to locate these people and special assistance given to assure that they obtain services. Furthermore, special consideration must be given to the way services are currently structured to assure that they do not inadvertently discriminate against these groups.

READING 3.1

A Miracle Story / Rosalie K. Jackson
Rosalie Jackson suggests that, considering the hardship, it is perhaps a miracle that any black person has managed to survive to old age. In this selection she creates a detailed background to a dynamic portrait of the black elderly.

I am going to talk about what I call a "miracle story." The fact that any black person has survived in America (and I use the word "survive" advisedly) to live to the age of eighty or ninety years is indeed a miracle. What do I mean by miracle? What are the implications of survival for the emotional needs in older black adults? Let's think about a black person who is eighty-eight years of age. That means he or she was born in 1886 in America. That's the reconstruction period. Reconstruction days for black people in America were difficult days. There was so much ambivalence—slaves, then freedom—they were working through a lot of things in those days. By the time this eighty-eight year old person was in his pre-teens America was in the Spanish-American war. This black person was a young adult around World War I in 1914–1918. Having come out of slavery, he was poorly educated. There were few jobs for any Americans, to say nothing of black ones; white men were marching off to war, becoming

From "New Ideas for Better Serving the Older Adult." Used by permission of the author.

lieutenants and sergeants. The few black men who were conscripted or called up were the cooks, message boys, and a few of them served in regiments. But the majority served in menial jobs. Today this person is in a nursing home or a board and care home or in a ward. He is now eighty-eight in 1974.

Back in 1886 there were some positive things going for him mental health–wise. People had tight family ties; black Americans lived in extended family units. They were very religious. They had faith that things would be better and they really believed that God would take care of them. So they survived. These were positive aspects in those days. They knew nothing but hard work and hard times, but they possessed positive factors—the adaptive mechanisms prevalent in the black races—long muscles, diminished amount of skin fat, the ability to sweat and adapt to a climate—just as other races have adaptive mechanisms to stay alive. Blacks in America for their own mental health and survival took on the practices and the adaptive mechanisms to stay alive. Uncle Tomism was a survival technique.

Let's move to more recent times in America. When this eighty-eight year old black American was hitting middle-age, there was the Great Depression. They were scrounging not only for their mental health but also for basic physical comforts. By World War II this person was over the age level to serve. He was fifty-five years old in 1941. The climate of the country which had contributed to poor mental health was shifting, was getting a bit more relaxed; jobs were opening up a bit, and the war brought great industrialization. I guess I am suggesting that in the majority culture mental health and physical comforts are tied in with economic state. The blacks had survival skills but not some of the creature comforts and job securities the rest of America had at that time. With World War II, our fifty-five year old black person migrated from the South to the city where there are factory jobs. For the first time he isn't chopping cotton and doing menial jobs. He is working in industry, in the shipyards, perhaps, and may be able to buy a piece of land and property and begin to get into the economic base of the nation. But he is fifty-five and at age forty-five, chronic diseases set in. The grim reaper takes its toll earlier with black Americans. So a good percent of blacks never become eighty-eight.

There has been some social legislation providing Social Security and some other benefits for all of the people and pension plans developed in some parts of the country. But remember, this black person, uneducated and unskilled, is still at the bottom of the ladder. This person can't move with the times. When the boys came marching home from war, the first fired were older people, and the older black in particular. If he managed to hold on to a job cleaning offices at night, that was at least a stable economic base. If they were lucky, the black people went back to menial jobs. I am leading up to how one develops status. We know that one of the tragedies of aging in the white American is to have been the president of a large firm, and to end up retired and occupying a chair on the board at eighty-eight. But that eighty-eight year old black American never had status, so therefore his mental health is slightly different.

With two-thirds of this man's life over, America is in good times; TV is becoming universal, and showing how everybody is living. But there is nothing on the screen that applies to anything that is happening to this group. Science and technocracy have come to the country, and the good times are rolling. One of the best things that happens to the older black American is things most people look down on. That would be the social programs . . . the things that guarantee you a little bit. For many black Americans the Social Security check is the biggest amount of money they ever had in their lives. When we think about the negative aspects of Welfare and how terrible it is we should remember that the little pittance everybody is getting, $167 or $121, is still more than many of the older generation has ever had or made. Medical care, the ability to go to the doctor and complain like everybody else, were things that were denied to poor people. But the adaptive mechanism of black Americans was herb medicine, to treat your own. These are the positive skills that people develop to survive and adapt. All this helps explain how a black person lives to be eighty-eight years old in 1974.

Hear now the story of Mrs. Blue, who is a 93-year old black. We know she is that old because of the events she can relate. She shares with us about herb medicine so if you try to give her your pills, you will be made to remember that she has been self-medicating all her life. How can you fight her? I can get knowledge from these old people about living and survival and about getting by. Mrs. Blue knows about the medicines. In an accident she burnt her foot badly and had to go to the hospital. They wanted to keep her there a long time. She said, "No. If I stay here longer, I'll die because you won't let me get up and walk on my foot." The doctor explained that his regimen would save her life. Nevertheless, every night she walked around that bed all night to keep her circulation going, to avoid pneumonia. She didn't know why she was doing it all, but she had a history of observing. And through her self-regimen she got out of the hospital sooner than they predicted.

I am sharing with you survival, and mental health practices, and common sense and things that have helped people to live to be eighty-eight and who now are in your care, under your jurisdiction. What I am suggesting is that you owe to that person some respect for his adjustment. If you managed to stay alive through this period (and I haven't mentioned discrimination, Ku-Klux-Klan, poor housing, or the whole gamut of destructive influences) then numerous obstacles had to be surmounted. Have respect for the old person's intellectual functioning, capabilities. In working with the older blacks, remember that little story about Mrs. Blue.

We should consider losses further. After forty-five, health begins to go, and chronic illnesses begin to set in. The implication here, it seems to me, is that you must listen all the more. Remember that the eighty-eight year old was never a master of the English language, so listening implies a deeper meaning. Help people with recalls, which sharpens what they want to say.

What about the implication in loss of family ties? Children of this eighty-eight year old black would be in their sixties, because they bred early, and many times they outlive their children, there may be only grandchildren left. We know great-grandchildren and grandchildren are very mobile; they have active lives and little time and even less living space to have extended family persons living with them. So the modern way of life has led to isolation of both black and white older Americans. What about the implications of loneliness? If the older person is isolated and separated, then TV is a form of involvement; it is something to listen to, and I suppose even talk to. TV still isn't enough, because people need to be touched; they need to be interacted with. The mental health implication for an old man having outlived all of his friends is that you listen to him, let him tell his stories and this enhances his status; it is important.

What about the implications in recognizing managerial skills? Managers are hard to find. We are used to so much incompetence that we are almost appalled if all goes well. Let's think of the managerial skills of older black Americans. What are the managerial skills of a woman who raised twelve children on next to nothing, who fed, clothed, housed them, disciplined them, and brought them up to standards that are mostly absent today? I am suggesting then, that a person who has managed a household has given reason for a status of respect and dignity.

And then there are the implications in de-emphasizing failures. I did a study in 1971 in Los Angeles with the Meals-on-Wheels program. I needed data for my study. These people are black and Mexican-American older citizens. We talked about lacks and about positive things. One woman said to me, "It sure is good to be free." She meant freedom from all the burdens and responsibilities she had as a manager. It is good, she was saying, to have no one but oneself to look after. So there are some positive aspects to aging. But she complained about lack of transportation. These are the trade-offs. Never having driven (black women were not that independent) it was transportation that they needed most of all. Of all the things that older black Americans need, transportation is the first. Eighty-eight percent of the people found transportation the number one problem. In the bus that picked them up for Meals-on-Wheels in Los Angeles they were trying to bribe the driver to take them other places but they didn't succeed.

The second thing I found in my study was that seventy percent of the people I asked, "How do you feel?" answered by saying, "I feel fine." Then I had another question later that asked, "Do you have any of the following illnesses?" Although five or six illnesses, such as heart trouble, hypertension, diabetes, etc., were cited repeatedly, they always presented them- selves as "doing fine." I had a difficult time dealing with that. But compared to what they had been accustomed to, they *were* doing fine. When a person says he is doing poorly, talk with him about what that means; and if a person says he is doing fine, in comparison to what is he doing fine? You always have to put the answer in context as you seek the identity of that black American.

When I think of a mentally healthy person, I think of a person who has enough to make him happy, who wants to share, wants to give. We, as helpers, supply some of those things, and when we understand the background of this person, we can supply some of this status.

The older black American now is adaptable, but the new generation as it ages will have its own bitterness and frustrations that it will go through. The old ones worked through their bitterness a long time ago.

The last thing I want to talk about is the need of being touched, and the need for sensuality and sexuality. Remember also that the status of child bearing in this group is going to be different from the cohorts of today. Also a good deal of a person's sexual identity for the cohorts of 1896, was evaluated on the basis of the number of children one produced. Another of the implications for mental health of older black Americans is the fact that for this group the idea of potency, of manhood and womanhood is tied up in the role of parent.

Individualize your clients; don't stereotype them; listen to them; put your client in proper context; learn about them, then relate to them appropriately.

Questions 3.1

1. Jackson describes several historical events that have had an effect on the quality of life for blacks in the United States. Discuss these events and their implications for the black elderly.

2. Because of their minority status in the United States, blacks have developed special adaptive mechanisms and survival techniques. Discuss what minority status means. How does it create a double bind for an older black person? As human-service workers, why should we concern ourselves with such causes and effects?

3. Jackson points out that the emotional needs of the black elderly are related to the unique experience of being black in the United States. Identify those factors discussed in the article that are related to the emotional investments of blacks.

4. Group task—Develop a position paper based on the following statement: Black elderly in the United States should be accorded the same treatment as any other elderly group in the United States.

READING 3.2

The Older Woman/Irene de Castillejo

Living to old age brings gains as well as losses. In this selection Irene de Castillejo eloquently presents some positive models of aging.

It would seem easy enough for me to write on "The Older Woman" since I am one, but perhaps it is for that reason I find it difficult. One can really only see situations clearly when one is outside them, not when one is in the middle of living them. However there is no help for it. When I have passed the stage of being an older woman I shall also be beyond writing at all.

It is obvious that there are two distinct classes of older women: the wife and the mother on the one hand, and the professional woman on the other, although today these two merge more and more. It is with the former that I am most familiar.

The fundamental truth to remember in thinking of woman irrespective of the role she plays, is that her life's curve, unlike that of man, is not a slow rising to the zenith of power followed by a gradual decline in the later years. The curve of a woman's life span follows more nearly the pattern of the seasons. She almost literally blossoms in the spring, but the long summer which follows is a very slow ripening with nothing much in the woman herself to show for it. If she lives a traditional family pattern she will be giving all the sap which rose so abundantly earlier to nourish her offspring, materially, emotionally and spiritually.

Then suddenly her children are all grown up, gone on their separate journeys, and she finds herself bereft. The apparent purpose of her life, for which she had strained every nerve, is

From *Knowing Woman* by Irene Claremont de Castillejo; copyright 1973 by the C. G. Jung Foundation for Analytical Psychology. Reprinted by permission.

snatched from her with the attainment of the goal. She feels stranded on the mud flats, while the river races by bearing away each new craft as it embarks, and she no part of the flowing waters. What then? What can happen then, with another thirty or forty years still to run and no one needing her? Even her husband has centered his life on his career and other interests apart from her while she was occupied with the growing family. At the best his need of her is not absorbing enough to assuage her aching emptiness.

What then? This is the crucial moment in the life of any wife and mother. It is then that she may notice, almost by accident, that from where the early blossoms fell fruit is hanging and almost ripe. Unsuspected fruit, fruit which has swelled and grown unheeded, is now ready and waiting to be plucked. The autumn of a woman's life is far richer than the spring if only she becomes aware in time, and harvests the ripening fruit before it falls and rots and is trampled underfoot. The winter which follows is not barren if the harvest has been stored, and the withdrawal of sap is only a prelude to a new spring elsewhere.

Conscious modern women of course know these things. They prepare for the autumn before the long dry summer is over. But far too many women still feel that life is finished at fifty and that vibrant loving ends with the menopause. This last bogie should be swept away at the outset. It is utterly untrue.

You may know some version of the famous story of the young man who asked his mother at what age women cease to be interested in sexual intercourse. "I do not know," she replied, "you had better ask your grandmother." "How should I know?" she answered gruffly. "Great Granny may be able to tell you." This is perhaps not as far-fetched as would appear.

It is true enough that some men cease to be interested sexually in women when their physical fertility is ended, causing their wives, who have a recrudescence of sexual interest at this time, great distress. Such a situation is the survival of an inherent primitive pattern where sexuality was for humanity, as it is for animals, only a matter of procreation.

Since the age of chivalry and the development of romantic love, sex has become very much more than that. And with the discovery and spread of contraceptives sex has entered a new phase. The contraceptive can certainly lead to irresponsibility, license and a devaluation of sexuality. In fact it often does so. But on the other hand it opens the door to immensely heightened emotional experience where sex ceases to be solely a biological function, and becomes an expression of love in its own right. In this context age with its absence of fertility is irrelevant.

This cultural achievement gives mankind a chance of healing the cleavage between body and spirit which has been fostered for centuries by the Church, and may enable us to weld once more the two together.

In this whole development the older woman is actually at a great advantage. She does not need the contraceptive, and I believe this is one reason why a woman's most profound and meaningful sex life often occurs after fifty when she is no longer caught in the biological net. For the first time she is able to give herself in the sex act completely free from fear of conception, a fear which in countless women does still operate beneath the surface, even when reason and science assure them that they have taken the most complete precautions.

Moreover to a great many women contraceptives, though accepted intellectually, are still unaesthetic, and to a deep basic feminine morality they are wholly unacceptable, all of which inevitably causes inhibitions so long as they have to be used. When once a woman is free to use her body as an expression of deep feeling, without its becoming the impersonal vehicle of nature's insistent demand for life and yet more life, she can transcend her earlier inhibitions and attain physical expression of an emotional relationship beyond anything of which she had ever dreamed.

Do not misunderstand me. It is a grave mistake for a woman to look for some great spiritual experience in sex at any age, or even to assume that she ought to have such a thing. All assumptions about sex are disastrous. They tend to lead to disappointment and recriminations. To my mind most modern books on sex do more harm than good for this very reason: they fill women's heads with assumptions and expectations which actually prevent experience at its fullest. It is one's own personal experience that counts and it should not be measured up against any generalization. The statistical so-called normal man or woman does not in fact exist, and it is foolish to weigh our actual living experience against such a mythical figure.

Sex delight is like happiness. It does not come when sought. It is not until a woman ceases to strive for her own sensual satisfaction, but allows the voice of her heart to speak to her man through the medium of her body, that she finds that heart, spirit and body are all one.

Important as the heightening fulfillment of sex may be, it is none the less only a small part of the ripe autumnal fruit to which I have alluded. A woman's liberation from the service of nature's purposes frees an enormous amount of energy for something else. A man at fifty is probably at the height of his intellectual or administrative power. A family woman at the same age may be aware of an entirely new stirring. Latent possibilities dance before her unbelieving eyes.

I recall one such woman seated on the lawn of her house one summer evening holding forth to her family. I say holding forth but she was certainly not laying down the law. It was almost as though a dam had burst and a torrent of ideas came tumbling out to which she herself seemed to be listening with the same astonished amusement as were her hearers. She simply emanated vitality and I remember her ending up with the words: "I have no idea what is going to happen but I am quite sure something is." And as I watched and I listened so was I. She did in fact become a writer some ten years later.

The expression "change of life" exactly fits the situation. The menopause does not spell the end of life but a change of direction, not a living death but a change of life.

If this were more generally understood I am convinced that women's menopause problems would rapidly diminish. Glandular changes are inevitable but it is woman's own dread of this mysterious change in the whole tenor of her life which, I am sure, brings about the neurotic state she fears. No, change of life means an enormous release of energy for some new venture in a new direction.

The direction in which the newly released energy will flow depends of course entirely on the type of person and the particular gifts with which she has been endowed. Some may develop a latent talent, painting, writing or some such thing. Voluntary societies serving social, political and cultural causes of all kinds abound with such women. But these only cater for the more conscious and extroverted type of woman. There are innumerable others who can find no outlet. They suffer deeply, for energy which finds no channel in which to flow seeps into the ground and makes a marsh where nothing can be planted, where only slime and insects breed.

Women who find they are no longer vitally needed by their families yet have no other place where they can give themselves, sink into lassitude and finally fall ill. The magnates who organize society have hardly begun to notice this happening. The autumnal energy of countless older women escapes silently down the kitchen sink along with their tears.

Not only is the nation poorer for its loss, the wastage is double, for these women who could have been healthily active and useful become a wholly unnecessary burden upon the health services, while as likely as not their frustration poisons the atmosphere of the home. Swamps breed mosquitoes. Uncanalized, wasted energy breeds gloom and nagging.

Part-time work is at least one answer to this problem, but part-time work is not easy to find. Industry seems to frown upon it and our modern passion for degrees and paper diplomas shuts many a door. It is not sufficiently recognized that running a home can afford very valuable experience in organization, and particularly in handling other people with diverse temperaments. The mother of a family is generally adept at that very difficult accomplishment of attending to half a dozen things all at the same time, an asset by no means to be despised if diverted to other fields.

That society is gravely at fault in not providing outlets for the older woman's energy is unquestionably true. But her real problem is to discover in which direction her newly released libido wants to flow. Libido is like water, it always seeks its proper level. No amount of coercion can make it flow uphill.

So long as a woman is fulfilling her traditional role of bringing up a family, she is carried along by the stream of life. Indeed she has no alternative. She goes with the stream even though cooking and cleaning and changing diapers are not at all her ideal occupations. She has no real choice. But she herself develops as the family grows and she learns to meet the demands as they arise. Changing diapers gives way to helping with obstreperous homework and providing meals for expanding appetites in every field. But when all this is past and the river flows on without her, her own little stream of energy is dammed up. If she is fortunate the waters will rise till they are strong enough to burst out in a channel of their own.

What the channel will be depends on her concern. Even today, when education does its best to divert women's activity into every branch of industry and moneymaking, there are still older women who slide happily into the estate of grandmother because their children's children do in fact become the centre of their interest and their concern. Dedicated grandmothers who gladly put themselves at the service of the future generation without trying to run the show themselves are a boon to any family, but they are becoming increasingly rare. Like maiden aunts they are dying out, and the services which both maiden aunts and grandmothers used to give as a matter of course and with genuine devotion now frequently have to be bought with money. We all know what a poor substitute that is and how expensive.

The modern trend seems to be in the opposite direction. More and more mothers wait with impatience for their children to be grown and gone. Then at last they feel free to carry on with the career which family demands had forced them to abandon. These women are faced with relatively little conflict. They nearly always succeed in finding an outlet before the problem becomes acute. As the children grow they dovetail the new life into the old so that there is no traumatic moment when they feel deserted.

The ones who cannot look forward to any vibrant future or any sphere of usefulness to which they can give themselves, are those with whom I am particularly concerned here. For them especially is the surprise and delight of discovery. And for them above all is the paramount need to know what is and what is not their true concern.

. . . In the case of woman, the outstanding almost invariable object of her concern is, as we all know, the person or persons whom she loves. This is true right through her life. It is, I repeat, the essential ingredient of her nature. When she is true to herself love is her primal driving force. Love and the service of those she loves, I mean a wholly personal love, not the love of causes or of country. I believe this to be true for all the various ranks of women, and it is as true of professional women as of wives and mothers. It is not always apparent that this is so. We are all very good at covering up our mainspring. But I have yet to meet the woman who did not know in her heart that love is her main concern and that the secret of her success in any field was her personal love in the background.

Men really can give themselves to a cause, working wholeheartedly for it and inspired by it. Unless their ingredient of masculinity is very great, women cannot. If one is allowed to penetrate their secrets one finds beneath their apparent impersonal enthusiasms some very personal love, the existence of which makes them feel whole and gives them the energy which enables them to act.

The schoolgirl will work double for a teacher whom she loves. The career woman will either have a person who is the focus of her love at work who provides her dynamism, or some love outside which is her stimulus. It may be a lover in the background or children for whom she needs to earn.

Wherever I look I meet this incontrovertible fact that a woman always needs some person to do things for, even though to the outsider there is no apparent connection with the loved person and what she may be doing. We all know how difficult it is for a woman even to cook a meal for herself. She cannot be bothered. A bit of bread and cheese will do. But if there is someone to cook for she prepares quite elaborate dishes with delight.

The same prevails throughout. The work of a woman, whether factory hand or professional, will be quite different in quality if in some way she can connect it with her love. I have talked with women artists, painters, singers, actors. They all agree that art in itself is seldom quite enough. Beneath their devotion to their art is some person whom they love and for whom in some mysterious inner way they perfect their art. Even the nun, who is an extreme case of selfless devotion, is contained in and inspired by a very personal love of Christ. I suspect that men are far more singlemindedly purposeful.

The need to have someone to do things for comes out in most curious places. I recall a woman who was threatened with blindness which only an operation could prevent. Operations of any kind had always been anathema to her, and the thought of an eye operation was more than she could face. She raged internally at the meddlesomeness of doctors. Why couldn't she be allowed to go blind in peace? Then suddenly she realized what she might be doing to her children and grandchildren if she went blind. A blind old grandmother was the last thing she wanted to impose on them. Her torment ceased. She entered hospital without a further qualm. She had found someone to have her operation for.

This tendency only to be able to do things for someone whom one loves makes it difficult for a woman to know what she herself really wants. She is often accused naturally by men of futility or hypocrisy, because when asked what she wants to do, she replies "Whatever you like." But it is not hypocrisy. She really means that her desire is to do what he wants. It has not occurred to her to have any special preference. Even if she knew she wanted to dance it would give her no pleasure to do so if her lover was longing to watch a cricket match. This adaptability is not unselfishness and has no particular merit. It is the way a woman functions. Perhaps I am describing the last generation. I think it possible that the present generation of women not only know themselves better but are far more decisive than the last, thus changing their relationship with men. Whether the change is for the good, or rather a disaster, is still an open question. Perhaps it is both.

However this may be, the older woman's dilemma is precisely here. If no one whom she loves wants her services there is no one to do things for. There is in fact no reason for which to live. She is faced with an entirely new situation in which for the first time maybe she has to discover what are her own wishes, her own tastes and in which direction her energy, with no love focus to act as magnet, will consent to flow. It is fascinating to notice how a widow will sometimes reverse the habits of a married lifetime after her husband's death. The extent to which she does so is the measure of her earlier adaptability.

In the following poem I have tried to express an old woman's bewilderment. It is called "The Last Years."

> Now that my loves are dead
> On what shall my action ride?
>
> I will not make my children
> Lovers nor tune my time
> By footsteps of the young
> To ease my solitude;
>
> But sing of springs, forgotten
> In slow summer's tedium,
> And autumn ripe with fruit;
> Of winter branches, bare
>
> Beneath the storm, bowed
> With weight of rain, and after,
> Lifting knotted fingers
> Towards a translucent sky;
>
> And wrest from the gathered sheaf
> Forgiveness, buried in the heart
> Of every grain, to knead
> My bread for sustenance.

> My action, sharing bread,
> Love becomes ability
> To bless, and be, in blessing,
> Blessed.

To go back and collect up one's past as this poem suggests, writing it down in poems or as good prose as one can achieve, has in itself a healing effect. I believe one has to return to one's past, not once but many times, in order to pick up all the threads one has let fall through carelessness or unobservance.

I believe above all one has to return again and again to weep the tears which are still unshed. We cannot feel all the grief of our many losses at the time we suffer them. That would be too crippling. But if we would really gather our whole lives into a single whole, no emotion that belongs to us should be left unfelt.

Moreover, the review of our lives enables us to notice the constant repetition of the same pattern of happening, met by the same pattern of behavior. Seeing this we cannot help being struck by the apparent purposefulness of every detail of our lives even though we do not like our fate. Those who do in fact gather up and write their story are enormously enriched. And women for whom nothing is worth the effort unless it is for the sake of someone they love, can write their outer or their inner story quite deliberately for their own grandchildren (if they have any) to read when they are grown up. If there are no grandchildren, most women will need to find someone else to write it for.

What fascinating pictures of antiquated ways of living we should have if this were done more often. Every single person has the material for at least one book. It is, I think, important that publication should not be the aim. Too many books are published already. Too many mediocre pictures are put upon the market. No, the aim is creativity for its own sake. The grandchildren or some other persons are merely the excuse which the aging woman needs to enable her to make the effort.

Creativity once begun goes on. Nothing is so satisfying to the human soul as creating something new. If the old can become creative in their own right they are lost no longer. We all long to see our works in print, I know, but this is not the point. It is the act of creation which counts. Every act of creation adds to the creativity in the world, and who knows if it has some similar effect as the ritual breathing towards the East at dawn of those primitive tribes who believe that their breath helps the sun to rise.

Unless some outer activity claims her, the family woman may make the discovery earlier than either men or professional women that libido changes its direction as old age approaches. It is a change that all must encounter sooner or later: at some time or other outer activities lose their glamour and the inner world demands attention. So strong is this demand that the old who refuse to turn their faces inwards, clinging desperately to outer values even though they watch them daily slipping from their grasp, are frequently made ill. Forced by illness or accident to be inactive, they are given the opportunity which they had been unable to take of their own free will, to ruminate and ponder and put forth new shoots in an unaccustomed inner world.

Illnesses at any time of life should not be merely cured, but utilized for growth in a hitherto unknown field. Particularly does this apply to the aging, whether man or woman.

If the old can become creative in their own right, they are, as I have said, lost no longer, but above all it is imperative that the older person should have a positive attitude towards death. The young can forget death with impunity. The old cannot. They are fortunate indeed who have faith that they will not be extinguished when they die, and can look forward to a new beginning in some other dimension or some other realm. But faith is a gift. Like love it comes by grace. No amount of thought or striving can achieve it: which paradoxically does not mean that there is no need to strive. We get from life in the measure with which we give to it, and our fundamental attitudes demand unceasing strife. But this is only preparing the soil. The actual planting of a spiritual seed like faith is beyond our control. It comes when it will.

To those who have been denied such faith I would ask, is it not a fact that the people who accept death most readily are the ones who have lived most fully? I do not mean necessarily the people who have done the most. Outer visible achievement is no criterion of living fully. The life of a great business magnate whose industry has erected huge buildings, set innumerable wheels whizzing and employs thousands of people, may have been so narrowly focused on the gain of material wealth that the riches of the spirit, art, music, literature and the warmth of human contacts, may have escaped him altogether. This is not full living.

At the opposite extreme I recall Spanish beggars seated on the cathedral steps, idly watching the passers by, receiving as though it were their lawful due occasional gifts of alms with a dignified "God bless you." How well the beggar must know those oft recurrent faces, nearly as constant in their daily presence as the stone saints and gargoyles behind him, the hourly chiming of the cathedral bells and the chant from within the church. What a setting in which to dwell and ponder! Does this man live fully? I do not know, but Unamuno, one of Spain's greatest writers, believed he did. Unamuno even declared that the most interesting philosopher he had ever met was a beggar, one of a long line of beggars.

I am not advocating beggary, but neither it nor visible achievement is any criterion of the quality of living. There is no yardstick for the surmounting of obstacles, the wrestling with angels and the transcending of suffering.

There is no yardstick for the measurement of others, but maybe for ourselves there is. One's yardstick is one's full capacity to be as complete a person as within one lies, and that includes becoming as conscious as it is possible for one to be in order to bring out and develop the buried talents with which one was born, and in order to realize one's own innate knowledge.

The more diverse the talents of any person, the more difficult may be the task. We only have a certain amount of psychic energy and throughout our lives we have to choose the road we will take, abandoning the fascinating paths in other directions. But the development of an ability to choose, and the consistent following of the path chosen, may be a large part of becoming as whole a person as one can be. So also is our flexibility a very real asset. The man or woman who has chosen the wrong path by mistake, and we all make mistakes, may need to retrace his steps and start again. This needs courage and should not be mistaken for the idle whim of the dilettante. Moreover, many people follow a vital thread towards a wholly invisible goal. We cannot possibly judge the value of their achievement.

To be conscious is not in itself a goal. It is possible to be a highly conscious person without one's character being influenced at all. Consciousness is not enough in itself. But one cannot develop a gift if one does not know that it is there, so to be conscious is indispensable. Many of us, through ignorance of our own capacities, only allow a small part of ourselves to flower. Neither can one lop off a branch that is marring the beauty of a tree if one has not noticed its presence and seen that its unbridled growth is spoiling the harmony of the whole. Or it may have to be sacrificed because it is impeding the growth of other plants.

Our individual psyche is very like a garden. The kind of garden will be determined by the nature of the soil, whether it is on a mountain slope or in a fertile valley. It will depend upon the climate. Green lawns flourish in England. In parts of Spain to sow a lawn is to make a present to the wind, for literally the seed is blown away.

Climate and geology are powers beyond our altering. They are the conditions we have been given to make the most of it, and for some the task is immensely harder than it is for others. The slopes of arid hills in Spain are a marvel of man's endeavour. Every inch is terraced with little walls of stones so that not a drop of the rare precious rain shall be lost in tumbling streams but held for the thirsty vines and olive trees. All honour to such gardeners. Some of us dwell in more temperate climes where the task is not so hard, but any gardener will know the unceasing vigilance which is needed to tend a garden, wherever it may be. Weeds are never eradicated once for all.

So, too, our psyches. They also can be invaded by pests from other gardens which have been neglected, making it harder to maintain the health of ours. Indeed, to maintain our psyche or our garden free of pests is a responsibility to our neighbours as well as to ourselves. Some gardens are more formal than others. Some have corners deliberately left wild, but a garden with no form and no order is not a garden at all but a wilderness.

The psyche which is a total wilderness ends in the asylum or burdens its family with unhealthy emanations. The well-tended but over conventional garden, on the other hand, may have no stamp of individuality upon it. It expresses the psyche of the mass man, and suburbia is full of them. The garden which is tended with care yet is not quite like any other garden for it conveys the psyche of an individual who has become a mature personality from where the scent of honeysuckle and roses and wild thyme will perfume the air for all around.

But gardens cannot grow without earth, and the loveliest flowers thrive on soil that is well manured and black. Dirt has been defined as matter in the wrong place. Manure is not dirt when dug into the borders. And rich emotional living in the right places is as indispensable for the flowering of wisdom in old age as the purity of the air and the brilliant sunlight of consciousness. No flower and no wisdom was ever reared on a ground of shiny white tiles washed daily with antiseptic.

It is the older person, whether man or woman, who has the need and the obligation to tend the garden of the psyche. The young are generally too immersed in active living; study, work, careers, and bringing up a family absorb all their energies. Indeed, a too early absorption with their own psyche may be an actual poison for the young. It may deprive them of the essential spontaneity which is needed for living. Actual experience can never be replaced by thinking about life or examining inner motives. To be ever conscious of the possible hazards before us snatches away our power to leap. We can only live fully by risking our lives over and over again.

It is in the latter part of life that people need to turn attention inwards. They need to do so because if their garden is as it should be they can die content, feeling that they have fulfilled their task of becoming the person they were born to be. But it is also an obligation to society. What a man or woman is within affects all those around. The old who are frustrated and resentful because they have omitted to become in life the persons they should have been, cause all in their vicinity to suffer.

Being is not the same as doing. Most people have had to sacrifice in some direction their capacity to do, but none are exempt from being to the full. There can be no limit to one's endeavour to become more and more aware of the depths of one's own psyche, discovering its lights and its shadows, its possibilities of unexpected vision as well as its dark regions.

The old woman, like the old man, needs to turn her natural receptivity towards the inner voices and inner whisperings, pondering on the new ideas which will come to her if she is attuned to her own inner self. Mrs. Moore, in E. M. Forster's *Passage to India,* was doing precisely this in her sudden and unexpected refusal to be drawn into the whirl of outer events. But we should not expect the insights of the very old to be revealed to the rest of us. There may be weeks and months or even years of slow, quiet gestation in the minds of quite old people. To speak of half-formed ideas is to destroy their growth as surely as to burn a seedling with the sun's rays shining through a magnifying glass. The very frailty of age guards its secrets.

Indeed, the insights of the very old may never quite reach the level of consciousness where they can be clothed in words. But this does not mean that they are not at work beneath the surface. The conscious mind is only a small part of our total psyche.

The very old, those who have given up all interest in the outer world even to the stage of being withdrawn from any point of contact, may still be receiving and quietly nurturing within themselves new insights which will enable them to meet the unknown future. One wonders sometimes what holds them here. Perhaps they are not ready. They cannot die till they are ready. I have often felt that modern medicine is very cruel to the old for it keeps them here when they are longing to be allowed to go.

But perhaps longing to go is not the same as being ready to meet the other side. I doubt if science could keep anyone alive if in this sense they were truly ready for their death.

It is a fallacy that the old are necessarily lonely when they are alone. Some are. But never those who are quietly pondering, preparing themselves, albeit without deliberate intention, for their coming death. They need long hours of solitude to round out their lives within, as they have earlier done without.

There is a lovely little book, *All Passion Spent,* by Victoria Sackville-West. She tells of an old lady after the death of her husband with whom she has shared a long life. Her children hold a family council. What can be done with mother? They plan it all out. She shall stay with them and their growing families in turn so they can share the burden of looking after her and keeping her from feeling lonely.

The plan is unfolded to the old lady who, to the amazement of her children, thanks them politely and declines their offer of hospitality. It transpires that for years she has been longing to have a little house of her own where she could live alone and undisturbed with her thoughts. Miraculously the chance had come and nothing should cheat her of it now.

This old woman had the good fortune to know her own mind, which many of us do not. Many old men and women are cheated of their essential solitude, and kept continually focused on outer things by the mistaken kindness of the young and their own unawareness of their need to be alone. We die alone. It is well to become accustomed to being alone before that moment comes.

Old age is the time of reckoning, our achievements balanced by our needless omissions and our mistakes. Some of our mistakes are hideous, but this is no reason for not facing them. Some we would never know if our children did not tell us the awful things we had done to them without realizing the dire effect of our advice, the example of our behavior or our condemnation.

The old are generally too much shielded. The next generation fears to hurt them. I say the next generation deliberately for it is seldom the young who overshield the old. The vital calls to live of the young are more likely to make them callous, which is really far more healthy. It is those who are already advanced in middle age, often themselves already older women, who over-protect the very old. Nothing must be told to worry them. Frequently they are so pampered and humoured that they are turned into querulous children.

Indeed, it is more often than not our own dislike of feeling hard, rather than genuine affection, which makes us so falsely kind. Moreover there is no need for us to take upon ourselves the responsibility of sheltering the very old from worry. Griefs do not shatter them as they do the young. They have their own protection from those emotions which are more than they can bear. It is not our task to turn them into breathing fossils.

That is no kindness to the old. Rather it is cruelty because it deprives them of their power still to grow. It is an unpardonable belittling of the role of the aged, for it is they who, whether they can formulate it or not, are in fact the depositories of wisdom. Very often it is they who have lived more than those who shelter them. To the older woman who has the aged in her care I would say: Be careful not to spend more energy upon the very old than you can rightly afford to do. Your own life too makes claims. Deep thought and wise judgement are needed to give them libido where it is really due. If too much is given to the aged at the expense of the giver it will only breed bitterness, and that helps no one.

The care of the very old is a terribly difficult problem and every case has to be dealt with on its own merits. Many family women find an old parent a good substitute for the children who have grown and gone. Many others who have had no children turn the parent unwittingly into the child they have never had. In either case the old person is wrapped in cotton wool which he or she has not the strength to throw aside. They can very easily become victims, rather than grateful recipients, of our over-coddling.

And so they end their days either with a complacency to which they have no right, or in puzzled resentment that the young do not give them the love they thought they had deserved. There are no deserts in love. Greater outspokenness is better for everyone concerned, though the young might certainly temper their frankness with the constant remembrance that the old have done their best. Deliberate malice on the part of parents is, I believe, very rare. The vast majority of parents undoubtedly do the best they know. And as undoubtedly the next generation will have found it wrong, and rightly so. To be a parent is the most difficult task in the world. For a parent not to be understanding enough cripples. To be too understanding imprisons.

I have yet to meet the parents who have not made serious blunders with their children in one direction or the other. The childless in this are fortunate. The false steps they have taken in life are likely to have had less dire consequences on others.

I think it is important that mistakes should be brought out into the light of day, for how otherwise may they be forgiven? Forgiven by those sinned against but also forgiven by the sinner himself. This is something very different from complacency for it implies full consciousness and condemnation of the sin. To forgive oneself is a very difficult thing to do, but perhaps it is the last task demanded of us before we die. For the man or woman who can forgive him or herself can surely harbour no vestige of rancour against any other.

Impersonal forgiveness is very like love, but love on a higher plane than the personal love which women above all find so necessary. It is Agape as distinct from personal Eros. It is the charity spoken of by St. Paul. It is only possible for those who are completely on their own thread to God. No little isolated ego can forgive itself. In the last verses of the poem quoted the old woman found forgiveness of herself as well as others to be her inspiration and her goal.

And so, in the end, if endeavour is unceasing and the fates are kind, almost without noticing how it happened an old woman may find that love is still, as it always had been, the centre and the mainspring of her being, although, along with her years, the word has grown in meaning.

Questions 3.2

1. **The lives of many older women have followed the traditional family pattern. What are some traditional roles for elderly women in U.S. society?**

2. **Menopause is a universal experience for women. de Castillejo seizes the phrase "change of life" as exactly fitting the event. Why?**

3. **de Castillejo regards reminiscence and a "turning inward" as a need of older people. What factors discussed in the article contribute to this need?**

4. **One problem de Castillejo cites is the tendency of the previous generation to over-protect, even pamper, the elderly. Discuss the implications of this tendency for those who work with the aged.**

READING 3.3

Retirement to the Porch

Rural people, despite their relative isolation, have social systems that support them throughout their lives. This article shows how the front porch becomes a stage for social reciprocity.

Oftentimes, when people get on in years, they are relegated to the back room. But in Laurel Creek, West Virginia, they are usually accorded an honored place on the front porch. In that small, rural Appalachian settlement, according to sociologist-anthropologists John Lozier and Ronald Althouse of West Virginia University, there is a definite cultural phenomenon they call "retirement to the porch."

The front porch, which used to be an important place for socialization regardless of age, is now "useless for most Americans. New houses are built with a vestigial stoop in front, and outdoor leisure life focuses on the back yard or patio. The wide front porches of older houses often stand empty, if they have not been enclosed to provide more 'useful' interior space," Lozier and Althouse point out.

Observing. Well, the front porch is still a tradition for Laurel Creek senior citizens. (Lozier and Althouse have limited their reportage to the male inhabitants.) Typically, a man will begin to spend time on the porch when he is no longer competing for regular work. From his vantage point, he observes activity on the road and swaps tales with those who stop, often hitching a ride into town with them. In those first years, he arranges for occasional paid or volunteer work through social interactions initiated on his porch. "As long as he is active and able," say the investigators, "it is important that he continue to be available to help others and to provide for himself, associating with others in a way that is established from patterns of reciprocity in earlier years."

When his health begins to fail or when others relieve him of some of his obligations, he begins full retirement to the porch. He then can draw on the social credit he has stockpiled over the years, say Lozier and Althouse. It thus becomes acceptable to ask passersby he knows to pick up his groceries or to spend a few more minutes visiting. If his presence on the porch has become usual, a sudden absence causes community concern. After a reappearance on the porch following a health crisis, "there is an increased urgency about providing him with appropriate social interaction."

When he is close to death and spending most of his time indoors, whenever possible, those who care for him will bring him out on the porch. Such an appearance will be broadcast throughout the community, and "for a couple of hours, perhaps, he will receive his final public attention."

Not all old people receive such solicitous attention. Those who have recently moved into the neighborhood ("cash-ins," Lozier and Althouse call them) have weak social networks and don't spend much time out in front; in fact, they often live in trailers or in other porchless dwellings. Then there are the "no-counts," people who have never earned much social standing and who can't start now simply by parking a rocking chair out front. Others have always stuck to themselves and have never been involved with the community at large. For a successful retirement to the porch, a person needs to have a good amount of social standing.

Laurel Creek provides much more than the rudimentary services to many of its old people. All elderly people deserve at least that much, say the investigators. "What is required for successful old age is the continuing existence of community or neighborhood systems which can recognize and store credit for the performance of an individual over a whole lifetime and which can enforce the obligation of juniors to provide reciprocity. Without such a system, the help that is provided to an elder robs him of his dignity, for there is no recognition that this is his due, and not a form of charity," conclude Lozier and Althouse.

Questions 3.3

1. What are some positive social functions that retirement to the porch serves?
2. Lozier and Althouse distinguish between accumulated social credit and charity to elders. Why is this an important distinction?
3. Having some knowledge and understanding of the community or neighborhood system in which one works is very important for human-service workers. Why?

PART TWO

PROVIDING COUNSELING SERVICES TO OLDER ADULTS

With the increase of the elderly population and the problems older adults experience, efforts have been increased to meet their needs through new programs and services. More and more people are becoming involved in the provision of services to older adults. The remainder of this book focuses on how we help older people through a number of direct and indirect means.

In Part Two we cover the various methods of helping older people on a one-to-one or group basis. There are a variety of problems faced by older people that may require direct assistance through individual or group counseling.

The importance of reaching out to older people and the means through which this can be accomplished are discussed in Chapter 4. Chapter 5 includes a review of the basic principles and techniques of interviewing older adults. Group work techniques that can be used with older adults are reviewed in Chapter 6. Chapter 7 presents techniques that should enable the worker to help older clients and their families deal with the various role changes and crises that occur within the family at this time of life. Methods for working with the terminally ill and dying are discussed in Chapter 8.

cHApTER 4
REACHiNG OUT TO
oldER AdulTs

Those working in the field of aging have become aware that older people do not always receive services to which they are entitled. Over the years studies have shown that, as new programs for older people have been created, only a small fraction of those eligible actually make use of the services. Those providing the services have concluded that a major reason is that older people often do not know about the services or need assistance in obtaining them. In this chapter we will discuss how outreach services are conducted and how they can be used to enable older people obtain the services they need.

The Need for Outreach Services

In the field of human services, providers generally assume that individuals in need of services voluntarily seek them out. Recently we have become aware that many people do not know about the existence of service programs; consequently, we can no longer assume that potential clients know how or where to obtain services. This is particularly true for older people. Studies have shown that a great many older people are not receiving services that are available to them. There are several explanations. Today's older people were socialized throughout life to be self-sufficient and independent, and many would find it degrading and humiliating to seek assistance from social agencies. More important, perhaps, is the fact that many older people do not use services because they do not know about them, or, if they do know about them, are not able to obtain them.

Very often when services are initiated for the elderly, an agency or program is inclined to use mass media to solicit elderly participants or clients. However, studies have shown that mass media are an ineffective means of reaching older people. Many older people do not own televisions or radios or do not receive daily newspapers. Even if they do have them, many, due to sensory losses characteristic of later life, do not use these resources. In addition, many older people are illiterate or do not speak English. Consequently, media are not effective in communicating with them.

If programs are to be effective, special efforts must be made to inform the elderly about services and assistance that will enable them to make use of these programs.

The Purposes of Outreach

The basic function of an outreach service is to locate and inform older people of services that may be available to them. The specific purposes of an outreach program will vary, however. Sometimes outreach is conducted to provide older individuals information about special programs, such as nutrition programs, or it may have a more general purpose, for instance, as part of an information and referral service. In this instance, the purpose of outreach is to help with a specific problem by informing older people about the available services in the community. Outreach to older people has also been done on a national basis, for example, the Supplemental Security Income Alert aimed at making people aware of a federal program to increase their income level.

Some outreach programs are directed to the entire elderly population of a community, whereas others may be aimed at a subgroup or target population of the elderly, such as the poor, minorities, isolated, or handicapped. In recent years, for example, much of the emphasis has been focused on locating the isolated or "hidden elderly." Large numbers of older people have become recluses or withdrawn from the mainstream of society; they have lost contact with friends and neighbors and have infrequent contacts with other people. The purpose of outreach is to attempt to get these elderly people back into the mainstream of life by helping them become involved in social interaction.

Providing Outreach Services

When outreach is offered as part of a program for older adults, it requires concerted effort to actively seek out older people who may be in need of programs or services. Outreach service includes face-to-face contact with older individuals to make them aware of services. It will also involve helping individuals decide whether they want to receive services and then providing assistance so that they may obtain these services. Much time and planning is needed to successfully implement an outreach program.

Whatever the purpose or scope of an outreach program, there are four basic steps involved. First, the **target population** (the group to be served by the program) must be located. Second, the older person must be contacted and made aware of available services. Third, assistance must be provided to ensure that the older individual has access to services. Fourth, a follow-up contact should be made to ensure that the older person received the service. Each of these steps will be discussed in detail below.

*Locating and Identifying
the Target Population
of Older Adults*

Outreach services are somewhat unique in the realm of human services, as they involve provision of an unsolicited service. Consequently, a major function of an outreach service for the elderly is the location of older people in the community. The first step in most outreach efforts is to define the target population for whom the services are intended. For example, are you attempting to reach all people over 60 or 65 years of age, or are you looking for those who are isolated or low-income elderly. Once a target population has been defined, then a systematic plan for locating individuals in the community is required.

One can begin outreach by attempting to get the names of older people from the many social service agencies that exist in the community. Much time and energy will be saved if these agencies are involved in efforts to identify members of your target population. Agencies that deal with elderly clients are public welfare or social service agencies, Social Security offices, public-health services, visiting nurse services, hospitals and medical institutions, the Red Cross, the Salvation Army, and community action programs.

Unfortunately, large numbers of the elderly population are not part of the existing service system, and consequently you cannot rely solely on this means of locating elderly people in the community. Moreover, it may be difficult to get such information from social agencies, for very often they are prohibited by agency or public policy from disclosing the names of individuals receiving their services. Sometimes, however, employees of these agencies will unofficially provide the names of older people or direct you to sources where they can be obtained.

A very important means of locating older people, particularly the hard-to-reach, will be through informal communications systems in the community. In small towns and rural areas it is particularly likely that people know each other or have indirect contacts with each other, for example, contacts through extended families. Very frequently in those areas social contacts are interrelated and overlapping; people in the community belong to the same clubs or go to the same churches, for instance. Very often if you make these indirect contacts aware of your purpose, they can be instrumental in helping you locate older people in need of services.

In urban areas there are many individuals in the community who are not part of the social service system but who, by virtue of their position or the nature of their employment, have frequent contacts with the elderly, usually consumer–provider contacts. Such people may be able to easily and quickly identify those elderly who may be potentially isolated or in need of services. Grocers, druggists, barbers or beauticians, and delivery people may have this kind of information. Very often delivery people are the only contacts that isolated elderly individuals have with the outside world. Other sources might be mail carriers, police officers, ministers, private physicians, local politicians, service organizations (such as American Legions, VFW, Elks, or Moose), public libraries, and bartenders. These sources should be explored in efforts to locate older people.

In other instances, the only means by which you will be able to locate the target population will be through a door-to-door canvass of the community. This method is very time-consuming and requires careful planning. Very often, even with a door-to-door canvass, it is not productive to randomly search the entire community. It is generally more worthwhile to search those parts of the community where older people are more likely to live, such as the center or older neighborhoods in the city, resident hotels in center cities and in rural areas, isolated farms. Census tract data and city or county planning officials can help pinpoint where the older population of the community is concentrated. When you do a door-to-door canvass in large neighborhoods or communities, it may be helpful to subdivide the areas to be searched and start with the sections with the highest concentration of elderly and end with those with the lowest concentration.

Contacting and Informing
Older Adults about
Community Resources

Once you have identified members of the target population of elderly and know where to locate them, the next step in outreach is to make personal contact with individuals. The purpose of this contact is to provide information about service. Sometimes the information is general—about all services in the community; sometimes it is about a specific program for which you would like to recruit older adults. Even if the worker is making a contact to inform an older person about a specific service, having initiated the contact, the worker has the responsibility to obtain information about the individual's needs and to try to help with those needs even if they are not met by the worker's program.

Three major skills are needed to effectively carry out this phase of the outreach service. One is being able to identify social services in the community that are available for older people. This involves having specific information about services, including who provides them, who may receive them, and the steps an individual must take in order to obtain them. Another skill is gathering information, that is, being able to solicit pertinent information from the elderly person that will enable you to make some formulation about his or her immediate problems or needs. The third skill is setting priorities. After helping the individual identify problems, the worker must help establish which needs should be dealt with first. Some problems can be dealt with immediately and quickly; others are more long-range in nature and will require a series of activities to be resolved. A good strategy is to begin by trying to help with those problems for which you can provide an immediate solution and then setting some time frame for those that may take a longer time to resolve.

In carrying out the contact and information phase of an outreach service, one should keep in mind that the first contact with the older person is a crucial step. It requires much skill, because it involves an invasion of privacy and perhaps an effort to change the person's prevailing lifestyle from uninvolvement with social services to involvement through taking help. The worker will need to be tactful, as many older people are reluctant to let strangers into their homes or to share information with them. Often these concerns are realistic, as many older people are prey to such crimes as vandalism and assaults. Many fear for their safety. Other older people have unrealistic fears, may be depressed, or feel rejected. Every effort should be made to avoid causing an already withdrawn older person undue concern or further reinforcing negative feelings about the outside world. Some things to keep in mind when making a first contact with the older client are as follows:

1. *Try not to appear at the home of an older person without some prior notice of your visit.* The best introduction is through someone the older person already knows and trusts. If this is not possible, the outreach worker should inform the older

person of the impending visit either by letter or by phone. A letter should be short and simple. For example:

Dear Mr., Mrs., or Miss ——,

The [name of agency or organization] is in the process of making contact with elderly individuals in the community in order to discuss the availability of social services with them.
Your name was given to us by ——. I would like to visit you in your home and discuss our program with you. I will be in touch with you by phone in the next few days to set up a time when I might visit you.

Sincerely yours,

This letter will serve as an introduction when you phone or arrive at the older person's home. For example, you could begin such a visit by saying, "Hello. I'm Mrs. Jones. I mailed you a letter last week about our program. Could I talk to you further about it?" When approaching the home of an older person, the worker should have some form of identification verifying that he or she is a bona fide representative of a specific program in the community.

2. *When doing outreach, don't rush the visit.* Plan to spend more than 15 minutes with the older person. In addition, try to help the older person feel comfortable and relaxed with you. Be conversational. You might begin the conversation by talking about things of interest to the older person, such as the picture on the wall or the flowers in the yard, just to show that you are interested in the person as an individual. The contact that you make may be the first conversation this older person has had with another person in many weeks, or even months; you will need to be tolerant, for some older people may take advantage of your presence and monopolize the conversation. If you sense that the individual has the need to talk, try to allow time for this.

3. *Don't pressure communication.* If the person prefers not to communicate, it may be best to reschedule the visit.

4. *Be a doer not just a talker.* In short, find a need the older person has right now and attempt to meet that need with a service. This is the most effective outreach tool of all. Simply by doing a small favor you will break down much suspicion and reluctance. You begin to become a friend—someone who helps by doing something rather than talking about it.

The major purpose of the outreach contact is to inform the older person of the various services available in the community. During the process of getting acquainted and talking about problems or needs, you will obtain information that should help you to identify a problem that is pressing. Your next step is to identify an agency or program in the community that may be able to help with the problem and to explain the service of that agency. In doing this, be sure you have current information about the service being provided and don't misinform the older person.

In addition, do not make promises you cannot keep. Don't guarantee that a person will receive a service, as many times technicalities may prevent actual receipt of services. You are discredited as a helper if you make promises you cannot keep. For example, if you identify as a potential need transportation services to a physician, then you should say that *you will attempt* to get the person connected with an agency that may be able to provide this service. In talking to older people about income programs or other programs where there may be eligibility requirements, you should say that the person *may be eligible* rather than stating emphatically that he or she is eligible for the service. Many times we think a person is eligible but when the circumstances are presented to the agency, it may determine otherwise. In order not to raise false hopes, make clear that this is a service for which eligibility must be determined.

Workers sometimes will find that even though older people need services, some may choose not to obtain them. You should explore the reasons for such a choice. Sometimes it's based on fear or misunderstanding. Once this has been explored and misgivings or misunderstandings dealt with, if the individual continues to refuse, this wish should be respected. The older person should be left with information (a card or phone number) on where to find the service in case of a later change of mind. Very often pride or guilt will prevent older people from accepting services.

*Providing Assistance
to Older Clients*

Once a worker has made the older person aware of services and he or she has agreed to obtain them, the next step in outreach is ensuring that the services are actually received. Very often such assistance requires the worker to make a referral for the older person. This may involve making a call to an agency and talking to a representative of the agency about the circumstances, or setting up an appointment for the older person to go to the agency or for a representative of the agency to come to the older person's home.

Once a referral has been made and an appointment set up, the worker may have to help the older person actually get to an agency. This may involve trying to locate a volunteer service in the community that provides transportation, or the outreach worker may have to take the individual to the agency.

Sometimes older individuals who have never been to social agencies feel more comfortable if someone goes along with them, so that here again the outreach worker may need to find a volunteer or accompany the older person. In this particular step, the outreach worker should examine with the older person any obstacles that may prevent use of services and try to help eliminate such barriers so that the older person can have access to the services.

Following Up on
an Outreach Visit

The final function of outreach is to make sure that the client has actually received the service. This involves a contact a few days following the initial visit. The follow-up contact may be done in several ways. It can be done by telephone, that is, making a call to the older person's home or to the agency to make sure that the appointment was kept. It could also involve just dropping by the client's home, again on a social basis, to see how the older person is getting along and what happened with the agency. The major emphasis for follow-up is to make sure that nothing hindered the older person's receiving the service. If, for some reason, the older person or the agency did not follow through on the referral, then it is up to the outreach worker to determine the reason and to provide additional assistance, resources, or moral support to ensure that this does not happen again in the future.

If the agency fails to carry out its part once the outreach worker has made a referral, then it may be necessary to make a second contact with the agency. If the worker feels strongly enough about it, it may be necessary to inform the administrator of the agency about the situation.

Summary

Many older people do not seek out social service agencies when they are confronted with problems and need assistance. Outreach services that locate, contact, inform, and assist older people to get them to use existing programs is a means of assuring that they receive services to which they are entitled. When new programs are established for the elderly, efforts will be needed to inform and encourage them to use the programs' services. In this chapter we have attempted to spell out why outreach services are needed for older people and the steps necessary to provide these services.

READING 4.1

Herbert Simpson, Case Study
This case study illustrates sustained casework service to an ill, socially isolated man in his late 70s, living in a cheap hotel and in need of nursing home care.

Referral   On October 29, 1962, Mrs. Andrews, a friendly visitor for the agency, telephoned concerning Mr. Simpson whom she had heard was ill and alone. She did not know Mr. Simpson but had heard of his condition from a cousin of his who lives in another state. Mrs. A

Reprinted by permission from *Casebook on Work with the Aging,* Family Service Association of America, 1966.

wanted the agency to investigate his situation but she recognized that Mr. S might resent a caseworker's visiting unless he wanted a contact with the agency. Mrs. A got in touch with Mr. S and reported later that he was willing to talk with a caseworker. The case was assigned to a male worker because Mr. S resided in a "sort of a flophouse" and home visits were indicated. A letter of introduction was sent to Mr. S, informing him of the time of the visit.

Summary of Casework Activity from November through January 1, 1963   Mr. S was visited weekly at his hotel. At times, I increased my visits to twice a week in order to help him in periods of anxiety and depression. Mr. S telephoned me when he felt particularly upset. I gave him my home telephone number and I encouraged him to use it whenever he wished.

Background Information   Mr. S revealed little regarding his own parents. His father came to this city at an early age from Virginia. His mother was twenty years younger than his father. Mr. S was the sixth child in a family of seven children. His siblings died at early ages and Mr. S was the only child in the family from his sixth or seventh year. He vaguely described his mother as a domineering woman; his father was described as a hard-working man who, in his later life, was let out of his job with no financial consideration from his employer of many years. Mr. S was responsible for his parents' care after his father's retirement.

Mr. S married at the age of twenty-one. He and his wife resided with his parents because he was earning only $15.00 a week and could not afford separate quarters. One child, John, was born to Mr. and Mrs. S. When John was six years of age Mr. and Mrs. S separated, and eventually Mrs. S obtained a divorce. John lived with his mother for approximately one year. He then lived with Mr. S and did not return to his mother's home. Mr. S lived with his son continuously until 1950.

Prior to his son's marriage, Mr. S devoted his life to John. He would not go out during his son's pre-adolescent years without him. Mr. S's mother would suggest to him that he had a life to live apart from John. They did many things together and were quite close. John's marriage did not interrupt this close attachment. Mr. S moved in with his son and daughter-in-law when they married. Mr. S secured a loan so furniture could be bought for their home. He paid $12.00 for board and room to them to help out as his son was earning only $15.00 weekly during the depression years.

Mr. S was an integral part of his son's family for many years. He told of the money he provided for the family, because of his son's inability to earn more than minimal wages. John had left school at the age of fifteen against Mr. S's wishes. Mr. S obtained a "hard" job for him in the hope that this would motivate John to return to school. Mr. S thought that John's lack of education has always precluded his economic advancement. Mr. S revealed little information regarding his relationship with his daughter-in-law. He refers to her only from the time when in 1950 she asked him to leave the house. Mr. S was involved in an argument between his daughter-in-law and his granddaughter, Jane. His daughter-in-law became angry at him and requested that he leave. Mr. S moved to his present hotel room and did not again reside with his son's family.

Mr. S's relationship with his grandchildren was described as very good. He would spend his week-ends taking them to parks, to shows and·to visit various parts of the city. When his grandchildren began school he supplied lunch money, carfare and incidental money for them. Both his son and daughter-in-law were employed and frequently he would remain at home to see his grandchildren off to school. He would neglect his business to go after them when school was out for the day. Mr. S felt closer to his grandson, mentioning the boy would insist on remaining up until Mr. S returned to the home at night. Mr. S would only have to say "time to go to bed" and his grandson willingly went. Mr. S and his grandson shared the same bed for many years because of small living quarters.

Mr. S continually worried about his son. Prior to John's marriage, Mr. S could not sleep until John came in at night. He had fears that John would be injured in a car accident. As a corollary of this fear, Mr. S felt John could not take care of himself in most situations.

Mr. S's only other living relatives are second cousins who have resided in another state for many years. His last visit to them was in 1946. They have remained in contact through periodic letters. Recently, his cousins have sent Mr. S small sums of money.

Employment   Mr. S had been self-employed for thirty-one years as a tailor until the time of his hip fracture in 1960. He began work at the age of fifteen after quitting school. For a short time, he was employed as a bookmaker, but his mother made him quit this work and his father secured employment for him with a tailor. Mr. S worked in tailoring shops until he opened his own business at the age of fifty-three. Mr. S managed fairly well financially, but he encountered some problems because of the location of his business. He depended entirely upon his personal relationships with men customers to keep the business open. His decision to work for himself came late in his life after years of long hours and low wages. Frequently he had opportunities to secure jobs which would pay him more money than he was earning in his independent business, but Mr. S declined. He indicated he had some feelings of being taken advantage of by employers. He also felt he was not good enough as a tailor to work for someone else. He mainly viewed his employment as difficult.

Health   Mr. S maintained good health until his seventy-eighth year, although he indicated a long history of needing laxative pills. Since 1954 he has had regular colonics for constipation. In 1954, Mr. S had prostate surgery. In 1958, a blood clot developed in his right leg and he began to have difficulty walking. In 1960, Mr. S fell and fractured his left hip. He remained in a nursing home for four months. Medical care then became sporadic. Because of a lack of money for private medical care, Mr. S bought patented medicines for his constipation and dizzy spells.

Social Relationships   Mr. S has had a minimal amount of experience in social interaction with other people apart from his family. He has never belonged to any organization or church group. His concern about the expense of such activities was believed to forbid this. For a period of five years (1951 to 1956) Mr. S played pinochle every Friday evening with three other men who also had businesses in the building. These occasions were quite meaningful to Mr. S as he had the opportunity to relax, drink some beer and "be out with the boys." Because of the death of one member of the group and the failing health of others, the card games stopped.

Mr. S has had few close friends during his life. He relates this to his disinterest in talking and spending time with people. He dated one woman after his divorce, but she was of the same religion as his wife and he did not wish to become involved with religious matters.

Current Financial Situation and Living Arrangements   Mr. S indicated that he earned enough money to keep his business going and to save some money. He does not remember exact income sums for any period of time. It was not possible for him to save because he spent money on his son's family. At the time of his hip fracture, he had approximately $1,500 in savings. He paid for the convalescent period in the nursing home out of these savings. He began receiving $70.00 a month Social Security upon his release from the nursing home. He believes that once his funds to pay his nursing home care were exhausted he was discharged to return to his hotel room.

Since his hip fracture, there has been the increasing problem of sufficient funds to meet his needs. Mr. S would have his Social Security check cashed by his son. He let his son keep all the money because of his fear that someone would break into his room and steal it. Mr. S kept a cane propped against his door while sleeping. If the cane fell, he would awaken and scare off whoever was attempting to enter.

Mr. S had a small, sparsely furnished room in an antiquated hotel in the central section of the city. Toilet facilities were located down the hall, and shared with the other people on the floor. He paid $12.00 a week for the room. He formerly ate in neighborhood restaurants, using a walker to go outdoors. When walking became too difficult, he had meals brought in from the restaurants, but he could not afford the additional expense. He thought the hotel employees took advantage of his disability by charging him more than the actual cost of the food and asking for tips. He frequently telephoned his son, asking him to bring in food.

At the time of my initial contacts, Mr. S's chief concerns were his failing health and his financial problem. He complained of being constantly dizzy and having problems of incontinence or constipation. He fell frequently. On my first visit, I had to obtain a key to his room as Mr. S had fallen out of bed and could not get up. He also was having recurrence of his prostate difficulty. He was aware that he needed to change his living arrangements as his incontinence had, on several occasions, created problems with the hotel employees. He focused on the emergent need of "something being done right away." At first he thought any plan would be satisfactory to him. I discussed the need for a medical assessment of his condition.

When I inquired about his financial situation in order to explore his eligibility for financial supplementation from the state Division of Aid for the Aged, he was resistant to applying to that agency. He thought the agency would demand financial assistance from his son, and while he had no objections to that, he thought such a request would increase his son's marital difficulties.

I learned that Mr. S had applied to the Aid for the Aged in February. According to the report received from that agency, an initial investigation revealed he had a bank account and an insurance policy. He refused to sign a release form for the bank to disclose the amount of his savings. He had given the insurance policy to his son. Mr. S withdrew his application, stating that he was returning to his son's home to live.

Diagnostic Impressions   Mr. S has had a continued pattern of loss and increased social isolation for many years. He has a history of poor family relationships as a result of his interference in his son's family and his infantilization of his son. Throughout the years he has apparently been giving to his son's family which created some conflicts as this perpetuated his close attachment to his son and permitted little growth of his son toward maturity. Mr. S has viewed his son as an inadequate man, and dominated by women. As Mr. S became more dependent because of his poor health, he made more demands on his son, both for financial and emotional support which his son could not meet because of his own family and financial situation.

Mr. S has maintained an anal character structure throughout his life. He has used compulsive activities to ward off any feeling of anxiety about himself or those close to him. His main conflict may have been around his own sexual identity and feelings of self-worth and self-esteem. He had many problems relating to women, perhaps as a derivative of his close attachment to his father. He views his own mother as domineering and controlling.

At this time Mr. S's defensive structure has altered due to his deteriorating physical condition. He is ambivalent and tends to provoke competitive situations. His concerns over his bowel movements may indicate a breakdown of his control over his inner aggressive thoughts and fantasies. His anger is projected onto his son. Mr. S may see himself failing as a parent since his son will not provide for him as he provided for his parents. Mr. S's relation to his son is a hostile dependent one.

The treatment focus will be to provide, after evaluation of both his medical and social conditions, the necessary resources to meet his basic needs. A primary focus of treatment will be to strengthen his compulsive defenses. His anxiety may be bound, which will permit him to deal more effectively with his reality situation. Mr. S should be helped to express his anger at his need for dependency gratification and his feeling about death.

Plans for Medical Care   I was in touch with the Board of Health, the office of the City Physician and the Visiting Nurse Association. A nurse visited Mr. S on November 27 and on December 3; she recommended that the city physician visit him. The physician visited on December 6 and on December 20; he recommended that Mr. S should be placed in a nursing home. His physical condition was not considered to be serious, but his lack of mobility and his inability to care for his basic needs precluded his remaining in a hotel room. His physical condition, his history and attitude toward relationships with other people ruled out foster family care at this time.

Selected Interviews   Two interviews [January 17 and 21] are given to illustrate factors relating to Mr. S's need for assistance, his relationship with his son and with me.

January 7   I referred Mr. S to the Nursing Home Division.

January 17   Prior to my regularly scheduled visit on this day, Mr. S telephoned requesting that I visit him immediately. He was ill and wanted to go to the hospital. When I arrived Mr. S was waiting for me anxiously. His private physician had been in the building and stopped in to see him. To Mr. S's physical complaints his doctor said he needed to be in a hospital and then left. Mr. S's main concern was that he had not had a bowel movement in three weeks. Mr. S telephoned his daughter-in-law while I was there. She refused to come to the hotel to see him, advising me that she was caring for her grandchild and had enough worries without Mr. S always calling. Mr. S's son was at work and could not be reached. I contacted the City Physician's office and made arrangements for a doctor to visit Mr. S. If hospitalization was necessary, the doctor would telephone for an ambulance. Mr. S became much calmer. He felt I was willing to help him. Later when I telephoned Mr. S he stated that the doctor had been to see him. The doctor indicated he ought to go to the emergency ward at the hospital, but no arrangements had been made. Mr. S was upset and anxious as to what was wrong with him. He had talked to his son. I could meet his son this evening if I came to the hotel because his son was going to take him to the hospital.

When I arrived Mr. S was preparing to leave with his son. Mr. S introduced us, but his son barely acknowledged the introduction, seemingly being annoyed with his father's demand to go to the emergency ward. Mr. S was admitted immediately to the emergency ward and an examination was begun.

Then I had an opportunity to talk with John. He is a slightly-built, passive man. He tended not to want to talk with me regarding his father. I first had to speak directly of my concern regarding Mr. S. I gave recognition and reassurance to John for the difficulties he had had in the past years as he had attempted to meet his father's needs. I stressed the assistance he had been to his father, and mentioned perhaps he was doing what he could. This enabled John to become less defensive as he began to tell me of his difficult home situation, particularly in regard to his daughter and her dependence on him since her separation. He mentioned his own marital conflicts which have been accentuated by Mr. S's and his daughter's emotional and financial situations. John spoke in elusive and general terms, but he was trying to tell me why he could do no more for Mr. S. . . .

While we awaited word from the examining physician, John several times went into the examining room. Once, upon returning, he said he thought Mr. S would be staying since his clothes had been removed. It appeared to me that John was anxious to leave because seeing his father in the examining room was upsetting to him.

I referred to John's concern regarding Mr. S's physical condition. His only concern regarding a nursing home placement was that he would not be able to visit his father. I expressed my thinking about the importance of John being involved in any planning. My mention of the emotional support Mr. S needed from his family elicited John's telling how dependent and demanding his father had become. He had not thought this might be related to Mr. S's aging and physical deterioration.

The doctor advised us that Mr. S was in good health for a man of his age. He did have a very slight cardiac condition. Mr. S would not be hospitalized as no bowel impaction was found. Mr. S was to be given an enema. The doctor thought that Mr. S's problems were more social than medical. He said he ought not to be living alone, and that he needed companionship.

John appeared to be chagrined by the doctor's statement. He did not answer the doctor, and became impatient to take his father back to the hotel. When Mr. S came out, his son had left to pay the charge for Mr. S's examination. Mr. S was smiling and he mentioned as he looked at John across the lobby, that John looked older than he did. John returned Mr. S to the hotel. Mr. S said he hoped I would be able to find a nursing home soon for him.

January 21   Mr. S was very anxious as to when he would be going into a nursing home. He was quite fearful of what it would be like. He did not want to be chained to a wheelchair. He had fallen twice since my last visit, and saw himself as being immobile shortly. He has been eating much better and sleeps through the night. Our talking about his visit to the hospital was reassuring to Mr. S as he knew that his general health was good.

Mr. S was openly hostile towards his son. He had thought, in the past few days, his son's attitude was changing to that of wishing Mr. S were out of the way. He was able to express this feeling to his son as he knew his son wanted him to stay in the hospital. Mr. S's recent telephone calls to his son asking for food, money, and a visit have been met with statements that his son would come when he could. Mr. S wanted me to tell John how he feels. Mr. S has never been able to tell John how he feels. They have never been able to talk to each other. Mr. S cried for a time, then said his grandchildren never come to visit him. He had not done anything to harm them. Mr. S added that other people visit, like Mrs. Andrews, and I visit him and bring him coffee and doughnuts. Mr. S again said how much he enjoyed my coming to help him. He had told his son how good I was. Sometimes he got angry with me for not working out the nursing home arrangements fast enough. He was impatient when things never were done on time, even when he was a tailor. Mr. S related his growing feeling that his son was doing all he could. The pressure John was under sometimes was hard for John to handle. Mr. S continued stating how his son's attitude has changed towards him. Mr. S was ambivalent regarding his relationship with his son. At times he was angry at his son for not doing what he wanted him to do, at other times he realized that his son was doing all he could.

I discussed his ambivalence and Mr. S agreed that he felt both ways at different times. What he feared was that once in the nursing home, his son would not visit him. I said perhaps he was also thinking that I might not visit him. Mr. S asked if I would; he was not certain that I would as I had other things to do. I said that I would visit. Mr. S thinks that he is going to the nursing home to die. Sometimes he wants to die, but he cannot. This was up to the Lord. I related to people thinking about death as a natural result of growing older. Mr. S never thought about death before, but now he was so lonely and miserable that he wanted to die. (The feeling of loneliness and isolation from his family and friends is perhaps connected to his thoughts of dying.) Mr. S commented that maybe if he could do something he would enjoy life more. I mentioned he had sewn a button on my suitcoat some weeks ago, perhaps his tailoring skill could be utilized in the nursing home. Mr. S smiled and said he might not be able to sew in a zipper, but he could cuff trousers.

Mr. S's rent was due today. His son had given him money to pay the bill. He wanted to go to the lobby with me to pay it. He said to the desk clerk that I was the man who was going to get him out of the hotel.

Summary of Contacts from February through September 19, 1963   The investigation by the Nursing Home Division of the Department of Public Welfare involved contact with Mr. S's son. Although I had not seen John since Mr. S had been taken to the hospital, I had sent John a letter explaining our planning for Mr. S. John kept his appointment with the Nursing Home Division. The caseworker's evaluation of John was that he was quite guilty over not being able to do more for his father. John was relieved to learn that his income precluded a regular financial contribution to Mr. S.

At the time of moving to the nursing home, Mr. S became more concerned about his son's reaction than his own. He spoke of his growing awareness of his own needs which could not realistically be met by his son. In efforts primarily to protect himself from his disappointment with his son, Mr. S began to express much anger at his daughter-in-law. His expressions of anger at the caseworker increased also. He thought the plans were not proceeding fast enough. The acceptance of both his projected and direct anger permitted Mr. S to tell of his disappointment at not having his more infantile expectations met. His ambivalence as to whether the caseworker cared for him or wanted to be rid of him became apparent. To strengthen the positive relationship which existed, I accompanied Mr. S to the nursing home on February 20. Mr. S's son could not go because of his employment. Mr. S needed many reassurances that he was making the right decision. (The Nursing Home Division of Public Welfare applied to Aid for the Aged on the date Mr. S was admitted, according to the law which permits AFA financial supplementation after a person is a patient in a nursing home.)

Mr. S was anxious about my seeing him at the nursing home. I visited him weekly. At first, unless my visits were prompt Mr. S would interpret lateness as a rejection of him. He utilized these interviews to tell me of his fears of death. He developed an idea that his son would divorce his wife, and then he and his son could live together again. Mr. S talked of the losses he had experienced through separation and death. He seemed to be working through some aspects of his suppressed grief in a derivative manner to arrive at adequate conclusions to his own life experiences. His feelings of anger at his son abated noticeably as he began to express his feelings of loss.

John continues to visit Mr. S regularly, bringing cigars and candy. Mr. S has demanded less of his son as he expressed the feeling that his son is an adult not "the little boy he knew." His grandson also began to visit Mr. S which led to Mr. S taking much pride in his grandson's athletic ability, and in sharing in his grandson's adolescent activities. Mr. S and I often discussed adolescent boys' behavior. Mr. S raised questions about boys' activities today as against what his parents permitted him to do. Mr. S had some apprehension that his son would not be able to understand his grandson and let him grow up to be a man. Mr. S complains of dizzy spells the week his son does not visit as he had planned. My making the connection between these two occurrences has resulted in Mr. S's feeling that I was beginning to know him.

Mr. S has many unresolved feelings regarding his dependent financial situation. The financial arrangements are that Mr. S will sign his Social Security check over to the nursing home. The state Division of Aid for the Aged provides the remainder of the monthly fee. Mr. S's bank statements are sent to him and he continues to pay his hospitalization insurance.

Mr. S's relationship with the other patients developed into a parental configuration. He talks of the other men as being helpless, dependent sons. He rarely speaks about the women patients. Mr. S has particularly transferred his parental feelings towards one middle-aged man. Mr. S has recreated his own earlier relationship to his son in an appropriate setting where these feelings are helpful. Mr. S relates well to the nurses and attendants. They encourage Mr. S to care for himself whenever possible.

Mr. S has not mentioned being constipated for some time. He states certain foods will bind him, but he will eat them. He has gained weight. A staff physician visits weekly, and Mr. S has been given needed medication. Mr. S takes this as a reassurance that he is not as physically ill as he thought he was while living in the hotel.

I have continued to give support and reassurance that the nursing home is the "best place" for him. Mr. S has become more aware of me as a person, frequently asking about my family, car, and where I buy my clothing. Mr. S continues to test my interest in him by asking for my help in writing letters. A recent occurrence was his challenging me to play pinochle. Mr. S is becoming very competitive, but this attitude is directed to his relationship with me and not to his other relationships.

Questions 4.1

1. There were several dimensions to Mr. S's isolation. Discuss these dimensions and their causative factors.

2. How did the worker overcome impediments to service delivery to Mr. S? What were some sources of these impediments?

3. By aiding Mr. S, the worker was of indirect service to others as well. Discuss this interdependent constellation.

4. Which purposes, or goals, of outreach did this worker attempt to achieve? Was he successful? Why or why not?

chapter 5
interviewing
older adults

Workers in human-service agencies serving the elderly are often required to conduct interviews for a variety of purposes. This chapter offers concepts and methods for effectively conducting interviews with older people.

Purposes of Interviews

An interview is a purposeful and organized conversation. It is different from a chat or small talk because it always has a specific purpose. It has a particular form and usually includes a beginning, middle, and end, each of which is clearly defined.

Interviews with older people are conducted for many reasons. Perhaps the most important principle in interviewing is knowing why the interview is being held. Interviewing without a purpose usually misuses everyone's time—the service person's as well as the client's. The length, content, and format of the interview are determined by its objectives.

Some of the purposes for which human-service workers interview older people are:

1. *Providing information.* Workers sometimes conduct interviews with older people to explain the organization they represent. For example, someone who is interested in joining a community group for older people may want to know some facts about the program, such as the costs of belonging; the activities; when, where, and how often it meets; the names and interests of some of the other

members; and the goals of the program. In such an interview, the worker explains the agency and its services to the older person while also learning something about the potential member's interests. The worker explains the purposes of the organization in terms of the client's needs and interests.

2. *Eliciting information.* The largest numbers of interviews are designed to learn something about the person being interviewed. Most human-service agencies need information in order to effectively serve older people. In a public assistance program, for example, the worker needs to know about the older person's financial resources and social and economic requirements. In a mental-health program the interview is designed to find out about the emotional problems facing the older person, and the interviewer will want the answers to such questions as: What are the older person's emotional problems? How long have they persisted? What possible solutions might there be for them? In what ways may the organization help the older person overcome them?

3. *Solving problems.* Sometimes the goal of the interview is to help older people resolve some of their social and emotional problems. Interviewers may try to help older people adjust to new life situations after they lose spouses or relocate in new communities. At other times, the interview is designed to help clients understand and deal more effectively with their feelings of depression, loneliness, or isolation or to help them find alternatives to their living situations through homes for the aged or other group programs. Therapeutic counseling and other change-oriented interviews fall into the category of problem solving.

Most interviews are conducted for one or a combination of the three broad purposes of providing information, eliciting information, or solving problems. It is critical for interviewers to understand their own purposes, the older person's objectives and reasons for participating in the interview, the goals of the organization or agency for the interview, and the potential results of this planned and purposeful conversation.

Some workers act as if it is always useful to gain information about older people for their organization's records, and so they question the older person extensively and prepare detailed records on their responses. However, it is often wiser to limit the amount of information one gathers from older people. Only that information necessary for the purposes of the organization and for providing effective services to the client should be sought. Effective workers gather as much of the information they need as possible—but no more. Revealing and interesting information is not always the information that should be pursued. Information becomes old quickly, and dated information loses its utility. In addition, most workers should not want to know about problems the client faces if they are not relevant. Information is best collected on a "need-to-know" basis. In other words, workers should find out what is needed, but they should not probe for the simply interesting and titillating.

The information gathered from people in interviews may be used to help the clients solve problems or for referrals to other programs and services, providing appropriate releases are obtained and confidentiality is observed.

Conducting an Interview

Length

Although there is no way to fix a proper length for all interviews, there are some helpful principles that interviewers can follow. One is that the time used for an interview ought to be variable. Some interviews can be satisfactorily conducted and concluded in ten minutes; others may require more than an hour. A useful guide is to ensure that the interview is not rushed and that the interviewee has ample opportunity to answer relevant questions. It is probably wise in most situations to allow 30 minutes to one hour for an interview. Spending less than 30 minutes with a client may insult some people, but allowing more than an hour may encourage both the interviewer and the interviewee to engage in small talk or purposeless conversation. If there are limits to the time the interviewer will be available, those limits ought to be made clear to the interviewee at the beginning. Such information helps interviewees plan their time effectively and use interviews for dealing with their most pressing questions and issues.

Where to Interview

There is extensive discussion in the literature of counseling, social work, and psychology about the best places for conducting interviews. Some think the interviewee's home is the ideal place; others think that the worker's office is best; and still others choose neutral sites, such as restaurant tables, park benches, or special interview rooms in the agency's offices. In fact, there is no single best place for an interview. Each site produces different results, and the choice of the site depends on the purposes of the interview. If the interviewee is unusually anxious for the worker to see his or her home, if it is difficult for the interviewee to travel, or if the interviewer wants to observe or interview the whole family, then a home interview is ideal. However, if the older person wants to avoid interruptions from family members or if the subject of the interview is likely to be emotionally charged and confidential, then the worker's office or a neutral spot is best. If the interview is to inform the interviewee about the agency or institution, it may best be conducted on the site so that the worker can show the older person the facilities instead of simply talking about them. If the interviewee wants to talk to the worker but wants the family to remain unaware of the interview, a neutral site might be best.

How Many Interviews
Are Necessary?

The number of interviews necessary depends on the purposes of each interview and the problems being addressed. There is no need for a series of interviews to introduce an older person free of emotional problems to an agency or institution's program if the person learns everything in one session. If the problem is continuing and unlikely to be resolved through one or two interviews, a series of eight or ten contacts may be necessary. But just as there is no reason to believe that every problem can be resolved in one conversation, neither is there reason to believe everyone who comes to a human-service organization for help needs a lengthy series of meetings with a professional worker.

Ethical Foundations
of Interviewing

An ethical human-services worker always remembers to follow two basic concepts of interviewing when working with older people as well as with clients of other ages. The first is the principle of **confidentiality,** which means the worker does not reveal information that is secured in the interview to outsiders. The material may be shared with other professionals, if the interviewee grants permission, but not with the general public unless the information is changed, omitting specific details such as the identity of the interviewee, address, age, and so forth. Then the information is shared only for educational purposes. Human-service workers have ethical obligations and commitments similar to those of ministers, physicians, and attorneys when collecting information from clients. Frequently they do not have the same legal protections, however, and they must take special precautions to be clear about their ability to maintain confidentiality. Sometimes courts can force social workers and other human-service workers to reveal information that they would rather maintain as confidential. It is unethical for clients to be told that anything they reveal will be protected when that is not true. The client decides how much to tell the worker, but the worker should promise no more confidentiality than it is possible to deliver.

A second ethical principle of interviewing is **self-determination.** It is the client who decides what to talk about, it is the client who decides how much to share with the interviewer, and it is the client who decides what to do next. Human-service workers do not direct the lives of those they serve. Instead, they help them overcome their problems by offering information, providing opportunities to reach new decisions, and otherwise assisting their clients. Human-service workers are ethically bound to help those they serve achieve the things they want in the ways they want to achieve them, so long as the client's goals do not violate the rights of others.

Interviewing Skills

A variety of skills are required for effective interviewing. Of course, each interviewer proceeds in a particular way, but effective interviewers tend to stick to a number of principles and exercise certain skills that enable them to be effective.

1. *Achieving a positive relationship between the interviewer and the interviewee.* The interviewer must communicate a concern about the interviewee's needs. The interviewer must accept the interviewee as a human being and treat the individual as one who is important and worth the interviewer's time and effort. Similarly, before effective interviewing can take place, the interviewee must accept the interviewer as someone who wants to and can help, and whose interests are similar to those of the elderly person.

2. *Defining or clarifying the problem.* With this skill the interviewer helps the client precisely define the problem that is faced. It may be as simple or fundamental as learning about the agency's services, or it may be a complex set of emotional concerns. This means the worker must take time to assist the elderly person in the clarification. Sometimes simply spelling out the issues resolves the problem immediately. Sometimes when people are helped to face matters directly and clearly, they realize their problems are not so difficult, and they feel better

quickly. In any case, it is almost impossible to effectively help people who face what they perceive as a multitude of problems. The older person who is concerned about loneliness, rejection by children, finances, health, and many other problems cannot stop thinking about most of them long enough to resolve any one of them. That is why the third principle of interviewing is also significant in helping people solve their problems.

3. *Partializing.* The worker attempts to help the interviewee with **partialization,** or cutting the problem into pieces in order to deal with its aspects one at a time. Again, simply being able to identify the elements of a problem and work on them as a series of concerns is often sufficient to overcome the difficulties. Many times, people are overwhelmed by problems hitting all at one time rather than about the specific problems themselves.

4. *Setting priorities, or distinguishing the order of importance of problems.* Once the client understands the problems in pieces in a series, the worker can be effective in helping the client set priorities for problem solving. Many people can be helped to determine what is most important so that they can work on solutions in an order of descending importance. Putting things in order and taking problem solving one step at a time is an important interviewing skill.

5. *Communicating effectively.* Competent interviewers speak loudly and clearly; avoid jargon; maintain eye contact with those who are being interviewed; and know when to be quiet so that the interviewee has an opportunity to participate, change the direction of the conversation, object to the subject being discussed, or otherwise maintain control over the interview. Older people frequently feel themselves inferior to professionals in human-service agencies when they are interviewed. Sometimes they suffer physical losses of hearing. Sometimes, also, generational differences make it difficult for old people and human-service workers to communicate in the same language, particularly when both use their own colloquial speech. For that reason effective interviewers pay careful attention to their skills in communication and adapt themselves to the needs and capacities of the older people with whom they are speaking. Figure 5.1 illustrates some of the principles of the communication process. The reading that follows this chapter, called "Guidelines for Interviewing Older Adults," stresses effective communication with the elderly.

6. *Summarizing.* An effective interviewer summarizes the interview and helps the client understand where the interview has gone, what conclusions have been reached, and what problems remain to be resolved. Again, simply pointing to the achievements of the interview and the solutions that have been reached in the conversation can be an important part of the resolution of the problems that the interviewee faces.

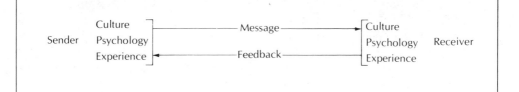

Communication takes place between two or more people who comprise two or more entities. The sender transmits a message to a receiver, and the receiver provides the sender with feedback. Messages are sent in terms of the sender's own culture, psychology, and experience. Senders say what they mean in accord with their understandings of the ideas and words. Receiver's hear or understand messages in terms of their own culture, psychology, and experience. A sender must understand a receiver in order to communicate effectively. Feedback is the primary source of clear understanding.

Figure 5.1   A Simple Model of the Communication Process.

Recording Interviews

Working in a human-service agency and conducting interviews often means that the worker must prepare a record of the interview. There are various forms for maintaining interview records, and they vary from agency to agency. The traditional practice in some human-service programs has been to record almost verbatim or to process record. Detailed files are then constructed for each client or client family for the agency's archives. This kind of interviewing is generally avoided in modern human-service programs. It is now more typical for interviewers to prepare organized summaries that aid the agency, cooperating human-service workers, and subsequent workers, should the interviewer no longer be available to help the client. The focus is on maintaining sufficient information to ensure that the client's interests and needs are served but not so much that it will prevent the agency and other workers from ever looking back at the material.

We would also like to point out that the amount of note taking done during the interview should be minimal. You may need to jot down dates, addresses, and names, but constant writing during an interview may denote to the older person lack of interest on your part.

Figures 5.2 and 5.3 are examples of formats that may be used in making records of interviews. Figure 5.2 is a sample interview face sheet. Most human service agencies try to maintain factual material on each individual, family, or group with whom they have contacts. Sometimes the face sheet is an index card, other times it is more detailed. The agency will want to record the names of the client or client family or group and the means for reaching them by telephone or mail; usually the names of the spouse, close relatives, or children of the client will also be recorded.

I.   Identifying Data:

        Name(s)   Telephone

        Address

        Alternate telephone and address (business, relative, home, etc.)

        Name of family members in client's household

II.   Presenting Problem, Concern, or Need That Brought the Client to the Agency:

III.   Worker and Client-Determined Goals:

Figure 5.2   Sample Interview Recording Format: Face Sheet.

It is occasionally useful to keep information on the problem or need that brought the client to the agency in the first place, and that may be briefly noted on the face sheet. Modern practice sometimes leads to a listing of the objectives or the service that is being provided by the agency.

Figure 5.3 is a form that may be used for individual interviews. It is not desirable, of course, for the interviewer to complete such a form during the interview itself. The form is completed shortly after the interview with information from the interviewer's memory or from brief notes taken during contact with the client. The format is a simple one and suggests that the interviewer maintain information on the key points of discussion, progress toward meeting the goals of the relationship with the agency, modifications in those goals, and future action that is anticipated.

These are only sample forms; each agency develops its own, some of which are more complex and some simpler. The forms shown here may be adapted for individual, family, or other group interviews.

Some interviewers use automatic recording devices, such as audio or video tape recorders, which have the advantage of collecting very detailed and complete information, when they function correctly and are properly placed and employed. Our experience is that it is generally not useful to employ audio or video tape recorders when interviewing clients, because they tend to inhibit some people from communicating. Older clients particularly tend to resent taping. Audio recorders also collect more information than necessary for effectively helping those who are served. The equipment is expensive and subject to breakdown.

The exception to this general principle, in our experience at least, is the occasional use of audio or video taping to help clients see themselves as others might see them. If one wants to show clients how their depressed communications sound to others, an audio tape recorder can help. If one wants to show clients how they communicate with hostile facial expressions, videotaping them in an interview situation can be useful. Or if one wants to show a family what its interactions are really like, audio-video tape recording can be an aid. But for normal recording brief notes or outline recordings are probably sufficient.

Family Interviews

Much of the discussion of interviewing implies that one human-service worker meets with one other individual and conducts an interview. That is frequently the case, but increasingly interviews are conducted with larger groups of people, as Chapter 7 explains. For example, many older people are interviewed as couples. In some circumstances one older person and a son or daughter are interviewed together. On occasion even larger family units are interviewed. Much depends on the circumstances, the needs of the clients, and the agency's goals. For example, if the interview is focused on helping an older person decide whether or not to enter a residential institution, it is sometimes useful for a child to join in the interview and participate in

---

Date of Interview _____ Time _____ Location _____

Client's Name(s) _____ Interview No. _____

I.   Key Parts of Discussion in This Interview:

II. Worker and/or Client Evaluation of Progress toward Determined Goals or
     Modification of Goals:

III. Action Taken, Anticipated; Plans for Follow-Up, Subsequent Interviews,
     Referral to Other Resources:

Figure 5.3   Interview Form.

the discussion. The child may have financial obligations for the housing arrangement, but even if that is not true, many offspring still have feelings of guilt about their parents' entering a residential institution.

If the problems are emotional in nature, they may emanate from conflicts between the older person and other members of the family. When that is the case, many human-service workers find it effective to talk to the older person along with other parties to the conflict in order to resolve the difficulties. Many older people are members of large constellations—for example, a grandfather, son, daughter-in-law, and grandchildren—all living together. In those cases, effective service can be provided with family interviews involving everyone. Human-service workers must understand that interviews are not always events that involve only two people.

Effective family interviewing uses all the principles of interviewing already discussed, as well as some of the concepts of serving older people through groups, discussed in Chapter 6, and some specific family intimacy methods, discussed in Chapter 7.

The following guidelines for interviewing older adults provide a good summary to this chapter.[1]

Guidelines for Interviewing Older Adults

1. In identifying the problem, get to know and understand the older person. What is his or her background—cultural, religious, financial? Will this affect how the person perceives the problem? Do you see the problem differently? Attempt to assess the strengths and weaknesses of the older person that will either delay or aid in solving the problem.

2. When determining what should be done, be aware of the available resources. Together with the client make a plan of action to resolve the problem, based on knowledge of the problem. Be sure the client is in agreement with the goals.

3. In implementing the plan, methods and techniques can be utilized effectively only after certain basic principles are understood and put into practice. Some of these principles are:
    a. Form a positive relationship. The older person's ability to accept help and to improve is dependent on the strength of the relationship with the helper. It may take more time for the older person to accept a new relationship. Understand this and be patient.
    b. Stimulate the client's motivation to accept help. Recognize the fact that an older person can change and utilize the client's strengths to help bring about change.
    c. Older people communicate in ways that are sometimes difficult for those

[1] Adapted from material prepared by Anita Harbert for training human-service workers.

younger to understand. The older adult may deny the need for help or for a helping relationship while discussing the situation but may reveal the opposite desire in behavior. Older people often speak and move more slowly and often need time to think things over; always remember this when speaking to them. Also, older adults may show their acceptance and appreciation of the worker in less verbal ways. For example, appreciation may be expressed by a gift. The tendency for older people to reminisce may require more time and listening skill, but this is normal behavior for older people. Tolerance of such behavior is a means of building trust and confidence between you and the client.

Getting the older person to accept needed help will depend on your ability as a practitioner. The more knowledgeable about techniques, the more skillful you are, the more likely you are to succeed in your efforts as a helping person.

Techniques used to bring about change depend on the personality of the client and the particular goals. Some techniques that can be used are:

1. Always include the client and important other people in planning and establishing goals.

2. Let the client make his or her own decision.

3. Gather information about the problem accurately and try to assess implications of this information to the individual or group.

4. Obtain any additional information needed to understand the problem; speak to other people or groups when appropriate.

5. Explore possible alternatives for solution of the problem with the client or client group.

6. Explore with the client the consequences of the decision, and if a wrong choice is made, help the client with it.

7. Don't misrepresent things; don't give false assurance. For example, if you must send an elderly person to a state mental hospital, don't give a false impression of what it will be like. If you don't know what to tell the client, just say you don't know and deal with the client's having to leave home. Don't make an elderly person think he or she is going some place temporarily when you are making a permanent arrangement. It is hard to say to a weepy person, "Your family doesn't want you." But in the long run, it's less painful than the client's learning you were dishonest.

8. Don't imply you know all the answers and what is best. Listen to the individual; hear out the client's ideas and perceptions of the problem and its solution.

9. Reaching out is important to engage those older individuals who can't express

their need for help, those who are too depressed and feel helpless, and those who don't know the available resources. This involves your being visible, flexible, creative, and sincere in your offer for help.

10. Work with groups of individuals when possible.

11. Obtain community involvement and community support for what you do.

12. Sometimes you will need to be an advocate or broker for the elderly; other times, a social activist.

13. The timing of what you say or do is of the utmost importance. Don't talk of relocation in a time of grief. Being prompt and keeping appointments is crucial. Some aged, like children, may tend to take what you say literally. I recall a situation when an older woman got up early and dressed every day for two months, because a relative said she would come and get her in a few days. She wanted to be ready, but the relative never came.

14. Follow through on referrals. Make sure your clients obtain the needed help or resources; don't let them get lost in the shuffle. Be certain the older person doesn't misunderstand directions.

Some skills involved in implementing these techniques are:

1. Ask open-ended questions rather than ones producing yes or no answers. For example, "Have you thought about what you might like to do, and would you tell me about it?"

2. Try to guide the individual to a decision by making suggestions rather than giving advice. Bad advice discredits you as a helping person.

3. Don't take over! Give the client a chance to talk.

4. Convey concern, warmth, acceptance, and understanding, and learn to read between the lines of what is said; try to understand unspoken communication.

5. Instill trust and confidence in your relationship to clients or groups by being consistent, honest, and patient.

6. Keep in check your own feelings of anger and frustration toward the client.

7. Reserve judgments.

8. Don't impose your own values on the client.

9. Be realistic. Don't always be bright and cheerful. Don't be afraid to discuss unpleasant aspects of the client's life; you may be the only person who gives the client this opportunity.

10. Exercise judgment in determining if a plan is realistic in terms of resources and/or time. For example, some elderly like to postpone changes in their physical environment as long as possible. You must be the one to set a time limit or help the individual understand one already established. Although a building is to be demolished on July 2, Mrs. Jones may not want to move out until September, when she can go to live with her nephew. She must be helped to understand that this is not a satisfactory plan and something must be arranged temporarily. Similarly, patients who want to remain in the hospital when the physician wants to discharge them must be helped to accept the necessity of change.

11. Learn to assess whether the group or individual has the capacity to achieve the desired goal or will need outside assistance.

These are some skills and techniques you can employ in your helping role. There are others. Direct service will not of itself solve the problems of the aged, but if you can provide services effectively, it will at least help people deal with their difficulties.

As practitioners trying to help the elderly meet the problems of life, we have the responsibility to keep abreast of the needs and problems of the aged. We must keep in constant communication with those who best know these needs—elderly people themselves. We must not have a "communication gap" with them. In working with the aged, listen to what they say and to what they don't say. Frequently they will spell out their individual needs. Then, too, as you listen to more of the aged, you may find several older people with similar needs and no way to meet them. It is only with a clear understanding of such needs that we can best know how to help and the methods to obtain what is needed.

READING 5.1

Mary Miller, Case Study

In this case study we see how a social worker deals with the problems of dependency, declining physical strength, and approaching death, through a series of problem-solving interviews with an 80-year-old woman.

July 20, 1962. Summary of Previous Contact.   Case was opened on May 27, 1958 upon referral from Dr. Stein to help Mrs. M make better living plans. Mrs. M resisted our help and though we made many overtures to her, we were not able to be of any assistance. In 1960, after Dr. Stein again intervened and after a hospitalization and a stay at the nursing home, Mrs. M

Reprinted by permission from *Casebook on Work with the Aging,* Family Service Association of America, 1966.

was more willing to be helped to make other living plans. She was placed in the Mann foster home on June 28, 1960. She made a fairly good adjustment there although she was difficult in that she made many demands. Going to the doctor's office represented a social event for her and she had a number of doctors whom she visited regularly. When her strength began to fail and it was apparent that she would soon be needing more protective care, an application to the Jewish Center for the Aged was started. She was very reluctant and ambivalent about it, but she did fill out the forms. On April 18, 1962, she suffered a severe heart failure and was hospitalized. Though she returned to the Mann foster home, she actually needed more care and shortly thereafter when it became known that the Manns would be closing their home and going to Europe for two months, she was able to accept nursing home care for herself, until such a time as she would enter the Jewish Center for the Aged. On July 1, 1962 she entered the Eaton Nursing Home. *Case transferred to ongoing worker.*

Summary of Contacts from August through November.   At the beginning of this period, Mrs. M had a great need to express hostility towards the previous worker. She was gradually helped to recognize and then to express that her negative feelings were probably an expression of her own resentment about having moved into a nursing home with so many senile people. I felt that this had threatened her image of herself as a still competent person who has managed her life well and wants, at least within limits, to continue to do so. To know what is going on around her, to be in the know about decisions about her own situation, is symbolic to Mrs. M of being in control and having some mastery over her environment.

Much time was spent at the beginning of my contact in letting Mrs. M talk about the various steps she had taken in the last few years: giving up her own home, going to a foster home, then a nursing home and eventually going to the Jewish Center for the Aged. I explored at length her feelings about the changes, her resistance to them and how she had overcome this and made a good adjustment. I gave Mrs. M much recognition for these achievements and I felt that my attention and understanding meant acceptance, love and proof of her worthiness. I made sure that the visits were regular on a weekly basis and that I would always be exactly on time. I always found her ready and waiting for me, dressed in what I later found out from her were her prettiest dresses. After testing me out for a number of weeks, Mrs. M finally said rather exuberantly, "I have found another angel." It was at this time that she asked directly whether I would take her to see the urologist (this was an absolute necessity according to her doctor, Dr. Allen) and the following two or three interviews were used to help Mrs. M accept that Mr. Adler, owner of the nursing home, would be the one to take her. Although she was initially resistant to this, she finally was able to accept it, showed tremendous pride in her own ability to have accomplished this and seemed to begin from then on to identify more with the nursing home and accept the owners as another part of the entourage of people who help make her life more pleasant. Until then, Mrs. M had had heart attacks at least twice weekly which sometimes necessitated a doctor's coming on an emergency basis or which sometimes could be handled by injections. From the latter part of September to November she has had only one very mild attack and her physical condition improved markedly to the point where she could go downstairs at least once a day. By the end of October, the possibility of reducing my visits from weekly to bi-monthly was carefully discussed with Mrs. M and she was able to see this as a step ahead in her progress and a sign that she was becoming stronger and more capable.

Diagnostic Impression.   Mrs. M is seen as a very narcissistic person who has tremendous negative feelings about getting old and ill. She has the capacity in a way to supply many of her own narcissistic needs by reiterating over and over again that she reaps the benefits of being good and deserving. Doing things for her means to her love and acceptance and she therefore needs to praise her nephews and exaggerate their feelings for her in order to keep up her self-esteem. This defense was supported by me throughout and the general goal was to help Mrs. M use her defenses and her image of herself in a constructive manner. Towards the end of the period, it was gratifying to see Mrs. M become more and more positively interested in her surroundings and those around her, and to express an exuberance of positive feelings, not only towards me but towards her nurse, the Adlers, and even one or two of the nursing home residents. The knowledge that she has been able to make several extremely difficult changes in the last few years and has weathered them successfully is giving her strength and confidence that she will be able to do the same with the next step which would be entering the Jewish Center for the Aged.

My plan is to continue visiting on a bi-monthly basis unless the situation changes.

Summary December through April, 1963.   Early in this period Mrs. M requested directly to be seen again on a weekly basis. Although she had been proud at first that she was gracious enough and strong enough to permit me to see her only bi-monthly, she apparently had become dependent enough on the weekly interviews so that she felt not seeing me was a great loss. Around January she also began to have symptoms of congestive heart failure (fluid accumulation in legs and lungs). She was taken to the hospital early in February and again late in March by Mr. Adler (in accord with arrangements made by me, Dr. Stein and Dr. Allen) to have her chest tapped which each time brought marked improvement regarding her shortness of breath.

The regular weekly interviews centered largely around three main areas:

1.   Her future life at the Jewish Center for the Aged, and preparation for it.

2.   Her feelings about being in the nursing home where she felt she "did not really belong" because she is mentally so alert; also her feelings around some of the comparatively minor dissatisfactions which came up weekly in this regard.

3.   Her feelings about her failing health and the possibility of approaching death.

In regard to the first area, Mrs. M brought out in practically every interview that she was quite aware that she would have to fit into the rules of the Jewish Center for the Aged, and this was explored with her. She came to see it as a task which she would be able to shoulder as a mature person who could take responsibility for her own actions. This was emphasized by me because to have this self-image enabled Mrs. M to function quite adequately in other areas too.

However, I also explored her negative feelings about being in a dependent state and eventually having to die in an institution. She herself brought this up repeatedly, usually relating how her grandmother died in her mother's arms, while her mother in turn died in her home and how she had not expected to "end like this." I verbalized some of her feelings for her because it was difficult for her to do so. She responded always in a very positive manner to this, such as either pressing my hand or eagerly calling her favorite nurse to show me off or something of this sort. I felt that for her to be able to express some negative feelings and have them accepted was very therapeutic for her. Also my undivided personal attention in the interviews was a real nourishment to Mrs. M's ego.

Mrs. M still showed exaggerated sensitivity to any slight, however unintentional [incidence]. For example, she had a small amount of cash which the Adlers, owners of the nursing home, kept for her. When she wanted to give her favorite nurse $5 for Christmas, she was told by the Adlers that she really could not afford this. Mrs. M was highly indignant and showed considerable spirit in her resentment. I helped her see that the Adlers meant well and had a point in their position, but I also supported her wish and her right to show her gratefulness to the nurse in this particular manner. I felt it was extremely important for Mrs. M to retain some control over her own affairs and in this regard I had at the beginning particularly discussed the financial situation with her (for instance, our managing her finances) as something which she had delegated to us because she has come to recognize and accept her present limitations.

I explained to the Adlers that for psychological reasons, Mrs. M should be permitted to dispose of the money they were holding for her as she wished, without question.

I also learned sometime during this period that Mrs. M still had $100 in her checking account and she insisted that I withdraw it for her. We discussed this at length and agreed that $50 would go into her account with us and the other $50 we would keep for her in cash to spend as she wished. The following week I learned that Mrs. M had laid in a good supply of cold cream and other cosmetics (bought by the nurse) so she would be well supplied when she went to the Jewish Center for the Aged. This again gave Mrs. M a sense of mastery which gave a great lift to her morale.

Interview of March 23.   When I entered the room, Mrs. M greeted me warmly, saying she had checked with the nurse several times to be sure this was the day I was coming. She added that she had so much to tell me, that she wanted to have the nurse call me the day before; but then she thought that there were others who needed me also and so controlled her impulse.

I complimented her on this and then said that I could see she was unusually anxious to talk to me and wondered what was uppermost in her mind. Somewhat irrelevantly she said that Mrs. Adler always seemed to be gone from the home when she wanted to talk to her. She immediately added that she realized that the A's had their own affairs to take care of, their son in college, their daughter planning to get married soon and besides, they themselves had not been married too long (both had been widowed and were recently married). When Mrs. M went on to talk about the A's family life, I interrupted to say that she was really saying that they are leading a happy, exciting life and were neglecting and deserting her. I said I thought this made her feel she was not considered important and worthwhile anymore, it reminded her more fully of how helpless and dependent she was now. I added that this was something that she does not really want to face because it not only reminds her of what she has lost or had to give up: her mother, her husband, her home and belongings, but also of her failing health, her age and inevitability of approaching death. I said that this makes her very angry, makes her feel frustrated and helpless. Like everyone else, she wants to blame someone for the unpleasant things which are happening to her because they are so difficult to accept. Mrs. M said this was just how she felt quite often and it was good to have one's inner feelings understood. She added that when she gets so angry, she also feels guilty. I said that this meant that she realized that there was really no one to blame and that this recognition was a sign of her maturity and understanding.

When she later complained about the food and the delay in getting attention at times, I said that part of her resentment about this was because she had always been so independent, and had been so well able to manage her own affairs and to take care of herself that it was now doubly difficult to eat what someone else cooked and at a time which someone else decided on and to have to wait a long time sometimes for someone to bring what she wanted. This makes her feel that no one cares, that she is nobody and that she is being depreciated. Mrs. M nodded and then continued by saying that her mother died in her arms after she had cared for her and waited on her day and night for a long time. I answered that she wished she had a daughter or a niece to be at her side constantly to make her feel loved and protected and that she is therefore unusually sensitive to anything that looks like a "slight." It again reminds her that this wish cannot be fulfilled. Maybe she wished that Mrs. A or I or the nurse could be like a daughter to her and be there all the time, but here again I thought that she had strength to face this maturely, it just cannot be. Mrs. M answered that at times she realizes and can face that she cannot have what she wants but at other times she gets so angry at those around her, that she can hardly control her wish to "tell them off." I said it was alright and quite natural to get angry when our wishes do not get fulfilled, but that she always regains her perspective and this again is a sign of her good sense and her adequacy. She answered that she and everybody else knew she really did not belong here with so many senile people. I picked this up by saying that her original anger was a reaction to being brought here and seeing these other people, it may have frightened her and she may have feared that she might become like them. She denied this, saying she knew she would not become like them ever but admitted that it is an unpleasant reminder of approaching death.

I said that it had been comforting to her mother to have her daughter by her side when death came and that she herself may be afraid she has to face it alone. I said that it is frightening at first thought to think of death, that no one knows what it will be like to die. She mentioned that she had not kept a kosher home but had always led an honest, good life and hoped that God would approve of her. I said that this bothers her a great deal, she has fears God might be displeased with her and yet she seems to have a feeling that He will understand. I said again that we all have to face leaving this world at some time and that she has fears and anxiety about it which are difficult to put into words. Mrs. M took my hand and pressed it and we sat like this in silence for a while. When I said goodbye to her, she pulled me down to kiss me on the cheek and said that she thought God had been good to her today.

Towards the end of March and early April, Mrs. M was showing some signs of confusion and for the first time on April 3, she did not "dress up" for me, which had become quite an important factor in our relationship. She would often wear beautiful dresses which I had never seen on her before and she would be thrilled with my appreciative comments. In turn, she was extremely aware of my appearance and what I wore and I felt that her approval of my appearance raised her own self-esteem.

Interview of April 3.   Mrs. M seemed somewhat confused, at the beginning, but became more alert as the interview went on. In talking about a very religious newcomer to the home, she began to talk about her feeling about God in relation to not having kept a kosher home. She expressed her belief that God would see deeper than outward conformity to religious obser- vances. I verbalized for her that she had feelings about meeting God and helping her express more of her concern about her failing health and what it meant to her. She brightened up considerably after this, expressed her relief about being "understood" and that she could talk about what she called "inner feelings." She repeatedly expressed her dependence on her "social worker" and how I was all she had and then would talk about her mother and how at her death she could not see for some time how it would be possible to live without her. Again I expressed for her that now that her health was not as good as before, she was thinking more of her mother and her death and again she related, as she had several times before, how her grandmother died in her mother's arms and her mother died in Mrs. M's home and how she had never thought that she would have to end in an institution. We faced together that she had no child to take this role with her, but that in her social worker she had a good substitute.

Much of what Mrs. M expressed in this interview I felt as a plea not to desert her and I assured her of my continued availability and that in an emergency I could be there within a very short time. Throughout this interview, I felt as if in a sense we had worked through a mourning reaction "in advance."

By implication I had the impression that Mrs. M sees the Jewish Center for the Aged as the "home" where she would like to die and we explored again as we had before her feelings about the Eaton Nursing Home and her still looking forward to a "future."

Although in general I feel that Mrs. M is slipping, it is remarkable how she can perk up within an hour's time and how some of her old spirit returns after she has released some of her negative feelings.

Interviews of May 1 and May 8.   During this week Mrs. M's edema became more and more pronounced and she was becoming more and more anxious to have Dr. Stein see her. During the first visit she was still reluctant to go into the hospital as a clinic patient but since in several telephone talks with Dr. Stein I learned that this would be the only possibility for her, she finally gave her consent on May 8, saying "I'll let you be the boss now."

There were numerous telephone calls during this period, to the hospital, to the doctor, to the nursing home, and to the nephew in Alabama.

These two interviews consisted largely of my holding Mrs. M's hand, telling her that she would have good care, and reassuring her that both Dr. Stein and I would stand by and see her.

May 9.   Mrs. M taken to the hospital.

May 10.   Visited Mrs. M but I could not be sure she recognized me. I stayed a while, patted her hand telling her who I was, and that I was there and would come again. She kept repeating between moans, "I am not the boss any more."

May 14 and May 16.   Visited Mrs. M in the hospital. Again I doubted that Mrs. M recognized me. In the last visit she kept repeating, again between moans, "God is good, God is good."

In a telephone talk with Dr. Williams who was Mrs. M's staff doctor, he stated that if the fluid removal does not help there is no hope. Apparently she did not respond to medication as they had hoped. He thought that within three or four days they should know whether she will recover sufficiently so that she could go back to the nursing home. He stated that the bed sore she had was the worst he had ever seen.

Mrs. M died on May 19, 1963.

Questions 5.1

1. Discuss how the caseworker helped Mrs. M define her problems. In what ways did the caseworker build a trusting relationship at the same time?

2. Mrs. M's physical problems were, on the whole, insoluble. What problems did the caseworker help Mrs. M solve? Discuss the caseworker's use of partialization in helping Mrs. M deal with her feelings of anger.

3. Which of the 14 techniques of Guidelines for Interviewing Older Adults did the worker use in Mrs. M's case?

4. Do you feel the caseworker was successful or unsuccessful in helping Mrs. M? Upon what evidence do you base your decision?

CHAPTER 6
SERVING GROUPS of
older adults

As earlier chapters have shown, growing old in the United States has many physical, psychological, and social consequences. One of the social results of aging for some people is the loss of familiar and pleasant group contacts, with loneliness as a result. This chapter discusses some of the group needs of older people and some of the programs human-service agencies use to help older people replace former group associations with new ones. It also describes the ways human-service workers may help older clients overcome a variety of social and emotional problems through group services.

Everyone has some concept of what a group is—it's simply people doing something together. However, as it is used in this chapter and in relation to human services in general, the term *group* means any association of three or more people that comes together to meet some of the needs of the participants. As we will explain, this coming together may be voluntary, or it may result from some efforts by a human-service worker. The kinds of groups we are talking about specifically usually have no more than 25 or 35 members—more than that may be better described as a crowd.

Changes in Group Associations during the Later Years

Retirement has social as well as economic consequences for older workers. Thus older people who have been employed often miss their associates just as much as their pay checks after retirement.

The deaths of friends, colleagues, and relatives also signal the loss of group contacts for older people, as the social circle begins to narrow in the later years. Some older women who are housewives lose the close association of their children, who become adults and leave home to begin work or families of their own, although for some the families of their children create an ever-widening circle of associations. Some older women become very close to their married daughters, in contrast to the estrangement they might have experienced during their daughters' adolescence. Men, too, may find that their children's adult years provide them with new and different associations or loss of association.

Loss of association through widowhood is a common accompaniment of aging for both men and women, although many more women than men are widowed. In addition, the changes in U.S. mobility patterns mean that many older people find themselves either left alone in communities where they have spent most of their lives but from which most of their relatives and friends have departed, or, often equally difficult, in new residential areas or different parts of the nation, such as Arizona, California, and Florida, which tend to attract retired older people.

Another major cause of change in group associations for the aged results from people's becoming less mobile as a result of physical disability. They may be unable to enter and leave buses, go up and down stairs, or walk long distances. Some must give up driving because of hearing and vision losses.

In addition to the physical barriers, there are also social and psychological reasons for changes in group associations, as discussed in earlier chapters. Economic factors, such as insufficient funds for transportation, offering or repaying invitations, or dressing satisfactorily, also play a role in modifying the group associations of older people. Psychosocial limits, such as feeling one lacks adequate social skills or being unable to hear or see well enough to be an effective social companion, may also reduce social contacts.

For all of these reasons, aging often leads to major modifications in the group association patterns of older people. For many, the loss of associations with friends and families is the most difficult part of growing old. Finding new and satisfying relationships with others may be an older person's most important social need.

Individuals often take steps on their own to achieve solutions to their lack of group associations. Some join social, religious, and political groups; others become devoted to pets. Some are exploited by commercial enterprises, such as dance studios, which promise but often do not deliver social contacts. People who face emotional and physical problems because they are lonely may find that group associations go a long way toward helping them overcome their problems. Other older people have emotional and physical difficulties requiring socioemotional treatment, which often is best carried out in groups with the help of a human-service worker.

Some Examples of Groups
for Older Adults

There is a wide variety of group activities for older adults sponsored by community centers, senior citizen centers, nursing homes, hospitals, and virtually every other kind of organization serving the elderly. The following are some examples of ways in which groups of senior citizens are served by human-service agencies:

1. Three older women who live in the same section of a nursing home form a friendship group. A nurse or aide meets with them regularly and helps them plan activities, discuss current events, carry on arts and crafts activities, or simply share **reminiscences.**

2. Four older men who live in the same condominium in a large resort city play cards together each afternoon. They are a close-knit group; the recreation director of their housing complex simply makes the facilities for their games available to them.

3. A social worker organizes a current events discussion group in a neighborhood center that deals with different subjects each week, with each discussion led by a different group member or a guest.

4. Terminal cancer patients on a hospital ward meet for an hour and a half each day under the leadership of a nurse to talk about their anxieties, fears, and plans for their families.

5. A group of recovered alcoholic veterans meet daily in the hospital with their social worker, who helps them plan for departure from the hospital and return to their own homes.

6. Ten emotionally disturbed older men in a state mental hospital meet twice a week under the leadership of a psychologist, to learn to face reality.

Each of these is an example of a group meeting the needs of older adults. Some of the groups are natural, or organized by the members themselves; others are formed, organized by outside agents to meet one or several needs of the members through professional help. (The two types will be discussed in detail later in this chapter.) Whatever their origins, groups play an important part in the lives of older people. They are increasingly used to help older people deal with social problems, obtain information that they need, and enjoy the company of peers through activities. The variety of groups used by older people to help themselves is wide, and the purposes for groups organized under the auspices of human-service programs are extensive—as extensive as the needs and problems of aging people discussed in this text.

Self-help groups are usually formed by and for their own members so people with similar problems can help one another overcome them. There are "Lost Chord" groups for laryngectomy patients, Alcoholics Anonymous groups for those who drink to excess, and varieties of other efforts to help people help themselves. Professionals may organize these groups, but the impetus is for those in need of help to help one another, rather than for someone who is free of the problem to help the victims.

In this discussion we place emphasis on the ways workers may help older people resolve some of their needs and enhance their lives through group services. We stress the formed group, because that is characteristically the kind of group served by a professional worker. However, natural groups that are already organized often lay an excellent base for groups served by professionals. For example, look at the following situation:

George, the social worker in the Veterans Administration Hospital, noticed that Charlie, Jerry, Bill, and Bob usually ate together, shared cigarettes, played pool with one another, and spent their evenings together watching television. All were older veterans who had faced emotional crises that caused them to enter the hospital. Now they were no longer so upset that they had to remain in the hospital, but neither could they return to their families, who lacked room and the desire to house them. So George created a "discharge planning group" for the men to help them find ways to learn enough to leave the hospital. The patients talked about leaving the hospital, where they would go, how they would live, and how they would obtain services from social workers such as George. They met for an hour each day with the worker and practiced cooking, traveling by bus, visiting the bank, and other practical but critical activities for men who would live outside hospitals. After four months they all left the hospital for rooming houses, hotels, and apartments close to one another. They promised to get together often and did so, first with George's help but, as they became acclimated to their new environment, later on their own.

Thus the dichotomy between the natural and the formed group is often false. Sometimes the best formed group is one that begins "naturally."

Understanding Group Life

Before anything else, human-service workers for the aging must understand the group lives and group needs of those they serve.

Effectiveness in working with older people in a variety of situations means that the worker, whether a gerontologist, nurse, social worker, recreation leader, occupational or physical therapist, or teacher, must become aware of the group dimensions of the aging person's lifestyle, problems, needs, and potential services.

Too often, directors of programs for the aging, arts and crafts personnel, homes for the aged staff members, and hospital employees think of clients or patients only as separate individuals. While it is true that each older person who participates in a program is an individual with special characteristics, needs, and potentials, there are profound effects from the groups with which each is involved.

Professionals trying to understand older people ask about their physical conditions, their emotions, and their incomes; they make socioeconomic diagnoses often without asking about group associations. However, group relationships may be the most significant part of life for some older people, and it may be those groups that they use for most of their emotional support. Therefore, fully understanding an older person requires knowing about that person's group associations as well as about his or her personal life.

The Dimensions of Group
Associations

Everyone has group associations, and for most of us they are numerous. With only a little imagination, you can think of at least half a dozen groups with which a typical older person might be associated: Family and neighbors constitute important associations. Most older people belong to at least one, and often more, organized social or service groups. Informal groups of friends and those with whom they worship are other examples. The loss of affiliation with or changes in these groups can have great impact on people of all ages; they can be especially difficult for older people, who have fewer opportunities to initiate new patterns of association and few outlets for building friendships.

Knowing about an older person's group life can often help a human-service worker understand the client's physical and emotional needs more fully.

For example, an effective worker in an institution for older people will understand the residents and the context of the formal and informal groups with which
they associate. The ward in a hospital, the wing in a home for the aged, the classes and
other activity groups in institutions are all sources of group contact for those who are
served by the institution, and they must be considered significant factors. Of course,
informal group associations also should be studied. Group life analysts should look at
the informal and voluntary groups created at mealtimes in institutions, at the groups
of people who prefer to spend time with one another (as George found a group of
friendly veterans) when they have free time, and at choices of friends within neighborhoods, centers, or institutions.

Some Purposes of Groups

The second step in providing services to people through groups is the development of group services with and for the older people who are being helped.

Knowing the group's goals is the first step in effective group work with older
people. There must always be a set of specific objectives for the individuals in the
group, for the group as a whole, or for both together. Although some human-service
workers act as though group involvement is always good, it is not true; groups are not
always helpful. It is impossible to know whether or not groups aid the clients without
also being clear about the goals they are aiming for.

Human-service workers with groups should have specific goals for their groups
that are within the context of the goals and objectives of the agency or association
employing them. Workers must keep those goals in mind at all times when organizing
and serving older people through groups.

There are many different types of group goals. For a friendship or social group of
older people in a small community, the objective may simply be friendly and effective
use of leisure time. For others, such as the recovered alcoholics in a hospital, the goal
may be to help them leave the institution. The goals may be simple or complex, global
or specific, but there ought always to be ends in mind when groups are begun.

There are many purposes for groups. In some institutional settings, groups may
be used to improve the social skills of the members in order to help them find less
intensive care. In an institution for convalescents, the staff may use groups to educate
patients about how to overcome some of their health problems by using the medicine
and other therapies prescribed for them. In these cases the goal is education, and the
group members learn from one another as well as from staff members and others who
may be brought to the group as advisors or resource people. The group solves the
problems of some individual patients while also improving the operations of the
institution.

In a home for the aged or a nursing home, group activities may be designed to
provide members with self-directed and pleasant recreational, educational, and so-

cial activities to enrich their lives. In hospitals that serve the terminally ill, the groups may be designed to help older patients come to terms with their feelings about death.

Since the vast majority of older adults live outside institutions, it is the community group that is critical. As we have said, group programs may be organized in urban neighborhoods, rural senior centers, apartment houses, condominiums, churches and synagogues, and various other places that house or attract older adults. Often such programs are sponsored by service centers or senior service programs within their own facilities. At other times, they operate as extensions of senior programs sponsored by community centers, governmental recreation departments, or other human-service organizations that are able to extend their efforts away from their own facilities.

In community programs for older adults, the goals may be social and recreational in nature. Some community groups are organized to achieve social action goals, such as developing better programs and services for aging people and their communities. Some programs organize groups of aging people who become lobbyists to work with state legislatures or city governments in defining and working to overcome the problems of older people as well as other groups in the community.

Goals and objectives are set for groups of older people that are in consonance with the purpose of the organization that sponsors the group and in line with the interests and wishes of the members of the group themselves. A crucial element in effective human-service work with older people is the opportunity for the older people to set their own objectives, modify the objectives developed by the sponsoring organization, and control the operation of their programs.

Various Names for
Group Services

Through the years in the literature of the service professions, a variety of names have emerged for the kinds of activities this chapter describes. Some organizations and service programs call these activities *group therapy;* others use the term *social group work.* Others may refer to programs in terms of the specific method that is used, such as *Transactional Analysis, sensitivity training, Gestalt therapy,* and so on. We prefer to use a more general phrase, *working with groups,* as our way of describing all of those approaches to serving people through group methods.

The principles offered in this chapter are fundamental to all forms of group services. We think there are more similarities between the various methods than there are differences. It is important for knowledgeable workers in the service professions to avoid becoming committed to one approach to helping people through groups if that one approach excludes all others. It is better to know a range of group methods, from therapeutic intervention to recreational programs. Then the worker can use the system most appropriate to the group's needs. The key to providing services to groups is to provide the service that members need.

The needs of many older adults are frequently better served through recreational and social groups than through insight-oriented or treatment-directed group therapy programs. Although large numbers of older people face serious emotional problems, people who serve such clients ought to consider a range of means for aiding them. At times the support of friendly peers and participation in satisfying activities are sufficient to help older people overcome some of their depression and other problems.

For example, Mrs. Jones, a depressed 63-year-old woman, was referred by the community mental-health center to the community center for group activities. The worker had several groups in which he could place Mrs. Jones—one, an insight-oriented group for depressed widows, helping them to adjust to their loneliness and isolation. However, the worker chose to place her instead in an arts and crafts group that was in the process of learning pottery-making skills, an activity similar to others that had interested Mrs. Jones as a younger woman.

After six weeks of three sessions of pottery making per week, Mrs. Jones's depression abated. Although she did not confront her loneliness directly, she substituted for it group associations and an activity that interested her. Therefore, she became less lonely and, perhaps, had less reason to be depressed.

Of course, other people with emotional problems may want to talk them out and will need a therapy-type group. Many different kinds of groups can be effective in helping older people deal with their feelings and their problems.

Some Basic Concepts for Working with Groups

Serving individuals effectively in groups requires that the human-service worker understand and master a variety of concepts and skills. The following analytic approaches are fundamental in helping people through groups and are useful in informal education and recreation groups, hospitals, and institutions of all kinds.

Differentiating between Natural and Formed Groups

Earlier in this chapter we distinguished between natural and formed groups. However, workers must keep in mind that there is a continuity between them; many times formed groups are created over the base of a natural group. **Formed groups** are simply those that are organized by someone outside the group; they do not develop spontaneously. For example, therapy groups serving older people in community mental health centers, when those groups are selected by and organized by psychologists, social workers, or other therapists, are formed. So is the group of people living on the ward in a mental hospital, who are assigned there by some outside agent, such as the director of treatment services or the head nurse. A community senior center crafts group that is selected by the instructor is also formed.

Natural groups, on the other hand, are those that are constructed by the members of groups themselves. These are, for example, groups of older men who bowl with one another and who develop teams on their own. The groups of older women who hold weekly card games or regular morning conversations are also natural.

The key question is who organized the groups—the members or someone else. Those who work professionally with groups have different opinions about the value of working with formed or natural groups. Probably, the forming of a group ought to depend upon the purposes of that group. It is easier to form a group for specific objectives, because the worker then knows that the group will consist of individuals with similar needs or problems. Moreover, the group will be relatively homogeneous; for example, people who are physically handicapped, of a somewhat similar age, or of the same sex.

Natural groups are often divergent. However, natural groups often have the advantage of having already overcome the need to develop cohesion (see Figure 6.1) and, therefore, they may move more rapidly through group development processes than would the formed group. On the other hand, it is more difficult to develop specific

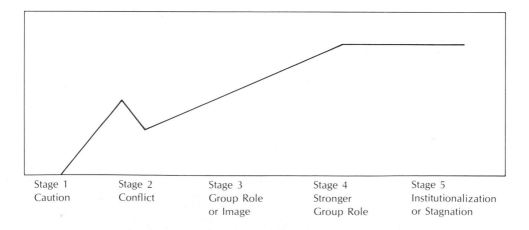

Stage 1	Stage 2	Stage 3	Stage 4	Stage 5
Caution	Conflict	Group Role or Image	Stronger Group Role	Institutionalization or Stagnation

Groups proceed through an uneven series of stages, from caution to stagnation. The line of development is not straight nor is it continuously upward, as the graph demonstrates. An upward line illustrates the development of greater group strength while a downward line indicates a retreat from group feeling.

Figure 6.1   Stages of Group Development.

objectives and methods for a natural group, since it will already have some of its own that may be different from or counter to those of the worker. For example, the discharge planning group in the Veterans Administration Hospital, mentioned above, might decide that they preferred to spend their time finding ways to avoid leaving the hospital, an objective directly counter to that of the social worker.

We have found that the best groups are those that are formed on the base of natural groups. The group's objectives are always a combination of those selected by the group members themselves, along with the human-service worker. However, it is often difficult to find that kind of combination. In actuality, most groups are initiated by human-service workers.

Selection or Nonselection?

There is little conclusive research that guides the worker in the formation of groups. Much of the information is conflicting, and it is hard to know who to put into a group to achieve what results. We can observe groups and understand why they behave as they do, but it is almost impossible to predict how individuals will behave if we put them together in a group. It may be that human beings are too complicated, particularly when they interact with others, to make them behaviorally predictable. The outgoing individual may be stoic in the group; the shy person may assume leadership. The dynamics, or patterns of relationships, among as few as five or six group members are so varied and the potential numbers of relationships so great, that many group service specialists believe it is best to abandon any efforts to develop perfect combinations of group members and leave the development of groups to natural member choices or random selection. The late Dr. Eric Berne said, in his *Principles of Group Treatment* (1969), that he preferred and found greater success by randomly selecting members than by trying to choose the best people for a group.

So we believe that if, for example, you want to organize a group of older men for a current events discussion group at a senior center, you shouldn't try to construct the absolutely perfect group. Look instead for a number of men who want to spend their time together and enjoy each other's company, and work with them as a group. That would be a natural group building into one that is formed. Or select every tenth name from the center's card file and invite those people to join. You will save time and achieve results that will equal or better any efforts to design the perfect group.

Stages of Group Development

Virtually all observers of group behavior recognize that groups grow and develop through a series of stages. Various models have been developed in the United States to illustrate those stages.[1] Although these models differ in their descriptions of group development and in the number of stages through which groups grow, all students of the subject tend to agree on some core ideas. Figure 6.1 illustrates the fundamental idea of group development.

Stage 1. One of the core ideas is that groups begin with a quiet, cautious stage, in which the members do not want to make emotional commitments to other members or to the group itself, because they are busy solving some of their own emotional reactions to being in the group. Groups at the first, cautious, stage cannot usually carry on concerted action. The group is so incohesive that it is best to treat any decisions it makes as only tentative. When the group "grows up," which means moving toward cohesion and group self-confidence, it may want to change those decisions. Therefore, those who work with groups have learned that it is best not to elect officers or develop rigid programs or constitutions and generally to avoid making many specific plans during the first stage.

Some older people remain at this cautious stage for a long time, and some groups of older people never move beyond it. When the group is heterogeneous, and people are uncertain about one another or suspicious, caution becomes the prevailing pattern.

Stage 2. Most observers of group behavior think that the first stage is followed by increasing **group cohesion** and group purpose. Some members, of course, remain cautious and uninvolved, but those who are most interested in the group's progress and growth and in reaching the group's objectives move toward closer relationships with one another and a more united spirit. However, that spirit is also characterized by a second level of **group conflict.** The conflict may be overtly expressed in shouting matches, schisms over decisions, and other differences of opinion. It may also be personal. In some groups of older adults, some members may want to remove others from the group, or they themselves may leave, if they are not satisfied with the officers who have been elected or with those who have taken leadership. In other cases, the conflict is covert and submerged, and the members may try to undermine one another outside meetings. Sometimes the conflict is not conflict at all but simply passive unwillingness to participate in the group's activities or a kind of negativism in reaction to the suggestions of the majority about what the group should do.

Conflict is a normal phase in group growth. It is not pleasant for either the worker or the members, and some groups fall apart over their conflict. Some groups even move back to the cautious first stage, because the conflict is so painful. Sometimes the conflict lasts for a long time, sometimes it is very brief. Groups that succeed have their conflicts, resolve them, and move ahead. In some cases groups of older people become fixed in a conflict stage and use the meetings for airing disagreements. Occa-

---

[1] Faculty members at the schools of social work at the University of Michigan, Boston University, and Tulane University, among others, have developed and published theories of stages of group development. The material presented in this chapter was influenced most by the theories of Dean Emeritus Walter Kindelsperger of the Tulane University School of Social Work.

sionally, group members enjoy the conflict, because they find that they are paid attention to when they argue. Some older people report that no one who is younger takes them seriously enough to argue with. The following example from a group of older adults illustrates the struggles that may arise at the second stage:

Seventeen men were present at the third meeting of the Friendship Club. Mr. Stein began the meeting by announcing to the group he was leaving for a six month stay in Florida and that they would therefore have to choose a new vice president. The president, Mr. Bluestone, was present for the first time since the club opened for the year.

Mr. Bluestone sat next to the worker, and Mr. Stein sat next to Mr. Bluestone. Throughout the meeting there was an undercurrent of struggle between these two men, in terms of control of the group. On the whole, Mr. Bluestone appears to be more in control; he went so far as to tell the worker that the success of the club depended on the power wielded by the president.

Mr. Bluestone insisted that the group needed a treasurer and attempted to appoint one. Mr. Levinson declined, as did Mr. Steinberg. Finally, since no one would accept the position, Mr. Lieberman agreed. Actually, Mr. Lieberman is very unpopular with the men and strong feeling was expressed later by Mr. Kletz, Mr. Shiff, Mr. Steinberg and several others that the fact of Mr. Lieberman's being treasurer might prevent the club from getting new members. Mr. Lieberman and Mr. Shapiro are considered [misbehavers] in the group, but no action is taken against them, and a great many times it appears that the members give in to the whims of these two in order to get rid of them. Mr. Shapiro insisted that he wants to go to the old men's home to visit two former members of the club. Although someone had very recently made a visit to the home and had made a report Mr. Bluestone gave Mr. Shapiro seventy-five cents to cover expenses of a visit.[2]

Stage 3. As the group grows to greater cohesion and begins to resolve its conflicts, it reaches another stage, one of **group solidarity,** in which a **group role** or an image is developed. At this stage group members begin uniting in their desire to carry on a variety of activities. There are healthy debates about issues affecting the group, but they are carried on within the context of democratic decision making. The members may argue over issues, but they remain friends after decisions are reached. Sometimes group role behavior is demonstrated by the group's agreeing on a series of activities, a name for itself, or a service role in the community. At other times a group role is developed through the selection of leaders satisfactory to and in line with the needs of the whole group. In any case, the group's behavior and attitudes are much better spirited and more committed to a group purpose than in the first stage and not nearly as conflicting as in the second stage.

The most effective groups are those that have reached Stage 3. The group does not dominate the lives of the members, but it is sufficiently important to them for their

[2] Taken from *"The Friendship Club," Records of Social Group Work Practice,* Gertrude Wilson and Gladys Ryland.

activities to succeed. Groups in Stage 3 have good attendance, high degrees of camaraderie, and high degrees of satisfaction with participation in the group.

Stage 4. There are differences of opinion among analysts about the fourth stage of a group's behavior. Some define it as a time in which the group becomes so dominant for the members that it virtually takes over their lives. Others think that the dominance of the group over the lives of the members is only an advanced manifestation of the third stage of development. However they define the stage, most group experts agree there is a time when the group becomes too important, when members lose their individuality to the group, and when group decisions are made to preserve the group more than to carry on useful activities for the members.

Stage 5. The fifth stage of development is institutionalization, in which the members turn the group's program into ritualistic, repetitive activities. They resist adding new members and trying new things. The group is comfortable. It may continue indefinitely; many such groups persist for decades. The Wednesday night men's poker group is one example of an institutionalized group; weekly bingo games organized by older people are another. Such groups are not harmful, but the members do not learn from them or change through them.

*The Human-Service Worker
and the Various Stages
of Group Life*

Human-service workers who serve groups of older people must use everything they know about working with the needs and problems of older people to assist the group. They must assist at all stages in various ways.

In the first, or cautious, stage the worker helps the members overcome their suspicions of one another and helps them feel comfortable together. Sometimes the worker accomplishes this by introducing the people to one another by making name tags, serving refreshments, introducing activities that can interest the members in continuing with the group, and in other ways helping them feel less cautious and more confident with one another. The worker wants the members to become friends and makes every effort to move them in that direction.

At the second, or conflict, stage the worker can help the group express its conflicts and handle them in ways that do not destroy the group. The worker needs to understand the reasons for the conflict and may help the group understand that it is simply passing through a normal stage of development. The worker might minimize the conflict, suggest solutions to differences of opinion, and otherwise lead the group toward better and more productive behavior.

In the third stage the effective worker advises the group on increasing its efficiency by showing it how to choose activities and helping it develop means for carrying out those activities in useful ways. For instance, the worker might help the members plan a trip, a social activity, or a game night. In a therapy group the worker might introduce useful information that will help the members understand their feelings and discontents or suggest bringing an outside resource person to the group to help members deal with personal problems that are troubling them. One of the goals of the human-service worker at the third stage is to help the group avoid entering institutionalized behavior by encouraging it to add new members, helping it to look for and carry out new activities, and helping it maintain some dynamism before its program becomes ritualized.

The worker's goal in the remaining stages is to help the group members continue to learn and continue to grow, because the human-service worker with the aged believes that older people can continue to develop socially and emotionally, even though their physical circumstances are declining.

At the fourth stage of the group's development, the worker becomes more of a consultant to the members—particularly the leaders—and less a leader. Informal and formal training for the members may be offered directly or arranged through other resources. Ideas for programs may still be offered, but they are less important as the group more clearly becomes the members'. The worker also cautions the members about institutionalization and helps them develop the skills necessary for making their own group analyses and diagnoses. In this stage some workers drop out of active roles with groups and attend meetings only occasionally, when their help is needed.

If the group moves into the fifth, or institutionalized, stage, it probably will not make effective use of human-service agencies or workers, since it simply does the same things over and over again.

Degree of Activity
of the Worker

Figure 6.2 illustrates how the degree of the worker's activity is related to the social health of the group members at each stage. This chart shows that the worker moves from being a controller with a group that is out of touch with reality to serving as an enabling observer with a Stage 3 group that is eager and competent to participate.

Many human-service workers want to know more about how they can play their roles with groups. As Figure 6.2 indicates, it is not possible to give a single answer to that question—the worker's role varies from group to group and from time to time within the same group. When the group is new or when it is composed largely of people who cannot control their own activities, the worker is very much a "leader," someone who essentially directs the group's activities. With a group that is competent to meet its own objectives, the worker is simply a guide or advisor.

It is important to remember that not all groups pass through all these stages of development, although they do not skip any stages, either. Some groups remain fixed

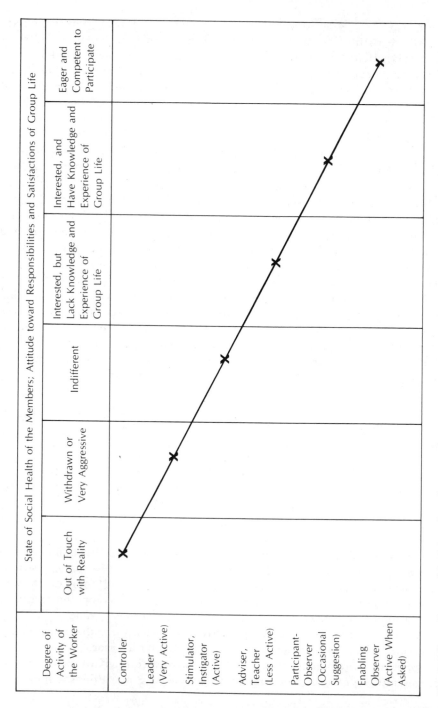

Figure 6.2   Degree of Activity of Worker As Indicated by Social Health of Members. (Source: Gertrude Wilson and Gladys Ryland, *Social Group Work Practice*, Houghton Mifflin, 1949. Reprinted by permission.)

at the first or second stage. Other groups move ahead and then slip backward from cohesion and competence. Not all groups move through all the stages at the same speed. Some, when they are faced by external crises, move rapidly through all the stages. Others may require years to reach the third stage.

These stages of development are real; groups pass through them and observers of group behavior can see them as the group develops. On the other hand, they are metaphors for group behavior. There are no explicit demarcations between the stages. Neither is there always agreement by experts looking at the same group about when a group reaches a given stage. Human-service workers should look at these stages as a guide for understanding and effectively working with groups rather than as a precise scale for defining social phenomena.

Some of the Dynamics of Groups

As we mentioned earlier, there are many ideas about the dynamics of groups. Some of the significant variables and knowledge about them are outlined here. Some are observable, some are speculative. An effective worker with groups needs extensive knowledge of the **group process** and group behavior in order to organize, understand, and help groups. Some of the suggested texts on services to groups that follow this chapter may be of help to workers who are new to serving groups.

Size   Group size is one element that affects group behavior. Specialists who work with groups argue about the optimum number of participants. Some think that 10 is ideal, but 9 or 11 appear to work equally well; it is the approximate number of 10 that seems effective. Others say that a group ought to have an uneven number of participants—perhaps 7—so that there are no tie votes when the group makes a decision. But a group that votes four to three is a group that ought to discuss its differences some more; almost half its members are dissatisfied.

Most observers of groups would define efforts to select the perfect group size as almost magical. They think no one can really say what is ideal, and trying to come up with the ideal number is almost impossible. But some principles of size seem to be agreed upon. For example, there are some practical issues. A group of older people must be small enough so all the members can hear and see one another well, which can be crucial problems for some groups. A group cannot be too large for the available meeting space.

The smaller the group, the stronger the impact the group has on the individual members. A very small group will put heavy pressure on individual members. This is particularly true with treatment groups. If the group's purposes are best served by a strong effect on the members—for example, a group designed to educate older people about medicine and to obtain agreement and compliance about their prescriptions—

then a group of, say, 3, 4, or 5 is ideal. On the other hand, if the purposes of the group are best served by reducing the pressure on individuals—for example, an informal group that anyone can attend and participate in modestly—then 12 or 15 could be better.

The optimum size for a group also depends on the social health of the members. People who feel comfortable in large groups and social situations will feel comfortable in groups as large as 50 or 100, a not unreasonable number for a drop-in, informal program in a senior center. Those who are intimidated by large groups and massive social situations may prefer and best be served by more moderate-sized groups of 6, 7, or 8.

Subgrouping   A normal occurrence in all group behavior is that of subgrouping, the phenomenon through which individuals organize themselves into fragments of the total group. In any group relationships among all the members are not as intense as they are between some of the members. Therefore, pairs, trios, and quartets of members may form themselves and become very important to the individual participants. Individuals in these situations deal with the total group through the small group with whom they happen to work. Most people cannot form close relationships with all the members of the group and, therefore, develop familiar and friendly contacts with much smaller units.

One of the things the human-service worker must be careful to do is avoid the negative connotations and conflicts caused by cliques, which are a form of subgroup. The worker also must be careful to watch for isolates, individuals who are not participants in any subgroup, and help them find a place.

Conflict   As we discussed, differences of opinion and differences of choices are normal phenomena in any group. Conflict is necessary to help a group develop. A group does not survive to the third stage without engaging in some kinds of conflict. Conflict has the value of focusing issues, helping people align themselves with others in subgroups, and providing the basis for making decisions.

Leadership   Leadership is a complex phenomenon that is described and discussed in hundreds of volumes in the social and behavioral sciences. Those who work with groups need to recognize leadership as an important phenomenon in the group. We are speaking here of member-based peer leadership—those members of the senior citizen group who are followed by other members, and whose suggestions and directions are followed by the group members. The human-service worker or the employee of the sponsoring agency is a separate dynamic, whose task is to help peer leadership achieve some successes and to ensure that the leaders help the group in meeting its objectives.

The Human-Service Worker   The human-service worker constitutes a dynamic in the group's development, and the effectiveness of the worker has great impact on the success of the group. The effective worker carries out all the activities that have been described and uses all the skills of working with individuals, working with the community, and acting on his or her understanding of older people.

Program   Perhaps the most significant of all the dynamics is the program, or the activities in which the group engages. The group is always involved in some kind of program, whether it is group discussion, decision making, talking about problems of living, informal socializing, or more fully developed and planned activities. The worker with older people ought always to be aware of the program of the group, know what the group is doing, and be able to help the group define, plan, and carry out a clear, conscious program that meets its objectives.

A major principle of programing in working with groups is involvement of the members. The members should be involved to the fullest extent possible—in line with the social health of the group—in deciding what the group is going to do. The worker plays the role of an expert resource or consultant, helping the group choose alternatives, articulate its wishes, and channel its desires into specific program activities. The program of activities must be within the group's financial, social, and emotional capabilities, in consonance with the agency's objectives for the group, and in line with the objectives the group members have determined for themselves. Program activities may be divided into the following categories:

1. *Planning.* This is the opportunity for the members of the group to decide what they want to do, when they want to do it, and how they want to do it. The program may be as complex as a political campaign for new services to the aging or as simple as a trip to a neighboring city to visit another group of older people. The planning process itself is crucial, because it ensures that the members develop their own program and that the activities are pertinent to the needs, capabilities, and interests of the members.

2. *Games and sports.* Group activities for people of all ages frequently revolve around games and sports. Many older adults enjoy such activities and join groups so they will have opportunities to participate. The human-service worker will often want to help the group engage in sports and games that are new to them rather than the more familiar kinds so that all the members will have a common base for participating and an equal chance to succeed and will engage in activities that are different and special for the group. The group may want to start with familiar activities in which members are already likely to participate, such as cards and bingo, which have value for older people because they are familiar. But even if the group sponsors these, the worker will want to be sure that the group moves ahead to other activities or at least will want to alternate the famil-

iar with the new to help the group grow in their understanding of and exposure to activities. A "new" game for many older adult groups could be backgammon, which is ancient in its origins but newly popular. Tripoley is a commercial game that combines a number of familiar card and dice games. Kickball is a gentler version of baseball. Long-distance running is one of the world's oldest forms of recreation, but it is newly popular, particularly with older men.

3. *Music and dance.* Music and dance activities have a number of possibilities for helping groups of older people. At times expert outside resources are needed to help with music, instruction, and other elements necessary for carrying out the activities. Sometimes musical activities in senior centers and other community-based programs for older people are almost infantile—group singing, for instance, is conducted in a style more appropriate to nursery-school-aged children than to groups of adults. There are adult ways to sing and adult ways to lead singing, and groups that can use such activities need help in adapting them to the characteristics of their members. Senior adults may prefer a wide range of musical activities, from seminars on classical music to discussions with folk singers. Some groups seem to focus on choral singing and rhythm bands, which are all right in some ways but should not be the totality of the music program.

   Older members of groups can learn square dancing, folk dancing, and modern dance, and they also can teach them. Culturally based dancing may be quite effective with groups of older people who represent a variety of ethnic communities. They may provide a channel for members to talk about and deal with their differences.

4. *Excursions.* Trips to both nearby and distant places have often been a part of programs designed for older adults. These are frequently effective, particularly when they introduce older people to new experiences and when they provide opportunities for travel outside the limits of possibilities for individuals. An excursion may be as simple as a field visit to a factory, a farm, or a park, or as complex as travel to foreign nations by ship or air. Senior groups both enjoy and learn from such programs. Of course, costs, safety, health services, special arrangements for physical disability, and proper supervision are important aspects of planning trips and excursions.

5. *Cultural activities.* Many groups of older people enjoy current events discussions, book reviews, films and subsequent discussions about them, and dialogues with political figures. Opportunities to discuss, challenge, and learn are often welcomed by older people and ought to be considered part of the possible program for group activity.

6. *Arts and crafts.* Some of the most successful programs for older adults provide them with opportunities to engage in arts and crafts activities. These might include painting, leather craft, ceramics, and weaving. The emphasis in a good

program of arts and crafts should be on activities that provide the members with opportunities to learn from one another and to share in the development of the activities and the objects. Group art activities are often neglected but frequently are quite useful. For example, a group-created plaque for the agency might have more meaning for the group than ten keychains for the individual members.

7. *Therapy and discussions.* For many groups the program needs to be dealing with the problems they face with loneliness, economic insufficiency, poor health, and emotional disturbances. In such cases the worker assists the members in coping with their problems constructively by helping them to clarify precisely what the problems are and what solutions there may be. At times the group provides an opportunity for members to simply get their problems on the table, which in itself can be very helpful.

Within each of these opportunities for programing, human-service workers may want to call for advice and assistance upon experts, for instance, travel agents in the case of excursions; occupational therapists for arts, crafts, dance, and music programs; physical education teachers and physical therapists for sports and games; and any number of other people who have special knowledge. Psychiatrists and psychologists can sometimes give excellent help to treatment groups. The specialists can help the worker and the group determine the best activities and describe the resources that they might want to use.

Effective workers are willing to use specialists who can aid their groups; not every worker can be an expert in all of the activities suggested here. The human-service worker who knows something about politics, dance, crafts, *and* therapy is rare. A group with a worker who is a specialist in music may have little need for musical activities but a great need for therapy. Therefore, a responsible worker should make sure the members have access to resource people who can assist them with activities that are designed to help them meet their needs.

Summary

This chapter has discussed the group needs of older people and has provided a brief review of concepts useful in serving people through group methods. The roles played by human-service workers with groups of older people are covered, as is the range of activities that may be useful with groups of older adults. Group services are frequently an important part of the responsibility of the worker and of the organization serving older citizens. The concepts of working with groups specified in this chapter are applicable to group services with people of all ages, and can be applied to working with older people who have some of the specific problems discussed in Part Four.

READING 6.1

Peer Group Counseling for Older People / Elinor Waters, Sylvia Fink, and Betty White

Group work with the aged can take on many forms for a variety of purposes. In this article Waters, Fink, and White give a detailed description of a group treatment program for the elderly they developed in Michigan.

Group Counseling as a Treatment Modality

Although psychological help for the elderly can be offered in many ways, group counseling may be the treatment of choice for a variety of reasons. Certainly issues of loneliness and alienation can be meaningfully dealt with in a group situation where counselees have an opportunity both to realize that others share their concerns and to develop new and meaningful relationships with their peers. Additionally, group counseling offers the advantages of efficiency and economy.

A few attempts at providing such services have met with considerable success. Klein, et al. (1965), reporting on their use of discussion groups in centers for older people, wrote that members gained a more realistic view of their situation, increased their sense of inner resources, and added to their capacity to relate warmly to others. At the same time, the stress of loneliness and the sense of futility were relieved by identifying their strengths and focusing on the preservation of their existing health. In an earlier study, Kubie and Landau (1953) reported that through discussion groups elderly people were able to recognize and resolve their individual differences, share perspectives about public assistance, and talk about the problems of preventing deterioration. Similar good results were reported by Fast (1970), a chaplain in a church retirement home, who formed small groups of the residents to enable them to share their sense of loss of usefulness, independence and self-esteem. Fast noted that the retirees had felt isolated from interpersonal experiences and that the small-group milieu afforded them the opportunity of sharing their philosophy of life with each other.

If Kahn's (1975) predictions are correct as to how mental health services will be provided for elderly people in the future, then the Continuum Center program described below may be a portent of things to come. It embodies many of Kahn's recommendations in that it is primarily a preventive program which focuses on the healthy, rather than the pathological, aspects of personality, and on the psychological and social factors in people's lives, rather than on their biological make-up. It also involves minimal interruptions by reaching people in familiar, non-medical settings in their own neighborhoods.

The Continuum Center's Approach to Group Counseling

Before describing the Continuum Center's work with older people, it may be helpful to give some background information. The Continuum Center of Oakland University is an adult

From *Educational Gerontology*, Vol. 1, Issue 2, 1976. Reprinted by permission of Hemisphere Publishing Corporation, 1025 Vermont Avenue, N.W., Washington, D.C. 20005.

counseling and leadership training center, designed to assist people of all ages and stages of life in self-exploration, planning and decision-making. The Continuum Center came into existence in the fall of 1965 as a women's center. Over the years it has diversified its clientele and operations so that it now serves men as well as women from young adulthood to old age. Most of the Continuum Center's counseling is done in small groups led by carefully selected and trained paraprofessionals working under the supervision of professionally trained staff members.

Since 1972, the Continuum Center has been offering time limited group counseling programs for older people affiliated with various community centers in the metropolitan Detroit area. Some of these centers have a religious affiliation, some are municipally funded, and others have labor union backing.

Each program consists of a series of seven two-hour sessions. During the first part of each session all clients meet in a large group of between 12 and 30 people in order to be introduced to a new exercise or approach to communications. Following this general presentation, participants join their small groups of five or six clients and two paraprofessional group leaders. Within these groups they have an opportunity to talk about their own needs, values, and problems as they relate to the materials introduced in the large group. We have found this combination of large and small group work to be particularly effective. The large groups are well suited to presenting information and the small groups to providing an opportunity for counselees to personalize the information which has been provided.

Perhaps this general statement will become clearer if we focus on some of the specific exercises and approaches used in the Continuum Center programs. A week before the program begins, an orientation session is held to acquaint potential group members with the operation of the program in order that they can decide if they wish to commit themselves to regular attendance. At this orientation session, a staff member explains the overall goals of the program and encourages potential participants to talk by asking each one to state "what this center means to me ———." The focus on listening to others is introduced by asking each member to repeat the statement made by the previous speaker before giving his/her own. This exercise encourages everyone's participation, fosters listening, and underlines the positive, important place the center has in the members' lives.

At the first regular session, participants are asked to join in a values clarification exercise, the forced-choice strategy adapted from Simon, et al. (1972). Group members must move to one side of the room or the other in order to indicate which of two words or phrases (e.g., Cadillac or Volkswagen, dancing shoes or house slippers, loner or grouper, bubbling brook or placid lake) they are most like. This activity not only serves to encourage self-exploration but also serves as an ice breaker and a vehicle for precipitating involvement.

At the next session, participants are asked to spend five minutes in the small group talking about people and experiences which have been most significant in their lives, ending with what is most important to them at the present time. This encourages participants to talk about themselves, to focus on strengths they have developed, and to look at and listen to each other. Throughout this exercise, group leaders model reflective listening.

Later sessions provide an opportunity for counselees to talk about helpful and unhelpful forms of interpersonal assistance, and to experience dependence upon and responsibility for others by going on a "trust walk" in which one member of a pair closes his/her eyes and is led by the other. Several other activities are included to heighten self-esteem. Each time the small group meets, a naming exercise is done to insure that everyone knows everyone else's name. This exercise usually proves to be reinforcing, as many group members who claim they are too old to learn find they are able to remember all the names. The sessions end with a Strength Bombardment activity, adapted from McHolland's (1972) Human Potential materials wherein each person lists their own strengths on a piece of paper and other group members add strengths they have observed during the program.

Follow-Up Counseling

After each of the group counseling programs for older people, many members have expressed a desire to continue meeting. Since group discussions often bring personal issues to the surface we think it is important to provide people with opportunities to pursue these issues. Therefore we arrange for a Continuum Center counselor to be available for individual or small group counseling for a limited period after each program ends. Very few of the older people avail themselves of the opportunity for individual counseling but approximately one-third continue with small group work. This suggests that part of the oft-mentioned reluctance of older people to seek psychological help may be related to the form in which it has been available, that is, on an individual rather than group basis. The follow-up groups provide an opportunity for continued self-exploration and problem solving. Additionally some members' interpersonal communication skills develop to the extent that they gain the confidence necessary to enroll in the training program to become paraprofessional group counselors.

Program Evaluation

In assessing the impact of the counseling program we have had input from three different sources: (1) client written and verbal self-report data, (2) group leader reports on client behavior in the group counseling situation, and (3) observations from staff members of the host institution on behavioral changes they see in participants as they engage in other activities at the center. Let us deal with these sources one at a time.

Self-report data is obtained through feedback sheets collected at the end of each program as well as from verbal reports made on an on-going basis. General response to the program has been positive, as participants report increased self-confidence ("nothing has really changed but I feel better about myself" or "I've gained new courage"), feelings of warmth and closeness towards their fellow members and the community center in general ("I've made a friend," "I feel closer to this group than to anyone I know"), and willingness to try new behaviors ("who would have ever thought I would learn about myself at 69!").

At some of the programs for older people a ladder profile was administered at the first and last session. This profile, adapted from Saltz (1968) requires clients to indicate the rung of the ladder which best describes how they see themselves in the areas of general self-esteem, energy level, relationships with family and relationships with people outside the family.

Among the older people, the area of greatest change seems to be that of relationships with family members, although the data here has been too sparse for statistical analysis. Our preliminary explanation is that older people who experience self-exploration and interpersonal communication activities learn in the program to express their positive and negative feelings. This practice enables them to speak more directly to their family members and to harbor fewer resentments, which results in generally improved relationships.

In our efforts to gather information about the effect of the program, we are trying to focus on observable behavior changes. At the end of each session group leaders rate participants on how often they speak during the session, show recognition of other group members, demonstrate interest in other group members' problems, respond in a helpful manner to others, volunteer information about themselves, and do not exhibit disruptive behavior. Group leaders also write reports on their clients at the end of the program and have noted many changes which do not lend themselves to statistical analysis. Many clients improve their physical appearance dramatically during the course of the program. One attractive 68-year-old woman who participated reluctantly at first and mentioned fears of touching, especially of men, later joined a square dance group. Some participants add new activities to their lives. One woman who was initially so shy that she looked down in her lap most of the time and never responded verbally to the group, began to write notes of her impressions to the group leader. After she had received several of these notes, the group leader asked for permission to read them to the group and the response was very positive. Toward the end of the program the leader asked the woman to read her own notes to the group, and this led to an increased interaction. The group feedback on her writing ability so encouraged her that she began writing a column for the community center newsletter of which she later became editor.

Clearly a goal of the program is to help participants increase their level of functioning outside of the counseling group as well as within it. In an effort to assess this at a relatively simple level we have devised a rating scale on which staff members of the community center, who are not involved in any way in the counseling program, are asked to rate participants before and after the program on their overall appearance, their level of social interaction, energy level, degree of optimism–pessimism, and level of self-esteem as indicated by the extent to which they speak highly of themselves. No statistical analysis is yet available on this data. There is, however, some impressionistic data which is encouraging. The director of one of the centers reported a "warmer atmosphere" in the center after the first Continuum Center program which manifested itself in more seemingly animated conversations in the lounge and more friendly greetings to newcomers. A librarian who periodically visits another of the centers with a bookmobile, and knew nothing of our program, asked the director what had happened because some center members had begun to ask for specific books, particularly psychology books.

An unexpected development was the presence and impact of handicapped persons in some of the programs. Recent participants have included people who are partially sighted, blind, stroke victims and arthritics, as well as people with cardiac problems and other disabling diseases. Severe hearing loss proved to be the greatest drawback to participation in the program because of the emphasis on verbal communication. Blind people were able to learn the names of their fellow participants, to identify who was speaking, to listen to others, and to be generally active in both large and small group activities. The presence of blind people who were leading active and relatively independent lives was reassuring and encouraging to others fearful of losing their eyesight.

The findings described here will meet few, if any, rigorous standards of research. They are, however, sufficiently encouraging that we want to continue with the programs and develop more systematic ways of assessing their impact.

Use of Paraprofessionals

As noted above, the Continuum Center small group counseling is provided by trained and supervised paraprofessional peer leaders. The value of peers as counselors has been demonstrated with varying populations, and may be especially important in dealing with older people. In a discussion of the need for counseling of the aged, Pressey and Pressey (1972) noted the value of using older counselors who have shared some of the same life experiences as their clients. In our work at the Continuum Center, we have found that the modeling effect of elderly group leaders is extremely valuable. It is difficult for clients to say that they are too old to learn when their group counselors range in age from 55 to 77, and are clearly launched in new directions.

Selection Procedure

Potential peer counselors are drawn from the pool of program participants. Group leaders and project staff look for the following indicators of group leadership potential: regular attendance; ability to learn and use the program material; willingness to self-disclose; ability to listen to, and empathize with, other group members; and a general emotional investment in the program. Project staff invite potential trainees to the follow-up counseling groups mentioned above, which provide an additional opportunity to assess their helping skills and group participation. If this assessment is satisfactory, the counselor invites the potential peer counselors to consider enrolling in the training program.

The final step in the selection procedure is an orientation session designed to familiarize trainees with each other, the trainers, and the training methods. As part of the orientation, trainees are asked to engage in video-taped "mini" interviews which are then viewed and discussed in order to familiarize trainees with the use of videotape replay as a learning tool. At the end of the session trainees give brief statements of their learnings from the day and make a final decision about participation in the training program.

Training Design

For those who agree to participate, the training program has several general objectives: (1) to reinforce in potential group counselors their already existing qualities of genuineness, empathy and non-possessive warmth; (2) to develop their communication skills; (3) to help them become facilitators who can encourage their clients to think through alternatives; (4) to increase their self-awareness and self-confidence; and (5) to teach some principles of group dynamics.

The training program consists of ten five-hour sessions on a twice per week basis. Because of the highly personal nature of the training, participation is limited to between eight and twelve trainees. The program coordinator and counselors, who have previously worked extensively with the trainees when they were program participants, usually function as co-trainers. The training design combines didactic and experiential procedures. The approach is an eclectic one, drawing upon materials from adult education, group counseling, and humanistic psychology. Aside from the orientation session described above and the final session, which is devoted to trainee evaluation and assessment of readiness to group lead, the balance of the sessions follow a similar pattern.

Morning sessions are devoted to development of counseling skills using an adaptation of the Systematic Human Relations Training Model (Carkhuff, 1972). We lead our trainees through the steps of attending, observing and reporting of helpees' physical behavior, repeating helpee statements verbatim, identifying feelings and major content, and making responses which are action-oriented to encourage helpee growth steps. Throughout this skill training, trainees are encouraged to evaluate their own performance and are given feedback by the trainers and the other trainees. Skill practice during the eighth session varies somewhat, in that helping pairs are asked to have a five-minute interview, during which the helper attempts to use any of the full repertoire of interchangeable and action-oriented responses in "counseling" the helpee. This interchange is videotaped and critiqued by, first, the helper and then the trainers and other trainees.

Afternoon sessions are devoted to videotaped small group leadership practice sessions. This change from the structure of the morning underlines the importance of the specific helping skills learned, and increases the attention span by providing a change of pace, a particularly relevant issue with older people. Materials used are from the counseling program, as we think trainees can learn skills more easily using familiar materials.

At the end of the morning session trainers announce the names of the people who will be working as leaders that afternoon. Trainers then meet with the designated leaders in a mini-clinicing session to go over the rationale and approach to the exercise they will lead, and to encourage co-leaders to plan ways of working effectively together. This brief clinicing also serves as a model of the longer clinicing sessions for group leaders which precede all counseling programs and are a central part of our ongoing supervision of group leaders. Following the lunch break all other trainees have some common experience from the program agenda followed by a videotaped discussion of their feelings about the experience in a small group. The entire videotape is then replayed and critiqued by trainers and trainees.

We have found that the opportunity to see and hear oneself is an invaluable learning tool as trainees can observe their responses, comment on their accuracy and effectiveness, and suggest alternative responses for themselves. They also get feedback from their peers, who have been members in the groups they led, and from the trainers on what they did and what else they might have done. Both trainers and trainees may stop the tape at any point to ask a question, to comment on verbal or non-verbal behavior, or to make a group process observation. This broad range critiquing of the tapes enables trainers and trainees to comment on issues of timing or pacing of responses, and to underline the importance of open-ended questions. Because of the value of positive reinforcement, trainers stop the tape and comment equally about good interventions and poor ones.

In addition to reinforcing constructive and effective counseling responses, trainers underline a variety of issues throughout the training program for older people. Since the trainees will work in group settings within the community centers and in the counseling program, trainers highlight group dynamics issues as they arise during the training. Sometimes trainers deviate from the agenda to comment on group norms, to identify the developmental stages of group process, and to focus on interpersonal group interactions. Trainers also emphasize the importance of co-leadership in group sessions and encourage effective cooperation through the use of specific step-by-step procedures.

Supervision and Inservice

The training program for older people is truly a preservice experience. Continued supervision and inservice programs are necessary for reinforcing basic helping skills and increasing trainees' level of functioning.

The clinicing sessions mentioned above provide the primary avenue for both supervision and inservice training. During these sessions, group leaders and staff consultants evaluate the effectiveness of the previous session, discuss any problems within the groups or between co-leaders, and review the agenda for the day. Additionally, inexperienced group counselors are initially paired with experienced group counselors from other Continuum Center programs, prior to being paired with their own peers. Aside from the obvious on-the-job training implications, such exposure of younger men and women to their older peers affords several secondary gains. The older group counselors, and the group members as well, experience a young person who does not reject them for the usual age-biased reasons, while the younger person has the opportunity to work with older people who are dynamic, vital and striving for continued growth. Supervision is also provided in the feedback given to group counselors following site visits by the program coordinator and staff counselors to the small groups.

Special inservice workshops run by Continuum Center staff and outside consultants are offered to older group counselors on a regular basis. Recent sessions included a presentation of the communication model of Satir (1972) and a discussion of Transactional Analysis terminology and concepts.

Outcome for Group Leaders

As noted in the program evaluation section above, various informal measures seem to indicate that the counseling program has beneficial effects on the program participants. The same can be said for the effects of training and group leading on the older people who function as paraprofessional group counselors. In the most recent training program a checklist of behavioral observations was used to assess the impact of training. Trainer ratings were made after each session on the quantity and quality of group participation, level of counseling skills displayed, and ability to express feelings and to evaluate their own performance. Forward movement was shown on most measures. A few brief anecdotes will serve here as examples of the changes we see and as a wrap-up to this paper.

A retired 75-year-old English teacher had a difficult adjustment to retirement, hating the age-segregated housing for older people that isolated her from young people with whom she'd shared so much of her life. She recently negotiated a move back to an urban university neighborhood and thus increased the sense of self-esteem and control over her life that has developed as she learned and used skills in her new role as group leader.

Another peer counselor entered the program after seeking help from an audiologist for a hearing problem. She had a slight hearing loss, but was suffering mostly from isolation and estrangement following a long illness. Initially quiet and shy, she gradually gained a feeling of confidence and excitement. She has recently become an ombudsman for Citizens for Better Care, and a resource person for Wayne State University classes on aging while continuing her group leading role. An initially quiet and unassuming woman recently modeled in a fashion show after complaining that clothes are always displayed by young, thin people.

A retired shipping clerk with only an elementary school education was the first older paraprofessional we trained. He has initiated several Continuum Center programs, provided out-reach counseling to widowers, and enrolled fellow retirees in college classes in the community center over which he has presided. He reports that his new learning and career have helped establish a deep bond with his adult children who are all professional people.

These individuals all express delight in finding a rich exciting part of themselves and amazement at being able to begin a new career that is helpful to others.

Bibliography

Carkhuff, R. R. 1972. *The Art of Helping.* Amherst: Human Resources Development Press.

Fast, Jay H. 1970. The Role of the Chaplain. *Guidelines for an Information and Counseling Service for Older Persons.* Durham: Duke University Center for the Study of Aging and Human Development.

Kahn, Robert L. 1975. The Mental Health System and the Future Aged. *The Gerontologist.* Vol. 15, No. 1, Part II, 24–31.

Klein, W. H., Le Shan, E. J., Furman, S. S. 1965. *Promoting Mental Health of Older People Through Group Methods: A Practical Guide.* New York: Mental Health Materials Center, Inc.

Kubie, Susan H. and Landau, Gertrude. 1953. *Group Work with the Aged.* New York: International Universities Press, Inc.

McHolland, James D. 1972. *Human Potential Seminars.* Evanston: James McHolland, Human Potential Seminars, Kendall College.

Pressey, Sidney L. and Pressey, Alice D. 1972. Major Neglected Need Opportunity: Old Age Counseling. *Journal of Counseling Psychology.* Vol. 19, No. 5, 362–366.

Saltz, Rosalyn. 1968. Foster Grandparents and Institutionalized Young Children: Two Years of a Foster-Grandparent Program. Unpublished report of the Foster-Grandparent Research Project, Merrill-Palmer Institute, Detroit, Michigan.

Satir, Virginia. 1972. *Peoplemaking.* Palo Alto, Calif.: Science & Behavior Books, Inc.

Simon, S. B., Howe, L. W. and Kirschenbaum, H. 1972. *Values Clarification: A Handbook of Practical Strategies for Teachers and Students.* New York: Hart Publishing Co.

Questions 6.1

1. How does working with groups differ from family interviewing as described in Chapter 5?

2. What interviewing skills can be applied to working with groups?

3. Using the group counseling program as a model, suppose you had been asked to design a group program for older people in your community. Which techniques would you incorporate into your program? Which would you exclude? Justify your choices.

chapter 7
serving older adults
and their families

Thinking about the older client means thinking about the client's family, too. For almost all older adults, the family is a crucial reference point. Many older people's lives have meaning primarily in the context of their families; failing to take the family of the older client into account may cause a human-service worker to neglect the most important parts of that client's life. This chapter opens with a discussion of the older person and his or her family. The concepts in this chapter should be applied to all work with older people.

Families and the Aging

The family is the most important institution in American life. Although in recent years there has been extensive discussion of and reporting on the changes in the family system, those changes, though real, have not negated the importance of the family for most Americans. Certainly, as the nation has changed from a rural to a metropolitan society, the *extended family* has become less pervasive—the family that consists of several generations and several households with grandparents, grandchildren, parents, aunts, uncles, cousins closely involved—than the *nuclear family*, which includes only the husband and wife and their children. Yet many older clients grew up in a time when the extended family was the typical family of significance for all people. Although the extended family has disintegrated because of increasing population mobility—with children leaving their birthplaces and, consequently, leaving the

older adults behind—maintaining connections with it is an important part of the lives of older adults, no matter how frequently or infrequently there are actual contacts with that family. Even when there is minimal present contact, reminiscence among the aged is often about their family lives.

Family Patterns in the
United States

Of course, family has a variety of meanings for Americans. Family patterns may vary between rural and urban groups, among various ethnic groups, and among older people in the various regions of the United States.

Generally, family life, particularly extended family life, is stronger in rural than in urban areas. Secondary institutions, such as governments, social agencies, and civic clubs, may have greater significance and impact on the lives of people in metropolitan areas than they do in rural areas, where the family sets behavioral norms for its members, where economic problems are resolved through borrowing and lending among family members, where home may be the house where one grew up, and where face-to-face communications and contacts are regular, almost daily in some cases. In urban areas, family contacts and extended family influences may be less significant because of other types of relationships. Neighbors or business associates may play a more predominant role than family in urban areas.

Ethnicity and Families

It is a general concept that the more ethnically identified a family, the closer the links among members of the family, including the extended family. For example, Italian, Polish, Jewish, and other ethnically identifiable families in urban and metropolitan areas who maintain strong ties with their ethnicity are likely to be more closely oriented to the extended family than people whose identities are less ethnically specific or who have assimilated into the broader culture of the United States. For an Italian-American family in an urban area, continued adherence to ethnically oriented diets, regular attendance at Roman Catholic services, attendance by children at parochial schools, and residence in neighborhoods that are largely Italian-American are signs of continuing identification with the ethnic group. Jewish families that continue to observe religious holidays, attend services regularly, and, in the case of Orthodox or Conservative Jews, maintain dietary laws, are likely to remain closely tied as well to the extended family.

Although the form of expressing ethnicity and concern for the extended family may vary, every ethnic group, whether Asian-American, black, Chicano, American Indian, and so on, may be characterized by strong interest in the family. It is often the older family members who hold the extended family together and who provide the basis for adherence to ethnic identifications. For instance, celebration of American Indian customs by families otherwise assimilated into the general U.S. culture are often maintained to satisfy and cater to grandparents. For some families, it is the older family members who hold everyone together by remembering and reminding younger family members about birthdays, anniversaries, and other events that require acknowledgement or celebration, and which, in their turn, maintain family solidarity.

Socioeconomic Level
and Family Life

There is some evidence, too, that the lower the socioeconomic level, the more significant the extended family is. Daughters may use their mothers and grandmothers for information on appropriate child-rearing practices rather than texts by psychiatrists and pediatricians. Fathers and husbands may want to emulate their own fathers in recreation, employment, and family life patterns. The differences may result from differences in education or many other reasons on which one may speculate, but when encountering an older client from a lower- to lower-middle socioeconomic level, a worker may expect that the family will be of great importance. Since human-service workers are more likely to come into contact with less affluent clients, recognizing the importance of and understanding the family in relation to the older person are crucial.

Changes in Family Life
Encountered by the Aging

Changes in family life during the older years are both positive and negative. Retired couples, for example, have more time to spend with each other and in leisure-time pursuits that appeal to them. Some of the more burdensome aspects of adult life, such as raising children, competing economically, and taking responsibility for community activities, are reduced during the senior years; for some older adults, those changes increase freedom.

The following discussion focuses on some of the problems reflected by changes in family life in the senior years and some of the ways human-service workers aid older people and their families in overcoming those problems.

Leisure Time

Perhaps the best known characteristic of retirement is increased leisure time, which most recognize is both an advantage and a problem for retired older adults. Human-service workers with the aged are often occupied in developing and organizing leisure-time programs for older people. Some of the principles of organizing those services and some discussion of the range of them are found in Chapter 14. In many ways the worker is most valuable by helping the senior adult identify and make use of leisure-time programs of a group or individual, formal or informal, structured or unstructured nature.

Marital Difficulties
and Retirement

Although they are less well known, marital problems resulting from retirement are encountered by many older adults. There is a variety of reasons for these difficulties, some of which are well understood and obvious. A typical situation might be seen in the following example:

Mr. Alexander retires at age 72 after 40 years of marriage to the same woman and an equal number of years of time-consuming work that kept him out of the house all day every day except Sunday afternoons, when he usually napped to rest from that morning's golf. His life with his wife was confined to dinner, after-dinner television, holiday activities, and an occasional Saturday night social event with friends or relatives. For all those 40 years Mrs. Alexander occupied herself with civic clubs, visits with her sisters, child rearing (her youngest daughter had left home 15 years earlier) and household management tasks. Now Mr. Alexander is home all day. He plays golf three times a week and bowls twice, but he can't bowl and play golf all day every day. He plays no musical instruments, rarely reads, and cares little for the company of the few men in his neighborhood who are also retired. He is at home with nothing to do, and his being there interferes directly and critically with Mrs. Alexander's routine. The result—bickering, mutual criticisms, or sullen stares—is unlike anything they had experienced in their previous years of marriage.

Retirement alone is not the cause of their problems. The two have also gone through some sex-role changes that almost guarantee a clash when they find themselves confronted with one another over long periods of time.

Sex-role Reversals in the Later Years   Psychologist David Gutmann (1975) reports that as men age they become, in contrast to younger men, more interested in love than in conquest for power and more interested in communicating with others. They become less personally sensual and more generally loving. Young men are more interested in sex—even procreative sex—while older men become more interested in food, pleasant sights, sounds, and human associations.

Women move in the reverse direction. As they age, Gutmann says, women become more aggressive, less sentimental, and more domineering. In later years, "The older wife becomes something of an authority to the husband. . . ." According to Gutmann the relationship that began the marriage is almost completely reversed.

Sex   There are also distinct changes in the sexual inclinations and behavior of older people. Seymour Kornblum and Geraldine Lauter, two community center workers with the aged, report:

As a man grows older, certain physical-sexual changes become evident. The prostate gland often enlarges and its contractions during orgasm are weaker. The force of ejaculation weakens, and the seminal fluid is thinner and more scant. Orgasm is slower in coming and may not last as long as it once did. Erections are less vigorous and frequent, although the potential remains the same. The aging man may lose his erection rather rapidly after ejaculation and be unable to attain another for several hours, or even days. Studies of older men reveal that impotency increases steadily with age reaching 50 to 70 percent at age 75.

In contrast to men, women demonstrate few changes in the pattern of their sexual response as they grow older. . . . A woman's sexual desire ordinarily continues undiminished until she is 60 years or older, after which it declines very slowly, if a suitable outlet is available. . . . There is no time limit drawn by advancing years to female sexuality (Kornblum and Lauter, 1976).

Thus the retired couple may have significant psychosexual needs with which human-service workers can help.

Working with the Retired Couple   The human-service worker may help the couple become aware of and able to deal with some of their personal marital problems through some of the interviewing or counseling methods suggested in Chapter 5, or through a group program for couples with similar characteristics and problems, such as those discussed in Chapter 6. If leisure-time programs are indicated, the worker may help the couple make contact with them and may even lead the couple to them. Such programs may be recreational, educational, or oriented to political or social action.

The couple needs help in understanding the problems associated with their new relationship but, perhaps more important, they need help in adjusting to the changes in their circumstances. Certain kinds of marital and family counseling methods may prove helpful with retired couples. One approach that may help Mr. and Mrs. Alexander would be an opportunity to reminisce, with the help of the worker, on the reasons for their marriage in the first place. That may help them regain some understanding of why they have remained together as long as they have, what they have in common, and what they feel for one another.

Of course, all of their problems are not those of leisure-time or emotional difficulty. Perhaps a physician could help Mr. Alexander understand his waning sexual powers. Physicians with special knowledge may be able to help him restore his sexual functioning. Counselors on sexuality may be able to help the Alexanders find alternative ways for providing each other with sexual gratification.

New Relationships with Children

Aging makes for major differences in the relationships between parents and children. Some are obvious: Children grow up and leave. They become independent socially, economically, and geographically, with many relocating long distances from their parents. Outright estrangement is a common phenomenon in American families, with children and parents barely communicating by mail, telephone, or personal visits. There are also some less obvious changes that occur with the entry into the senior years by parents.

Closer Ties   For some older women relationships with their daughters become closer than during the daughters' adolescent and young adult years, when they themselves were younger. The grandmother has a useful contribution to make as a babysitter and a counselor. Daughters probably ask more advice about child rearing from their mothers than from any other source. The mother and her married daughter may also have more in common in the later years of their relationship. Both have husbands, both may have had children, both are or have been employed. There is a good bit to talk about and much to share. Some older women report that their daughters provide them, through the daughters' contemporaries, with an ever-widening circle of friends among both young and old women.

Men have similar positive changes in their relationships. Older fathers and their adult sons may share household chores, experiences in work and community affairs, and recreational activities such as hunting or fishing together. The tensions that may have existed between the father and his adolescent son may disappear when both become adults.

Such changes are generally pleasant for both parent and child and are not likely to come to the attention of human-service workers. The family has found some satisfactions on its own and has developed a pleasant reaction to the later years without the intervention of any outside agency.

The Two-Way Guilt of Parents and Children   By contrast, for many families the later years are a source of increasing and unpleasant reminiscences about past unkindnesses perpetrated by children against their parents and parents against their children. The reminiscence, so characteristic of the later years, is a source of anxiety and tension rather than pleasant memories.

Although aging is the normal result of time passing, many children think they are responsible for the problems their parents face. The problems are physical and social results of growing old, but the children, nevertheless, feel guilt. In many cases, younger family members do not feel they are doing all they can for the older relative. Sometimes their resources or the availability of community resources are insufficient, and family members are burdened with the feeling that they have not satisfactorily aided their elders.

Older people often feel guilty, too, toward their children and other younger relatives. They dwell on the unkindnesses they have committed or imagine they have committed against the younger generation. Though it should be obvious that people cannot live together over decades without occasionally being less than kind, reminiscence about outbursts of emotion and denials of affection can lead to disabling feelings of guilt on the part of older people.

In many situations the human-service worker's primary role with the family is to help the older and younger generations speak with one another about their feelings, particularly their guilt feelings. The human-service worker may be able to arrange opportunities for the older and younger family members to confront one another directly and to explain why they do not want their older (or younger) counterparts to feel guilty.

For example: Mrs. Carter visits a human-service worker in a family service or community mental-health agency and talks about her overwhelming sense of guilt toward her son, William, whose career plans she criticized when he was a child and whom she rarely supported in his educational activities. When he married, she was critical of his choice of a spouse, and although she attended the wedding, she did not do so enthusiastically. In recent years, the families have been closer. Mrs. Carter has come to care deeply for her daughter-in-law and for the couple's children. She has helped when she could, and she has learned to be proud of her son's career. But she feels guilty about those earlier unkind and inaccurate judgments about her son, his career, and his wife.

The human-service worker with Mrs. Carter could serve her best by bringing her together with her son and letting them talk things over. The son may deny having ever been disturbed by his mother's negative attitude. And the worker can be helpful to the client by helping her understand the normal reactions parents have toward their sons' departures from the home and selections of careers that may be unfamiliar to their parents.

Even more beneficial might be introducing Mrs. Carter into a group of women with similar concerns and backgrounds who can help her overcome her feeling of being unusual and unkind to her son and his family.

But the guilt associated with aging among family members goes in both directions. A typical case is: Mrs. Hellman develops cancer of the breast and requires surgery, long hospitalization, and extended care in a nursing home. Her small health and hospitalization insurance benefits run out quickly, and she is forced, before recovering, to obtain medical assistance from her state welfare department. Her daughter and son-in-law have a comfortable income but little more than enough to provide for food, clothing, and shelter for their own family of four. They feel guilty about their mother's seeking and obtaining public assistance, which is for some a demeaning course of action. (See Chapter 12 for a more detailed discussion of financial assistance programs.)

In a case such as that of Mrs. Hellman, the social worker with the public welfare department would find it necessary and beneficial to the family to alleviate their guilt—to explain that, without drawing on financial assistance programs, many families would find themselves destitute and still unable to care for the health costs of a close family member.

In other cases, children feel guilty about the normal onset of aging in their parents, as if, by misbehavior as children or lack of attention as young adults, they caused the problems. Such families may be helped by conversations with a human-service worker or by group sessions with other children of aging persons.

Families Arriving for Service

One of the observations that many human-service workers in health and welfare agencies make about old people and their families is that help is frequently sought not by an older individual alone but by an older adult and the total family.

Visit the waiting room of any large hospital, particularly one that cares for serious illnesses referred to it by family physicians, such as a university hospital, and you will find family groups waiting for an older person's appointment with a physician. Such hospitals frequently must build waiting rooms larger than usual, with seating for many more people than their patient load. That is because their patients may come with as many as five or six family members. Public welfare departments experience the same phenomenon and so, on occasion, do mental-health and family-service agencies.

At times there are practical reasons for the mass entry into the agency. The older person cannot drive, public transportation is inadequate, or the family wants to make sure that the older person can negotiate the complexities of entering and using a health or social service agency's programs.

Just as often, however, the reasons are emotional. The older person is afraid to go for help without the support of at least one, and probably more, family members, or the family members are unwilling to let the older person obtain the services without their presence. Family ties are so close, particularly in times of crisis when health or social services are needed, that the whole constellation is involved.

Situations such as these offer excellent opportunities for human-service workers to meet and work with the total family around the social, cultural, and psychological problems associated with use of the service. Helping the family use the hospital properly, helping the family understand what is happening in the hospital, and helping the doctor understand the larger family constellation may have value in curing the patient of his or her problems.

Economic Insufficiency

As we have mentioned, economic need is one of the greatest problems of older adults. Chapter 12 discusses some of the programs established to help people overcome that need. However, beyond concrete financial assistance, there are service implications for helping older people and their families deal with the problems of economic need.

For example, education is one need. Frequently families with older adults will need help in finding ways to better use the money they have. Conserving resources by purchasing goods and services at the lowest possible cost is an important consideration for older people, who frequently find themselves short of funds for the first time in their memories.

Human-service workers can aid older people and their families by informing them of consumer information and by helping them develop knowledge about the best places to shop, organizations that provide discounts to senior adults, and the principles of comparative purchasing. Many older widows, who have had little experience in handling finances, can dissipate their limited resources by bad choices of housing, clothing, or savings programs. Advice from consumer experts and the assistance of consumer advocates, which can be brought to the attention of older people and their families by human-service workers, can make a significant difference.

Institutionalization

Few issues cause as many feelings of guilt on the part of children or rejection on the part of older people as institutionalization in homes for the aging. The range of such institutions is great. Some are excellent, and some are scandalously inadequate, as newspaper readers will testify.

The human-service worker has a variety of roles to play working with the family around the need for and alternatives to institutionalization (see Chapter 13). For one thing, the worker must help the older person and the family decide whether or not institutionalization is absolutely necessary. If so, why? If not, what are the alternatives available and how realistic are they? Although unhappiness for both the family and the older person is a characteristic of the institutionalization process, the worker can be helpful in minimizing the guilt felt by the family and the anger felt by the older person. Perhaps even better, the worker can be effective in locating an acceptable alternative to institutionalization, such as foster care, continued residence with the family, an apartment with associated assistance from a community agency, or relocation to another community with other family members. All may be realistic alternatives.

Emotional Problems

One of the key methods for helping older people and their families is family group therapy or family counseling.

Family methods are designed to solve the emotional, social, or, more generally, family problem that is being experienced by older people and those around them by dealing with the whole constellation that experiences the difficulty. Experts in family counseling believe it is better to help the whole family discuss a problem situation than to discuss it with only one or two family members, particularly when much of the conversation will be about others who are not present. Therefore, the human-service worker enters into the family constellation and assists it in dealing with the problem.

Essentially, family therapy combines the techniques of interviewing with some of the understandings and methods of working with groups.

The methods for dealing with family problems through family therapy are several. They include those that have been developed by Walter Kempler, Nathan Ackerman, Virginia Satir, and many others.

Summary

Human-service workers who hope to assist older people and their families in overcoming problems must understand the total family and the total family context in order to provide help to the family system.

This chapter has covered the various ways in which families function and has provided details on the reasons families play crucial roles in the lives of older people. Means for working with total families have been suggested. The subsequent chapters provide information on ways of working with older people through direct and organizational services and describe the service programs available for older people and the means for using them.

READING 7.1

The Rehearsal / Christina Flynn

In this selection Christina Flynn reminisces about growing up in an extended family.

Rehearsal time for Grandpere's small family orchestra was at ten o'clock every Sunday morning in the kitchen. All the heavy maple chairs were moved to the sides of the room to make way for folding chairs and for the music stands of his five sons and their instruments. The jockeying for position in the semicircle intrigued me. The final seating arrangements always looked the same, so why all the shifting around?

The first violinist passed out the scores. I thought my eldest uncle had written the music. Grandpere finally raised his baton and the music was on—so beautiful to me. Not so to them, for all quarreled when the music was stopped by the conductor. They quarreled in French, so I never knew what their problems were.

Meanwhile, Grandmere and two daughters prepared Sunday dinner on a big black iron stove using big black iron pots.

Left over in the crowded kitchen was one small unoccupied place I claimed for my own use when the music was a dance tune. Oh to be a famous dancer some day! Why not start now, I fancied, moving to the music.

Sometimes there were other things to do, such as investigate the huge pockets of the overcoats hanging on a corner rack, or try on enormous felt hats also hanging there. I never dared to open the ice box door, a large piece of furniture built of maple wood, lined with tin and painted white. I know because I peeked once when someone else, an aunt, opened it.

Occasionally I would sit in Grandmere's maple rocking chair to galloping music for an imaginary trip, careful to keep the horses at a quiet trot, lest she invite me to halt too soon. Tiring of travelling I might choose to stand in front of the ice box and look up at a pencil drawing hung above it. My oldest uncle had drawn this large picture of a boy riding a bicycle with huge front wheels. I pondered—that bicycle does not look like the ones the boys my age are riding.

From *Reflections,* 1975, edited by Graham Rowles. Reprinted by permission of Clark University and the author.

And another place drew my attention—the shelf over the kitchen table where two treasures were kept: one a clock from Canada with real gold designs on it and the other a little black iron night light, about seven inches high, in the shape of a gnome wearing a pointed hat and smoking a cigar, a wick that when lighted gave a warm faint glow over the kitchen, regularly welcoming home the orchestra from evening playing engagements.

After what seemed a long concert, the conductor brought it to a close. Then promptly each player gathered up his instrument, placed it in its case. The chairs were folded and all equipment taken to the store room.

The kitchen was cleared. Pots on the stove, their covers now removed, sent fragrant steam streaming to the ceiling! My two aunts replaced the kitchen chairs and set the table for dinner.

Presently Grandmere called us all to the table with a cheerful, "Bonne appetite mes enfants!"

Questions 7.1

1. The objects that surround people help observers define them. How does the setting help define this family as extended?

2. Discuss the clearly delineated role structure in this family. How do these roles help define individual identity within the family constellation? Behavioral norms?

3. Using the knowledge you have about changes in American family patterns, discuss the kinds of changes you would expect this family to have experienced between the time described and now.

READING 7.2

Counseling with Older People and Their Families / Jean Leach

In this useful and practical article Jean Leach outlines areas of special difficulty for the elderly individual who needs help and the helping roles of the human-service worker.

This paper will attempt to share some of what the family agency has learned in counseling with older persons and their families when they are confronted with a problem that they cannot solve without outside help. This situation in and of itself is difficult for most older persons who have been accustomed to solving their own problems and who are not attuned usually to the use of any professional services except those of their physician or lawyer. Sometimes they have a trusting relationship with their clergyman and from time to time shared some of their concerns with him.

From a paper given at the Institute for Coordinators and Directors of Senior Centers, sponsored by the New Jersey Division on Aging—May 11, 1966, Trenton, New Jersey. Used by permission of the author.

The Request for Help

Most counseling agencies find that the request for help to or for the older person often comes from his relatives—his adult children or grandchildren or a niece or nephew. Frequently, the request is made without the knowledge of the older person, and often the applicant is uncomfortable about his request for help, feels he is being somewhat disloyal to discuss the older person's problem with an outsider, or inadequate because he has been unable to solve the problem through his own efforts. Sometimes the family postpones requesting help long beyond the point when it might have been most effective. Often the expenses required to maintain the older person have constituted an undue strain on the resources of a young family. Sometimes the young relative is not able physically or emotionally to provide the care the older person requires.

Behind the request for help for the older person the caseworker often will find the applicant's deep sense of loss or his fear of the impending loss of the relationship with the older person as it has existed in the past when it was meaningful. He has known the older person as an adequate, independent, mobile person; and he is now reacting with grief to what the loss of these capacities mean to him. This is particularly apt to be the case with adult children or grandchildren or contemporaries who have had a close and meaningful relationship with the individual over a period of years. The caseworker must be sensitive to such feelings on the part of the applicant, if he is to be of service to the family.

Focusing the Relationship

The caseworker considers it his first task to get to know the *person with the problem*. This includes developing a relationship with the older person as well as those family members and friends who are actively involved in his life and who need to be understood and taken into consideration as a plan is made with the older person. The concept of planning with the person rather than for him often is difficult for families and even other professionals to accept. In their minds the request for outside help is necessary only because the older person can no longer solve his problems through his own efforts, and the alternative from their viewpoint is to take over and plan for him. Dr. Maurice Linden recently commented that in working with an older person it is necessary to make a plan, not to hatch a plot.

Caseworkers proceed with the conviction that every human being wishes to operate to the maximum of his capacities throughout his life, and that this wish does not diminish or disappear as one's physical and emotional resources dwindle. In fact, it is demonstrated over and over that this intensifies as one feels himself slipping or becoming more isolated. Often this accounts for the dogged determination to do for himself or to proceed in his own way which characterizes the eccentric, the recluse, or the "cantankerous" older person.

The caseworker's first task always is to make contact with the client, and sometimes under these circumstances this is achieved by commenting on some object or belonging in the room or house which seems to have particular meaning to the older person—e.g., his well-cared for plants, his well-read books, a figurine in a prominent place, a piece of jewelry, a picture on a nearby table, etc. Often the older person can talk more easily about these objects than he can

about himself, and in so doing, he begins to share with the caseworker something significant
about himself and his earlier life. This can be the beginning of a bridge to him which will lead
to the relationship necessary to help him with his current concerns.

Reactions to Loss

As has been noted many times, the central dynamic of aging is the struggle to cope with
loss—not only of health, but also of one's important relationships, and one's sense of usefulness
and importance. Not infrequently an older person experiences a marked loss of income and
prestige as he retires from his work. In order to cope with these losses and the anxiety they
engender, the individual not only employs his usual defenses against anxiety but also often
acquires some new defenses in a desperate effort to protect himself against further hurt. It is for
this reason that the older person sometimes appears walled off and impervious to further
onslaughts from the environment. Behind this mask, however, is the frightened individual,
trying desperately to hang on and to protect himself. The caseworker who recognizes this
moves slowly and gently and, above all else, tries to convey through his manner that he wants
to understand the older person's anxieties and his struggles to cope with the fears that haunt
him day and night. In an effort to reverse the person's sense of helplessness which has been
deepening as his losses increased, the caseworker begins to demonstrate his conviction that the
older person is capable of planning for himself, even though he may need the help of others to
carry out his plans. Sometimes this is extremely difficult to accomplish because the older
person seems to be almost beyond such reassurance. This is particularly true with those
seriously withdrawn persons who appear almost frozen.

When a person has become markedly withdrawn and seems to have pulled into himself, it
is difficult to gain enough information from him, even to know how he is managing the tasks of
daily living. Does he have any close relatives or friends whom he trusts? Does he have a
church connection he values? Does he have a doctor whom he sees with any regularity? What
are his financial resources? Caseworkers have learned that as people lose their important family
and personal relationships on which they have depended the most, and as their sense of
isolation increases, they usually transfer their dependency to those persons in their environment
who can be counted on to appear regularly and to provide them with some important small
service which is essential to their survival—e.g., the milkman, the grocery boy, the elevator
operator, the postman, the newspaper boy, the delivery boy from the pharmacy, a neighbor, or
some small boy in the neighborhood who runs errands. It is the grocer who knows what the
older person has been eating. It is the druggist who knows what medicines have been ordered
and by whom. It is the milkman or postman who often is the first to notice that the person must
be unable to get to the door. In order to reconstruct what the older person's life must be like, the
caseworker may need to contact some of these persons who provide the environmental and
emotional supports which keep the person alive. Some older people are sufficiently intact to
manage their daily living on their own, but transfer a tremendous amount of dependence to
their physician, lawyer, broker, or friends. In all this behavior one can observe the struggle to
maintain oneself and one's identity, even in the face of the most painful losses. As one older

retired man put it—"Aging is the process of doing without—without energy, friends, money, health, etc."

The Need for Prompt and Careful Evaluation

We have found that it is important for the caseworker to respond promptly to the request for help to the older person. As stated before, many such requests have been postponed too long; when they finally are made, it is important for the agency to move quickly to establish a meaningful contact with the older person and his family. What needs to be guarded against, however, is precipitant action before the situation is understood sufficiently. It is particularly important to avoid uprooting the older person from his familiar surroundings without careful preparation for such a move, because such sudden shifts undermine the person's usual defenses and create so much anxiety that personality deterioration may result. Sometimes a medical emergency or even an environmental event, such as a fire in the client's apartment, makes it necessary to move the older person without warning or preparation; but when these occur, we should anticipate and help others to understand the kind of disorientation which may occur as an immediate reaction to sudden uprooting.

Caseworkers attempt to maintain the older person in his own familiar surroundings for as long as possible. In order to do this, they introduce a variety of supports, such as homemaker service, casework service, a volunteer who will visit regularly, financial assistance, home medical care, a hospital bed or some other equipment which will enable the person to remain at home, etc. Even when an eventual move has to be made, these services help to maintain the status-quo while the situation is being evaluated to determine how the older person can be maintained with the greatest degree of contentment and adequacy.

The Implications of the Diagnosis

Caseworkers attempt to maintain the older person in his own familiar surroundings for as order to fully understand their older clients. In particular they need to understand the implications of the medical diagnosis in order that they will know how to understand what they are observing in the patient's behavior and what to expect. If the patient is suffering from an insufficiency of blood to the brain, or if he has suffered a cerebral accident which has affected his memory or judgment, these will need to be taken into account in planning with him. If his attention span or performance span are shortened, he will be unable to tolerate an hour's interview. If he has experienced a memory change, he may forget that the caseworker is coming to see him, the content of their last conversation and what he has already discussed. It often appears that caseworkers are more alert to the effect of physical handicaps, such as deafness, defective vision, and crippling than they are to the effects of diseases which bring about brain changes or loss of energy. Unless the caseworker consults with the physician to inquire about what should be anticipated and to share what he is observing, his expectations of the client may be excessive and his plans doomed to failure. One of the caseworker's main tasks is to help others to understand the client, and this obviously is impossible when the caseworker does not understand. When aging is complicated by organic brain changes, the caseworker will need to proceed differently than when the problem arises from a physical disability which does not involve organic brain changes. . . .

In considering the issues involved in staffing services to older persons, we are reminded of the importance of a continuing relationship for the client, which will serve the purpose of helping the older person to have something which sustains while so much of his life experience is changing and so many of his relationships are terminating. This is particularly important to the client who has withdrawn from others in a self-protective manner and who needs to be encouraged to run the risk of investing his energies and feelings in a new relationship, if his disengagement is to be interrupted. Out of our conviction that continuing relationships are of vital importance to most older persons, we sometimes overlook the equally important function of a short-term relationship for some older persons.

In this connection we need to apply some of what we have learned about short-term counseling services to younger persons. We know that such help is particularly acceptable and appropriate for clients who have demonstrated strengths in their capacities to solve problems throughout their lives. People who pride themselves on their ability to help themselves often expect and wish to continue in this way throughout their lives. They often are unhappy in any situation which requires their enforced dependency. If they bring themselves to request help from others at any point in their lives, they want the provider of services to recognize their independence and their good capacities. They may accept suggestions, but want to be free to choose among them, and may see no reason why they should inform the counselor as to their final decision. Such older persons often can use help at intervals rather than on a continuous basis. They are reassured by the caseworker's recognition of their ability to carry on between contacts without outside help. Some of these older persons enjoy the responsibility of providing some volunteer services to a community program, as this is tangible evidence of their continuing adequacy. Sometimes caseworkers encourage volunteer activities as part of the treatment for such older persons. Beyond this, many older persons have a kind of wisdom which is much needed in solving today's complicated world problems, and their talents should never be ignored. Another group of persons who use short-term services more easily than continuing services are those who shun close relationships and feel more comfortable when they maintain some distance in their relationships. Many people are reluctant to commit themselves to an indefinite plan for service and prefer a time-limited arrangement.

What seems clear is that people of all ages wish to remain in control of their own lives. They want to make decisions for themselves, once they have demonstrated their ability to do so. They expect to seek expert counsel on matters on which they are uninformed, but they do not anticipate that this will commit them to a plan for continuing relationship with an outsider. If caseworkers want to make themselves useful to these older persons, they must respect their wish for separateness and their reluctant decision to accept help when we have demonstrated some awareness of their feelings and of their usual contribution. . . .

Thus, it is demonstrated that in serving older persons, helping agencies must be extremely sensitive to the individual differences of their clients—and must have access to a range of services appropriate to their varying needs at different points in their lives. To the extent that it is understood that older persons often prefer to participate in all aspects of plans which concern them, and in addition, continue to be able to contribute in a meaningful way to the solution of problems, agencies demonstrate their confidence and conviction in the flexibility and enduring capacities of the human personality. When this is not understood, rigid and inflexible patterns of service emerge and make it difficult for older people to make the contribution of which they are capable.

Questions 7.2

1. Leach points out that most often the request for help comes from someone other than the elderly client. What are the ethical obligations of human-service workers in such cases?

2. Reaction to loss is an important dynamic of an older person's need for help. Discuss the patterns of behavior such reactions can take for the older client and his or her family.

3. The human-service worker with the aged usually encounters conflicting needs. On the one hand, there is a need for independence; on the other, there is a need for care and support. How can you deal with such conflicts?

4. Leach maintains that a caseworker attempts to maintain an elderly client in familiar surroundings as long as possible. Discuss the services that your community provides to support this goal.

CHAPTER 8
working with terminally ill and dying older adults

One of the realities of working with older people is the fact that some will die during the course of a human-service worker's contacts with them. Other older clients will be terminally ill over long periods of time while workers are in contact with them and their families. For those reasons, human-service workers involved in helping the aging must become familiar with and capable of dealing with older clients who face terminal illness and death.

The taboos associated with terminal illnesses and dying are numerous. They are so strong that many social workers, physicians, nurses, and others who are required to become engaged with dying people actually do their best to avoid contact with the processes of death and with the dying. Studies in the social and behavioral sciences point to the difficulty professionals have in dealing with the issues surrounding the last stage of life.

The following excerpt is from David Sudnow's *Passing On: The Social Organization of Dying* (1967). Sudnow studied the way death was handled in two hospitals and described the ways in which health professionals handled dying patients:

Of the professions, clergymen and morticians work most directly and effectively with the realities of death. It is also they who are often most willing to deal directly with the families of the dead. However, dying people and their families need help from professionals in addition to clergymen and/or morticians. There may be times when those two groups are less well prepared to help the family with its needs than are others. However, for most people, including professionals in the fields of health, welfare, education, social work, and other human services, death is an issue that causes anxiety and fear.

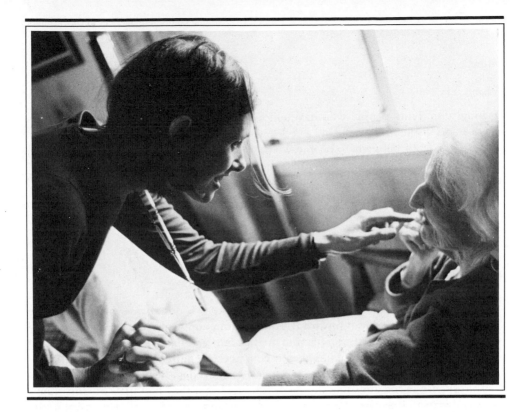

One of the most comprehensive books ever written on the subject, Robert Kastenbaum and Ruth Aisenberg's *The Psychology of Death* (1972), includes some speculation about the reasons for the aversion to working with and dealing with death and dying.

First of all, human-service professionals, particularly those in mental health, have the luxury of being able to avoid death, according to Kastenbaum and Aisenberg. Ministers, medical personnel, and morticians must deal with it.

Second, death is not an "interesting" intrapsychic problem. That is, it is a reality problem that cannot be cured through psychoanalysis, group discussion, psychotherapy, and the like. Feelings about it can be dealt with, and people can be prepared for its eventuality, perhaps, but it cannot be averted in those who are actually in the process of dying.

Third, death does not involve a common, mass ritual in the United States as it has at other times and in other cultures. The public funeral, the casket shop, and the deaths of people one knows throughout one's life are more common in less developed nations such as India and those of Latin America. Mass deaths caused by epidemics, natural disasters like floods and earthquakes, or war are not common in the United States, and neither is death among the young; therefore, people do not see death and can avoid it. Many American adults have never been to funerals and some people manage to avoid all funerals throughout their lives, other than their own.

Fourth, the United States is an achieving society that focuses on making progress and on improvement. In such a context, there is little desire to talk about or deal with death. Death is unproductive, a sign of failure for some professionals. Some think that working with dying people who have emotional problems related to their death is obscene and disgusting.

Finally, death happens to people who are relatively unimportant in most cases, that is, the old, who are, as this text has made clear so many times, often not considered important in our society. The old are devalued, it is the old who usually die, and, therefore, little emphasis is put upon death.

Feelings about Death

Fear and Anxiety

There are differences in feelings about death, but it is not always easy to measure accurately people's attitudes toward it. Kastenbaum and Aisenberg report on a study by psychologists Irving Alexander and Arthur Adlerstein of the attitudes toward death of 50 male college students. They used a questionnaire, the Semantic Differential Technique, and a polygraph, which measures psychogalvanic skin response.

In response to the questionnaire, most claimed that they had little anxiety about death and viewed it as the natural order of things and as God's will. However, in the Semantic Differential Technique, words that were related to death were evaluated as bad and potent by the subjects. And when terms associated with death were used, the psychogalvanic skin response of the participants was significantly different from the times words not usually associated with death were used.

It is possible that most people want others to believe they feel acceptance of death compared to fear of and anxiety about, but they may not be responding with total honesty. However, a study of older people by J.M.A. Munnich (Kastenbaum and Aisenberg, 1972) found that two-thirds of older people felt acceptance of or acquiescence in thoughts of death. Kastenbaum and Weisman found apprehension about death minimal and found that there was much more apathy and acquiescence than anxiety.

Some studies have shown that those who live alone fear death more than those who live with families, friends, or in institutions.

Disengaging

Some older people recognize that they are dying, accept that fact, and begin to **disengage** from friends, relations, and regular activity. Others, although they may recognize that death is imminent, remain involved in daily activity.

There is some indication that personality characteristics, such as aggressiveness, irritability, and narcissism; the capacity to avoid acquiesence; and acceptance of life as it is can, in themselves, be deterrents to death. Morton A. Lieberman (Kastenbaum and Aisenberg, 1972), in a highly significant study, reports on people in nursing homes and public housing facilities and finds that those who coped with changes in their situations and with crises in aggressive, irritating, narcissistic, and de-manding ways were those most likely to survive crisis. In other words, the more accepting, acquiescent, and tolerant were less likely to survive. Being pleasant and good seemed to be associated with earlier death.

Confronting Death

Although the intensity and nature of anxiety and fear of death differ from indi-vidual to individual, it is reasonable to assume that they are virtually universal phenomena. Human-service workers who have difficulty confronting death or who fear dealing with it should not consider themselves either unusual or incapable of serving older adults who are terminally ill. Such workers are representative of the total population, which has characteristically feared the termination of life. Since fear of death is normal, human-service workers should not be surprised about their fears; they should be capable of dealing with their reactions sufficiently to help the terminally ill and their families.

In reality, dying is no more difficult to handle than are other kinds of disabling, human, real problems that can arouse the anxiety of almost everyone, such as pov-erty, sexual dysfunction, and conflict with the law. Most human problems arouse anxiety in most people, which means only that workers frequently deal with prob-lems that cause anxiety to them as well as to their clients.

Death is quite different from other crises in the life-span. The major difference is its finality. As individuals we cannot resolve this crisis. We can only choose whether or not to accept and prepare for it. It is universal—all people must anticipate it as their fate—and there are no personal witnesses to its exact nature. Although highly articulate professionals and others—Professor Lois Jaffe, a social worker who recently died of leukemia, comes to mind—can testify about the phenomenon of dying, no one can write about the realities of death.

Death Prevention

Human-service professionals in fields such as health, welfare, and rehabilitation view death as a mortal enemy. Most such programs are directed toward the preserva-tion of life. Therefore, social workers, physicians, nurses, rehabilitation counselors, and all others who serve the aging take, as their fundamental task, preventing the death of their clients.

Death prevention is accomplished in many ways by effective human-service workers.

Accidents

Accidents still remain the most common cause of death for older people, and the most common cause of their accidents is the automobile. Therefore, older people die more commonly from automobile accidents than from all of the crippling and life-ending diseases.

Of course, auto accidents in old age are much different from those occurring in the younger years. It is often the lack of coordination or muscular skill and the incapacity to react instantly to dangerous conditions that cause accidents among older people, rather than the risk taking that can be the source of automobile accidents for young people. Chronic illness, failing eyesight, poor hearing, and other conditions associated with aging can cause the death of older drivers and their passengers.

Older people are also highly prone to accidents in the home, especially falls. Many older people fall out of bed or down stairs, slip on rugs or in the bath, and suffer broken limbs or injured joints.

Educational activities about accidents and accident prevention in the home and on the road may help prevent the deaths of some older people. Helping older people find alternative means of transportation, safer housing, and other accident-preventing resources may also be valuable.

Suicide

Suicide is a major cause of death among older people. In fact, the highest suicide rate for all age groups is 27.9 per 100,000, and this rate is for people 75–84 years of age.

The figures cited are for men and women combined. When they are separated, it is interesting to note that the male suicide rate at age 75–84 is 47.5 per 100,000, which represents a dramatic increase over suicides among men 55–74, which are approximately 37 per 100,000. For women, however, the suicide rate at ages 75–84 is 6.4 per 100,000, representing a decrease from those 55–74 years of age. In fact, the suicide rate for men moves steadily upward throughout the life-span, while for women it rises to approximately 10 per 100,000 in the middle years, 35–64, begins declining at age 65, and continues to decline for the balance of the senior years. Precisely why that is true is not absolutely known.

There is some disagreement about the reasons for such high suicide rates among people 75–84. Some have speculated that retirement and the associated loss of role and income that go with it cause people to terminate their lives. However, retirement usually comes much earlier than age 75.

Some theoreticians believe that all suicide among the elderly results from emotional illness and disturbance. Kastenbaum and Aisenberg report some belief that after age 60 the majority of suicide attempters are in a depressive stage of a manic-depressive psychoses, a few others have organic psychoses, and yet a few others a transient confusion that is organically based.

Those who terminate their own lives usually have one of the three elements delineated by Dr. Karl Menninger—the wish to kill, the wish to be killed, or the wish to die. Most believe that as age increases, the first two elements decline among those who commit suicide, while the third, the desire to die, increases.

Suicide prevention by human-service workers includes a variety of steps, depending upon the kind of agency with which the worker is affiliated. This might include the telephone reassurance effort—trying to guarantee that contact is maintained with the older person as a means of helping the person overcome any fear, depressions, or desire for self-destruction. It can mean simply being available to talk over life and the future with older people and having time to talk to people who may be troubled. It may mean "crisis intervention" services—helping the person who is contemplating suicide avoid a positive decision to do so at an appropriate time, thus preventing the act from taking place.

Performing One's Job Well

Death prevention is perhaps best accomplished by simply doing one's job well. That is, the worker employed in a hospital or other health setting may prevent death by making certain that the client has all of the health resources, nutrition, medical care, and other physical elements necessary to remain healthy or to become restored to good health. Human-service workers make major contributions toward curing individuals who are ill by serving as liaisons between the patients and other professionals and, at times, by serving as **advocates** for patients, ensuring that professionals know about and work to overcome the older clients' health problems.

In the field of recreation the human-service worker may help prevent death and prolong life by assisting older people in finding pleasure in life through activity and companionship and otherwise finding and maintaining good reasons for living, which can, in many ways, contribute to the prolongation of life.

Social workers in mental-health programs may help maintain life through suicide prevention activities, such as those discussed above, and by helping older people overcome the socioemotional problems that may interfere with the maintenance of and continuation of life.

We may summarize by saying that death prevention is a major role of the human-service worker with the aging and that effective performance of duties with one's client is a major way of preventing death.

Working with the Terminally Ill

Not all deaths can be prevented, and, as we indicated above, the human-service worker must come to terms with the fact that individual death is the fate of all of us.

Dying is not an aberration; it is a normal state of life. It is more imminent for aging people, but it is the reality that must be faced by all. Therefore, patients and clients as well as workers in health settings, nursing homes, group projects, and all other service agencies must be aware of and deal realistically with the fact of death.

Effectively working with the terminally ill requires some understanding of the emotional processes of dying that are coming to be identified by students of the growing field of **thanatology.**

Perhaps the most widely studied and best-known student of death and dying is Dr. Elizabeth Kübler-Ross (1970), a European psychiatrist who has developed an international reputation as an expert on working with the dying. Her several books and articles are illuminating for those who work with the dying. Kübler-Ross has identified five stages of dying, which are accepted by many professionals as those through which dying people pass. These stages are:

1. *Denial.* The person refuses to acknowledge the reality of impending death, whether he or she has learned about it accidentally or intuitively or has been told about it by a health professional.

2. *Anger.* The patient becomes a blamer—of physicians, the environment, the family, even God. The patient wants to know why he or she is dying and strikes out against the injustice of life and death.

3. *Bargaining.* Fate is offered a bargain. The patient essentially promises to lead a different or better life with the understanding that life will continue.

4. *Depression.* Denial no longer works, and it is replaced by fear, guilt, and feelings of unworthiness. Communication with the family and others begins to come to a halt.

5. *Acceptance.* The patient gives in to death. He or she is not happy with life's ending, but neither is there a willingness to fight death any longer.

Robert Kastenbaum suggests that one must understand these stages in relation to other phenomena. It is likely that people die differently from different diseases and that the stages do not have the same effect for the cancer victim as they might for the victim of coronary disease, which is more crisis-oriented. Men and women may go through different stages on the way to death. Different ethnic groups may also experience different stages; just as funeral practices among various ethnic groups differ widely, so may the process of dying.

Furthermore, the personality of the dying person will affect the kind of death he or she experiences. The acquiescent personality will be likely to treat death differently than the battler. Kastenbaum says that the reflective person dies differently than the impulsive, the warm human differently than the aloof. In other words, personality has an effect on death.

Finally, the place of death has different effects. Whether one dies in a hospital, at home, or in a nursing home will have some impact.

In any case, the process of dying is, for many people, multifaceted. It passes through phases and it changes through time. The human-service worker must be prepared to deal differently with different patients during the various stages of their dying.

Dealing with the Practical
Consequences of Death

Though death is not a problem like the adversities that happen by chance, since it is a natural stage of life, it poses crises for the dying patient and those around the patient. Therefore, there are practical, critical realities that human-service workers with dying patients must help their clients manage.

Those who work with terminally ill people find that they have many concerns over and above their physical condition, comfort, and immediate health. Those with families will want to be assured that their spouses, children, or grandchildren will be cared for when they die. Others will be concerned about close friends or people with whom they have lived in recent years. Still others will want to have some assurance about the disposition of their financial resources. It often makes no difference how many or how few those resources are; the older person is concerned about them even if they are modest.

Funeral Planning

Some older people who are dying are deeply concerned about—perhaps preoccupied with—the disposition of their remains. They want to know where they will be buried and the kind of funeral they will have, and they will want to settle in advance other practical issues surrounding the physical fact of death.

It is often possible for the human-service worker to help the aging and terminally ill client with these practical problems. The worker can help the client obtain information on funeral and burial plans and may help the client choose a grave site or mortuary.

Burial and funeral customs carry many cultural connotations that will be important to the dying client. Where the funeral will be held, what kind of clothing the body will carry, whether the casket will be open or closed, who will officiate, whether or not the body will be embalmed, and whether or not there will be an autopsy are issues that may make a great difference to the client.

Some ethnic groups think cremation is objectionable; others object strongly to concrete crypts and caskets; still others find the whole idea of burial distasteful.

Clients divide along socioeconomic, cultural, and regional lines on these matters, which make significant differences to dying people. The effective human-service worker must be able to help the client make satisfactory decisions about them.

Legal Assistance

The human-service worker may help the dying client obtain legal help for preparing a will, which is the usual means for guaranteeing that money and property will go where the client wants them to go. When such matters can be handled prior to death, it is often reassuring to the older person to know, with some security, what will happen to his or her resources after death.

Helping older people cope with the practical realities of death may, paradoxically, prolong life by reducing anxiety and helping the client feel mastery over the situation. If nothing else, the human-service worker can assist the dying patient to feel in charge of his or her own life and the tasks at hand.

Psychological Assistance

Treating the Dying Person As a Whole Organism   Human-service workers must understand that dying people are people first, and only secondarily dying. Those who are near death have the same sets of emotions, needs, and concerns that all human beings have. Therefore, human-service workers must deal with terminally ill and dying people as those who are facing a special crisis but as individuals who have feelings; interests in other people; physical, emotional, and social needs; and who regard themselves as human beings with full identities not as corpses. The perception of the client as a dying organism may exist more in the mind of the professional serving the person than in the mind of the dying patient. That is, Mr. Smith will think of himself as Mr. Smith not as a dying body.

With that in mind, effective human-service workers deal with terminally ill and dying people through the same kinds of interventions and methods they might use with any other older person. These include interviewing individuals or families, doing group work with older clients, developing leisure-time activities, providing health services and mental-health services, where those are indicated. Everything this volume says about serving older people applies to older people who are dying as much as to those who are not. After all, we are all dying—some perhaps more immediately than others.

Older people who are dying need some kinds of help that are different from that required by others. They may need to reminisce, and may need simply to be listened to and spoken with by human-service professionals.

In some cases, the dying patient will have become physically less attractive than formerly. People who develop facial cancers may have only part of their faces, which may seem repugnant to some. It is critical that the human-service worker not reject the client because of a poor appearance. Others may be bedridden and, in most cases of dying older patients, physical appearances are not pleasant. The human-service worker must find opportunities to help the dying patient maintain some elements of a positive self-image through friendly contacts with peers, group programs such as some of those described in Chapter 6, friendly conversations between the worker and the client, and positive relationships with family members.

Avoiding Somberness   An important principle in working with aging people is to avoid somberness or sadness when that is possible. Obviously, sadness surrounds the lives of people who face death as well as their families. One does not treat dying frivolously, because that would be cruel. On the other hand, treating dying people as if they had already died is even worse. That would involve never making jokes, never challenging, arguing with, or treating as viable organisms those for whom death is imminent. Dying people are not dead, and they want to be treated as whole human beings while they live. Therefore, it is inappropriate to continuously, consciously, and totally avoid laughter, disagreements, and other human responses that are normal with everyone else.

On the other hand, false cheerfulness is equally inappropriate and is best avoided. Sometimes false cheerfulness in the face of terminal illness is more offensive than anything else. Being accepting, friendly, and responding to the human needs of the dying patient are some of the keys to effective human-service work with clients.

Helping the Families of Terminally Ill, Dying, and Deceased Older Adults

Effective work with terminally ill and dying patients does not end with the patient; it extends to the family, which encounters problems with both practical and emotional elements surrounding the loss of a parent, sibling, or spouse.

Practical and Financial Problems

Some of the practical problems that cause concern for older people are discussed earlier. Matters such as burial, wills, and the like have their effects on family members also.

The financial difficulties surrounding the care of a dying person whose life lingers is also of significance to a family. Some of the ways of handling such costs and obtaining extra resources to provide care are discussed in Chapter 12. Human-service workers must be aware that long and lingering death may wipe out the financial resources of both the aging person and the family.

There has been extensive writing, research, and legislation on the "right to die," which deals with the power of an ill person to terminate his or her life if it is no more than a physical existence—if the person is terminally and irreversibly dying. Definitions of *life* and *death* are currently the subject of considerable legal dispute. Some states have absolved physicians of any criminal or civil responsibility for patients whose irreversible conditions are ended by the withdrawal of "life-support" systems such as respirators or other devices that artificially maintain heart function. Ordinarily these legal rulings make it possible for a person to be allowed to die if brain function has ceased. Counseling with patients or families about the patient's right to die will become an increasingly important role for human-service workers.

Serving the Families
of the Dead

Human-service workers often find that their work goes on after the older person's death. There may be a need to counsel family members about their feelings toward the deceased parent, spouse, sibling, or other relative.

At some time in the dead person's life, some or all of those people probably treated the deceased with unkindness, and the recollections of those unkindnesses may cause guilt feelings. Cases of depression among widows and widowers because of unkind actions—for which the deceased can no longer absolve them—are among the most significant causes of emotional breakdown among survivors. It is often the task of the human-service worker to assist families and friends in handling their feelings about such matters.

There is also frequently a need to provide programs for survivors. Some community centers have provided outreach programs for widows and widowers that help them make the transition from marriage to single life, helping them to occupy their time and, at times, averting emotional or physical breakdowns. At other times, such outreach programs can help surviving family members cope with the financial difficulties associated with the death of a spouse or parent. One community center used a team of volunteer widows to locate and help other widows deal with the consequences of their widowhood, which seemed to have positive results for those who volunteered (see Chapter 14).

Summary

Dealing with death is one of the requirements of effective human-service efforts with older people. It is a task that initially may seem unpleasant or undesirable to the human-service worker. However, it is an essential element in serving the entire later stages in the life-span and it can be, for many older people and their families, the most important of the ways in which the human-service worker intervenes.

READING 8.1

The Social Worker's Role / Leon H. Ginsberg

This article provides directions on the various ways social workers can assist clients or families of clients to cope with death and dying.

There is a dual reaction to death. On the one hand we may be astonished at how rapidly we forget those who have died and how rapidly others are likely to forget us. On the other hand dying and death itself have permanent effects—obviously on the person who dies but also on his or her family and others closely associated with the dying or dead person. The role the social worker plays in dealing with the dying and those affected by their deaths is the subject of this discussion.

It seems odd and perhaps anachronistic to discuss this topic. Although most social workers serve dying patients and their families in one way or another, it is clear that most would rather not. Like all the other human service professions (with the exception of funeral service) that ought to confront death and dying forcefully and directly—social work tends to avoid it. And that should not be considered unusual. Death may be viewed as the ultimate enemy of professions such as social work, nursing, and medicine. Admitting that it exists is a kind of insult.

Death does not fit the models for treating social problems most widely accepted in social work theory and practice today. The typical problems addressed by social workers are poverty, disease, crime, loneliness, and interpersonal conflicts—all of which may respond to strategies of elimination or amelioration, which are the usual goals of social workers when they confront social problems. Death, though it may be handled more intelligently and more humanely, is final, nonpreventable, universal, and irreversible. It requires a strategy of acceptance and adjustment. Death can be viewed as the ultimate defeat for a social work client, and it is not one taken lightly by the social workers who serve him. The client's defeat is also, in part, the worker's defeat.

There was a time in the development of social work strategies and philosophies when programs associated with death and dying could have been more in keeping with the established ways of thinking. That was during an era when social workers spoke about helping people to accept and adjust to certain conditions such as poverty, illness, and physical handicap. That is, social workers sought ways to enable people to function more effectively within

From *Social Work with the Dying Patient and the Family,* edited by Elizabeth E. Prichard. New York: Columbia University Press, 1977. Reprinted by permission.

the parameters of certain kinds of problems, among which dying might be included. But that attitude has changed, and social workers are now less willing to help people accept severe personal and social problems. Social workers believe that it is much better, in most cases, to help individuals and families change their situations. It is much more desirable to change the facts of the society so that the situation no longer exists. Such a philosophy helps enormously when dealing with many phenomena. It sees to it that efforts will be made to create lasting changes and to ensure that problems will be finally overcome, not just for the individual but for society as a whole. But death is not one of those phenomena.

When I first studied social work in the late 1950s, we were still learning, in dealing with public assistance clients, to help them prepare reasonable budgets to live within very small monthly grants. But we changed that approach in the 1960s. Although I suspect there remain many workers in public assistance programs who help families with the realities of small welfare grants, the official strategy of professional social workers is to talk about the need for improving the system through programs such as guaranteed minimum incomes, better assistance grants, and social action activities designed to modify the distribution of wealth in the United States. Because of these changes and the new strategies of social change and social development, strategies aimed at helping people accept and live with problems are less well accepted than they once were.

Learning to accept and to deal with irreversible problems such as death and finding ways to make sad and difficult situations less so are essential in services to the dying and their families. For that reason it may be that most current social work problem-solving strategies do not fully lend themselves to this problem, although death and dying are among the most common phenomena with which professional social workers must deal.

It may also be true that social workers, like other health professionals, are psychologically set in a manner that makes it difficult for them to deal with the problems of death and dying, and they may be psychologically less adequately prepared for such problems than other professionals are. Social work may be the most optimistic and future oriented of the human service professions. Social workers seem to believe that improvement is possible, no matter how pervasive a problem might be; the notion that certain problems have always existed and will continue to exist is not acceptable. It is one of the lessons we have not wanted to learn from the sociologists and anthropologists who provide us with much of our theoretical background. I have encountered this nonacceptance of certain social problems as the normal state of affairs among social workers in this country, among social work Peace Corps volunteers overseas, and among social work educators. I remember my own experiences in East Africa early in this decade when I was enraged by the high infant mortality rate. I could not be comfortable in a situation that found the majority of children dying before they reached the age of five. A social worker who had spent many years in Africa responded to my rage by saying simply that one must learn that all people die, some young and some old, but they all die. For social workers all social problems are, by definition, phenomena to be battled and reduced, not facts to be accepted and dealt with as the realities of the situation. That may be more true for North American social workers than for others, but, of course, we are talking about social work in North America.

Death Prevention

Social workers can be and are effective professionals in death prevention. That is true within a number of institutional frameworks and could be true in many others. In the normal course of counseling and guiding, in helping people with emotional problems, through their work in mental health programs and family service programs, social workers can prevent suicide and the psychological depression that often leads to death from so-called normal causes.

Social workers also play active roles in suicide hotlines and suicide prevention centers around the United States. They take part in providing the 24-hour answering services, referral activities, and counseling programs designed to help those contemplating suicide and to prevent it. Such activities are in keeping with social work philosophy and typical social work practices.

Social workers are also effective in maternal and infant care programs, which also prevent death. They want to maintain life and have skill in doing so through the kinds of programs mentioned here.

Social workers also have a major role to play—and it has not been played so heavily as it might be in the United States—in the prevention of industrial deaths and accidental deaths in nonindustrial settings. It seems clear that accidental death, both on and off the job, has a high degree of social content. That is, death in industry, death on the highways, and all accidental deaths are frequently related to the emotional state of the persons who suffer the accidents, the other relationships among group members on the job, and the social structure of the place where the accidental death occurs.

This is not to deny that many deaths result from unsafe plant conditions in industries, from unsafe automobiles, and from the imprudent use of drugs and alcohol in connection with dangerous work and recreation. But each phenomenon has social components, and social workers can be effective in reducing the incidence of accidental death if their services are called upon.

In some countries large numbers of social workers are employed in accident prevention programs, particularly in industries, and provide major inputs in planning for industrial safety and preventing accidents.

Social workers can, I am suggesting, be highly effective in preventing accidental death within and outside industry.

The Social Worker with the Dying Person

Large numbers of social workers work in hospitals and outpatient programs helping patients with both physical and emotional problems. Many are highly effective, and more could be effective in serving the needs of dying persons, which implies a number of activities—among them the help with the acceptance of death mentioned earlier. That is, an effective social caseworker (or a group worker dealing with groups of dying persons) can help serve the needs of those who face lingering deaths. This service can include counseling that enables people to plan intelligently for the balance of their lives and for the lives of those around them, such as family members, so that they can come to terms with death. It is possible and often desirable to use other resources, including religious resources, for those who need or can use such services.

There appear to be "stages" in the dying process. Kübler-Ross (1970) indicates that the stages—she identifies five—range from denial to acceptance. Anger, bargaining, and depression intervene between the two extremes. There is an obvious role for social work services at each of these stages, and it may be that social workers must learn that there are stages to dying in which they may be helpful, just as there are stages of development during the rest of the life span in which they are of service to individuals and their families.

The dying person has not stopped living. He or she often needs help in planning and coming to terms with reality just as other clients do. Social workers can provide this assistance.

Services to the Families and Other Significant Persons in the Lives of Dying Persons

Death has its personal elements but is also a social phenomenon. That is, whereas it is an individual who dies, his or her death has its effects on family members, employees, employers, and friends. In many situations the needs of those around the dying person for the services of social workers may be as great as or greater than the needs of the dying person.

Again social workers can provide a variety of services, such as casework or counseling with individual family members about their own emotional reactions to the death of a family member, as well as help with practical matters such as future budgeting and living arrangements. Death often brings change in the lives of those around the person who dies. Social workers can provide guidance or at least someone to talk with about whether or not the living situation should be changed, whether or not the work situation should be changed, and the like.

In addition many individuals in the United States are employed by small, individually owned firms. The death of the owner or manager of a small firm creates significant needs on the part of his or her employees. Social workers can counsel and assist these employees, who are significant others in the lives of deceased employers.

In the other direction social workers can work with the employers of employees who are dying. Employers can be assisted in adjusting a dying person's work schedule and assignments as one means of helping him or her adapt to reduced health and the process of dying. The dying person may need vocational rehabilitation services, just as those who are temporarily ill or newly handicapped might.

In such roles social workers can be important mediators between employees and employers when death faces one or the other participant in an employment situation.

Services to the Families of Those Who Have Died

Social workers can also help the families of those who have died. The range of skills and of problems of this group may be larger than those of any of the other client systems social workers might serve in dealing with death and dying. For a variety of probably valid reasons, most discussions of death deal with older people or at least with adults. Of course, they constitute the "normal" dying population, but they are not the totality of that population. Infants, young children, adolescents, young adults die too—anyone may die at any time, an obvious statement but one we are reluctant to make and even more reluctant to accept.

It is likely that the extraordinary death causes the greatest social and emotional trauma to the significant others in the former life of the dead person. How many marriages terminate after the unexpected or accidental death of a young child? What happens to the parents of children who are believed to have committed suicide, an increasingly more common phenomenon and a leading cause of death among young people? How easy is it for them to escape the guilt that may be justified or unjustified but that must always exist? What happens to families who experience automobile accidents in which only some of the family members die? What are the emotional reactions of the surviving family members?

The trauma associated with the deaths of persons who would not normally be expected to die is great and often demands the kinds of services that social workers can provide.

The same kinds of needs for counseling services exist with families of older persons who have died. A 60-year-old widow may face the same trauma at the loss of her husband as a 30-year-old widow would, and the same is true for widowers. Perhaps the shock and change are even greater because of the longer marriage and because of the long years of emotional and economic dependence.

There are also a number of practical matters that many families must face. For example, large numbers of American families have virtually no savings to use in supporting themselves once the breadwinner has died. Social Security is not available to younger widows and older children, both of whom may have been supported nicely but precariously on the monthly income of the breadwinner. These great problems associated with economic and social changes may be reduced by the services of social workers, who can help families locate alternate financial resources or modify their living patterns to conform to reduced incomes.

The Social Worker as a Member of the Team

The best assistance social workers can provide to the dying is indirect. That is, they can serve the dying as members of teams of treatment specialists. While dying in itself is a physical phenomenon, it always has its social components. Physicians, nurses, psychologists, clergymen, and others dealing with the dying patient and his family, as well as the families of persons who have died, need to understand and work with these social components. Social workers can contribute to their knowledge as part of the team effort. Social workers can be an important part of the treatment team dealing with dying persons and with death.

Macroplanning

Much of the foregoing discussion has dealt with the microlevel aspects of death and dying, the ways social workers may serve individuals and their families when death and its consequences are being faced.

There are, however, macrolevel considerations as well. Probably not enough general programs dealing with death are available. Not enough services are designed to provide guidance in dealing with the problems of the dying and those who face the deaths of those around them. There are inadequate resources to which they may turn for assistance and guidance. We need more information on death—not just the simple demographic facts of death but the emotional phenomena and the social problems that arise because of it. There is a need for social research on death and dying and for programs in mental health and family service agencies dealing specifically with death. There could be groups of dying persons and of their family members receiving social work services. Groups of people who have recently experienced death in their own families might also be excellent vehicles for helping with the problems related to death. Broad educational programs on death might also meet major needs. Our social welfare services are willing to prepare parents, through family life education programs, for the births of their children, for the facts of marriage, and for retirement. But few educational programs deal with death and dying. Perhaps such programs of education and service in our communities are needed.

Conclusions

It is clear that social workers have many roles to play in death and dying—from counseling with dying persons to planning educational programs for the community.

It is also clear that more needs to be known to meet the needs of those who are dying and those who play other roles in the lives of the dying. Social workers now make and have additional contributions to make in these areas.

But we need to know and learn more about death and dying. We need to confront the phenomena of death and dying directly because they cannot be neglected in a profession that deals with the social components of human existence.

Reference

Kübler-Ross, E. 1970. *On Death and Dying.* New York: Macmillan Company.

Questions 8.1

1. The author suggests that social workers have not been as active as they might be in this service area. What do you think can be done to make human-service workers more sensitive to this problem?

2. In the article the author suggests that com-munity education is one way social workers can become involved in services provision in the area of death and dying. Discuss the kinds of community education programs that might be developed for older adults and their families.

READING 8.2

The Ritual Drama of Mutual Pretense / Barney G. Glaser and Anselm L. Strauss

"Make-believe" is a part of every child's life. In this selection Glaser and Strauss show that dying patients and hospital staff often cooperate in pretense that ignores the realities of dying and death.

When patient and staff both know that the patient is dying but pretend otherwise—when both agree to act as if he were going to live—then a context of mutual pretense exists. Either party can initiate his share of the context; it ends when one side cannot, or will not, sustain the pretense any longer.

The mutual-pretense awareness context is perhaps less visible, even to its participants, than the closed, open, and suspicion contexts, because the interaction involved tends to be more subtle. In some hospital services, however, it is the predominant context. One nurse who worked on an intensive care unit remarked about an unusual patient who had announced he was going to die: "I haven't had to cope with this very often. I may know they are going to die, and the patient knows it, but (usually) he's just not going to let you know that he knows."

Once we visited a small Catholic hospital where medical and nursing care for the many dying patients was efficiently organized. The staff members were supported in their difficult work by a powerful philosophy—that they were doing everything possible for the patient's comfort—but generally did not talk with patients about death. This setting brought about frequent mutual pretense. This awareness context is also predominant in such settings as county hospitals, where elderly patients of low socioeconomic status are sent to die; patient and staff are well aware of imminent death but each tends to go silently about his own business.[1] Yet, as we shall see, sometimes the mutual pretense context is neither silent nor unnegotiated.

The same kind of ritual pretense is enacted in many situations apart from illness. A charming example occurs when a child announces that he is now a storekeeper, and that his mother should buy something at his store. To carry out his fiction, delicately cooperative action is required. The mother must play seriously, and when the episode has run its natural course, the child will often close it himself with a rounding-off gesture, or it may be concluded by an intruding outside event or by the mother. Quick analysis of this little game of pretense suggests that either player can begin; that the other must then play properly; that realistic (nonfictional) action will destroy the illusion and end the game; that the specific action of the game must

Reprinted by permission from Barney G. Glaser and Anselm L. Strauss, *Awareness of Dying* (Chicago: Aldine Publishing Company); copyright © 1965 by Barney G. Glaser and Anselm L. Strauss.

[1] Robert Kastenbaum has reported that Cushing Hospital, "a Public Medical Institution for the care and custody of the elderly" in Framingham, Massachusetts, "patient and staff members frequently have an implicit mutual understanding with regard to death . . . institutional dynamics tend to operate against making death 'visible' and a subject of open communication. . . . Elderly patients often behave as though they appreciated the unspoken feelings of the staff members and were attempting to make their demise as acceptable and unthreatening as possible." This observation is noted in Robert Kastenbaum, "The Interpersonal Context of Death in a Geriatric Institution," abstract of paper presented at the Seventeenth Annual Scientific Meeting, Gerontological Society (Minneapolis: October 29–31, 1964).

develop during interaction; and that eventually the make-believe ends or is ended. Little familial games or dramas of this kind tend to be continual, though each episode may be brief.

For contrast, here is another example that pertains to both children and adults. At the circus, when a clown appears, all but the youngest children know that the clown is not real. But both he and his audience must participate, if only symbolically, in the pretense that he is a clown. The onlookers need do no more than appreciate the clown's act, but if they remove themselves too far, by examining the clown's technique too closely, let us say, then the illusion will be shattered. The clown must also do his best to sustain the illusion by clever acting, by not playing too far "out of character." Ordinarily nobody addresses him as if he were other than the character he is pretending to be. That is, everybody takes him seriously, at face value. And unless particular members return to see the circus again, the clown's performance occurs only once, beginning and ending according to a prearranged schedule.

Our two simple examples of pretense suggest some important features of the particular awareness context to which we shall devote this [discussion]. The make-believe in which patient and hospital staff engage resembles the child's game much more than the clown's act. It has no institutionalized beginning and ending comparable to the entry and departure of the clown: either the patient or the staff must signal the beginning of their joint pretense. Both parties must act properly if the pretense is to be maintained, because, as in the child's game, the illusion created is fragile, and easily shattered by incongruous "realistic" acts. But if either party slips slightly, the other may pretend to ignore the slip.[2] Each episode between the patient and a staff member tends to be brief, but the mutual pretense is done with terrible seriousness, for the stakes are very high.[3]

Initiating the Pretense

This particular awareness context cannot exist, of course, unless both the patient and staff are aware that he is dying. Therefore all the structural conditions which contribute to the existence of open awareness (and which are absent in closed and suspicion awareness) contribute also to the existence of mutual pretense. In addition, at least one interactant must indicate a desire to pretend that the patient is not dying and the other must agree to the pretense, acting accordingly.

A prime structural condition in the existence and maintenance of mutual pretense is that unless the patient initiates conversation about his impending death, no staff member is required to talk about it with him. As typical Americans, they are unlikely to initiate such a conversation; and as professionals they have no rules commanding them to talk about death with the

---

[2] I. Bensman and I. Garver, "Crime and Punishment in the Factory," in A. Gouldner and H. Gouldner (eds.). Modern Society (New York: Harcourt, Brace and World, 1963), pp. 593–96.

[3] A German Communist, Alexander Weissberg, accused of spying during the great period of Soviet spy trials, has written a fascinating account of how he and many other persons collaborated with the Soviet government in an elaborate pretense, carried on for the benefit of the outside world. The stakes were high for the accused (their lives) as well as for the Soviet. Weissberg's narrative also illustrated how uninitiated interactants must be coached into their roles and how they must be cued into the existence of the pretense context where they do not recognize it. See Alexander Weissberg. The Accused (New York: Simon and Schuster, 1951).

patient, unless he desires it. In turn, he may wish to initiate such conversation, but surely neither hospital rules nor common convention urges it upon him. Consequently, unless either the aware patient or the staff members breaks the silence by words or gestures, a mutual pretense rather than an open awareness context will exist: as, for example, when the physician does not care to talk about death, and the patient does not press the issue though he clearly does recognize his terminality.

The patient, of course, is more likely than the staff members to refer openly to his death, thereby inviting them, explicitly or implicitly, to respond in kind. If they seem unwilling, he may decide they do not wish to confront openly the fact of his death, and then he may, out of tact or genuine empathy for their embarrassment or distress, keep his silence. He may misinterpret their responses, of course, but . . . he probably has correctly read their reluctance to refer openly to his impending death.

Staff members, in turn, may give him opportunities to speak of his death, if they deem it wise, without their directly or obviously referring to the topic. But if he does not care to act or talk as if he were dying, then they will support his pretense. In doing so, they have in effect, accepted a complementary assignment of status—they will act with pretense toward his pretense. (If they have misinterpreted his reluctance to act openly, then they have assigned, rather than accepted, a complementary status.)

Two related professional rationales permit them to engage in the pretense. One is that if the patient wishes to pretend, it may well be best for his health, and if and when the pretense finally fails him, all concerned can act more realistically. A secondary rationale is that perhaps they can give him better medical and nursing care if they do not have to face him so openly. In addition . . . they can rely on common tact to justify their part in the pretense. Ordinarily, Americans believe that any individual may live—and die—as he chooses, so long as he does not interfere with others' activities, or, in this case, so long as proper care can be given him.

To illustrate the way these silent bargains are initiated and maintained, we quote from an interview with a special nurse. She had been assigned to a patient before he became terminal, and she was more apt than most personnel to encourage his talking openly, because as a graduate student in a nursing class that emphasized psychological care, she had more time to spend with her patient than a regular floor nurse. Here is the exchange between interviewer and nurse:

Interviewer: Did he talk about his cancer or his dying?

Nurse: Well, no, he never talked about it. I never heard him use the word cancer. . . .

Interviewer: Did he indicate that he knew he was dying?

Nurse: Well, I got that impression, yes. . . . It wasn't really openly, but I think the day that his roommate said he should get up and start walking, I felt that he was a little bit antagonistic. He said what his condition was, that he felt very, very ill that moment.

Interviewer: He never talked about leaving the hospital?

Nurse: Never.

Interviewer: Did he talk about his future at all?

Nurse: Not a thing. I never heard a word. . . .

Interviewer: You said yesterday that he was more or less isolated, because the nurses felt that he was hostile. But they have dealt with patients like this many many times. You said they stayed away from him.

Nurse: Well, I think at the very end. You see, this is what I meant by isolation . . . we don't communicate with them. I didn't, except when I did things for him. I think you expect somebody to respond to, and if they're very ill we don't. . . . I talked it over with my instructor, mentioning things that I could probably have done; for instance, this isolation, I should have communicated with him. . . .

Interviewer: You think that since you knew he was going to die, and you half suspected that he knew it too, or more than half; do you think that this understanding grew between you in any way?

Nurse: I believe so. . . . I think it's kind of hard to say but when I came in the room, even when he was very ill, he'd rather look at me and try to give a smile, and gave me the impression that he accepted. . . . I think this is one reason why I feel I should have communicated with him . . . and this is why I feel he was rather isolated. . . .

From the nurse's account, it is difficult to tell whether the patient wished to talk openly about his death, but was rebuffed; or whether he initiated the pretense and the nurse accepted his decision. But it is remarkable how a patient can flash cues to the staff about his own dread knowledge, inviting the staff to talk about his destiny, while the nurses and physicians decide that it is better not to talk too openly with him about his condition lest he "go to pieces." The patient, as remarked earlier, picks up these signals of unwillingness, and the mutual pretense context has been initiated. A specific and obvious instance is this: an elderly patient, who had lived a full and satisfying life, wished to round it off by talking about his impending death. The nurses retreated before this prospect, as did his wife, reproving him, saying he should not think or talk about such morbid matters. A hospital chaplain finally intervened, first by listening to the patient himself, then by inducing the nurses and the wife to do likewise, or at least to acknowledge more openly that the man was dying. He was not successful with all the nurses.

The staff members are more likely to sanction a patient's pretense, than his family's. The implicit rule is that though the patient need not be forced to speak of his dying, or to act as if he were dying, his kin should face facts. After all, they will have to live with the facts after his death. Besides, staff members usually find it less difficult to talk about dying with the family. Family members are not inevitably drawn into open discussion, but the likelihood is high, particularly since they themselves are likely to initiate discussion or at least to make gestures of awareness.

Sometimes, however, pretense protects the family member temporarily against too much grief, and the staff members against too immediate a scene. This may occur when a relative has just learned about the impending death and the nurse controls the ensuing scene by initiating temporary pretense. The reverse situation also occurs: a newly arrived nurse discovers the patient's terminality, and the relative smooths over the nurse's distress by temporary pretense.

The Pretense Interaction

An intern whom we observed during our field work suspected that the patient he was examining had cancer, but he could not discover where it was located. The patient previously had been told that she probably had cancer, and she was now at this teaching hospital for that reason. The intern's examination went on for some time. Yet neither he nor she spoke about what he was searching for, nor in any way suggested that she might be dying. We mention this episode to contrast it with the more extended interactions. . . . These have an episodic quality—personnel enter and leave the patient's room, or he occasionally emerges and encounters them—but their extended duration means that special effort is required to prevent their breaking down, and that the interactants must work hard to construct and maintain their mutual pretense. By contrast, in a formally staged play, although the actors have to construct and maintain a performance, making it credible to their audience, they are not required to write the script themselves. The situation that involves a terminal patient is much more like a masquerade party, where one masked actor plays carefully to another as long as they are together, and the total drama actually emerges from their joint creative effort.

A masquerade, however, has more extensive resources to sustain it than those the hospital situation provides. Masqueraders wear masks, hiding their facial expressions: even if they "break up" with silent laughter (as a staff member may "break down" with sympathy), this fact is concealed. Also, according to the rules ordinarily governing masquerades, each actor chooses his own status, his "character," and this makes his role in the constructed drama somewhat easier to play. He may even have played similar parts before. But terminal patients usually have had no previous experience with their pretended status, and not all personnel have had much experience. In a masquerade, when the drama fails it can be broken off, each actor moving along to another partner: but in the hospital the pretenders (especially the patient) have few comparable opportunities.

Both situations share one feature—the extensive use of props for sustaining the crucial illusion. In the masquerade, the props include not only masks but clothes and other costuming, as well as the setting where the masquerade takes place. In the hospital interaction, props also abound. Patients dress for the part of not-dying patient, including careful attention to grooming, and to hair and makeup by female patients. The terminal patient may also fix up his room so that it looks and feels "just like home," an activity that supports his enactment of normalcy. Nurses may respond to these props with explicit appreciation—"how lovely your hair looks this morning"—or even help to establish them, as by doing the patient's hair. We remember one elaborate pretense ritual involving a husband and wife who had won the nurses' sympathy. The husband simply would not recognize that his already comatose wife was approaching death, so each morning the nurses carefully prepared her for his visit, dressing her for the occasion and making certain that she looked as beautiful as possible. The staff, of course, has its own props to support its ritual prediction that the patient is going to get well: thermometers, baths, fresh sheets, and meals on time! Each party utilizes these props as he sees fit, thereby helping to create the pretense anew. But when a patient wishes to demonstrate that he is finished with life, he may drive the nurses wild by refusing to cooperate in the daily routines of hospital life—that is, he refuses to allow the nurses to use their props. Conversely, when the personnel wish to indicate how things are with him, they may begin to omit some of those routines.

During the pretense episodes, both sides play according to the rules implicit in the interaction. Although neither the staff nor patient may recognize these rules as such, certain tactics are fashioned around them, and the action is partly constrained by them. One rule is that dangerous topics should generally be avoided. The most obviously dangerous topic is the patient's death; another is events that will happen afterwards. Of course, both parties to the pretense are supposed to follow the avoidance rule.

There is, however, a qualifying rule: Talk about dangerous topics is permissible as long as neither party breaks down. Thus, a patient refers to the distant future, as if it were his to talk about. He talks about his plans for his family, as if he would be there to share their consummation. He and the nurses discuss today's events—such as his treatments—as if they had implications for a real future, when he will have recovered from his illness. And some of his brave or foolhardy activities may signify a brave show of pretense, as when he bathes himself or insists on tottering to the toilet by himself. The staff in turn permits his activity. (Two days before he returned to the hospital to die, one patient insisted that his wife allow him to travel downtown to keep a speaking engagement, and to the last he kept up a lively conversation with a close friend about a book they were planning to write together.)

A third rule, complementing the first two, is that each actor should focus determinedly on appropriately safe topics. It is customary to talk about the daily routines—eating (the food was especially good or bad), and sleeping (whether one slept well or poorly last night). Complaints and their management help pass the time. So do minor personal confidences, and chatter about events on the ward. Talk about physical symptoms is safe enough if confined to the symptoms themselves, with no implied references to death. A terminal patient and a staff member may safely talk, and at length, about his disease so long as they skirt its fatal significance. And there are many genuinely safe topics having to do with movies and movie stars, politics, fashions—with everything, in short, that signifies that life is going on "as usual."

A fourth interactional rule is that when something happens, or is said, that tends to expose the fiction that both parties are attempting to sustain, then each must pretend that nothing has gone awry. Just as each has carefully avoided calling attention to the true situation, each now must avert his gaze from the unfortunate intrusion. Thus, a nurse may take special pains and announce herself before entering a patient's room so as not to surprise him at his crying. If she finds him crying, she may ignore it or convert it into an innocuous event with a skillful comment or gesture—much like the tactful gentleman who, having stumbled upon a woman in his bathtub, is said to have casually closed the bathroom door, murmuring "Pardon me, sir." The mutuality of the pretense is illustrated by the way a patient who cannot control a sudden expression of great pain will verbally discount its significance, while the nurse in turn goes along with his pretense. Or she may brush aside or totally ignore a major error in his portrayal, as when he refers spontaneously to his death. If he is tempted to admit impulsively his terminality, she may, again, ignore his impulsive remarks or obviously misinterpret them. Thus, pretense is piled upon pretense to conceal or minimize interactional slips.

Clearly then, each party to the ritual pretense shares responsibility for maintaining it. The major responsibility may be transferred back and forth, but each party must support the other's temporary dominance in his own action. This is true even when conversation is absolutely minimal, as in some hospitals where patients take no particular pains to signal awareness of their terminality, and the staff makes no special gestures to convey its own awareness. The pretense interaction in this case is greatly simplified, but it is still discernible. Whenever a staff member is so indelicate, or so straight-forward, as to act openly as if a terminal patient were dying, or if the patient does so himself, then the pretense vanishes. If neither wishes to destroy the fiction, however, then each must strive to keep the situation "normal."[4]

The Transition to Open Awareness

A mutual pretense context that is not sustained can only change to an open awareness context. (Either party, however, may again initiate the pretense context and sometimes get cooperation from the other.) The change can be sudden, when either patient or staff distinctly conveys that he has permanently abandoned the pretense. Or the change to the open context can be gradual: nurses, and relatives, too, are familiar with patients who admit to terminality more openly on some days than they do on other days, when pretense is dominant, until finally pretense vanishes altogether. Sometimes the physician skillfully paces his interaction with a patient, leading the patient finally to refer openly to his terminality and to leave behind the earlier phase of pretense.

Pretense generally collapses when certain conditions make its maintenance increasingly difficult. These conditions have been foreshadowed in our previous discussion. Thus, when the patient cannot keep from expressing his increasing pain, or his suffering grows to the point that he is kept under heavy sedation, then the enactment of pretense becomes more difficult, especially for him.

Again, neither patient nor staff may be able to avoid bringing impending death into the open if radical physical deterioration sets in, the staff because it has a tough job to do, and the patient for other reasons, including fright and panic. Sometimes a patient breaks his pretense for psychological reasons, as when he discovers that he cannot face death alone, or when a chaplain convinces him that it is better to bring things out into the open than to remain silent. (Sometimes, however, a patient may find such a sympathetic listener in the chaplain that he can continue his pretense with other personnel.) Sometimes he breaks the pretense when it no longer makes sense in light of obvious physical deterioration.

Here is a poignant episode during which a patient dying with great pain and obvious bodily deterioration finally abandoned her pretense with a nurse:

There was a long silence. Then the patient asked, "After I get home from the nursing home will you visit me?" I asked if she wanted me to. "Yes, Mary, you know we could go on long drives together. . . ." She had a faraway look in her eyes as if daydreaming about all the places she would visit and all the things we could do together. This continued for some time. Then I asked, "Do you think you will be able to drive your car again?" She looked at me, "Mary, I know I'm daydreaming; I know I am going to die." Then she cried, and said, "This is terrible, I never thought I would be this way."

---

[4] A close reading of John Gunther's poignant account of his young son's last months shows that the boy maintained a sustained and delicately balanced mutual pretense with his parents, physicians and nurses. John Gunther. Death, Be Not Proud (New York: Harper and Bros., 1949). Also see Bensman and Gaver, op. cit.

In short, when a patient finds it increasingly difficult to hang onto a semblance of his former healthy self and begins to become a person who is visibly dying, both he and the staff are increasingly prone to say so openly, whether by word or gesture. Sometimes, however, a race occurs between a patient's persistent pretense and his becoming comatose or his actual death—a few more days of sentience or life, and either he or the staff would have dropped the pretense.

Yet, a contest may also ensue when only one side wishes to keep up the pretense. When a patient openly displays his awareness but shows it unacceptably, as by apathetically "giving up," the staff or family may try to reinstate the pretense. Usually the patient then insists on open recognition of his own impending death, but sometimes he is persuaded to return to the pretense. For instance, one patient finally wished to talk openly about death, but her husband argued against its probability, although he knew better: so after several attempts to talk openly, the patient obligingly gave up the contest. The reverse situation may also occur: the nurses begin to give the patient every opportunity to die with a maximum of comfort—as by cutting down on normal routines—thus signaling that he should no longer pretend, but the patient insists on putting up a brave show and so the nurses capitulate.

We would complicate our analysis unduly if we did more than suggest that, under such conditions, the pretense ritual sometimes resembles Ptolemy's cumbersomely patched astronomical system, with interactants pretending to pretend to pretend! We shall only add that when nurses attempt to change the pretense context into an open context, they generally do this "on their own" and not because of any calculated ward standards or specific orders from an attending physician. And the tactics they use to get the patient to refer openly to his terminality are less tried and true than the more customary tactics for forcing him to pretend. .

Consequences of Mutual Pretense

For the patient, the pretense context can yield a measure of dignity and considerable privacy, though it may deny him the closer relationships with staff members and family members that sometimes occur when he allows them to participate in his open acceptance of death. And if they initiate and he accepts the pretense, he may have nobody with whom to talk although he might profit greatly from talk. (One terminal patient told a close friend, who told us, that when her family and husband insisted on pretending that she would recover, she suffered from the isolation, feeling as if she were trapped in cotton batting.) For the family—especially more distant kin—the pretense context can minimize embarrassment and other interactional strains: but for closer kin, franker concourse may have many advantages.

Oscillation between contexts of open awareness and mutual pretense can also cause interactional strains. We once observed a man persuading his mother to abandon her apathy—she had permanently closed her eyes, to the staff's great distress—and "try hard to live." She agreed finally to resume the pretense, but later relapsed into apathy. The series of episodes caused some anguish to both family and patient, as well as to the nurses. When the patient initiates the mutual pretense, staff members are likely to feel relieved. Yet the consequent stress of either maintaining the pretense or changing it to open awareness sometimes may be considerable. Again, both the relief and the stress affect nurses more than medical personnel, principally because the latter spend less time with patients.

But whether staff or patient initiates the ritual of pretense, maintaining it creates a characteristic ward mood of cautious serenity. A nurse once told us of a cancer hospital where each patient understood that everyone there had cancer, including himself, but the rules of tact, buttressed by staff silence, were so strong that few patients talked openly about anyone's condition. The consequent atmosphere was probably less serene than when only a few patients are engaged in mutual pretense, but even one such patient can affect the organizational mood, especially if the personnel become "involved" with him.

A persistent context of mutual pretense profoundly affects the more permanent aspects of hospital organization as well. (This often occurs at county and city hospitals.) Imagine what a hospital service would be like if all terminal patients were unacquainted with their terminality, or if all were perfectly open about their awareness—whether they accepted or rebelled against their fate. When closed awareness generally prevails the personnel must guard against disclosure, but they need not organize themselves as a team to handle continued pretense and its sometimes stressful breakdown. Also, a chief organizational consequence of the mutual pretense context is that it eliminates any possibility that staff members might "work with" patients psychologically, on a self-conscious professional basis. This consequence was strikingly evident at the small Catholic hospital referred to a few pages ago. It is also entirely possible that a ward mood of tension can be set when (as a former patient once told us) a number of elderly dying patients continually communicate to each other their willingness to die, but the staff members persistently insist on the pretense that the patients are going to recover. On the other hand, the prevailing ward mood accompanying mutual pretense tends to be more serene—or at least less obviously tense—than when open suspicion awareness is dominant.

Questions 8.2

1. Although the authors use the language of the theater when they speak of "drama," "props," "characters," "roles," and so on, they are describing behaviors that are quite real. What are some of the specific behaviors that contribute to the drama of mutual pretense, as described by these authors?

2. Adults engage in the drama of mutual pretense in settings other than hospitals, often to avoid uncomfortable confrontations. Observe the behavior of people around you carefully for a few days to indentify an example of mutual pretense. Report on your example. How did the participants illustrate any or all of the implicit interactional rules (to avoid dangerous topics, to discuss dangerous topics only when the pretense can be maintained, to focus on safe topics, to conceal or minimize interactional slips)? Did the context change to open awareness? Why or why not?

3. The drama of mutual pretense that surrounds a dying patient in a hospital can serve positive or negative functions for the patient. Discuss the range of good and bad effects of the drama.

PART THREE

PROGRAM PLANNING AND DEVELOPMENT FOR OLDER ADULTS

As we continue to understand the needs of older people, we become more aware that many necessary services are not provided by the community. Those helping older people need to be attuned to their unmet needs and understand the process through which these needs can be met.

In Part Three we illustrate how planning and program development and advocacy can be used to meet the needs of older people. Chapter 9 is a discussion of how to engage in the planning process. The various kinds of support services that may need to be developed for older people are discussed in Chapter 10. How to advocate in behalf of older people and teach them to advocate for themselves is covered in Chapter 11.

CHAPTER 9
PROGRAM PLANNING FOR
OLDER ADULTS

Many programs and services needed by older adults are not part of the existing network of social services. To effectively serve the elderly, it may be necessary to create or develop appropriate resources, services, or programs. Program development generally involves **planning,** the systematic process of decision making through which one makes rational choices among alternative problem solutions. The planning process enables the worker involved in program development to move through a series of steps leading to rational choices about the best way to meet the needs of the older adult. In this chapter we discuss the steps in the planning process—problem identification, problem analysis, involvement of vested interests, program implementation and evaluation—and how they are used in development of programs for the elderly.

Planning for Older Adults

Most of us engage in goal-directed behavior. We act in the present to secure desirable states of affairs in the future; this is planning. For example, many parents begin saving money when their children are infants to ensure their college education. These parents make decisions long before their children are of college age to achieve this goal; this is long-range planning. We also engage in goal-directed behavior on a day-to-day basis. For instance, you may plan at noon to attend a movie in the evening; this is short-range planning. Almost all processes of decision making can be considered as a form of planning.

One way to define planning is as a relatively systematic method we use to solve problems. It is decision making that enables us to decide what is to be accomplished and that results in the identification of priorities for accomplishing our objective. It occurs through a series of logical steps or a process that enables us to identify and select among alternative problem solutions. Planning is a process for fully determining a preferred course for future action.

Planning is a useful tool in the development of programs for older people, for it increases common understanding of the issues in the community and facilitates communication, which, in turn, facilitates decision making. In addition, in any community there are limited resources available for aging programs and planning ensures that these are well used. Problems and conditions vary from community to community, making it impossible to devise a universal solution for the problems of older people. Planning permits the design of programs that best suit the needs of the specific elderly population we are concerned about.

When we engage in program development for older people, we attempt to find the best solution to an existing service need. For example, the director of a meals program, in looking through the agency files, may discover that a number of older people who would like to receive hot meals aren't able to, because they cannot get to the meals program. After discussing this matter, the director learns that other meals program directors have identified a similar problem. The director of the meals program may then make contact with service agencies in the community to determine if they provide transportation to older people. If they do not offer transportation services either, the program director will probably conclude that transportation is a problem not only for prospective participants of the meals program but for all the elderly of the community, and something should be done about it.

The "something to be done" may involve any of a number of solutions. For example, in the situation stated above, the need perceived by the meals program director is for transportation services. However, does this mean that older people need access to public transportation or financial aid in order to use transportation? If older people do not have access to public transportation, then the service needed is a transportation system. If, on the other hand, they do not have money to pay for public transportation, then the service needed may be an income subsidy to be used for public transportation. The planning process enables us to make the correct choices among the various alternatives available.

The Planning Process

The planning process involves a series of logical steps that should lead to an ultimate goal. Morris and Binstock (1966) have identified six major steps in the planning process. They are: (1) problem identification, (2) problem analysis, (3) involvement of interested people, (4) development of a plan of action, (5) program implementation, and (6) program evaluation. They maintain that these are the logical steps to follow in the planning process, and, if carried out conscientiously, they should lead to rational decisions about program development. Although we will discuss them sequentially, in reality they may occur out of sequence. Moreover, planning is a continuous process; the final step of the process, program evaluation, provides feedback that should reactivate the first step, problem identification. (See Figure 9.1.) In other words, in evaluating whether or not a planned program meets its objectives, we may learn that it does not, and this may motivate us to go back and reassess the problem. Or we may identify another problem that may reactivate the process. Planning is not static but a fluid process. Each step in the process is discussed below.

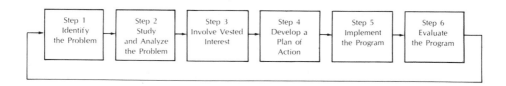

Figure 9.1   Steps in the Planning Process.

Problem or Need Identification

This step of the planning process helps to answer the question of what problems exist for the elderly. The problems addressed in program planning generally result

from the elderly's having **unmet needs.** Needs for most older people are basic requirements for purposeful independent living, such as adequate housing, income, and
basic material needs; psychological requirements, such as safety needs (need for
protection against damage or deprivation); the need for social interaction (sharing
love and social contact); the need to feel important or valued (achievement, accomplishment, and self-esteem); and the need for self-fulfillment (development of human
potential).

In the planning process these problems or unmet needs are identified in many
ways. Frequently they are observed by those attempting to provide services to older
people, for example, the director of the meals program mentioned above. Another
example of problem identification through service providers occurred in our home
state of West Virginia. Welfare workers attempting to provide services to older people
had begun to realize that many older people were forced into institutionalization,
because resources were not available in the community to provide supportive services
in the home. This was documented for a number of years by the welfare workers and
finally resulted in the department's development of a homemakers' service for older
people, which provided them with an alternative to institutional care.

Very often citizens in the community or national, state, and local government
agencies will identify unmet needs of older people. Gerontologists and the elderly
themselves may define problems. However the problem is identified, it is brought to a
level of public awareness that prompts us to act to alleviate or resolve the problem.

Problem Analysis

This step in the planning process deals with the question of how pervasive the
problem is in the community, what resources are available to respond to it, and
where available services fall short in dealing with the problem. The purpose of this
step is to identify priority unmet needs and to provide recommendations for how they
can be met through program development. There are three tasks involved in this step:
(1) assessing the needs of older people, (2) surveying available resources, and (3)
establishing priorities and making recommendations.

Assessing Needs   We suggested above that the identification of problems and
needs of older people can occur spontaneously as the consequence of observation
made by an individual. They can also be identified through a more formal method of
collecting information that permits a systematic analysis of the magnitude of the
need, its frequency, and the perceived seriousness of the problem. This is done
through an activity in planning called a **needs assessment.**

The needs assessment is a means of systematically collecting information about
the problems and needs of older people, as well as their service utilization patterns.
With this type of information at hand, a program developer may be able to assess the

nature of the program actually needed to cope with the problems. For example, in the meals program problem discussed above, we need to know if transportation is needed only for older people who want to participate in the meals program or whether it is a more general need of older people in the community. Do older people also need transportation in order to get medical care, to get to the grocery store, and so on? The systematic collection of data through needs assessment should help answer such questions and provide a clearer definition of the transportation problem of the elderly.

Four methods suggested by Warheite, Bell, and Schwab (1974) can be used to obtain information about the needs of the elderly adult: (1) the knowledgeable person approach, (2) the public hearing approach, (3) the social indicators approach, and (4) the direct contact approach.

1. *The knowledgeable person approach,* as the title suggests, involves obtaining information from those in the community who are in good positions to know about the needs of older people. The criteria for the selection of these individuals are logically based on the fact that they know about the community, older people and their needs, and patterns of services being received. Individuals who should be sought for such information are administrators and personnel of health and welfare agencies, aging-program directors and personnel, and the clergy. Both the public and private sectors should be used in trying to identify knowledgeable individuals. Information about the needs of older people can be obtained from these individuals through either mailed questionnaires or personal interviews.

    There are very obvious advantages to the knowledgeable person approach. First, it is relatively simple and inexpensive; second, it permits the input and interaction of a great many different individuals, each with an individual perspective on the elderly's needs in the community. This approach is not the best, however, because it tends to be based entirely upon the perceptions of those providing services. There is thus a likelihood that an organizational perspective will be presented, which may not reflect fully and adequately the needs of older people.

2. *The public hearing approach* relies on the perspective of individuals who are asked to assess the needs and service patterns of older adults in the community. It is similar to the knowledgeable person approach in that it is based on the views of individuals. However, some of the most serious disadvantages of the knowledgeable person approach are reduced by widening the circle of respondents to include the general population. Forums or hearings are planned around a series of public meetings to which all residents of the community are invited to come and express their beliefs about the needs and services for older people. This approach is flexible. It can be planned to elicit information from any member of the community willing to attend the meeting or it can be geared toward the elderly alone. If they are to be effective, public hearings must be well publicized. It will be necessary also to record the ideas, attitudes, and perceptions of those present.

Hearings are relatively easy to arrange and inexpensive to conduct. They provide an excellent opportunity for input from many segments of the community through a process that is very likely to bring into consciousness new ideas of previously unidentified needs of older people. They also aid in the identification of those citizens most interested in helping, who can be valuable resources for the later implementation of programs.

There are also shortcomings in this method. One of the most serious is the difficulty of obtaining representative attendance at public hearings. Only a partial view of the community's perceptions of needs and services will emerge unless the meetings are well attended by a broad cross-section of older people or knowledgeable citizens who are articulate in expressing their beliefs and in sharing their information. Still another disadvantage lies in the possibility that the meetings may heighten the expectations of those in the community in ways that cannot be met. Many of the factors associated with the problems of older people and the creation of programs to alleviate them are beyond the control of local agencies. Therefore, it is essential that expectations about what can be achieved be clearly spelled out to those attending.

The public hearings held prior to the 1971 White House Conference on Aging are an example of this method. The objective of the White House Conference and the general expectation of those who attended was to establish a national policy on aging. Public hearings were held all over the United States, and, on the basis of the information obtained and shared at the conference, recommendations for a national policy on aging were submitted to the president. The ultimate national policy never materialized, however, which may have been very disappointing to those who participated in the preconference activity and in the conference itself. Early in the public hearings sessions those who attended should have been made aware of what would be a realistic outcome.

3. *The social indicators approach* is based primarily on inferences of need drawn from descriptive statistics found in public records and reports. The underlying assumption of this approach is that it is possible to make useful estimates of the needs of older people by analyzing statistics on selected factors that have been found to be highly correlated with persons in need. Some of the factors commonly used as social indicators include the special arrangement of the community's people and institutions; the social or demographic characteristics of the population, such as age, race, sex, and income; and the general social conditions in which people live. For example, substandard housing, overcrowding, inside plumbing, accessibility to service, transportation, and economic conditions are factors that can be used. When they are analyzed as a constellation, they can provide important information about a community and the needs of those who live there.

There are many advantages to using the social indicators approach. The most significant is that such approaches can be developed from vast information sources already existing in the public domain, such as census reports, governmental agency statistics, and the like. Such information can generally be secured at relatively low cost. However, one of the most serious shortcomings is the fact that many of the indicators are only indirect measures of need and may not be accurate.

4. *The direct contact approach* is based on the collection of information about older people in the community through either personal interviews or mailed question-naires. This can be done by interviewing all the older people in the community or representative groups. The key to the success of this method is in obtaining pertinent information. The tendency is to ask a great many questions because they are interesting and so overburdening the older people with the demand for information that they may be uncooperative.

There are many advantages to using this approach. Properly conducted, this method of assessing need can provide the most valid and reliable information available about the needs and service utilization patterns of older people. On the other hand, it is costly and time-consuming. In addition, older people may be reluctant or refuse to participate in providing such information. Of the four approaches discussed, however, the direct contact approach is by far the best, for it provides information on needs as perceived by older individuals themselves; it should be used if at all possible.

Surveying Available Resources   A second type of information needed for a clearer understanding of the service needs of older people is an understanding of the current patterns of service provision in the community. A survey or overview of existing service patterns should provide information about the type of services available—for example, health, income, counseling, or recreation—and the pattern of utilization of these services by the elderly. Such a survey may provide a dual function, for in asking what types of services agencies provide to older people, we may also be enlightening them as to the needs of old people or helping them identify a potential client group.

Modification of the various needs assessment approaches can be used to obtain information about community services. The knowledgeable person approach would involve talking to those who know about agencies in the community; for example, the directors of the Council of Social Agencies or the United Way. Rather than a commu-nity forum, you may want to have an agency forum, with representatives of the various service agencies providing information about the services they provide to all those present.

Information on the availability of community services for the elderly can also be obtained from social services directories, information and referral agencies, social service councils, and even the phone book. By far the best method, however, is direct contact with the agency providing services, through either a mailed questionnaire or personal interview with the agency executive.

The type of information you may want to obtain when dealing directly with an agency in order to assess service gaps includes: (1) the formal objectives of the agency;

(2) a brief listing of services currently provided; (3) staffing patterns; (4) facts about clients, for example, age, sex, income, and geographic distribution; (5) the types of problems people bring to the agency; (6) the types of referrals that are made by this agency to other agencies; and (7) service gaps identified by the agency.

Setting Priorities and Making Recommendations   The final aspect of needs assessment is an analysis of the information collected about the elderly and current services. On the basis of this analysis priorities should be developed for meeting the needs of older clients. The results of the needs assessment would generally reveal that older clients have many specific needs. Unmet needs typically far outreach resources available to respond, making it necessary to define priority of needs.

An effort should be made to rank needs from highest to lowest. For example, the most pressing transportation need may be travel for medical care; travel to a nutrition program may be needed but less pressing. The need most frequently expressed by older people can be given a rank of 1, the next highest, 2, and so on. Ranking will provide a perspective of which needs should be given priority in program development.

Although some needs are given higher ranking than others, those given the highest ranking may not be the needs given highest priority in program development. As part of the decision-making process involved in setting priorities, information about available services must also be taken into consideration.

Sometimes a needs assessment may indicate that rather than developing a new program, alterations in some existing program may be all that is required to meet a service need of the elderly. If an existing agency agrees to provide this service, a new program has not been created but a new service has, and the ultimate goal has been achieved.

In setting priorities, the worker may also find that some needs of older people cannot be resolved through program development. Resolution of some service needs for the elderly is beyond the realm of local resources. For example, a major need of older people is income. Very little can be done through local programs to deal with this problem, except perhaps something with regard to employment opportunities for the elderly. In setting priorities you should make a realistic assessment of whether the need can be dealt with at the local level.

In summary, priorities should reflect prevalence of unmet needs, perspective of citizens as to the hierarchy of need, and the program's potential available to respond. The product of this step in the planning process is generally a report that ends with recommendations about the kind of program or services that should be developed to resolve the problem. The report, with its recommendations, is generally prepared for a board, agency director, committee, or planning council. The report should be written in a way that enables those for whom it is prepared to understand clearly how priorities were established and how they relate to the recommendations.

Involvement of Interested
People

The third step in the planning process addresses itself to the political aspects of program development. As we stated above, resources for program development are generally limited, and gaining access to such resources may be highly competitive. In addition, just because you and your agency or board may think new programs or services for older people are needed in the community, others may not feel this way. Consequently, it is advisable to gain community sanction and support for what you are doing. This is done by bringing together people in the community who both support and oppose your goals.

This is one of the steps in the planning process that very often falls out of sequence. You may start the planning process by bringing together relevant interest groups of the community; it may be they who initiate the planning process in the first place. At what point relevant interests are involved will depend on the circumstances surrounding your specific planning process, but they must be involved at some point.

You should attempt to involve key people in the community who support your program's planning goals, as very often they can open doors that are generally closed and expedite matters. In addition, they may be crucial for obtaining the resources needed to implement the program. Very often it is advisable to seek counsel or sanction from older people in the community, city or county officials, key social agencies, and potential funding agencies. One way of involving others is to establish an advisory or planning committee that works with you throughout the planning process. We would like to emphasize that when you are developing programs for older people, it is always "good politics" to involve them as much as possible in the entire process.

Involving those who oppose your effort is crucial to its ultimate success. By involving them you put yourself in a position to overcome their resistance to what you are trying to achieve. We generally overcome resistance by a number of means: obligation, friendship, rational persuasion, selling, coercion, and inducement (Morris and Binstock, 1966). However, we must have access to the person or group in order to overcome the resistance. By involving them you or those who support your efforts will have an opportunity to influence their opinion about what you are attempting to do.

Development of a Plan of Action

Developing a plan of action involves designing a program or service that, hopefully, will alleviate the problem you are concerned about. The plan of action contains four major parts: (1) goals and objectives, (2) strategies, (3) work plan, and (4) the budget.

Goals and Objectives   **Goals** establish the direction of your plan of action. They state what will be accomplished over the long run. For example, the purpose of a transportation service may be to increase the general mobility of older people in the community or to enable them specifically to participate in the activities of a senior center.

Objectives also establish direction, but they are short-range and are always measurable. There are two types of objectives: **impact objectives,** which define outcomes in terms of change expected in project participants as a result of project activities; and **output objectives,** which define outcomes in terms of the expected level of services or activities of the project.

In development of a plan of action we are concerned with output objectives. Good output objectives generally answer the *what, where, who, how, how many,* and *how much* questions. More specifically they should include: (1) types of services or activities to be undertaken, (2) expected level of effort, (3) target groups for the effort, (4) time period for the effort, and (5) cost. For example, a transportation program may have the following output objectives: The program is to provide, through Title XX funds, a $40 monthly cash subsidy to each of 100 low-income elderly in the community in order to meet their transportation needs. Or the program is to provide private volunteer automobile transportation three days a week for the 200 older residents living in one area of the community.

Once objectives are developed, they should be assigned priorities. The following factors should be kept in mind in creating **priority objectives:** The priorities among unmet needs should serve as a guide by defining the immediacy of the unmet need; the ability to mobilize resources; and the overall feasibility, given constraints such as political situations, staff, and the like. Other factors include order dependency (what objectives must be attained before others can be initiated); viewpoint of the advisory board; and finally, short-term or long-term commitments implied.

Strategies   Objectives define what is to be accomplished; **strategy** defines how it will be accomplished, the approach to be used. There are two basic approaches to responses to unmet needs: (1) delivery of services by an existing program, or (2) using staff time to develop new resources or improving existing resources operated by other service programs. Developing a strategy involves developing alternative approaches to meeting the objectives. The selection of the most appropriate strategy involves deciding which alternative approach best meets the various objectives. There may be several alternatives that can be used to meet your objectives; these should be examined carefully and assessed in terms of projected costs. Often the ideal solution or the ideal program design or objective is most costly, and frequently less-than-ideal means must be used because of the scarcity of resources.

If a new program is to be created, a funding strategy should also be considered. In order to get funding for new programs, it often will be necessary to submit grant proposals to federal or state agencies. Funding may also be available by requesting revenue-sharing money from the city government. Another alternative that should be explored is private funding sources, such as Community Chest, United Way, and private foundations.

Work Plan   The **work plan** provides more detail to strategy and becomes a framework for action by those who would implement the program. The work plan makes operational the output objectives and milestone dates for accomplishing them or for implementing the design.

The work plan should spell out the major nonservice and service tasks that must be achieved in order to conduct the new program, and anticipated dates for project task completion. If you hope to begin implementing your new program at the end of one year of planning and development, then all necessary nonservice tasks and sub-tasks must be identified and the dates they will be completed indicated. Service tasks are related to actual service delivery. The work plan is a tool for the planner as well as a means of indicating to others how the objectives will be achieved.

Work plans define, at a minimum, what will be done (tasks/services), how, when, where, and by whom. The work plan also provides the basis for developing a program budget.

The Budget   The final task in a plan of action is the development of a proposed budget. The **budget** should reflect as accurately as possible the amount of money that will be required to operate the program. In the planning process two budgets are needed. The first is an activities or service budget, which identifies how much it costs to provide a given service. The second is a line item budget, which projects the expected costs by type of expense, such as personnel or staff, rental, travel, supplies, and so on.

All four parts of the plan of action—goals and objectives, strategies, the work plan, and the budget—serve as the foundation and the blueprint for the final phases of the planning process, program implementation and evaluation.

Program Implementation

The program implementation step of the planning process involves carrying out those activities necessary to prepare for actual provision of services to clients. The implementation step involves securing staff, facilities, equipment, and supplies—all things essential to the actual program operation—as well as establishing policies and procedures to structure the program. It may also involve the establishment of the policy-making body and an advisory board and developing relationships with other agencies. This step includes activities to inform older people about the program and, finally, actual provision of the service.

Program Evaluation

The final step in the planning process, evaluation, assures accountability and feedback as part of the process. The purpose of program evaluation is to determine if the program goals and objectives are actually achieved. This step may begin when the program begins, because evaluations are built into the program's implementation as data are collected from the onset of the program.

At some point established in the work plan, the data collected for the evaluation are studied to see if the program has accomplished its objectives. The information

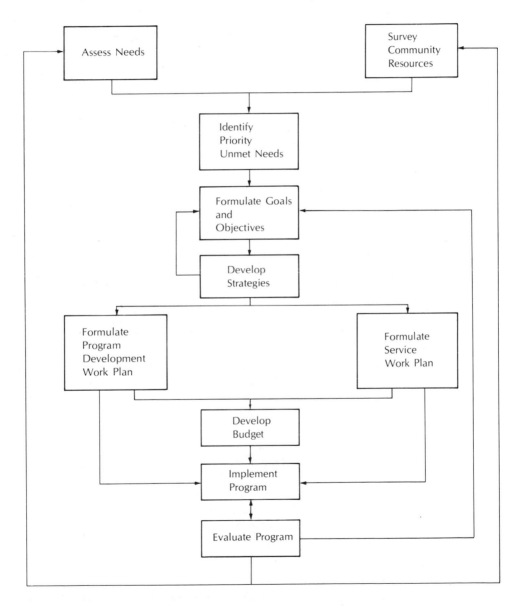

Figure 9.2   Relationships among Components of the Planning Process.

obtained in this step may be the basis for reactivating the planning process in order to achieve new goals or to modify the existing objectives.

Figure 9.2 shows how components of the planning process are interrelated.

Involving Older Adults in Program Planning and Development

As we indicated earlier, there is a role for older adults in the planning process. They can be involved in several aspects of program development, beginning with voicing their own needs for services. The needs assessment phase of program development, inasmuch as possible, should include the direct input of older individuals; several of the methods suggested above for gathering information on needs call for their direct input. Since older people usually are not involved in program planning, it may take an overall educational effort to elicit help and to get them to understand their role in the process and the need for their input in order for the program to succeed. To ensure participation it may be necessary to visit senior centers and other programs used by older people to explain the purpose of a needs assessment and encourage their participation. If mailed questionnaires are to be used, it may be useful to visit older people at agency programs or in their homes to explain the purpose of a needs survey and to solicit their support.

One way of assuring that old people will be involved in planning is by their participation on advisory and policy-making boards. Many federal programs for older people require that they be represented on such boards. To serve effectively as board members, the elderly may need some preparation, for many older people have not had such experience.

When older people become involved as board members, it will be necessary to provide them with an orientation to help them understand the purpose of the board, their role as board members, how the board is structured, how it will function, the nature of the service program, and the relationship of the board to program staff or a planner. If older people are being asked to serve on a policy-making board, it may also be useful to orient them to Robert's Rules of Order.

In developing an advisory board of older people, it will be helpful to have a board that is representative of a cross-section of the elderly population, including individuals with varied racial and socioeconomic backgrounds. You should probably seek out older individuals who are interested in such activities, will enjoy the experience, and have the stamina to carry out the responsibilities involved.

Summary

This chapter has provided some idea about the various tasks that must be undertaken to effectively develop programs for older people, with emphasis placed on involving older people themselves in the planning of programs for their benefit. In the next two chapters we discuss a number of programs that can be developed for older people. The reading that follows provides additional ideas about developing programs for older people.

READING 9.1

A Goal, a Program and a Community / Eunice H. Sluyter

In this article Eunice H. Sluyter provides a model for careful identification of service needs and development of programs.

The Federal and State grant of $93,335 would have been lost had not the Division of Family Services awarded those funds the summer of 1972 to the Community Service Council of Broward County. Broward, the only county in Florida to receive Title III funds for an Area-wide Model Project on Aging, was selected because of its "ever-increasing population" according to Mr. H. W. Thompson, Director of the Community Service Council.

A Project Is Conceived

To translate an idea into an effective program requires not just a person but the right person. Broward was fortunate to have that "right" person, Mrs. Nan S. Hutchison. Former Dean and Director of Student Activities at Broward Community College and Dean of Women and Director of Student Activities at Florida Atlantic University, Mrs. Hutchison was selected to direct the Model Project on Aging. Her approach to this pioneer assignment is summed up in a statement she made at that time: "Every program for the elderly must be geared to their particular set of circumstances. That's why we are going to every part of the county to find out what the specific needs of people are." These words proved to be the key to most of what has been accomplished in four years.

In order to "go to every part of the county" a task force was appointed by the Community Service Council with Hollywood Mayor David Keating as chairman.

A Survey Is Made

The first task was to learn the circumstances of the elderly. A 73-item questionnaire, designed to pinpoint actual need in the areas of nutrition, transportation and telephone availability, housing, health, and assistance, was compiled. This questionnaire was taken personally to 1,027 white, black, rich and poor older persons living in north central and south Broward County.

From *Aging* Magazine, June/July 1977. Reprinted by permission of the publisher.

Of those surveyed 52% lived alone and 75% said they wanted to participate in the proposed meals and companionship programs.

The survey had a dual purpose: first, to learn the actual needs of those 60 and over; second, to develop a statistically valid random survey of these persons to prove the needs of Broward's seniors to the Federal government's satisfaction. Research showed that 152,613 persons were over 60, comprising 24.6% of the population. The priority needs of those interviewed were health care, transportation, nutrition, education, recreation, and information and referral.

Those conducting the survey had experiences they will long remember. One surveyor found herself interviewing a retiree from the lobby of a condominium by telephone. Others found senior citizens wanted to talk about everything except the items in the questionnaire which would reveal their needs—in some cases their desperate needs. Yet other interviewers were invited to have snacks or lunch. Through conducting the survey, quite apart from the statistical results, much was learned about the senior citizens of Broward as people with pride, dignity, and courage.

A Partnership Is Formed

The needs of the elderly were verified, but to launch programs to meet these needs required funds. According to the Older Americans Act, recipients of Federal funds must match, by proportionate amounts, money received. This meant that 29 cities in Broward County had to be persuaded to raise 10% to add to the Federal grant of 90% that first year. This was no small task. Some city fathers were skeptical of new programs.

In Pembroke Pines a council member said, "Older persons have set aside a little nest egg for retirement and do not need a food program." Mrs. Hutchison pointed out that the survey revealed that 91% of the seniors were eating inadequately and only 4.6% knew they had a nutrition problem. The result of the discussion was to table the request for funds until a later meeting.

In Hollywood a barrage of questions had to be answered. Factual answers to probing questions laid the foundation for the partnership between the cities and the area agency on aging. One city was amazed to learn that there were 255 elderly persons with incomes below the poverty level living in their municipality.

The patient presentations of facts by the Executive Director and Task Force paid off. Wilton Manors, by a 3–2 vote, agreed to pay their share on condition that they receive a report of services to their residents over 60. The funds would be stopped if the services were not used. As a result of detailed reporting to municipalities in Broward, funds were approved in city after city. A partnership between the area agency on aging and the cities was formed.

Meanwhile Broward residents had to be made aware of the needs of the elderly in the county. The 1970 census revealed that 23,000 of Broward's 152,613 persons over 60 lived below the poverty level. In 1973, one year after the Project on Aging began, that figure had risen by 15%, according to the Area Planning Board.

In keeping with the original policy that "every program must be geared to their set of circumstances," the elderly were consulted privately and in conference. In February, 1973, the first Conference on Aging was held at Broward Community College, planned and organized by the Project on Aging. Some 227 seniors came together to discuss their needs. Matters discussed included the separation of young and old, the often unadmitted problem of loneliness, and the more tangible problems of transportation, health, and lack of money. Another haunting question, "What do we do with the elderly person who is not sick but has little money and nowhere to live?," had to be dealt with.

In 10 groups led by representatives from State and local service agencies, the circumstances of the elderly in Broward were more fully realized.

Programs Come to Life

The summer of 1973 was momentous. Florida's Division of Aging approved funds for the nutrition program. After much searching, suitable locations were obtained as sites. On Sept. 17, three nutrition sites were opened in the north, south, and central parts of the county. During the first weeks of the program, participants averaged 172 per day. By the fourth week 316 persons were attending; by the end of the eighth week, 714 people; and by the end of the tenth week, 894 people were coming daily. The success of the program was reflected in newspaper headlines such as "Turkey and Talk Bring Good Times for Elderly Hot Lunch Participants," "Hot Lunch Plan Enables Elderly to Find Friends," and "Lunch Program Brings Senior Citizens Together." New centers were opened in all sections of the county in churches, halls, and schools. By December, 12 sites were serving congregate meals.

At this peak of accomplishment Florida's Gov. Askew signed a bill assuring senior citizens programs for another year. Meanwhile the State Senate Special Committee on Aging met for three days to discuss "Transportation of the Elderly: Problems and Progress," with Senator Lawton Chiles presiding. Mrs. Margaret Jacks, Director of the Florida Division on Aging, summarized the challenge in one sentence, "Transportation is the lifeline of our senior citizens."

Three months later, in March 1974, the Federal government extended the Older Americans Act nutrition program through fiscal year 1977.

The promise of continued funding for the newly incorporated Areawide Council on Aging of Broward County, Inc. was good, and expansion possible. By mid-summer the elderly who had no means of transport were calling to make appointments to be picked up in small vans to go to the doctor, food stamp office, clinic, and nutrition site. Information and Referral staff were advertising their telephone number so that the elderly could learn where to go for help and advice. The home services coordinator was recruiting and training homemakers to assist needy older people in their homes. The mass media coordinator sent public service announcements to radio stations, releases to newspaper editors, and prepared newsletters, flyers, and brochures. Counseling and job placement staff were setting up locations for contacts with the elderly and seeking ways of helping retirees who wanted to get back into the work force.

Further Expansion

Legal Counseling, supported through Manpower funds, started in February, 1975. It was a rough start with no money for a desk, typewriter, or office. In spite of this inconvenience the legal counseling program thrived and after six months the staff moved into a building with their administering agency.

The Home Touch program began in September, 1975. It was surprising to learn of the numbers of houses with bad floors, lack of hot water, and rotting steps. Handymen repaired screens, stoves, roofs, leaking pipes, and electrical wiring. Many houses are being made healthier and safer for older persons who are now able to remain independent in their own homes.

Teenagers supplement the work Home Touch personnel do inside houses. On weekends groups of young people supervised by Specialized Urban Ministries paint houses, cut grass, and trim shrubs. Such tidying up has a chain reaction. The chairman of the Area Agency Advisory Council reported that an entire block of houses has improved because owners were impressed with the transformation of two houses brought about by Home Touch and the teenagers.

The Day Care Center had a slower liftoff. This program, opened in October, 1975, was designed for the frail elderly. Transportation was a problem because the elderly had to be brought to the Center. Many had difficulty associating such a Center with the elderly. However, after six months 15–20 persons were coming in daily. After the Junior Welfare League helped make possible a ramp, persons in wheel chairs added to the numbers.

Family members are now free to work or shop and not worry about the older people during their days out. On the other hand the older person finds friends, enjoys mental and physical stimulation, and has a change of environment.

Entertainment Is Planned —"Salute to Seniors"

From the very beginning Mrs. Hutchison recognized the importance of entertainment. Each year beginning in 1973 during Older Americans Month (May) community programs were planned and presented in the War Memorial Auditorium made available by the city of Fort Lauderdale. Printers donated tickets and programs, banks donated door prizes, senior citizens clubs provided ushers, and schools provided orchestras. Professionals including Jackie Gleason and June Taylor have helped make this annual event a very popular feature in the county for persons 60 and over.

Workshops Are Planned

Motivation and stimulation essential to the growth of any organization have been provided for professional personnel through a variety of workshops. Organized by the State and area agency, they have covered a range of subjects such as: "After Middle Age—What?" "Volunteers," "Understanding Older People," "Community Organization," "Reality Orientation," "Medicare and Medicaid," "Grantsmanship," and "The Aging Process."

Workshops held in Broward and neighboring counties have provided training as well as an opportunity to meet others working with the elderly.

Reassessment

Recognizing that years bring great change to communities, the State Division sent a questionnaire which the area agency on aging administered to 105 subjects in 1975. Had two years brought changes in the county? The updating confirmed the findings of 1973. The needs of the elderly were still for health, transportation, nutrition and recreation programs. As in the earlier survey other needs were noted. New plans were being written constantly to meet the needs. Two mini-centers in the north and south of the county were opened in the Spring of 1976.

Organization

To plan, coordinate, and evaluate the eight Title III and Title VII programs during the four-year period has required careful organization and wide community involvement. The selection of a grantee agency to administer and an advisory committee to monitor each of the programs has meant drawing upon the help of other agencies and many members of the community.

One of the reasons that the area agency's programs are meeting the real needs of the older residents of Broward County is that so many senior citizens serve on these Advisory Committees. The area agency itself has an Advisory Council.

In addition, the Board of Governors of the Areawide Council on Aging of Broward County Inc. meets each month to deal with policy, hear reports, and approve future plans.

A Goal Achieved

"Every program for the elderly must be geared to their particular set of circumstances." That this goal has been achieved is evident from the response of senior citizens as reflected in the following comparative figures:

Program	First Year 1974–75	Second Year 1975–76
Information and referral	11,323	23,490
Counseling and job placement	1,441	2,646
Transportation (round trips)	39,566	55,150
Home services	3,595	8,595
Legal aid (5 mos.)	1,343	3,224

In the first nine months of operation, Home Touch has surpassed its goal for a year by completing 543 units of service. In approximately the same length of time, the day care center has provided 12,969 hours of care to 175 participants. In the first nine months of its third year, the nutrition program served 221,301 meals.

The expansion of services to Broward's older citizens has been made possible through the Older Americans Act and other legislation. But not every community can boast of success equal to Broward's. Locally, the reasons may be summed up in community cooperation and dynamic leadership. The outstanding contribution of Mrs. Nan Hutchison, now Dr. Hutchison, was acknowledged in May 1976 when she was named "Outstanding Woman of the Year" for Broward in the Business Category. Her tireless effort to involve other community leaders has made the area agency's contribution to Broward County so significant. Under outstanding community leadership the community has responded, and the elderly have benefited.

Questions 9.1

1. Which of the four methods of obtaining information about the needs of older adults is used in this model? Discuss why it was chosen.

2. Although health care was the first priority item, a nutrition program was implemented first. What factors would account for this?

3. What is the stated goal of the program? What structures directed toward goal achievement were created within the program?

chapter 10
support services for older adults

Many of the physical, psychological, and social conditions experienced by older people create barriers to their use of services and programs. Agencies must sometimes provide supportive services to guarantee that older adults are able to use their programs. The primary service provided by an agency must often be supplemented with support services in order for the agency to respond effectively to the needs of older clients. In this chapter we discuss various types of support services that might be needed by the elderly and suggest how such services might be established as part of an agency's program. Information and referral, telephone reassurance and friendly visiting, transportation, shopping assistance, escort service, legal services, and protective services are discussed.

Information and Referral Services

Older clients in the community may need aid in finding resources to help resolve the many problems confronting them. They may be plagued with a leaky faucet or frustrated because precious eyeglasses are broken. An information and referral service can provide tremendous assistance to older adults with such difficulties by helping them find repairmen or professionals who can help deal with these difficulties.

Communities are dynamic places in which change and growth are constant, and the average person may find it difficult to keep abreast of all the changes in the service and business segments of the community. The major function of an information and

referral service is to collect accurate and up-to-date information about all resources available in the community and to make this information easily available to the elderly. The foundation of a good information and referral service is the development and maintenance of an accurate community resources file.

The Community Resources File

To serve older people effectively through information and referral, a community resources file must be developed. The development of such a file entails a systematic survey of the community in order to identify the various resources available. The community survey can be done by either mailed questionnaires or personal interviews. A good resources file is not limited to information about social service agencies; information about resources available from civic groups and organizations and the business community should also be included. A community resources file should be a comprehensive statement of all services and resources available to the elderly.

Some resources are informal in nature, for instance, an individual who is willing to provide material or financial aid to those in need. Information about such people usually is available only by word-of-mouth. Much exploration may be required to identify these resources, but it is well worth the effort if it helps provide assistance to an older person in need.

To establish a useful resources file, the following information will be needed: (1)

The name, address, and phone number of the agency, business, or individual providing the service or the resource; (2) the nature, amount, and duration of the service or resource provided; (3) the conditions or criteria an individual must meet to receive assistance or the resource; (4) the name of a contact person within the agency or business.

In order to effectively and efficiently serve older people, the information obtained about community resources should be recorded on 3 × 5 cards and kept in a card file for easy access. The information in the file is generally organized by grouping together resources available for a specific problem area such as income, health, housing, clothing, transportation, and so on. If a specific resource is available for several of these areas, then duplicate cards will be required, and they should be filed under the appropriate problem category.

Once the resources file is created, the most challenging matter is keeping it up to date. This may require a periodic survey of resources, or perhaps arrangements for the information and referral service to be informed by a resource provider in the event of some change.

Information and referral services lend themselves nicely to the use of volunteers. Once a resources file is established, volunteers can be trained to use it.

Information Dissemination

Information and referral services are generally provided over the telephone. A "hot line," "need line," or other catchy name is often used to call attention to the service and to publicize its phone number. The phone number for the information and referral service should be announced in the newspaper and on the radio and television. All service programs, hospitals, the police, and so on should have the number. Some information and referral services have developed decals that contain the information and referral service number, and these are posted in phone booths, public restrooms, grocery stores, and other public places.

The agency or individual providing the service must answer calls from clients who ask either about a specific service or where assistance can be obtained for a specific problem. The task of the information and referral worker is to attempt to identify, through the resources file, an agency, program, individual, or resource that can assist with the older person's problem and to share this information with the caller.

If resources are not available to deal with a problem presented by an older person, this fact should be noted, as it is a means of documenting the need for specific types of service in the community. Such information should be shared with appropriate individuals in the community concerned about such needs.

Telephone Reassurance and
Friendly Visiting

Telephone reassurance and friendly visiting are two support services ideal for volunteers, particularly elderly volunteers. As we indicated in Chapter 4, many older people live alone, and because of physical, social, or psychological barriers, they do not routinely have contact with others. Regular contact by an individual who is concerned about the well-being of the older person can be very meaningful.

Rather than waiting for the older person to call and express a need, as is the case in the information and referral service, a telephone reassurance service is designed so that the volunteer calls an older individual on a regular basis. The purpose of the call is to check on the health and well-being of the older client, especially the semi-ambulatory elderly. In addition, if the older person called is in need of some type of service or resource, the volunteer of the telephone reassurance program will attempt to have this need met.

Generally the telephone reassurance worker arranges for the older person to call in and inform the volunteer if he or she does not plan to be at home at the time of the regular call. If the worker has not been prewarned that the client will not be at home at the time of the scheduled call, an unanswered telephone is an alert to the volunteer to have another person, such as a social worker or a landlord, visit the residence to determine why the client was unable to answer the phone. Older people are prone to accidents in the home. Some are taken ill suddenly, and without such a service they may go many days without assistance.

A friendly visiting service serves the same purpose as telephone reassurance but is accomplished by the volunteer's actually visiting the home of the older person. Often, in addition to visiting the home, a friendly visitor may also correspond with the older client or send greeting cards. A friendly visitor may also do small chores for the individual while in the home.

Transportation Services

Transportation is another support service that may be needed by older clients. Many older people do not use agency services because they are not mobile for any of the many reasons we have discussed earlier. Assistance by increasing the mobility of older people is quite beneficial from a social, psychological, and physical point of view.

Each community has its own transportation problems. In rural areas older people may have to travel many miles to get to services and programs, and public transit may be nonexistent; older people living in more populated areas may have to travel only a few blocks, but getting to the transit line may be treacherous because of hills or heavy traffic. Several types of services may be needed to assist with the mobility problems confronting older clients.

Pedestrian Travel

Very often accessibility to services and programs may involve the need to travel on foot only a few blocks, but this can present problems to the older individual. Because of the physical changes that occur with age, frequently street curbs are too high, traffic lights too fast, and traffic signs unclear to the older pedestrian. The highest incidence of pedestrian death and accidents is among the elderly.

Government units should be made aware of these problems and encouraged to ensure safe travel by foot for older people by determining that: (1) they always have the right of way; (2) traffic lights are timed for their needs; (3) curbs are altered for the safety of elderly and handicapped individuals; (4) signs are placed or colored so that they are visible to older citizens; and (5) if at all possible patrolmen are posted at busy intersections and neighborhoods highly populated with older people.

If these options are not possible, then "people pools," "safety patrols," or escort services should be developed to assist older pedestrians move about.

Vehicular Travel

There are a number of ways assistance can be provided to older people who need to travel using vehicles. If public transportation is available in a community, the transit authority might be persuaded to (1) reduce rates for older patrons; (2) establish bus stops near facilities, programs, and services frequented by older people; and (3) provide shelters and benches at bus stops used by the elderly.

If public transit is not available, volunteer transportation services may be organized. This would involve soliciting the services of private citizens using their own automobiles to transport older individuals to services they may need in the community. The responsibility of the agency with a volunteer transportation service would be to recruit volunteer drivers and coordinate the services of the driver with the needs of older clients.

Many community organizations, such as private or parochial school systems, churches, charity groups, sheltered workshops for the handicapped, and federally funded community programs, own vehicles for transporting their clients. It may be possible to get these groups to agree to provide transportation for older people when their vehicles are not being used for other purposes.

Still another option is organizing an effort to obtain a bus to provide transportation services for older people in the community. This may mean several years of fund raising or obtaining grants from federal or state agencies.

Shopping Assistance

With the advent of the supermarket and the demise of the friendly neighborhood grocer, food purchasing has become a major problem for the elderly. Older individuals living in the center-city and rural areas are often the most likely to experience difficulty, since supermarkets are generally located for the convenience of suburban shoppers. Because older consumers are forced to use local grocers rather than chain stores, their food costs are often high. Shopping assistance to older people has several facets. The major problem for older clients is getting to the market or grocer, which may involve travel by bus or taxi or a long walk. Older people sometimes find it necessary to pay neighbors or acquaintances to transport them by private automobile. The reliance of the older person on any of these means of transportation increases their food costs.

Reliable and inexpensive means of transportation to the grocer sometimes can be dealt with through volunteers who will transport older shoppers. Some senior center programs operate mini-buses that transport older people to the market once or twice a week. In some metropolitan areas food store proprietors themselves operate such mini-buses. Store proprietors may be persuaded to reduce the cost of food for older shoppers to offset the cost of transportation.

Once in the store, an older shopper is confronted with another problem. How many older people need to purchase ten pounds of potatoes or a four-pound cut of meat. The tendency of markets to prepackage foods in quantities suitable for families of four creates a variety of problems for the elderly. First, having to buy quantities of food in excess of actual need increases the cost of the purchase. In addition, it creates difficulties in transporting purchases back to the place of residence. Because of diminishing physical strength an older individual may be forced to make several trips to the grocery store over a short period of time in order to obtain all of the necessary groceries. If the older person is paying someone for transportation to the store, he or she may shop for a month at a time and do without certain items until the next trip.

Food store managers should be made aware of the packaging needs of older consumers. For example, one or two potatoes in a package or a small quantity of meat are more suited to the needs of the older consumer. Some grocers have established senior citizen shopping days featuring discounts on food items, and some markets serve refreshments to older customers while they are in the store. The major task is to make the commercial businessperson aware of the needs of the elderly consumer group.

The inability to shop affects the eating patterns of older people and, ultimately, their basic health. Malnutrition is a serious problem among the elderly, and any assistance that can be provided in this area will assure better nutritional patterns in old age.

Escort Service

Escort service is another support program that may be needed by older clients. Many older people need to be accompanied by another person in order to get around, especially the elderly with physical impairments or language barriers. Many elderly are homebound because they cannot cope with physical obstructions such as steps, curbs, or getting into and out of buses or automobiles. Other elderly persons may use prostheses, walkers, canes, and crutches. Many ethnic and minority elderly do not speak English and have limited mobility because of their inability to communicate. The availability of someone to accompany the older person and to provide assistance so that he or she can leave home without fear of feeling humiliation is very beneficial.

Through an escort service the older person with physical or language problems is provided assistance in leaving the home and getting to the desired destination. Sometimes the escort will provide transportation in a personal automobile or an agency's automobile; accompany the older person on a bus, train, or plane; or walk with the client to the destination. When immobility is created by a language barrier, the escort should be bilingual to act as an interpreter for the elderly client.

Escorts may accompany older clients to a variety of places such as the grocery store, department stores, physicians' offices, hospitals, and service agencies.

Legal Services

As individuals move into old age, they are confronted with a number of tasks that require legal counsel. Until a few years ago the legal needs of the elderly received little attention from the legal and other professions; however, this situation has started to change. Older people are beginning to be viewed as a distinct client group with its own set of problems, such as taxes, wills, pensions, Medicare, Medicaid, Social Security, nursing homes, and involuntary commitment. The poor elderly in particular have little knowledge of their legal rights and are timid about consulting attorneys. In addition, older clients often cannot afford to pay fees for legal advice charged by most private attorneys.

Although free legal-aid offices to serve the poor have been established throughout the country, these services have not been widely used by older people. Many older people whose income makes them ineligible to use public services are still too poor to afford an attorney, so they do without legal help. At this stage of life there is a need to put one's affairs in order, and access to legal counsel can greatly facilitate the process.

A number of ways are available to provide legal services to the elderly. The services of retired attorneys or volunteers obtained through the Bar Association can sometimes be obtained for a few days a month. A growing trend, however, is to use paralegals or legal advisors to provide this type of service. Paralegals work under the supervision of an attorney and provide assistance with a number of technical problems that may confront the elderly, such as eligibility for Social Security and Medicare. Older individuals themselves can be trained to serve as paralegals. Sometimes law students, with an attorney's supervision, can also be used to advise older clients. Agency staff members, such as caseworker, information and referral specialist, or outreach worker, may help older clients obtain assistance with their legal problems.

Protective Services

Older adults at times are unable to act in their own best interests, and it may become necessary for another individual to assist them with the administration of their personal affairs. There are times when, due to physical changes, mental functioning, and extreme stress, older adults may not be able to make decisions about their own well-being. There are some older people who cannot function adequately in the home and must be removed to another living situation. Older people may be pressured by family members, or they may need to be removed from a nursing home for their own protection. There are instances where older people are harassed by salesmen and collection agencies. In all these instances court action may be necessary in order to protect the interests of the older person. In such a case the worker acts as an advocate and attempts to see that the older person's rights are not violated and that his or her interests protected.

Protective services are usually provided by workers of a social service agency. The worker must be able to assess whether an older person is capable of making decisions in his or her best interest. At times older people may not be able to function effectively, because they are demoralized by the seemingly endless circumstances that complicate their lives. At this point they are vulnerable and may agree to do things they will later regret and be unable to undo.

For effective protective services the worker may need to be able to demonstrate to the court or others in authority that the older person is not acting normally and is incapable at the time of exercising proper judgement. The older person may require commitment or someone to act in his or her behalf. Someone may need to be given the power of attorney for the older person. The worker in this service pleads the case of the older client in court. Very often in protective services it will become necessary to seek legal assistance in order to help the older person.

Summary

Many services can be made available to older people as a means of helping them cope with the complex matrix of problems confronting them. In this chapter we have discussed how several of the services, such as information and referral, telephone reassurance and friendly visiting, transportation, shopping assistance, escort service, legal services, and protective services can be provided to older clients.

The two readings that follow illustrate problems confronting the elderly. You are asked to identify support services that may assist elderly individuals in these circumstances.

READING 10.1

Aged Wanderer Baffles State / Thomas Grubisich

Thomas Grubisich highlights here some of the conflicts involved in providing appropriate services for needy individuals.

Charles E. Perkins has wandered into a crevice in society, and nobody seems to know how to get him out.

An 89-year-old former biochemist, he is highly intelligent and knowledgeable, friends and acquaintances agree. They also say he tends to "wander," has neglected to pay his rent (although he has the Social Security money to do so), doesn't take care of his laundry and other household chores, and sometimes won't bother to eat.

On the evidence of these people, the Fairfax Department of social services, and a 15-minute medical examination, the state of Virginia had Perkins committed, against his will, to Western State Hospital for the mentally ill.

At that point, the state found itself engaged in an unexpected and difficult struggle with a man who seemed to straddle the line society tries to draw between sanity and insanity.

A jury, hearing an appeal demanded by Perkins, overturned the state's decision to commit him. Then, minutes after gaining his freedom, Perkins disappeared, a victim of his tendency to wander on foot, along and across busy highways.

Thursday morning, Perkins was back in the hands of the state, but no one knew what to do with him.

What can be done with an 89-year-old man who is intelligent yet wanders off, who has no home (his belongings have been put in storage for non-payment of rent) but won't be placed in one supervised by the state, who has been declared mentally ill by a doctor and special justice but sane by a jury?

The Fairfax County department of social services told the court during Perkins' August 19 commitment hearing that Western State was the only alternative for him.

"I didn't belong there," Perkins said this week. "I was in a room with babbling lunatics. If you're not a lunatic, but you're subjected to that, you will be a lunatic before long."

Perkins told his court-appointed attorney, Robert C. Downs, "I'm not insane. I want to be vindicated."

He demanded an appeal, requesting a jury, a right no court official remembers ever being involved in a commitment hearing in Fairfax.

The jury listened to the same evidence offered at the original August 19 hearing and decided Perkins was right.

Perkins walked out of the courtroom a free man.

Michael J. Valentine, a Fairfax attorney who presided as a special justice at Perkins' first hearing, said he was dumbfounded and saddened by the jury's decision.

Valentine had ruled at the original commitment hearing that Perkins "has been proven to be so seriously mentally ill as to be substantially unable to care for himself."

After the jury reversed his ruling, he said, "It's not just a case of my ego being hurt by losing a case, but the system has worked a tremendous disservice. There he is, sitting on a bench in the courthouse with nowhere to go. The man needs help."

As Valentine was speaking, Perkins' court-appointed attorney was trying to find help. He left his client in a chair in the courthouse lobby and went to a phone booth to call charity shelters.

None of the shelters would take Perkins, either because they didn't have room or because of his reputation for wandering.

When his attorney came out of the booth, Perkins was gone.

"I couldn't find him," Downs said. "He had no money, no identification except the wrist band from Western State Hospital."

Twelve hours later, about midnight Thursday, Perkins was found by a policeman wandering the streets of Arlington.

It is not clear what happened to Perkins after he left his courthouse chair Wednesday afternoon. He apparently made his way to Washington, where he was picked up by police in the downtown area and taken to a charity shelter. He then apparently left the shelter and headed, on foot, to Arlington.

Arlington police turned him over to a county volunteer service, FISH, and at 2 o'clock in the morning, he was taken to the house of volunteer Helen McKinley where he spent the night.

He was then taken to Fairfax Hospital to wait for a new commitment hearing yesterday.

Perkins' attorney, Downs, said "This is the toughest ethical dilemma I've ever been in."

Downs fought hard for his client at the appeal hearing, but he, like Valentine, thinks Perkins needs some help.

At a new commitment hearing held at 6:30 a.m. yesterday at Fairfax Hospital, Valentine put off a decision on commitment after reaching a compromise with the 89-year-old man.

"I can't keep you against your will," Valentine said. "My suggestion, and strong request, is that you agree to stay here till Wednesday." He told Perkins that the county's department of social services would try to find some place for him other than Western State.

Perkins, a dignified looking man with a white mustache, said: "I'm not a convalescent, I'm in full possession of all my faculties." He acceded to Valentine's request, saying: "Anything I can do to assist you, I will be happy to do. I have an open mind."

The petitioner for yesterday's hearing was one of Perkins' friends, Martin Young of Arlington, a coworshiper at Calvary Baptist Church in Washington, a church Perkins had joined at the turn of the century.

Like Perkins' few other friends, Young had intensely mixed feelings about the man.

"Charles has a brilliant mind," he said, "but he has traits that didn't amount to a satisfactory old age. . . . Charles doesn't remember a lot of things, but I don't remember a lot of things, and I'm only 71."

Perkins' attorney marvels at the breadth of his client's knowledge. "I came down with something called cervicobrachialga," Downs said. "He gave me a detailed description of the problem. His explanation was so sophisticated, I couldn't understand it."

Yet, when Perkins disappeared after his successful appeal Wednesday, a worried Downs said: "I hope he doesn't get hit by a car."

Robert Craig, the manager of Willston Garden Apartments near Seven Corners, where Perkins lived up to the time of his commitment to Western State on August 19, said: "He's a nice person, a lovely guy. But he cannot motivate himself."

Craig was one of the chief witnesses in the original commitment petition of the department of social services. However, he failed to appear at the appeal.

At the original hearing, the department said it had considered all alternatives to commitment, and they were either inappropriate or Perkins had rejected them.

According to Alma Cohn, service supervisor at the department's Baileys Crossroads office, Perkins refused to consider staying at a hotel for the elderly in Winchester. A social worker is assigned to the privately run hotel, but residents are free to leave.

Perkins wants to stay in the Fairfax area—in an apartment of his own—because that's where his few friends live, and it's close to Bethesda, where, until recently, he and his estranged 86-year-old wife lived. Perkins was born and raised in Washington, but, other than the estranged wife has no known relatives in the area.

There are no supervised hotels for the elderly in Fairfax, though they are "desperately needed," according to Thelma Petrilak, head of the social services department's adult services. Nor are there any halfway houses for the elderly.

The department does have a federally assisted "companionship" program, where someone, often a student in social work, will spend up to 40 hours a week helping an aged person with household and personal chores.

Mrs. Cohn said this program wasn't appropriate for Perkins because "he wouldn't benefit from partial companionship. He needed a protective situation."

However, his friend Martin Young said, "He could make it with help 10 percent of the time. . . . If it was someone he had confidence in, a companion might be a solution."

When the social services agency reached an impasse with Perkins, it filed the petition to commit Perkins to Western State.

Officials in the hospital's geriatrics ward, where Perkins was sent August 19, said the institution tries to group patients according to similarity of problems, but that it was possible that Perkins encountered some patients with "active psychoses."

Director Hobart Hanson said, "It would not be at all unusual for a person of above average intelligence to resent being placed with people who have more severe problems."

Hanson said Western State is not a dead-end for a geriatric patient. After treatment, one-half to three-quarters of all new geriatric admissions return to their homes, if they have them, or are placed in an environment less restrictive than the hospital, he said.

Aged patients who have problems of memory or wandering—symptoms that witnesses at Perkins' first hearing said he showed—can make progress through "attitude therapy," Hanson said.

"Frequently it's a matter of reorientation," he said. "It's surprising that if you can get people back into a routine, how this often has an effective impact on their behavior."

Leaving his client at Fairfax Hospital this week, Downs paused in the corridor of the emergency ward and said, "It's kind of scary. This could happen to you or me."

Questions 10.1

1. **The attorney defending Mr. Perkins called the case "the toughest ethical dilemma I've ever been in." Discuss the ethics involved. What is the source of the dilemma?**

2. **On what do you think Mr. Perkins based his defense against commitment to the state hospital for the mentally ill?**

3. **Discuss the services available to Mr. Perkins and their appropriateness or inappropriateness in his case.**

4. **As a human-service worker with the elderly, what service(s) would you recommend for Mr. Perkins? Defend your choice(s).**

READING 10.2

The Elderly: Prisoners of Fear
This article dramatizes one area of victimization in which the elderly are particularly vulnerable.

When they go out—if they go out—they listen anxiously for the sound of footsteps hurrying near, and they eye every approaching stranger with suspicion. As they walk, some may clutch a police whistle in their hands. More often, especially after the sun sets, they stay at home, their world reduced to the confines of apartments that they turn into fortresses with locks and bars on every window and door. They are the elderly who live in the slums of the nation's major cities. Many are poor. White or black, they share a common fear—that they will be attacked, tortured or murdered by the teen-age hoodlums who have cooly singled out old people as the easiest marks in town. Except in a few cases, police statisticians do not have a separate category for crimes against the elderly. But law-enforcement officials across the nation are afraid that such crimes may be growing in number and becoming more vicious in nature. *Time* correspondents surveyed the plight of the elderly in three cities. Their reports:

New York: Charlie's Anguish. The couple inched painfully from Fordham Road into a wasteland of The Bronx. Clinging to each other for support, the old man and woman mounted a curb and struggled for a moment while she regained her balance. Then, slowly, they went on. Watching them shuffle into the shadows of late afternoon, Detective Donald Gaffney sighed heavily and said, "There goes prime meat."

In other rundown sections all over New York City, the elderly are indeed prime targets. Their chief tormentors are young thugs, who have even mugged a 103-year-old woman, stealing from her a couple of dollars' worth of groceries. In Gaffney's district, about 97% of the offenders are black, and 95% of the victims are white women—usually Jews who have stubbornly stayed on in once comfortable apartments while the neighborhood deteriorated around them. "Fagin wouldn't last up here for half an hour," said Gaffney. "He'd be calling us."

The blacks prey primarily on the whites not for racial reasons but because they are convinced that the old people have money stashed away somewhere—hidden in old shoe boxes, tucked under mattresses. The young hoods operate in raiding teams of three or four, or as many as ten. Typically, they have a morning "shape-up" in a local schoolyard to plan what they call a "crib job," because it is as easy as taking money from a baby.

The team will send its youngest, most innocent-looking member, often an eleven- or twelve-year-old, into a bank to spot a likely victim: a woman, say, who is cashing a money order or a Social Security check. When she leaves the building, only one member of the gang will follow her closely so as not to arouse her suspicions. The others trail far behind. When she gets into the elevator in her apartment house, two or three will catch up and board it with her and get off at the floor below hers. Then as she unlocks her door, they will suddenly appear in the corridor and shove her inside the apartment.

If threats do not succeed in producing valuables, one member of the gang will beat her—often someone under the age of 16 and thus a juvenile in the eyes of the law. The rights of juveniles are so well protected that it is next to impossible to send them away for any length of time. About 75% of the juveniles apprehended in The Bronx and brought into family court have been arrested before and let go, frequently several times over. Knowing how weak the laws are, many elderly victims refuse to prosecute their attackers, fearing that the hoodlums will soon be back on the street and might pay them a second and even more vicious call.

As a result, old people—black and white alike—live like prisoners in the decaying sections of the city. One woman was even afraid to put out her trash; she stuffed it in plastic bags, which she stored in a spare room. When one room would fill up, she would seal it off and start filling up another. At times she lived on candy bars, tossing coins out of a window to children who would go to the store for her. Visiting The Bronx, a reporter from the *New York Times* talked to Clara Engelmann, 64, who had moved her bed into the foyer of her apartment and slept fully dressed so she could dash out the door the next time someone tried to break into her bedroom—which had happened three times before. "They're not human," she cried. "They're not human."

To try to cope with the special problems of the elderly, New York police have set up senior citizen robbery units in all five boroughs. One of the units' main jobs is to persuade old people to bring charges against their attackers. The police make special arrangements to eliminate the tedium and confusion of court appearances. Detectives also lecture groups of old people on how to survive in the city (e.g., don't go home if you think you're being followed—find a cop). In addition, the police have created a few "safe corridors" for the elderly: thoroughfares in shopping districts that are heavily patrolled. Civic-minded youths, mostly high school students, have helped further by volunteering to escort old people to stores and social clubs.

The police are convinced that some progress is being made; but it is painfully slow. So far this year, although some 600 apartment robberies have been investigated in The Bronx, only 82 arrests have been made. Voluntary agencies do what they can to ease the plight of the elderly, but the scope of the problem is overwhelming.

Time Correspondent Mary Cronin last week paid a visit to the victim of one of the hundreds of robberies that are still unsolved. Charles Bertsch, 87, is a huge, hearty man who lives with a dozen cats in a cluttered Bronx basement apartment that he has occupied since 1911. The once prosperous neighborhood is now an age-blackened slum of begrimed apartment buildings lining rubbish-choked streets.

One morning Bertsch opened the door to let out Peggy, his dog, for her regular 10 A.M. walk. Says he: "The next thing I knew, I was here on the floor. Eight Puerto Ricans piled in and started hitting me with broom handles. They hit poor Peggy on the head with a hammer. They picked through this drawer and found $60 worth of quarters. Then one of them bent over me with a knife, holding it to my throat. 'Shall I kill him now?' he asked another guy. And the other guy said, 'No, the boss doesn't want him hurt.' "

They left Bertsch on the floor, his cats meowing around him. "Peggy was washing my face with her tongue," he recalls. It was 6 P.M. before he was able to struggle to his feet.

Now Charlie Bertsch, no longer so hearty and outgoing, has turned his place into a fortress. The day after the attack, Detective Gaffney came over with a load of plywood and, at Bertsch's request, nailed up all the windows. "That'll keep people from throwing fire bombs in," said Bertsch. He rarely goes out, getting food deliveries from a delicatessen, paying by check. Next year, he says, he plans to move. "There is no law here," said Charlie Bertsch. "I'm even afraid for the police."

Chicago: "Where Can I Live?" On the South Side, old people in the ancient apartment buildings look out of their windows early in the month, when the Social Security checks are arriving, and see the knots of young toughs keeping watch. On the West Side, gatherings of the elderly break up by 4 P.M. so that everyone can get home before dark. Walter Bishop, 72, a retired dry-cleaning worker, remembers how "on nice days and nights we used to take strolls and walks and things. Now I wouldn't go anywhere without a car. And after dark I don't go any place."

According to a recent survey by the Chicago Planning Council on Aging, 41% of the city's 518,000 residents over 60 feel that crime is their most serious concern. "Statistically speaking," says Robert J. Ahrens, director of the Mayor's office for senior citizens, "the elderly aren't victims of crime more often than other age groups. But the effects are much more severe. If a young woman is knocked down during a purse snatching, she gets up with a few bruises. If an

80-year-old woman is knocked down, she could suffer a broken hip, have to enter a nursing home, and risk losing her independence."

That is exactly what happened to one 72-year-old woman. A year ago, neighbors found her lying in her bathtub, blood clotted on her head, a stocking twisted around her neck, and her arms trussed behind her. She had lain there for two days. The next day, the doctors amputated one arm; recently they had to remove the other.

Some elderly people fight back. Not long ago, Gertrude Booker, 75, wrestled a husky teen-age purse snatcher to the ground before she decided that her pocketbook, which contained only bus fare, really was not worth fighting for. Jane Gilbert, 70, has taken karate lessons, and is determined to go out after dark, although she has been held up twice.

The residents of a public-housing project in a decaying area known as "Uptown" live under siege. Like combat soldiers, they recount story after story of how their friends have fallen victim to attacks; a deaf woman in her 90's who was mugged and cut on her forehead, another neighbor who broke a hip when she was knocked to the ground. Ann Lewis, 77, a spirited white-haired widow, was recently knocked down right in front of the main entrance to the project by two twelve-year-olds and dragged by her purse strap. "The fright has gone to my stomach," she said. "I'm scared. But I can't afford to live any place else. Tell me, where can I go? Where can I live?"

Oakland: The 17¢ Slaying. At first glance, everything looks quite normal. The rows of frame or stucco houses are cheerfully painted, the hedges neatly trimmed, the yards well kept, the whole neighborhood clean and tidy in the warm afternoon sun. But where are all the people? The streets are virtually deserted, the blinds drawn, the casement windows fortified with heavy iron gates. The section is an enclave in the slums of East Oakland, and the houses, owned mostly by elderly retirees, are preyed upon by teen-age thugs.

There is no explaining the cruelty of some attacks. Hildur Archibald, 91, probably did not see well enough to identify the assailant who invaded her home in July, and she surely did not have enough strength to resist. She was found lying on the floor of her bedroom, dead of multiple knife wounds. Robbery was the apparent motive, yet police confess they are not sure what was taken.

Elsie McIntosh, 72, was walking beside her apartment building last month when a 16-year-old boy ran past and grabbed her purse. She was knocked to the ground, injuring her head. Four hours later she was dead. Her pocketbook had contained 17 cents.

By dogged work, Oakland Police have managed to put away a score of the members of one black gang, Wolfpack I, that systematically terrorized East Oakland's residents last winter. But most of the dozen or so raiders who were under 18 when they were convicted will probably be back on the street within a few weeks, because of relatively light sentences.

"It's a sad commentary that the only way of stopping crime is locking up the offenders," says Howard Janssen, 33, a deputy district attorney of Alameda County. "But there are now only two solutions: letting them run wild and hurt more people, or locking them up." Given that choice, the elderly in Oakland—and other major cities—would have no trouble picking the solution.

Questions 10.2

1. Discuss the legal problems involved in crimes against the elderly as described in this article. Is there an advocacy stance a human-service worker can take?

2. What are some social consequences of the problem?

3. What services are currently offered to help the elderly?

4. Legislative solutions to this problem are distant solutions to an immediate problem. As a human-service worker with the elderly, what service(s) would you recommend to solve or alleviate this problem immediately? Defend your choice(s).

chapter 11
advocacy on behalf
of the elderly

Since older people have low status in our society, frequently they do not receive a share of available community resources and services. Those working with older people and the elderly themselves must act to ensure that appropriate resources are allocated for them. This chapter examines the need to advocate with and on behalf of the elderly. The various ways those working with the elderly can advocate for older clients and ways older people can advocate in their own behalf are discussed.

Why We Need Advocacy

With the civil rights movement of the 1960s, we became keenly aware of the need to ensure that disadvantaged groups in our society are given fair and just treatment. Older people are often treated in a manner that violates their basic civil and human rights. Older adults are extremely vulnerable, as they feel individually responsible for their status at this time in life and thus are not likely to challenge agencies or individuals that deal with them in an unjust or unfair manner. Therefore, in 1976 the Federal Council on the Aging reaffirmed, in a Bicentennial Charter for Older Americans, the following basic human rights for older Americans:

1. The right to freedom, independence and the free exercise of individual initiative. *This should encompass not only opportunities and resources for personal planning and managing one's life style but support systems for maximum growth and contributions by older persons to their community.*

2. The right to an income in retirement which would provide an adequate standard of living. *Such income must be sufficiently adequate to assure maintenance of mental and physical activities which delay deterioration and maximize individual potential for self-help and support. This right should be assured regardless of employment capability.*

3. The right to an opportunity for employment free from discriminatory practices because of age. *Such employment when desired should not exploit individuals because of age and should permit utilization of talents, skills and experience of older persons for the good of self and community. Compensation should be based on the prevailing wage scales of the community for comparable work.*

4. The right to an opportunity to participate in the widest range of meaningful civic, educational, recreational and cultural activities. *The varying interests and needs of older Americans require programs and activities sensitive to their rich and diverse heritage. There should be opportunities for involvement with persons of all ages in programs which are affordable and accessible.*

5. The right to suitable housing. *The widest choices of living arrangements should be available, designed and located with reference to special needs at costs which older persons can afford.*

6. The right to the best level of physical and mental health services needed. *Such services should include the latest knowledge and techniques science can make available without regard to economic status.*

7. The right to ready access to effective social services. *These services should enhance independence and well-being, yet provide protection and care as needed.*

8.   The right to appropriate institutional care when required. *Care should provide full restorative services in a safe environment. This care should also promote and protect the dignity and rights of the individual along with family and community ties.*

9.   The right to a life and death with dignity. *Regardless of age, society must assure individual citizens of the protection of their constitutional rights and opportunities for self respect, respect and acceptance from others, a sense of enrichment and contribution, and freedom from dependency. Dignity in dying includes the right of the individual to permit or deny the use of extraordinary life support systems.*

We pledge the resources of this nation to the ensuring of these rights for all older Americans regardless of race, color, creed, age, sex or national origin, with the caution that the complexities of our society be monitored to assure that the fulfillment of one right, does not nullify the benefits received as the result of another entitlement. We further dedicate the technology and human skill of this nation so that later life will be marked in liberty with the realization of the pursuit of happiness.

Those working with older people are frequently confronted with clear violations of their clients' basic rights. For example, older people may be denied services because they do not provide information requested by an agency, but at the same time they are not offered assistance in supplying the needed information. In nursing homes the elderly are frequently treated in an inhumane manner by personnel. They are also evicted at times without advance notice or due process. All these examples are incidents where the rights of the older person have been violated. In such cases, if the older person is unable to act in his or her own behalf, a worker must act as an advocate to protect the client's interests.

Moreover, lawmakers and public officials often forget the needs of older members of the population when proposing new programs and services for the community or state. They also lose sight of the fact that certain provisions or laws may have an adverse effect or create hardships for older citizens. Public officials must be reminded periodically of the needs of the older constituents in the community through advocacy by those acting for the elderly or by the elderly themselves.

Advocating for Older People

An **advocate** is one who defends, promotes, or pleads a cause. In this role the worker acts as a partisan in a social conflict and uses professional expertise in the interest of the older client. In the traditional advocate role the social worker acts as a representative for the individual client or family, fighting the client's battle with the agency. The ultimate goal, however, is that of showing the client how to fight the battles effectively.

Traditionally, advocacy has taken a personal approach, where the worker attempts to fight for relief of individual clients. In recent years the advocacy role has expanded so that the worker is one who also attempts to change the system. With the broader approach to advocacy, the individual's problem is seen in light of the social and political system that produced it, and in fighting for the cause that the individual client represents, the advocate takes on a prolonged, broader battle that may eventually lead to relief for many. Both approaches may be needed as you work with older people.

Understanding How to Act
as an Advocate

Advocating for older people involves a series of activities similar to those discussed in Chapter 5 as a problem-solving process: gathering information about the client's problem, making a decision about the type of assistance needed, determining how assistance will be provided, and providing the required assistance. The crucial aspect of the process for advocacy rests in the worker's ability to recognize a situation in which advocacy is required. To recognize such instances, the worker needs a solid background in civil rights legislation, welfare laws, housing laws, mental-health laws, and the like. The worker must understand that, in addition to denial of the right to services or of due process, dehumanizing treatment, where agency employees attempt to strip a client of dignity by needling, teasing, or humiliating through name-calling or derogatory remarks also violates civil rights. Another type of inhumane treatment may involve cross-cultural misunderstandings, in which workers of a predominantly white culture ignore or deliberately misunderstand behavior of ethnic or minority elderly and belittle ethnic approaches.

Once a worker has identified a situation that may call for advocacy, a plan of action must be developed in order to deal with the problem. A crucial decision is determining the level at which one should intervene for or with the client. Sometimes the only action needed is to reprimand or remind the worker of the rights of the elderly client; in other instances it may be necessary to call the incident to the attention of the agency's administrator. If this is not effective, it may then be necessary to initiate agency grievance procedures or even legal action.

In dealing with individual advocacy situations, the worker must also determine whether the individual case has ramifications of a broader nature and whether the older person might be better served by tackling the broader issue. For example, insufficient income is a problem facing a large proportion of the elderly population today. When confronted by older people with such a problem, workers frequently attempt to get temporary assistance. If an older person cannot pay for utilities, rent, or food, the worker is inclined to get some agency to pay the bill to relieve the immediate need. But the problem will remain the same next month and the next. Temporary assistance is a possible solution, but it is not a position of advocacy.

In a position of advocacy the worker should address the question of older people's being denied the right to overall well-being or a safe and secure life in old age. The worker must want to begin a concerted effort to lobby for higher income provisions for older people. Rather than dealing with an immediate problem, the worker is aiming for a long-range goal, which may involve legislative and policy change.

Developing a Strategy for Advocacy

Development of a strategy or plan is essential to success for advocacy. The worker and everyone involved should have a clear understanding of the goal and the means through which the goal will be achieved. A strategy involves the selection of techniques to be used in the approach to advocacy. For example, in order to bring about change, an advocate may begin by using a case conference to demonstrate an unfair law or policy, then move in turn to an interagency committee, a coalition, direct contact with elected officials, and finally to demonstration and protest. The strategy is to gather a broader and broader base of support as one moves through the advocacy process. Very often it may not be necessary to use the final technique, but it should be made clear to all involved that the extreme may be necessary in order to bring about change.

The above plan suggests that time is on the side of the advocate. However, those attempting to help older people may learn at the last minute that a piece of legislation that is detrimental to the good of older people is being considered and will come up for a vote in a few days or even the next day. In this case, it may be necessary to employ dramatic or drastic action quickly to influence the legislative vote. Public outcry in the media and protest demonstrations may be the only way to deal with such a situation.

In developing a strategy the worker must be conscious of factors such as timing, the commitment of those involved, and the strength of the adversary. In attempting to serve as an advocate on behalf of older people, the worker should keep in mind the following:

1. *Make an accurate diagnosis of the problem and form an effective strategy.* Mobilize allies and check to make sure you are not duplicating efforts being made by others.

2. *Know the system you are dealing with.* For example, find out about the welfare laws, the ins and outs of the rent control office, and landlord–tenant laws.

3. *Locate resources.* For example, be cognizant of legal services, legislators, citizens' groups, and sympathetic individuals within the bureaucracy.

4. *Weigh the risks* to yourself, your agency, and the individual. Plan to protect the most vulnerable from paying too high a price for too small a gain.

5. *Work for cooperation and voluntary change but be prepared for confrontation* if this alternative becomes necessary. Learn to work constructively with anger, hostility, and resistance.

6. *Don't get discouraged.* Change takes a long time. As you think you are making progress, other events will precipitate even more crises. The only rationale for continuing is that there is value in the struggle, and the ultimate end is worth the struggle.

Techniques Available
to the Advocate

A wide variety of techniques are available to the worker who engages in advocacy. The selection of which specific technique to use in an advocacy situation is complex. Many factors should be considered, such as the nature of the problem, the objectives of the worker, the nature of the adversary, the degree of conflict in which the worker wants to become involved, and the effectiveness of the technique. It is generally possible to use more than one of the techniques identified by Panitch (1974) listed below to address a problem that requires advocacy:[1]

1. *Study and survey.* The systematic gathering of information about the problem and sharing it with others is an important first step in advocacy for the elderly. The information obtained from such studies is generally applicable to other techniques of advocacy, as well as for educational and publicity purposes.

2. *Expert testimony.* Social workers as professionals and as representatives of their agencies can testify at public hearings and in political arenas—for example, legislative sessions, committee meetings, or special sessions. Workers very often have pertinent information about the magnitude of the problem and the injustice existing in current laws and policies that affect older people.

3. *Case conferences with other agencies.* If the worker learns that clients of a particular agency are being badly treated, a case conference with the worker, supervisor, and/or administrator of the agency can be requested to explain the problem. The goal of such a conference is to elicit information that may help clarify why the problem exists and to explore measures that can be taken to discontinue such treatment of clients.

[1] Adapted from *Social Work*, vol. 19 (May 1974), pp. 330–331. Copyright 1974 National Association of Social Workers, Inc. Used by permission.

4. *Interagency committees.* This technique is similar to the case conference in that agencies may bring up specific cases that are indicative of problems entailed in services provided by an agency. One of the advantages of this technique is that such a committee can be influential through peer pressure in getting other agencies to alter practices that are harmful to clients. This technique also makes agencies aware of potential problem areas for clients.

5. *Education.* Public education through the media is another technique that can be used to aid older people. Consciousness raising through meetings, panels, exhibitions, and press conferences can make the general public aware of problems confronting older adults. This technique can also be used to educate a target segment of the population about the issues.

6. *Position taking.* Taking a public stand on issues can have both internal and external advantages, as the worker or agency goes on record with regard to the issue. This technique also lets clients know where the agency stands on the issue and, in effect, provides moral support for them. Very often such stands can be communicated without cost on the radio or television or they can go on public record at meetings or in the agency's minutes.

7. *Appeal.* Most governmental units have procedures for reviewing decisions made by their representatives or employees. However, very often clients are not aware of such procedures, or they may be intimidated by testifying. With this technique the worker helps clients initiate an appeal and then acts as their advocate or defender at the actual hearing. If the appeals procedure does not satisfy the demands of the client and the worker, the next step may be to take the matter to court.

8. *Direct contact with officials and legislators.* Many times agencies can provide information about community problems for public officials. Agencies can have individual or group meetings with legislators on a regular basis in order to keep them abreast of current issues that affect agency clients. Individuals who serve in this capacity often are sought out by legislators when they have questions about upcoming laws and policies affecting older clients. In many cases these individuals have an indirect influence on bringing about change.

9. *Coalition groups.* An agency may become part of an ad hoc group committed to specific goals. The advantage of this technique is that it makes a specific agency less vulnerable to direct attack yet shows the community a cohesive group that supports a particular goal. Such coalition groups may become lobbying groups on behalf of the older client.

10. *Client groups.* With this technique the agency or the worker helps the clients organize in order to fight their own battles and acts as a consultant to the group, providing them with technical assistance and expert knowledge. It is very impor-

tant that a leader be found among the elderly who can act as a spokesperson for the group. It may be helpful if the group identifies other client groups in the community with a similar cause and forms coalitions around common issues.

11. *Petitions.* Circulating a document within the community is a means of obtaining the supportive signatures of the general population. Petitions are a way of informing the general public about the issue and showing officials that there is public support for it. Often volunteer private citizens who believe in the cause will circulate such petitions. In addition, it may be advisable to publish such petitions in the local newspaper to call attention to the issue and to make the public at large aware of the stand of a number of citizens in the community.

12. *Persistent demands.* This technique involves bombarding officials and legislators with letters, telephone calls, telegrams, and visits, and going beyond the usual channels of appeal. This tactic stays within the limits of the law, but it may verge on harassment or other extralegal means.

13. *Demonstrations and protests.* Marches, sit-ins, vigils, picketing, and the like are forms of nonviolent direct action public demonstrations. This technique should only be used with the full sanction and support of the agency. Those participating should be aware of the potential consequences of being part of such activity such as lay-off, eviction, or arrest.

Preparing Older People
to Act as Advocates

As we stated above, in the traditional role of advocate the worker acts as a representative of the client, but the ultimate goal is to show clients how to fight their own battles. The civil rights movement of the early 1960s and the welfare rights movements of the late 1960s demonstrate that client groups can advocate effectively in their own behalf and sometimes are more effective than professionals in bringing about change.

Civil disobedience, demonstrations, and "challenging the system" are seen by some as activities of the younger generation. This is no longer true. Ralph Nader, the consumer advocate, maintains "all over the country, older people are beginning to question their powerlessness and their exclusions. Common grievances such as inflation, consumer fraud, unfair taxation and poor medical care are forging a common consciousness of how powerful they could be if they united around these causes" (1977).

Older people are beginning to organize, voice their own concerns, and take action aimed at changing the laws in their own behalf. A classic example of such activity is the Gray Panthers, under the leadership of Maggie Kuhn, a national effort at advocacy for older people. Similar efforts are going on at the state and local levels.

Older people can become involved in advocacy in a number of ways. They can advocate in their own behalf, they can be trained to serve as advocates for other people, and, finally, they can become part of a coalition group whose goal is to influence legislators and other public officials in order to uphold and protect the rights of older citizens.

Organizing Older Adults

Older individuals must be brought together for the purpose of engaging in advocacy. The first step is to make them collectively aware of the need to become advocates through information calling this need to their attention. Older people can be informed through the media, town meetings, individual contacts, or talks given to organized groups of older people, such as senior centers, neighborhood centers, religious groups, and so on. Activity of this nature serves two purposes. It informs older people of their right to advocate as citizens and makes them aware of the need to act as a group.

The next step is attempting to bring individual older people together to discuss the issue of advocacy, for example, at a general meeting held in the community. The time, place, and purpose of such a meeting can be announced in the paper or when effort is being made to make older people aware of their potential role as advocates. Another approach would be to work through an existing group of older adults or through a coalition of groups. One of these groups can sponsor a meeting, inviting nonmembers to come and discuss the issue of older people's becoming involved in advocacy.

Once the elderly are brought together as a group, efforts must be made to get their collective commitment to the cause or to an advocacy stance. Some older people may not agree with this type of activity, while others will be supportive; a consensus either for or against becoming advocates must be elicited from the group. If the consensus is against, then the group will probably disband. If the group is for such action, they must then begin to develop a formal structure with identified spokespeople or a leader. The group may decide to elect officers and establish a committee structure in order to function effectively.

From this point on the function, purpose, and tasks of the group revolve around deciding on the issues or concerns for which they will advocate and the development of plans and strategies for making their positions heard.

Teaching Older People
How to Advocate

Once a group of older people have organized to become involved in advocacy, the worker's role becomes one of facilitator through consultation and teaching. The worker no longer advocates for the group but helps the group act in their own behalf. However, the worker probably has special knowledge that will be of assistance to the group, and it should be shared with them through an educational or consultation process. If the worker does not have the expertise or knowledge required to educate older individuals about how to become advocates, then it is his or her responsibility to locate resource people within the community who can do this and to coordinate such activity.

Older adults participating in advocacy should have a clear understanding of their civil rights as citizens of the United States and respective states of residence. They should also understand clearly the political structure of the state and national government and how contact can be made with legislators and other public officials. In addition, they need to know how to assess the strength of the opposition, how best to get their position heard, and how to apply pressure in order to obtain action.

As we have suggested, strategy is a key factor in bringing about change, and older advocates should be schooled in the art of strategy development. An effective way of teaching this skill is through simulation; that is, role-playing or acting out various strategies or approaches to problem resolution. If older people are to be successful as advocates, they need the kind of preparation that will enable them to succeed.

Older advocates must understand that success is not always possible when one enters the political arena. However, if they are well schooled, they should be able to gauge the likelihood of an activity's success or failure and weigh this in light of the long-term or short-term goals of the group. Success in bringing about change is not always the measure of successful advocacy. Gains may be achieved even with failures, for, if nothing else, public officials and others are made aware of dissent or counteropinions of older voters. Such knowledge may be the foundation for future successes in attempting to effect change for the elderly.

Summary

In this chapter we have provided some ideas about how workers can advocate for older clients and how older people can be helped to advocate in their own behalf. Two readings follow that demonstrate the changing attitudes of older people toward advocacy and illustrate how the elderly are beginning to fight back.

READING 11.1

Elderly in Bronx Monitor the Youth Offender Cases / Judith Cummings

This report could be regarded as a sequel to the report on youth crime against the elderly in Chapter 10. Judith Cummings describes one elderly group's response to this problem.

A group of elderly Bronx residents, convinced that youths charged with violent attacks on old people are getting lenient treatment in the city's courts, has organized a "case-watch" in Bronx courtrooms to determine whether any corrective measures can be taken in the criminal justice system.

They hope to generate stricter treatment of offenders through, they say, the systematic study they are making of how the criminal justice system fails to serve the elderly. The findings from their courtroom monitoring are to be used as documentation in their campaign to encourage overhaul of the system.

The decision to take collective action originated, leaders of the group said, in "spontaneous outrage" last fall over the robbery-beating of an 82-year-old Parkchester woman, charges to which 19-year-old Ronald Timmons pleaded guilty last week. His sentencing is scheduled for April 12.

"The laws are too lenient—for them, not for us," declared Ella Goldstein, an elderly Parkchester resident who has spent long hours in Bronx Supreme Court as a project volunteer.

"They can walk the streets," she said of youths who she feels are too quickly released despite charges that they have mugged and beaten elderly victims. "We can't."

She added, "We're afraid."

The presence of old people carefully noting courtroom developments and comparing notes has stirred a controversy in legal circles. Defense lawyers and others are questioning whether the open monitoring unfairly influences convictions, sentencing, bail and other courtroom decisions.

"Chilling Effect" Feared

Richard Gotkin, attorney for Mr. Timmons during pretrial hearings before his guilty plea, petitioned unsuccessfully to have the 12 to 20 elderly men and women who daily monitored the court barred from the jury phase, or, to at least, have them seated separately around the courtroom to "present a more natural appearance."

Mr. Gotkin puts it this way: "To have a particular group of people taking notes in unison, their heads bobbing up and down in unison, could have a chilling effect on juries."

The Bronx volunteers, led by a former Board of Corrections lawyer and sponsored by the East Bronx Council on Aging, were observed daily during the Timmons case sitting in the spectator benches of Justice Joseph P. Sullivan's court, taking lengthy notes on proceedings.

The project has so far participated in four cases in state Supreme and Bronx Criminal Court, none of which has reached a jury.

"I take down everything the attorneys and the judge say, as long as they don't repeat themselves," said Ann Rynn, a cheerful red-haired woman, who is a member of Parkchester's Project HAND senior center, the Helping Aged Needing Direction office that provides most of the pool of 70 volunteers.

William Arnone, the lawyer who is the director of Project HAND and organizer of the monitoring project, said he instructs the monitors to take special note of actions bearing on bail setting, plea-bargaining, exclusion of old people from juries, and "the whole question of delays—which is really an attempt to take advantage of the age of the witnesses, that they will expire or just become frustrated and give up."

He has devised a dozen simplified forms for the monitors to use, for "felony arraignment," "pretrial conference" and other proceedings. At day's end the volunteers, whose numbers in court shrink to two or three during jury selection and other less active phases, return to the bustling Parkchester center for the elderly above a bowling alley on Metropolitan Avenue and go over their notes.

"They've got to change the laws for these juveniles, definitely," said Ann DuBall. Like most of the monitors, she said she was not afraid of being marked as a target for possible retaliation.

"In that case, it's especially worth going out for," she said.

By arrangement with the Police Department's Bronx Senior Citizens Robbery Unit, the group receives immediate notice of any crime against a person 60 years old or older within the 43d Precinct.

In their largest turnout to date, 50 of them showed up last month for the sentencing of a High Bridge man, outside their region. Mr. Arnone said the turnout came at the request of the assistant district attorney prosecuting the case. But the prosecutor, a first assistant district attorney named Bruce H. Goldstone, said it was at their own initiative.

"Criminal Cowards"

The defendant, 22-year-old Benjamin Underwood, who was described by District Attorney Mario Merola as a "black belt karate expert," was given a maximum 10-to-30 year sentence by Justice Ivan Warner in a $6 mugging that involved fracturing an 83-year-old woman's jaw.

Leaders and members of the project said they were heartened when Justice Warner, at the sentencing, read to the crowded courtroom a statement calling such offenders "criminal cowards" and asking: "How much longer do we have to live in a jungle?"

Justice Warner, in an interview, said he would have given the same sentence with or without the presence of the 50 elderly persons. Noting that courtrooms are public places, he said that he welcomed the expression of community interest and suggested that more such activities could stimulate broader social action.

He added:

Maybe people will start asking other questions, for example, "We're sending this kid to jail, but what about his brother who's still on the street wandering around with no job, no school?" Maybe it will result in some public awareness and get something done.

"Improper Effect"

Justice Sullivan, in turning aside Mr. Gotkin's objections, also expressed a reluctance to restrict what he referred to as "the public's right to know." He added, nonetheless, that he reserved the right to reverse his position after a jury was seated, if it seemed necessary.

Richard Klein, a Legal Aid lawyer interested in the emerging issue, said the picture presented by large numbers of elderly people before juries was "likely to have a substantial and improper effect."

"The point is you see lots of people in the courtroom and one is bound to be sympathetic," he said. "The jury is there to see that that case is looked at fairly and objectively, and not to hold that individual defendant responsible for all the crimes against old people in the city."

The elderly volunteers have applied to several foundations for funds, according to Mr. Arnone, and to the Federal Law Enforcement Assistance Administration for $130,000 to set up a staffed office in the Parkchester community, to be identified by a sign saying, "Attack on Crimes Against the Elderly," the official name of the project.

"We want to make this a very visible effort by a community that's just had enough on this issue," he said.

Questions 11.1

1. In this example all of the elderly involved felt their rights were being violated, whether or not they, specifically, were victims of crimes. What rights are they concerned about?

2. Attack on Crimes Against the Elderly (ACATE) uses several advocacy techniques. Discuss these techniques and their effectiveness.

3. ACATE has created some controversy, a healthy sign of effective advocacy. Discuss the various positions taken in the controversy.

4. The ultimate goal of ACATE is overhaul of the criminal justice system. What outcomes do you anticipate as a result of their efforts? Why?

READING 11.2

Nobody (in TV) Loves You When You're Old and Gray / Bill O'Hallaren

Bill O'Hallaren presents here the reactions of some elderly groups to television images of the aged.

Lydia Braggar is the trim, feisty, seventyish Chairwoman of Media Watch, a nation-wide volunteer force created by the Gray Panthers to keep an eye on how television treats senior citizens. The Manhattan-based Mrs. Braggar has a speech she delivers around the country on what the watchers have discovered so far; its key passage is that old people as depicted on television are "ugly, toothless, sexless, incontinent, senile, confused and helpless. . . . Old age has been so negatively stereotyped that it has become something to dread and feel threatened by."

The Panthers, who describe themselves as "a movement, not an organization," have staked out positions on a number of issues of concern to older people (they are vehemently for national health insurance and against compulsory retirement) but it sometimes seems they put particular joy and zest into their struggle to shape television more to their liking.

Maggie Kuhn, the founder and leader of the Panthers, recently appeared on the Johnny Carson show and took the opportunity to give television in general a scolding for its treatment of the old. She then zeroed in on a character Carson portrays called Aunt Blabby, who is television's definitive silly old lady. Miss Kuhn sternly advised Carson that the nation is full of elderly women who aren't dingbats, and she demanded he raise Blabby's level of consciousness immediately. She even gave him a Gray Panthers' T-shirt to remind him of his older, non-senile viewers. So far it hasn't helped. Aunt Blabby is as hopelessly giddy as ever.

The Panthers are joined in their criticism of television's treatment of the old by such groups as the American Association of Retired Persons and the National Council on Aging. The latter has formed a Media Resources Center whose goal is to convince the public that old people aren't all silly, crazy and useless. As part of that task, in February, 1976, the Center set up a two-woman office in Hollywood whose sole purpose is to lobby television's creative community to do a little better by the old.

Helyne Landres, the head of the office, tells every TV executive who will listen that "there are 31 million Americans who are 60 or over, and 25 million of them are healthy, busy, functioning citizens. They aren't in rest homes, they aren't senile, and they have the economic potential to buy $60 million worth of goods and services every year. And that's not bubblegum."

Mrs. Landres and her associate, Nadine Kearns, offer a hotline service for TV writers and producers seeking advice on how to treat older characters. The questions put to them sometimes sound as though the callers were seeking guidance on the lifestyles of some fragile, alien culture. One writer said he was thinking of creating a scene calling for a room full of older folks and wondered if a doctor would have to be on the set. Another was curious if an 80-year-old could possibly rob a bank. Definitely yes, he was told, but Mrs. Landres added, "Please make it clear he was always a bank robber."

Indeed, as Mrs. Kearns explains, "One of our biggest objections is to the idea that people suddenly start doing dumb or terrible things because they are old. We never objected to the "Fernwood flasher" of "Mary Hartman, Mary Hartman" per se. What we didn't like was the implication that he turned flasher because he was old. They should have made clear he was flashing all his life."

"What I would like to see on TV," Mrs. Kearns continues, "is a sex scene in which a 65-year-old man kisses a woman. I don't mean giving a granddaughter a peck on the cheek, I mean kissing a woman because he finds her sexually attractive." She doesn't expect that to happen any time soon, because she is convinced that all a 65-year-old can yearn for on television is a better laxative.

Carson and Carol Burnett are prime targets of the Media Watch, largely because of their acid portraits of doddering ancients. Mrs. Jeanne Schallen, a Los Angeles leader of the Panthers, complains, "I wish Carol would be a little less vicious. She's funny but at terrible expense to the dignity of older people. There's got to be some realistic compromise between Carol's sour puss old lady and dreamy, fantasy Grandma Walton." Ironically, the militants believe that old people are rebuffed most harshly in television's most trivial area: The game shows. Mrs. Landres contends that the game shows by and large not only don't use older contestants but won't even let older people sit in the front rows of the audience. "I have spoken to every game show produced in town and everyone resists. One young woman said, 'Oh, all right, you can bring some of your old people down here and they can watch.' I said, 'They don't want to watch, they want to be contestants.' She acted as though it were the most idiotic request she had ever heard. 'We can't use old people. They're all senile, they talk too much, and they're too slow.' "

The nice old grandmother is a staple of TV commercials, and some critics believe she ought to get lost. Mrs. Landres contends: "The TV grandmother in the commercials is a woman of about 80. Chronologically she's at least a great, great grandmother. A real grandmother could be in her late 30's or 40's." Mrs. Schallen says, "You see these TV grandmothers in 1890s clothing and silly hats all agog over a sink cleaner, it makes you sick." She adds, "I'm 62, my mind never worked better, but when I take a prescription to the druggist, he treats me like an imbecile child. That's the way television has taught him to treat me."

A major complaint by militant oldsters is that when television isn't ridiculing the old, it ignores them. Says Mrs. Schallen, "In commercials, we're buffoons, in programming, we don't exist." Virginia Carter, Vice President of Creative Affairs for Tandem and TAT Productions, the Norman Lear Company, has investigated the subject for her boss, and believes there's validity to the complaint. One survey, she reports, "found that less than one percent of the continuing roles in drama and comedy go to women over 40."

Miss Carter adds: "We didn't know there were organized power centers that reflected the interests of older people, but we found that out in a hurry. There is enormous passion on the part of older people on this subject, and we share their view."

Miss Carter says it's the view of Tandem and TAT that ignoring the old on television isn't even good business: "When we do shows that reflect favorably on the old, we get a very positive response. If you ask any family what their real concerns are, what causes them grief or joy, the concerns of older people are right up there. The young worry about their older parents. The parents worry about their health; their economic survival. It's simply good sense for television to do shows about the concerns of the aged."

Miss Carter isn't worried that television might be knuckling under to still another pressure group. "The passions of people are the raw materials of our shows. When people come through that door spouting and flaming, we listen. If there is one person who is boiling enough to get through the door, there's probably ten million behind him."

There is, however, a worry on the part of some TV decision-makers that any pressure group, however innocently motivated, is a potential danger to free expression. Gordon Van Sauler, CBS's vice-president in charge of program practices, recently told a convention of CBS affiliates in Hollywood that the eventual goal of pressure groups is control of news and that CBS intends to put up a stout resistance. Jay Sandrich, a director for the Mary Tyler Moore company, attended an April seminar at the University of Southern California's Andrus Gerontology Center on the subject of the old and television. He said, "I heard a lot of legitimate complaints, understand how these people feel. But I came away wondering if they aren't really after creative control. I'm not going to have any group tell me what I can do, I won't let any pressure group tell me how to be creative."

Meantime, there are a couple of straws in the TV winds. Lucille Ball is scheduled to return in some specials this coming season in which she will once again be playing Lucy. She feared she was too old for the character and "tried a lot of other things lately, trying to play my age, trying to do something they would believe and buy. Well, they didn't buy it. What the people seem to want is Lucy, so I'm doing Lucy." Score one for 65-year-old comediennes. But another straw blows in a different direction. The movie "Logan's Run" is being adapted as a TV series. It's about a world in which no one lives beyond the age of 30.

Questions 11.2

1. Discuss the advocacy techniques, as listed in this chapter, the various groups of elderly have used and their effectiveness.

2. Controversy has resulted from advocacy pressure. Discuss the various positions taken in the controversy.

3. What are the goals of the advocates in this issue? What outcomes do you anticipate? Why?

4. Class project: Using technique 1, Study and Survey, develop a TV monitoring system that will provide information about TV's treatment of older people. Test the system for a week. How could you use the information obtained for effective advocacy?

PART four

service programs for older people

In order to help older people with their various problems, the worker must know the programs and services available in the community. Many federal, state, and local program. have been created to meet the needs of older people.

In Part Four we review service programs and illustrate how they can be used for specific problems experienced by older adults. We would like to point out that what is presented here i. what currently exists; programs may change over time, and it is the worker's responsibility to keep abreast of these changes.

We attempt in this section to elaborate on three major problem areas discussed in Chapte. 2: economics, physical and mental health, and leisure. Chapters 12, 13, and 14 discuss these problem areas, respectively, and the programs aimed at dealing with each. In addition, specific case examples are provided to illustrate how the worker can deal with the problems presentec to them by older adults.

CHAPTER 12
MEETING THE ECONOMIC NEEDS OF THE ELDERLY: FINANCIAL ASSISTANCE, HOUSING, TRANSPORTATION, EMPLOYMENT, AND TRAINING

Aging and Poverty

There is an almost direct relationship between aging and poverty in American society. A large proportion of the elderly become financially distressed when they grow old because of various factors. Most significant of these factors is retirement, whether mandatory or voluntary. Retirement not only reduces the income of older workers, it also affects their spouses and other dependents. Another cause of poverty among older people is widowhood, which causes financial need for the many women who outlive their husbands or, in fewer cases, husbands who outlive their working wives. Reduced work opportunities and lessened economic power lead to poverty for many.

When retirement or death do not cause economic problems for older people, health problems may; for many older people they are the most important source of financial difficulty. Those who do not use all their resources after retirement purchasing food, clothing, and shelter may use their savings and other funds to pay for medical care.

Financial distress is so common among aging people that many credit firms have automatically canceled charge accounts for customers who have reached age 65. Banks are reluctant to loan money to older adults because of the high incidence of poverty among them. The poverty associated with age is the reason that, in many cases, people first have contact with human-service workers and social welfare agencies when they reach the older years.

Some Typical Cases

There are a variety of typical cases one encounters among older people who face financial deprivation. Although each case of need is unique to the individual who faces it, and each individual feels differently about need than another might, cases of financial deprivation can be grouped into categories and generalized examples. Let us take a look at some fictional but not unusual examples of the kinds of financially needy older people human-service workers are likely to encounter.

Mr. Adams Loses It All   Mr. Adams is an older man who has been self-employed for most of his life. He suffers business or professional reverses and failures at about the same time he wants to or needs to retire. His business failures use up the savings that he has built up over the years, and he is left with only limited support from Social Security.

Mrs. Baker, Too Young and Too Old   Mrs. Baker is a widow whose husband left very little life insurance when he died. She is slightly younger than her husband, too young to collect full Social Security benefits. However, she is too old to begin work and has no work experience, and she has few personal or financial resources to fall back on. Moreover, she is ill herself.

Mr. Croyton and the Disappearing Pension   Mr. Croyton has worked for years in a factory and has built what he thought would be an excellent pension program through his employer's retirement plan. Then he retires and discovers that the funds have been invested in stocks that declined in value or that his money was misspent by officials of the plan. For whatever reason he will have much less money than he had hoped for.

Mrs. Digby's Illness   Mrs. Digby, a widow, has been left a substantial sum from insurance policies her husband purchased early in their marriage. But she develops cancer, which requires extensive surgery, hospital care, posthospital nursing home care, a move to a new house or apartment because she cannot climb the stairs in the house she owns, extensive equipment purchases, large amounts of medicine, and other costs that quickly reduce what appeared to be a sizable estate to nothing.

Mr. Epworth's Permanent Poverty   Mr. Epworth has been relatively poor all his life. Having always earned a marginal income, if any, he does not benefit during his later years from savings, life insurance policies, or social insurance. He is in his mid 60s and likely to be poorer than ever because he is old.

Programs of Financial Aid

The balance of this chapter describes the programs available for assistance to older people with financial problems in terms of the ways the typical cases would be helped by human-service workers.

Helping Mr. Adams

Changing business patterns, changing geography, and the passing of time cause many older businesspeople to have reverses or failures late in their careers. Mr. Adams has lost everything in his business, and the banks will not loan him money to start again, because they fear he may fail again or that he may die before he is able to repay the loan. He and his wife have enjoyed a secure and comfortable middle-class life; suddenly he finds himself in need of help and in contact with human-service agencies.

A human-service worker talking with the Adams couple would first attempt to assess the problems they face. Surely they have some emotional reactions to their new status, and they may well require some of the kinds of counseling discussed in Chapters 7 and 13; group activities, such as those discussed in Chapter 6; leisure-time activities, such as those discussed in Chapter 14; as well as other forms of nonfinancial assistance and support. But their fundamental needs are financial, and they are significant.

It is a principle of effective human-service work to try to help clients overcome their practical, financial problems before trying to deal with personal, emotional problems. It is doubtful that Mr. Adams and his wife can be helped very much with their emotional concerns until they know how they are going to pay for their food, clothing, and shelter. In fact, anxiety about money is their most serious emotional problem.

In what ways might a human-service worker help this older couple?

Social Insurance   The United States has had social insurance since 1935, when Congress passed the U.S. Social Security Act. The Social Security Act is amended almost every year and is certainly a very different program now than when it was first written, but it continues to represent the most important piece of social legislation in the history of the United States. Within it are all the provisions for the federal insurance programs, such as retirement, survivors, and dependents insurance; the public assistance programs; protective and services programs for children; and many other services directly or indirectly beneficial to older people that have been developed by the federal government.

When most people speak about Social Security, they mean the social insurance program. It is financed through the contributions of employers and of employees from wages. The employer pays a certain amount of money into the Social Security account of each employee, and the employee contributes an equal amount to the fund. Programs of this kind are not unique to the United States; virtually every nation of the world has some kind of social insurance program for employed people.

The fundamental idea of the United States social insurance plan is to provide a federal program through which citizens can buy low-cost, federally sponsored insurance against the common catastrophes people face. Because participation is mandatory for almost all employed people, the costs of purchase are very low. It is such a good insurance bargain that many self-employed people, including Mr. Adams, voluntarily participate in it.

The retirement, survivors, and disability insurance does exactly what it says—it ensures that participants will have some money for retirement, that their survivors will have some money to support themselves, and that they themselves will have some money to live on should they become disabled.

Social Security provides a retirement income for men and women who are either workers under the program or spouses of workers under the program when they reach retirement age. It provides benefits to spouses and minor children of participants when they die. It provides financial support for the life of the participant if he or she becomes blind or otherwise physically or mentally disabled. Participants also receive financial assistance to pay for the costs of medical care once they reach retirement age.

The amounts of the contributions and the age one must reach to receive benefits change periodically. Generally, however, the longer one has paid into the plan, the more one receives in benefits upon retirement or disability and the more the family receives upon the participant's death.

Because Mr. Adams had been a participant in the social insurance program and has now reached retirement age, social insurance would be a key resource for him and his wife. The human-service worker would help Mr. Adams apply for his benefits through the Social Security office in his community and, before very long, he would begin receiving monthly checks. If he had paid the maximum amount into the program for a long period of time, and recently, he and his wife could have the basis of a relatively adequate income.

However, social insurance is rarely sufficiently generous to continue a family's preretirement lifestyle. Therefore, most people also have life insurance, other kinds of retirement incomes, or savings, which, together with social insurance, will help them sustain themselves when they retire.

But Mr. Adams was not a compulsory participant in social insurance. If he had never participated, he would not receive any benefits at all. If his payments began only a few years ago, he will not receive very much money now. What can Mr. Adams do if social insurance for retirement purposes is, for any reason, insufficient to cover his and his wife's basic costs for food, shelter, and clothing? Where can he turn for help and what kinds of plans would the human-service worker help him develop? It is likely that the worker would know that retirement insurance through Social Security, even if Mr. Adams has the maximum amount, is sufficient for only a minimal amount of financial support. Therefore, some other resources would have to be explored.

It is likely that the human-service worker would help Mr. Adams compute his total assets to see what he already has. These assets would include, perhaps, his pension or retirement program, his savings, and whole life insurance policies that have built to some cash value. He may also consider limited employment, which is possible for beneficiaries of Social Security up to a specified maximum number of dollars per year.

Supplementary Security Income   If Mr. Adams's social insurance benefits are less than he would ordinarily need for his living expenses, public assistance is available to him. For Mr. Adams it would probably come out of a federal- and state-supported program called Supplementary Security Income (SSI), which has replaced state-provided public assistance or public welfare for older people. It is administered through the Social Security offices and is available to older and disabled people who qualify for assistance. In other words, he and his wife would be given a subsidy from

public assistance funds to make up the difference between his social insurance benefits and the amount of money they need for food, clothing, and shelter. Of course,
there are standard limits set on how much a married older couple needs and is
entitled to receive. The Social Security staff would tell Mr. Adams and his wife what
they are entitled to receive, based upon their circumstances.

Mr. Adams's Social Security retirement benefits would be based upon how much
he paid. His business failures would not affect his Social Security retirement benefits
at all. He could be extremely wealthy and still draw Social Security retirement
benefits; however, to receive Supplementary Security Income, he must demonstrate
financial need. Essentially, Social Security is for all those who participate; Supplementary Security Income is for those who need it, no matter how much or how little
they have paid in taxes in the past.

Disability Benefits and Aid to Families with Dependent Children   If Mr. and Mrs.
Adams had a child who was not employed and was living with the family, they might
be helped by the state public welfare department, which is responsible for providing
services to aged, blind, disabled, and mentally ill adults who do not have sufficient
income. Such a department is also responsible for providing support for dependent
children living in low-income families. Adult public assistance recipients now receive
their money from Supplementary Security Income, described above. However, the
state public welfare departments provide assistance to children, through their families, when they are poor.

If the state government's payments for Aid to Families with Dependent Children
(the name of the program) are more generous than the amount the Adams family
would receive from Social Security retirement funds, the difference between Mr.
Adams's retirement benefits and public welfare payments would be given to him by
the state department. If the Social Security benefits were higher, that is all the family
would receive.

Although most older people do not have dependent children of their own many
older people have young children such as nieces, nephews, grandchildren, or young
adopted children, residing with them. The fact that the child is living in the family
makes the family eligible for the aid program.

*Contrasts between Social Security Retirement, Supplementary Security Income, and
Public Assistance*   There is quite a bit of difference between the retirement benefits
from Social Security and those that are provided by Supplementary Security Income
or Aid to Families with Dependent Children. Those who receive SSI or public assistance funds of any kind must demonstrate that they have a need for help. They must
show that they do not have extensive savings or so much property that they could

convert it to cash for their basic living costs, and they must in other ways prove themselves "eligible." Many human-service workers in Supplementary Security Income and public welfare programs spend most of their time determining the eligibility of applicants for help. Such eligibility must be established very early—certainly before any assistance is provided—and it has to be regularly rechecked and reevaluated.

People have varying attitudes about Social Security retirement benefits and public assistance, too. SSI and public assistance mean that the person is poor, something that many older people find difficult to accept and to admit. Some people think that "welfare" places a stigma on those who receive it. They feel as if they have paid for Social Security retirement but are drawing charity from other citizens if they receive welfare. There is little validity to that distinction, particularly in a case such as Mr. Adams'. His federal and state taxes paid for his public assistance payments just as his Social Security contributions paid for his retirement. But there is a tendency for people not to view things that way. Very wealthy people are able to collect Social Security, but those of even modest means are ineligible for public assistance. One program is for everyone; the other for the poor alone.

Private Insurance and Savings   The human-service worker helping Mr. and Mrs. Adams will want to look through and reevaluate the kinds of life insurance they might have. Many wage earners buy life insurance at an early age in the hope that it will help provide for their retirement years. Mr. Adams is no exception, and the human-service worker, with the help of an insurance expert and perhaps the agent of the company that sold Mr. Adams his policies in the first place, would help him study the provisions of those policies. Many kinds of life insurance provide retirement income if the policyholder does not die first. Of course, some insurance policies—those known as *term*—provide benefits only upon the death of the insured person. But *whole life* or *ordinary life* policies can provide for retirement income as well. They are a form of savings.

Mr. Adams may also have savings accounts in banks or savings and loan associations; he may have stocks and bonds that can provide him with some help in his retirement years; he may have property such as a house, farm, or automobile that could be sold and converted to cash. Then he could use part of the money to purchase, perhaps, a smaller place to live or a less expensive car, and use the balance to pay for rent, food, and clothing.

Each case has to be solved individually, of course. It is an important skill of the human-service worker to help the older person facing financial need to list all assets, discover a variety of ways to best use those assets, and make a long-range financial plan for living satisfactorily within his or her means.

Job Training and Referral   But perhaps Mr. Adams, who may be in good health, would prefer working again to retiring.[1] If he is very old, it may be difficult for him to locate new employment. Even those employers without formal retirement restrictions may be prejudiced against older workers.

On the other hand, some employers prefer older workers, and job opportunities and training programs for older people do exist. Mr. Adams's state employment service will have information about potential employment for older workers as well as training programs for him. Senior centers in Mr. Adams's community may have special projects to locate and place older workers on jobs.

It is possible that Mr. Adams can locate training, part-time employment, or even full-time employment that can help him occupy his time while providing him with part of the income he needs to support himself and his family.

*Mrs. Baker—A Widow Faces
the World of Money*

Let's look now at the second typical case, Mrs. Baker, whose husband has died after losing most of the family savings and the business through which he employed himself for so many years. Mrs. Baker has a special problem—she is fairly young, or at least too young to receive all the benefits Mr. Adams was entitled to. Mrs. Baker is 58, she has never worked, and she has no work skills apart from those of keeping a home and raising a son and a daughter, both of whom are now beginning to establish themselves financially in their own families and careers.

Social Security for Mrs. Baker   Because she is so young and in good health, Mrs. Baker is ineligible for Social Security. All she will receive now is a little money to pay her husband's funeral expenses. Social Security retirement benefits, as well as Medicare under Social Security, cover the widows, widowers, and other survivors of employed people who have paid for Social Security benefits; however, they do not begin until age 60 for widows. The longer Mrs. Baker can delay receiving those benefits the better off she will be, because the payments are reduced for younger people. If she takes the benefits when she is 60 years old, she will receive less than she would receive if she waited until her 62nd birthday. If she waits until she is 65, she will do even better. In any case, Social Security cannot help her between now and age 60.

---

[1] Those 65 and over may work and still obtain Social Security benefits. According to 1978 guidelines distributed by H.E.W., the Department of Health, Education, and Welfare, a person 65 and older can earn $4,000 per year and still get all Social Security benefits. If earnings exceed $4,000, $1 in benefits will be withheld for each $2 earned above that amount. The annual exempt amount will increase to $4,500 in 1979, $5,000 in 1980, $5,500 in 1981, and $6,000 in 1982. Those under 65 can earn up to $3,240 and get benefits. Starting in 1982, there will be no limit on earnings for people 70 or older.

Public Assistance and Supplementary Security Income   The public welfare programs would probably not help her either. Mrs. Baker is an older person, she is a widow, and she needs money. But she is not old enough, nor is she handicapped, and if she does not live in a family with dependent children, there are no categories of public welfare that can help her.

Most state and local governments have assistance programs called General Assistance, which provide help to people who need it but do not meet any of the categories described for the federal public assistance programs. If Mrs. Baker's locality has a program of that sort, it can provide her with assistance until she is old enough to begin receiving Social Security retirement and/or public assistance for older people.

But general assistance programs are often very small and not very generous, because the money comes from local and state rather than federal sources. In most states general assistance payments are meager. They provide a few dollars, a few times, but not the steady pension-type payments that federally funded public assistance and Social Security retirement insurance provides.

Essentially, Mrs. Baker's case represents a gap in the financial support services available for older people. Unless she is sufficiently talented and resilient to enter a job-training program or to find employment with which she can support herself, she has some serious problems to face.

The human-service worker would want to help Mrs. Baker evaluate all of her assets, such as her husband's savings, life insurance benefits, or anything else he might have left to her. Perhaps her children will be able to help her, and perhaps she might live with one of them, although that might mean relocating.

When she becomes eligible for Social Security, Mrs. Baker may also become eligible for Medicare, the medical service insurance provided through Social Security. If she is terribly poor and has little to rely upon, perhaps she can receive Medicaid through the public assistance program, which is available only for people who are eligible—that is, very poor. However, if she becomes ill and there are no other resources, hospital care would probably be provided to her somewhere from public funds or charity hospital services.

However, she may have sufficient funds to continue participating in the family's privately supported health insurance policy. Such policies are sold to groups, such as employees of large organizations or members of professional organizations, by Blue Cross and Blue Shield, major life insurance companies, or special private health insurance companies. Many people receive health insurance coverage as a fringe benefit where they work. Even if they pay for it, they probably pay less than the full cost. After the death of her husband, Mrs. Baker could continue to pay into and receive benefits from his health insurance company. Other families pay for health insurance as individuals rather than as members of groups.

However, if she lives in a rural area where there are no publicly supported health services, if she is too poor to continue the health insurance, and if she is too young for

Medicare when she first becomes ill, the human-service worker may have great difficulty finding anything for her.

Other Resources for Employment and Assistance   Mrs. Baker would probably be referred to the state employment service by the human-service worker to see if there might be a job or job-training program for her. If her physical disability made it impossible for her to be employed without some help and training, her state's vocational rehabilitation program might be another resource to pay for her health care and, if feasible, some training for her. Vocational rehabilitation programs provide services to people who are unemployed because of disabilities. The rehabilitation program, which is supported by federal and state tax funds, is designed to provide the kinds of money, training, and other resources that people might need to make them employable.

There are a number of other resources that the human-service worker can explore for Mrs. Baker if she is ill. Many communities have special transportation to clinics and hospitals for older people; these are sometimes provided by charitable organizations and sometimes by governmental bodies. Home health assistants and visiting nurses can also be a help to a woman in Mrs. Baker's situation by coming to her house, helping her with her housework, making sure she has plenty to eat, and insuring that she follows appropriate medical procedures. These services are provided by public-health departments and a variety of other organizations and institutions.

Essentially, the human-service worker must know about all of the resources in the local community that can help older people.

Mr. Croyden and the
Vanishing Pension

Mr. Croyden is not alone—many American workers find themselves financially disappointed and disadvantaged when they retire, because their pensions are not as large as they had hoped. In some cases the pension funds developed by employers do not perform as well as they should; that is, the funds are invested in ways that do not lead to the kind of growth that had been anticipated. When pension funds are invested in stocks and bonds on the decline, all or most of the money in the fund may disappear as the stocks lose value.

Other causes of reduced pensions have included some criminal acts by pension managers that drained money from pension funds. Some public funds, such as those supported by state and local governments, may promise large pensions to workers, but if the tax receipts are not sufficiently high, the commitments cannot be kept.

Mr. Croyden's problems are relatively common. Human-service workers who work with older, retired people must know about all of the kinds of pensions and retirement plans and must understand that they differ significantly.

Pension Programs   Pension programs are an important economic factor for older people when they retire. Federal tax laws make it possible for individuals who are self-employed to establish their own retirement plans and not pay tax on the money they apply to their pensions when they earn it but rather when they withdraw it. Most people would rather pay taxes on the money they invest in pensions after they retire, when their incomes, and thus their tax rates are lower.

There are great variations among pension plans. Most governments, including the federal, state, and local governments, provide pension programs for their employees. Usually the employee and the employer both contribute a portion of each salary payment to the pension fund. The building up of the principal and interest permits the employee to retire with some income.

In some plans only the employer contributes. In others the pension is only good if the individual is employed by the company or government at the time of retirement, and retiring early or changing jobs before retirement may mean that all or a substantial part of the pension is lost. Some national pension plans are contributed to by both employees and employers and are "vested" to the employee. That is, everything that goes into the employee's account becomes part of his or her retirement program. In other plans the employee puts money into the pension program and can draw the money out upon retirement; however, the employer's part of the pension payments do not go to the employee but, instead, stay in the pension plan or go back to the employer if the employee leaves the organization before retiring.

Some people establish their own "pension fund" by saving money in bonds, stocks, or bank accounts.

The provisions and benefits of retirement plans are so variable that it is impossible to know how much an older person will receive upon retirement without studying the details of his or her retirement plan. Mr. Croyden knows his plan—or at least he thought he knew it until he found that he was about to retire without a pension.

Even though his pension is no longer there, Mr. Croyden probably has Social Security retirement benefits coming to him. They may not be enough for him to live on satisfactorily, but they are something. If his retirement benefits are low enough, perhaps he will also be eligible for Supplementary Security Income.

There are other kinds of aid that will help someone in Mr. Croyden's position. These are aid in the form of subsidies or services rather than cash.

Food Stamps   Older individuals whose incomes are low enough may be eligible for United States government food stamps. Essentially, the food stamps make it possible for people who need help to buy food with government coupons. The amount of food stamps changes periodically and is based upon needs. Because food is such a large item in any person's budget, food stamps are a useful way for individuals with low incomes to stretch the money they have. People can become certified for the stamps through state or local welfare departments.

Public Housing and Rent Subsidies   Mr. Croyden can, perhaps, find public or subsidized housing that will make it possible for him to get along on the limited funds available to him.

Public housing is housing that is owned and operated by governments. Usually federal funds subsidize the construction and operating costs of the housing, which may be run by the local government, the state government, or a private corporation. The rent in public housing is determined by the ability of the renter to pay, so people with little or no income pay very little or no rent. The amount of rent increases with the amount of income.

Public housing programs use large numbers of human-service workers, who help determine the eligibility of people who apply for the housing and conduct outreach, referral, and counseling programs for the housing residents. Other human-service workers organize and direct recreation and leisure-time programs within housing projects. Still others help organize tenant or resident councils that participate in making policy for and otherwise governing the public housing facility.

Most large cities have some form of public housing. Mr. Croyden, with his unexpectedly low income, might benefit significantly from public housing.

Subsidized private housing is owned by individuals or corporations. Usually in the form of apartments or apartment buildings but, in some cases, single family dwellings, this housing is available to low-income people at substantially reduced rents. Government funds, most of them from federal sources, are used to pay part of the rent to the landlord so that the economically needy person can live satisfactorily for affordable rent. Older people are among the primary beneficiaries of subsidized housing, which is available in most communities.

Because housing is such an important part of the budget of most families, public or subsidized housing can make the difference between success or failure for an older adult living on a limited income.

Transportation   Getting to work, getting to recreational services, and otherwise moving around is a significant expense for older people. Even those who are no longer employed need some forms of transportation. Transportation becomes an acute problem for many older adults who sometimes lack the funds, the physical coordination, or the eyesight to drive. For some older people, driving may be unpleasant or unwise. On occasion, they cannot maintain their licenses to drive cars because of health problems. Inadequate transportation can be a major social and economic burden for older people.

One of the biggest problems facing older people is that there are not enough public transportation resources. Transportation between cities and towns has become scarce and in many parts of the nation it is impossible to travel between communities without a private automobile. The railroads, which once carried a large number of passengers, now carry few. For many senior citizens who live in difficult-to-reach areas, taxis are the only reasonable form of transportation, and they are too expensive for most older people, particularly one who has the difficulties Mr. Croyden has.

There are a variety of ways in which transportation services have been provided to older people. Some public transportation systems, such as buses and subways, provide special reduced senior citizen fares during the nonrush hours. These are often an important aid to senior citizens. Some senior centers, departments of welfare, and other organizations serving the elderly provide tokens or other forms of direct subsidy to older people for transportation. Some older adult programs in local communities have developed special transportation programs providing buses, carpools, and other forms of transportation only for older people.

Mrs. Digby—Poverty through Illness

Mr. Adams, Mrs. Baker, and Mr. Croyden suddenly found themselves old and poor. Mrs. Digby began with substantial funds but slowly became poor because she was sick. Many older people who thought they had adequately provided for their financial needs for the rest of their lives become poor because of one or two serious incidents of illness. The health programs such as Medicare and Medicaid do not always pay for all the costs of an illness. Mrs. Digby, who thought she was doing all right, suddenly discovered that she was not yet old enough for Medicare, that she had too much money for Medicaid, and that she was terribly sick. By the time she was through with surgery, hospital bills, medicine, and all of the other things associated with a serious illness, such as the cancer she developed, she was poor—poor enough, in fact, for some of the programs for which her savings and her inheritance made her ineligible before.

Illnesses tend to equalize older adults. Mrs. Digby, who began in relatively good financial condition, suddenly found herself as dependent upon public assistance funds, Social Security retirement benefits, public welfare programs such as Medicaid, home health aids, perhaps public housing, and the other services described above as her less affluent counterparts.

It is very difficult for an older person to be both very ill and very wealthy. Whatever money was available is quickly exhausted. There are limits on the length of time private hospital insurance programs will pay and there are limits on the amount that major medical policies, which can cover catastrophes like cancer, will cover. With no new sources of income, Mrs. Digby's situation cannot improve. It is one of the facts of old age in the United States that illness can wipe out all but the greatest fortunes.

Mr. Epworth and Continuing
Poverty

Ironically, Mr. Epworth may have some advantages over the other cases mentioned here. Because his earnings have always been only marginal, he is likely to have had contacts with financial assistance programs before. He may already know how to ask for and receive help from the public welfare department, vocational rehabilitation, the state employment service, local churches and settlement houses, public housing, or any of the other resources already mentioned. Mr. Epworth is not entitled to any greater service or aid than any of our other hypothetical cases. He does not have as much to fall back on as some of the individuals with savings, private health insurance policies, or their own homes. However, he may have more experience with and less resistance to using public help when he needs it. Now that he finds himself old and in need, the shock of accepting public assistance is somewhat less than it might be for someone who had always been self-sufficient. On the other hand, there may be fewer programs of help available for Mr. Epworth than there were when he had the potential for employment. Being old and poor, even if one is accustomed to it, is often a problem of great magnitude.

Summary

Human-service workers must familiarize themselves with all the resources available to serve the financial needs of older people. They must understand poverty as the typical plight of the older person in American society. Those who are not poor before they grow old may find themselves facing poverty when they do. The causes of that poverty are many, but the result is that the older person must rely upon services and assistance from a variety of sources in order to survive.

The human-service worker helping older people in financial need will want to be aware of every available kind of service—help from family members including children, savings, public service programs, voluntary programs, special housing projects, programs through churches and a multitude of other efforts carried on by various governmental bodies and other institutions to help ease the way of the older financially needy adult.

It should be clear to all human-service workers who work with older adults that financial need is their most common and serious problem. They must expect older people to have financial need uppermost in their minds and must be both willing and able to counsel older people about such needs.

READING 12.1

The Life of Ma Parker / Katherine Mansfield

If this short story were a person, it would be approaching retirement age. Unfortunately, the problems of poverty the author portrays are still very much at work in contemporary society.

When the literary gentleman, whose flat old Ma Parker cleaned every Tuesday, opened the door to her that morning, he asked after her grandson. Ma Parker stood on the doormat inside the dark little hall, and she stretched out her hand to help her gentleman shut the door before she replied. "We buried 'im yesterday, sir," she said quietly.

"Oh, dear me! I'm sorry to hear that," said the literary gentleman in a shocked tone. He was in the middle of his breakfast. He wore a very shabby dressing-gown and carried a crumpled newspaper in one hand. But he felt awkward. He could hardly go back to the warm sitting-room without saying something—something more. Then because these people set such store by funerals he said kindly, "I hope the funeral went off all right."

"Beg parding, sir?" said old Ma Parker huskily.

Poor old bird! She did look dashed. "I hope the funeral was a—a—success," said he. Ma Parker gave no answer. She bent her head and hobbled off to the kitchen, clasping the old fish bag that held her cleaning things and an apron and a pair of felt shoes. The literary gentleman raised his eyebrows and went back to his breakfast.

"Overcome, I suppose," he said aloud, helping himself to the marmalade.

Ma Parker drew the two jetty spears [hatpins made of jet] out of her toque and hung it behind the door. She unhooked her worn jacket and hung that up too. Then she tied her apron and sat down to take off her boots. To take off her boots or to put them on was an agony to her, but it had been an agony for years. In fact, she was so accustomed to the pain that her face was drawn and screwed up ready for the twinge before she'd so much as untied the laces. That over, she sat back with a sigh and softly rubbed her knees. . . .

"Gran! Gran!" Her little grandson stood on her lap in his button boots. He'd just come in from playing in the street.

"Look what a state you've made your gran's skirt into—you wicked boy!"

But he put his arms round her neck and rubbed his cheek against hers.

"Gran, gi' us a penny!" he coaxed.

"Be off with you; Gran ain't got no pennies."

"Yes, you 'ave. Gi' us one!"

Already she was feeling for the old, squashed, black leather purse.

"Well, what'll you give your gran?"

He gave a shy little laugh and pressed closer. She felt his eyelid quivering against her cheek. "I ain't got nothing," he murmured. . . .

The old woman sprang up, seized the iron kettle off the gas stove and took it over to the sink. The noise of the water drumming in the kettle deadened her pain, it seemed. She filled the pail, too, and the washing-up-bowl.

It would take a whole book to describe the state of that kitchen. During the week the literary gentleman "did" for himself. That is to say, he emptied the tea leaves now and again into a jam jar set aside for that purpose, and if he ran out of clean forks he wiped over one or two on the roller towel. Otherwise, as he explained to his friends, his "system" was quite simple, and he couldn't understand why people made all this fuss about housekeeping.

"You simply dirty everything you've got, get a hag in once a week to clean up, and the thing's done."

The result looked like a gigantic dustbin. Even the floor was littered with toast crusts, envelopes, cigarette ends. But Ma Parker bore him no grudge. She pitied the poor young gentleman for having no one to look after him. Out of the smudgy little window you could see an immense expanse of sad-looking sky, and whenever there were clouds they looked very worn, old clouds, frayed at the edges, with holes in them, or dark stains like tea.

While the water was heating, Ma Parker began sweeping the floor. "Yes," she thought, as the broom knocked, "what with one thing and another I've had my share. I've had a hard life."

Even the neighbours said that of her. Many a time, hobbling home with her fish bag she heard them, waiting at the corner, or leaning over the area railings, say among themselves, "She's had a hard life, has Ma Parker." And it was so true she wasn't in the least proud of it. It was just as if you were to say she lived in the basement-back at Number 27. A hard life! . . .

At sixteen she'd left Stratford and come up to London as kitching-maid. Yes, she was born in Stratford-on-Avon. Shakespeare, sir? No, people were always arsking her about him. But she'd never heard his name until she saw it on the theatres.

Nothing remained of Stratford except that "sitting in the fire-place of a evening you could see the stars through the chimley," and "Mother always 'as 'er side of bacon 'anging from the ceiling." And there was something—a bush, there was—at the front door, that smelt ever so nice. But the bush was very vague. She'd only remembered it once or twice in the hospital, when she'd been taken bad.

That was a dreadful place—her first place. She was never allowed out. She never went upstairs except for prayers morning and evening. It was a fair cellar. And the cook was a cruel woman. She used to snatch away her letters from home before she'd read them, and throw them in the range because they made her dreamy. . . . And the beedles! Would you believe it?—until she came to London she'd never seen a black beedle. Here Ma always gave a little laugh, as though—not to have seen a black beedle! Well! It was as if to say you'd never seen your own feet.

When that family was sold up she went as "help" to a doctor's house and after two years there, on the run from morning till night, she married her husband. He was a baker.

"A baker, Mrs. Parker!" the literary gentleman would say. For occasionally he laid aside his tomes and lent an ear, at least, to this product called Life. "It must be rather nice to be married to a baker!"

Mrs. Parker didn't look so sure.

"Such a clean trade," said the gentleman.

Mrs. Parker didn't look convinced.

"And didn't you like handing the new loaves to the customers?"

"Well, sir," said Mrs. Parker, "I wasn't in the shop above a great deal. We had thirteen little ones and buried seven of them. If it wasn't the 'ospital it was the infirmary, you might say!"

"You might, indeed, Mrs. Parker!" said the gentleman, shuddering, and taking up his pen again.

Yes, seven had gone, and while the six were still small her husband was taken ill with consumption. It was flour on the lungs, the doctor told her at the time. . . . Her husband sat up in bed with his shirt pulled over his head, and the doctor's finger drew a circle on his back.

"Now, if we were to cut him open here, Mrs. Parker," said the doctor, "you'd find his lungs chock-a-block with white powder. Breathe, my good fellow!" And Mrs. Parker never knew for certain whether she saw or whether she fancied she saw a great fan of white dust come out of her poor dead husband's lips. . . .

But the struggle she'd had to bring up those six little children and keep herself to herself. Terrible it had been! Then, just when they were old enough to go to school her husband's sister came to stop with them to help things along, and she hadn't been there more than two months when she fell down a flight of steps and hurt her spine. And for five years Ma Parker had another baby—and such a one for crying!—to look after. Then young Maudie went wrong and took her sister Alice with her; the two boys emigrimated, and young Jim went to India with the army, and Ethel, the youngest married a good-for-nothing little waiter who died of ulcers the year little Lennie was born. And now little Lennie—my grandson. . . .

The piles of dirty cups, dirty dishes, were washed and dried. The ink-black knives were cleaned with a piece of potato and finished off with a piece of cork. The table was scrubbed, and the dresser and the sink that had sardine tails swimming in it. . . .

He'd never been a strong child—never from the first. He'd been one of those fair babies that everybody took for a girl. Silvery fair curls he had, blue eyes, and a little freckle like a diamond on one side of his nose. The trouble she and Ethel had had to rear that child! The things out of the newspapers they tried him with! Every Sunday morning Ethel would read aloud while Ma Parker did her washing.

"Dear Sir,—Just a line to let you know my little Myrtil was laid out for dead. . . . After four bottles . . . gained 8 lbs. in 9 weeks, *and is still putting it on.*"

And then the egg-cup of ink would come off the dresser and the letter would be written, and Ma would buy a postal order on her way to work next monring. But it was no use. Nothing made little Lennie put it on. Taking him to the cemetery, even, never gave him a colour; a nice shake-up in the bus never improved his appetite.

But he was gran's boy from the first. . . .

"Whose boy are you?" said old Ma Parker, straightening up from the stove and going over to the smudgy window. And a little voice, so warm, so close, it half stifled her—it seemed to be in her breast under her heart—laughed out, and said, "I'm gran's boy!"

At that moment there was a sound of steps, and the literary gentleman appeared, dressed for walking

"Oh, Mrs. Parker, I'm going out."

"Very good, sir."

"And you'll find your half-crown in the tray of the inkstand."

"Thank you, sir."

"Oh, by the way, Mrs. Parker," said the literary gentleman quickly, "you didn't throw away any cocoa last time you were here—did you?"

"No, sir."

"Very strange. I could have sworn I left a teaspoonful of cocoa in the tin." He broke off. He said softly and firmly, "You'll always tell me when you throw things away—won't you, Mrs. Parker?" And he walked off very well pleased with himself, convinced, in fact, he'd shown Mrs. Parker that under his apparent carelessness he was as vigilant as a woman.

The door banged. She took her brushes and cloths into the bedroom. But when she began to make the bed, smoothing, tucking, patting, the thought of little Lennie was unbearable. Why did he have to suffer so? That's what she couldn't understand. Why should a little angel child have to arsk for his breath and fight for it? There was no sense in making a child suffer like that.

. . . From Lennie's little box of a chest there came a sound as though something was boiling. There was a great lump of something bubbling in his chest that he couldn't get rid of. When he coughed the sweat sprang out on his head; his eyes bulged, his hands waved, and the great lump bubbled as a potato knocks in a saucepan. But what was more awful than all was when he didn't cough he sat against the pillow and never spoke or answered, or even made as if he heard. Only he looked offended.

"It's not your poor old gran's doing it, my lovey," said old Ma Parker, patting back the damp hair from his little scarlet ears. But Lennie moved his head and edged away. Dreadfully offended with her he looked—and solemn. He bent his head and looked at her sideways as though he couldn't have believed it of his gran.

But at the last . . . Ma Parker threw the counterpane over the bed. No, she simply couldn't think about it. It was too much—she'd had too much in her life to bear. She'd borne it up till now, she'd kept herself to herself, and never once had she been seen to cry. Never by a living soul. Not even her own children had seen Ma break down. She'd kept a proud face always. But now! Lennie gone—what had she? She had nothing. He was all she'd got from life, and now he was took too. Why must it all have happened to me? she wondered. "What have I done?" said old Ma Parker. "What have I done?"

As she said those words she suddenly let fall her brush. She found herself in the kitchen. Her misery was so terrible that she pinned on her hat, put on her jacket and walked out of the flat like a person in a dream. She did not know what she was doing. She was like a person so dazed by the horror of what has happened that he walks away—anywhere, as though by walking away he could escape. . . .

It was cold in the street. There was a wind like ice. People went flitting by, very fast; the men walked like scissors; the women trod like cats. And nobody knew—nobody cared. Even if she broke down, if at last, after all these years, she were to cry, she'd find herself in the lock-up as like as not.

But at the thought of crying it was as though little Lennie leapt in his gran's arms. Ah, that's what she wants to do, my dove. Gran wants to cry. If she could only cry now, cry for a long time, over everything, beginning with her first place and the cruel cook, going on to the doctor's, and then the seven little ones, death of her husband, the children's leaving her, and all the years of misery that led up to Lennie. But to have a proper cry over all these things would take a long time. All the same, the time for it had come. She must do it. She couldn't put it off any longer; she couldn't wait any more. . . . Where could she go?

"She's had a hard life, has Ma Parker." Yes, a hard life, indeed! Her chin began to tremble; there was no time to lose. But where? Where?

She couldn't go home; Ethel was there. It would frighten Ethel out of her life. She couldn't sit on a bench anywhere; people would come arsking her questions. She couldn't possibly go back to the gentleman's flat; she had no right to cry in strangers' houses. If she sat on some steps a policeman would speak to her.

Oh, wasn't there anywhere where she could hide and keep herself to herself and stay as long as she liked, not disturbing anybody, and nobody worrying her? Wasn't there anywhere in the world where she could have her cry out—at last?

Ma Parker stood, looking up and down. The icy wind blew out her apron into a balloon. And now it began to rain. There was nowhere.

Questions 12.1

1. Traditionally, day workers, temporary employees, migrant workers, and the like have fallen outside our benefits system. Discuss the special difficulties these individuals face upon retirement. What are some changes that have occurred recently?

2. The incident of the teaspoonful of cocoa poignantly dramatizes an attitude toward poor people shared by many in American society. Discuss this attitude and its implications for the human-service worker.

3. Ma Parker illustrates a common conflict for older people today: an identification with self-sufficiency in the face of diminishing personal resources. Using insights you have gained from Chapter 12, discuss this conflict.

4. Group project: Assume the literary gentleman referred Ma Parker to you for social service. Using information you have gained from this book, draw up a service plan for Ma Parker. How would you begin, what kinds of resources could you tap, what kinds of resistance and/or cooperation would you expect?

CHAPTER 13
MEETING THE HEALTH NEEDS
OF THE ELDERLY:
physical health,
MENTAL health,
institutional CARE

A common denominator for almost all aging people in the United States is declining health. Longer life often means affliction with diseases that strike older people more often than the young, including the major catastrophic illnesses and killers—heart disease, cancer, and stroke. Many other diseases first strike people in their later years, including diabetes, kidney disease, arthritis, and rheumatism. Circulatory diseases, such as hypertension and arteriosclerosis, are characteristic of aging, as are the normal declines in sight and hearing. The physical process of growing old inevitably includes a decline in health, as Chapter 1 explains more fully. Of course, the health problems of older people vary significantly between individuals. Some may be very healthy while others may be very ill, and these variations grow significantly as age increases.

Because declining health is so closely related to aging, health problems and the health services available to older people are important matters. Everyone who works with the elderly must know something about health problems facing those in the later years. Human-service workers who serve the aged must be able to interview older people about their conditions, must be able to help them obtain services to alleviate their problems, and must be able to make effective referrals to health services when they work in nonhealth-related services.

Body preoccupation is a health-related characteristic of aging. Older people, partly because they have more problems with and more concerns about their bodies and their bodily functions than younger people, may become preoccupied with bodily functions. They develop concerns about their bowel movements, bladder functions, digestion, and muscular pains. These conditions are often the product of physical

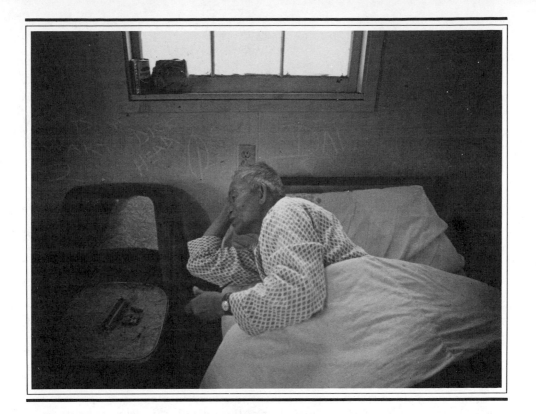

realities, but at times they are also a product of withdrawal into preoccupation with one's own body. Those without employment, recreation, families to rear, or relatives to care for may find themselves focusing their attention on themselves instead. The large number of television and radio commercials about patent medicines designed to overcome body discomfort on programs geared to older people result, in part, from the characteristic body preoccupation of older people.

So, for at least two reasons—the real decline in health faced by older people and the additional emphasis on their own bodily functions during the later years—health is a major concern of the aged and, therefore, of human-service workers who serve them.

Health Programs for the Aging

Because so many of the physically ill are older people, many health services and health service programs are devoted to the needs of older people in the United States, and most other industrialized countries.

Health Insurance

Private self-supporting health insurance programs sponsored by organizations such as Blue Cross–Blue Shield, private profit-making insurance companies, and nonprofit insurance organizations are the most common form of health programs available for older people. These provide for part of the costs of medical and surgical services for people who need hospital care. They ordinarily allow for the costs of hospital rooms, surgery, tests, and medicines; and, through "major medical" provisions, for the extensive costs associated with catastrophic illnesses, such as heart disease, cancer, and strokes.

Such policies cover a large part of the employed population of the United States. However, because they retire or otherwise find themselves unemployed, many aging people do not participate in group plans at work or can no longer afford such coverage on an individual basis.

Problems of Health Insurance for Older People   Health insurance serves primarily younger, employed people. It does so effectively in most cases, although it does not pay all of the costs of all health problems. However, it pays many of the costs of health problems that require hospitalization. Those who use it ordinarily are employed or are members of families in which at least one person is employed and, therefore, the balance of the costs can be paid out of income. Continuous, routine health care costs, such as prescription drugs, visits to physicians for less serious problems, and dental care, are also paid out of current income. Some tax advantage is available to employed people through deductions of part of their health insurance premiums and other medical costs.

However, these expenses pose significant problems for older adults, because usually they are not employed and therefore can pay neither the cost of the hospitalization premiums nor the costs of the additional, not-covered health-care expenses.

Medicare   To help older people handle the cost of their health care, the federal government has instituted a program, commonly called *Medicare*, which provides for hospitalization and other health services for people 65 and older. Employed people begin paying for the program through the Social Security program, and part of the annual contribution goes for Medicare. Upon retirement, people covered by Social Security are eligible for Medicare. Medicare covers the cost of hospitalization, surgery, and other expenses, much as a private health insurance program would. It also provides for extended care in nursing homes or similar facilities for aged people once they are released from hospitals. Whether they have been employed in the Social Security system or not, older people are eligible for Medicare when they reach age 65. There are frequent modifications in the Medicare provisions and changes from time to time in the extent of services provided and in the costs and benefits for participants.

Health Care through
Public Assistance

Older people with low incomes are often eligible for what is usually referred to as *Medicaid*, a program of health care for low-income people offered through state public welfare departments. This care, which is built into the Social Security Act under Title XIX, provides for hospitalization, prescription drugs, physicians' services, nursing home care, and virtually all medical necessities for low-income people in the United States. Low-income aging people are eligible for Medicaid when their own financial resources, private health insurance plans, or Medicare through the Social Security program are insufficient to meet their medical needs. Medicaid, or whatever name a state gives its program of medical services through public welfare, requires a means test—verified evidence that the person requesting help is unable to pay for it through his or her own or other available resources.

Medical costs are not a problem for all older people; many pay for health care from their own incomes or savings. However, they are a problem for most older adults. In fact, it is a common experience for older people to exhaust all of their savings because of physical illness. One or two encounters with severe health problems can lead to an exhaustion of such resources, no matter how great they may be initially.

Maintaining the Health of the Aged

Paying for medical services is, of course, only part of the problem of health care for the aged. More important, perhaps, is maintaining the kinds of conditions that make it possible for older people to satisfactorily survive and maintain high health standards. Occasionally, that means massive environmental efforts to eliminate air pollution, accidents, and inadequate nutrition, which can be the causes of ill health among older people and which can be eliminated. In other words, social efforts to eliminate or reduce illness can be more important than treating illnesses after they occur. The prevention of ill health becomes increasingly important for older people, who are more susceptible than younger people to complications from respiratory illness, epidemics, and other infections.

Inadequate social conditions and inadequate opportunities for recreation and other kinds of growth often make life more hazardous for older people. Poorly designed or poorly maintained intersections can result in traffic injuries or deaths that could be prevented if adequate crosswalks, signal lights, and other safeguards were provided. Insufficient recreational areas and facilities deny older people opportunities to exercise that might lead to illness or earlier death than normal. There is also some evidence that lack of social activities, as described in Chapter 6, can lead to loneliness and, in turn, to depression, illness, and death. The relationship between an individual's health, the environment, and programs of illness and disease prevention are closely interrelated.

As was pointed out in Part One, people age at different rates. Some people are very old and very ill at age 50, while others regularly engage in sports at age 80. Therefore, we must be cognizant of and account for differential rates of aging and different kinds of health problems within the older population.

Health Education and Individual
Responsibility

Many people of all ages do not have clear information on the differences between healthy and unhealthy living. In fact, many illnesses appear to be self-induced through overeating, excessive drinking, insufficient exercise, and other poor health habits. Human-service workers and others involved in preventive health care need to assist older adults, who are more susceptible to illnesses resulting from improper self-care than are younger people, and to educate them about the practices that can lead to better physical health.

Sometimes in group service programs, senior center educational programs, and other opportunities for education, information about good health practices can be taught. Some current research (Kass, 1975) indicates that seven rules for good health can help people live longer. Those 75 years of age and over who followed the rules were as healthy as those 35–44 years of age who followed fewer than three. At age 45 a person who followed at least six of the seven rules had a life expectancy eleven years greater than someone who followed fewer than four. The rules are simple and reflect more common sense than medical science:

1. Don't smoke cigarettes.

2. Get seven hours of sleep.

3. Eat breakfast.

4. Keep your weight down.

5. Drink moderately.

6. Exercise daily.

7. Don't eat between meals.

These rules appear to be more important than medical care and medicine in maintaining health and preventing illness. There is a special need for health services to reach out and provide direct services to older people, and, perhaps even more, to educate them in good health habits.

Humanizing Health Service

On occasion health service programs have to be humanized in order to make them effective and acceptable to older people. Older people are sometimes poorly treated in medical facilities. Some older people enter sophisticated clinics and complex hospitals for the first time when they reach the senior years and may find them difficult to understand and deal with. Frequently these facilities are complex; require intricate registration procedures; necessitate writing; and involve tests, treatments, and other procedures that are frightening and seem foreign to the older patient.

Furthermore, although many of those who have the most severe health problems are older adults, and older adults are very heavy users of health services, there are few health programs genuinely geared to the needs of older people. Experts in working with and talking to older people are sometimes needed to adapt services to the requirements of senior citizens.

Many health programs increasingly are using human-service employees to assist older patients with the health program. Sometimes human-service workers in such positions serve as guides and interpreters of the health program for older people.

Mental-Health Services
for Older Adults

The problems faced by older adults extend, of course, beyond physical ill health and physical declines. As Part One makes clear, emotional problems are also part of the experiences of older people in American society. At times these emotional problems result from physical illnesses. Being sick or watching one's physical capacities decline often leads to depression and other kinds of emotional disturbances. The loneliness and isolation experienced by many older people are also sources of mental distress.

Emotional problems are also connected, in some cases, with physical disabilities themselves. Arteriosclerosis of the brain, a severe health problem that is closely related to aging, has behavioral and physical symptoms. Simple senility is, of course, directly related to growing older. For these reasons programs of service designed to assist older people in meeting their mental-health needs and overcoming obstacles to adequate mental health are an important part of the human-service system for older people.

The Comprehensive Community
Mental-Health Center

Organizations called *comprehensive community mental-health centers*, funded by a combination of local (county and city), state, and federal funds, are designed to provide access to mental-health services to every citizen throughout the United States. The services provided include outpatient counseling, emergency care in general hospitals, day and night hospitalization, and, in some cases, halfway houses. Community mental-health centers also often have contacts with mental hospitals or jails, where some communities keep mental patients while they are waiting for transfer to a mental hospital or other facility, and they generally serve as the major mental-health program in the community. They provide educational and consultation activities to schools and other organizations. They often provide special programs for treating those addicted to alcohol and other drugs; direct or coordinate the efforts with sheltered workshops and other facilities for the mentally retarded or emotionally disturbed; and have close relations with employment services, welfare departments, rehabilitation programs, and a multitude of other services that can be helpful to older adults who face emotional problems.

The comprehensive community mental-health center is such an important service that it is useful for anyone seeking information about or referral to mental-health programs to contact the center first to find out the wisest course of action. Many times personnel at the center will ease the way for referrals of patients to special services or will be the provider of the services.

Mental-Health Workers

A variety of professionals and nonprofessionals work in the mental-health system in the United States. Some people believe that psychiatrists are the primary givers of mental-health services, but, in fact, a whole team of people provide services to those who face emotional problems.

Psychiatrists provide most of the private services for those facing emotional problems who pay fees for professional help. However, private mental-health services are only a small portion of the help provided, although psychiatrists are the most influential members of the mental-health field.

Most of the medical people who provide services in mental-health programs, for instance, mental hospitals, are physicians trained for general practice or for some speciality other than psychiatry. (A psychiatrist is a doctor of medicine who has completed a residency and other experiences in psychiatry and has been admitted for practice by the national certifying board in his or her specialization.) However, M.D.'s from all over the world, as well as doctors of osteopathic medicine, provide mental-health services of all kinds.

In addition to the psychiatrists and nonpsychiatrist physicians who provide mental-health services, nurses are also important deliverers of mental-health help. All registered nurses have some preparation in work with the emotionally disturbed, and some have special preparation at the bachelor's or master's level in work with mental patients. Nurses who specialize in mental-health work conduct counseling as well as providing nursing services to patients in mental hospitals.

Clinical psychologists are another important part of the mental-health team. They conduct psychological counseling and psychological testing, the results of which are of use to other professionals.

Social workers constitute a large proportion of those who serve the mentally ill.

Much of the direct individual and group work with patients in mental-health programs is provided by graduates of social work programs with bachelor's or master's degrees.

The mental-health service staff might also include rehabilitation counselors, occupational therapists, recreational therapists, licensed practical nurses, psychiatric aides, and outreach workers. These individuals have special roles to play and their impact on the patient may be most significant. In modern mental-health practices all of these professionals and staff members coordinate with one another and work together as a team. The literature on the "team approach" to the provision of mental-health services is extensive.

In any encounter with mental-health services, the typical older patient is likely to be helped by serveral members of the team. That is why modern treatment approaches require that everyone associated with a mental-health program be provided with training and guidance in working with the mentally ill. The switchboard receptionist can alienate an older patient to such an extent that the nurse, social worker, psychologist, or psychiatrist never sees the client. The cleaning crew in a mental hospital may so anger a patient that all the work done by the professionals is immediately undone. That is why a close, team relationship among all the members of the staff in a program serving the mentally ill or emotionally disturbed is essential.

Special Services

Family-Service Programs   Among the potential programs that can be of service to older people are those commonly designated as *family-service programs*, many of which are affiliated with the Family Service Association of America, a standard-setting and accrediting body. These programs provide a range of social services for families and help people of all ages. They can be particularly useful to older people in locating housing facilities, health care, leisure-time group activities, or other services. Family-service programs offer the services of social workers who can provide counseling, referral, and information on health, mental health, and housing.

Alcoholism and Drug Abuse   Older people may be addicted to alcohol and other drugs, such as barbiturates or even heroin. Although the emphasis has been on the drug problems of younger people, alcoholism frequently becomes most serious in the later years. With the exception of homes for the aged, there are few areas as heavily populated by older men as the skid rows of American cities. Of course, alcoholism is the typical health problem of the skid row resident.

Alcoholism, which typically begins at a much earlier age—perhaps in the 20s or 30s, or even younger—can often have its greatest impact and be most severe in the later years. The man or woman who needs a drink every evening at age 40 may begin needing a drink in the afternoon by age 45, no later than lunch a couple of years later, and at breakfast time by age 60. Alcoholism that may have been controlled in earlier periods may become pathological during the later years.

Alcoholism is not the only addiction faced by older people. Prescription drugs and dependence upon them—particularly amphetamines, barbiturates, and tranquilizers—may become a central part of the life of the aging person in efforts to overcome depression, loneliness, or physical pain.

Comprehensive community mental-health centers, family-service associations, mental hospitals, and some general hospitals have programs designed to help people with the problems of alcohol and drug abuse. But because the problems are widespread, difficult to treat, and poorly defined, there are many dilemmas for those who hope to provide services to those who face this set of difficulties.

Suicide Prevention   Among the most serious problems of older adults is suicide. A disproportionate number of the over 25,000 Americans who die from suicide each year are older. And the reported figures do not include suicides that are masked as deaths from other causes, such as single-car accidents. Therefore, the prevention of suicide is an important human-service for the elderly. Occasionally such services are provided through community mental-health centers and mental hospitals. In other situations they are provided by general hospitals and, perhaps the most sophisticated example, through telephone "hot lines," which attempt to convince potential suicides to change their minds or at least to delay deciding.

The Mental Hospital

Most casual observers of the mental-health treatment services in the United States do not realize that a large and highly disproportionate number of those incarcerated in public mental hospitals are older adults. The normal process of aging leads to some conditions, already described, that may be classified as mental illnesses. Some mental hospital wards are almost totally devoted to older people, particularly those that deal with the physical problems of mentally ill patients.

Over the years, the American public has had a variety of reactions to and relationships with mental hospitals. Initially these institutions were considered humane alternatives to imprisonment or to isolation in the attics and cellars of private homes, which had often been the fate of older people with emotional problems. Recently, however, observers of practices in mental hospitals began to discover that such institutions were often cruel to inmates. Social scientists who studied institutional life began to report that *total institutions*, to use Erving Goffman's term, were inherently demeaning and that it was, in essence, impossible to improve institutional life. Therefore, the trend in the mental-health field during the 1960s and 1970s has been to remove patients from institutions to a variety of other kinds of programs.

The Rights of Individuals in Mental-Health Programs   One of the responsibilities of human-service workers in institutions for the emotionally disturbed is to ensure that the legal rights of patients are upheld. There are examples of patients being physically beaten, having their personal property removed, being denied access to telephone and mail service, and being kept longer than either the courts require or their own conditions demand. It is crucial for mental-health workers to understand the rights of individuals in mental-health programs and ensure that these rights are upheld. Frequent Supreme Court decisions have added substantially to the civil rights of those whose freedom may have been denied for reasons of mental illness.

Older people in particular may find themselves incarcerated for long periods of time in mental hospitals, even though their only real problem is a lack of housing and an unwillingness on the part of their children to accept responsibility for them. The negative effects of mental hospitalization are so great that it is common to use all sorts of resources to avoid incarcerating a patient for any length of time. The process of "institutionalization" begins very early in the career of a mental hospital patient. Acclimating oneself to a mental hospital sometimes causes one to lose the abilities and social skills one has had in the past, and it is possible that before much time has elasped, the patient becomes capable of living only in an institution rather than in the free environment of the community. For that reason, in addition to trying to guarantee the civil rights of the patient, constant efforts are made to prevent and minimize mental hospitalization.

Alternatives to Institutionalization   One alternative to institutionalization is halfway houses, which are houses located in communities where mental patients can receive staff and other professional services after their departure from the mental hospital without the trauma of suddenly returning to their own homes. These institutions provide professional people to assist with counseling, food preparation, transportation, referral to education and employment, and other aids that can assist the older person in making the transition smoothly from the hospital to the community.

A similar set of arrangements is found in the *day hospital* and the *night hospital*. These kinds of services, which often are called *partial hospitals*, provide treatment and occasionally residences for half the time of the former or potential mental hospital patient. The day hospital may provide psychiatric treatment, occupational therapy, recreation, and education. Night hospitals provide residences for those who cannot live in their own homes; the patients work, study, or otherwise occupy themselves during the day.

These plans for partial hospitalization provide a compromise between complete residence in a mental institution and complete freedom, both of which may be impossible for some victims of emotional problems.

Institutional Programs
for the Aged

A small proportion—some 5 percent—of older adults live in institutions. Most of those who are involved in human-service professions believe that it is almost always best for individuals to live in their own homes and that institutional care for older people ought to be viewed as a last resort, after housing with friends, relatives, or alone is exhausted.

Of course, there are some cases when institutional care is almost required; for instance, when individuals must have constant and specialized health care under the supervision or administration of professionals or when they are senile and so confused that it would pose a danger to themselves or others to remain in a private residence. There are cases of older people turning on natural gas ovens and forgetting to apply the match, thus threatening themselves and those around them with asphyxiation. Some older people forget where they live. Others are sufficiently mentally alert to handle themselves in the environment but have physical problems that make it impossible for them to move around their own homes, apartments, or neighborhoods, because there are no special facilities for wheelchairs or other appliances. The physical handicaps associated with aging are often sufficiently serious to limit the possibilities for some people to remain in their homes.

Nursing Homes and Homes
for the Aged

There are two basic kinds of group living situations used by older people, the nursing home and the home for the aged.

The *nursing home* or, as it is sometimes called, the *extended care facility*, is an institution that provides nursing care to people who do not need the intense services of the hospital but who do need some nursing services they cannot provide on their own or that cannot conveniently be provided for them in their own homes.

Nursing homes are financed by payments made by the patients themselves or by agencies, such as public welfare departments, that provide service to the older patient. Some nursing homes are of excellent, almost luxurious quality, while others are barely adequate. Scandals frequently develop about the care provided to older patients in nursing homes.

The *home for the aged* is an institutional living facility for people who have the need for group or institutional living arrangements. Medical and other health services are available but are provided only when they are needed by patients who are ill. Other services, such as barber and beauty shops, recreation, education, cultural arts, and counseling are also available. Residents of homes for the aged come and go as they please, take their meals in the home, and are sometimes provided transportation away from the home by the institution itself.

There is an increasing use of human-service workers such as social workers in nursing homes and homes for the aged. Nursing specialists are almost always involved in both types of institution. The current trend is to provide personnel who can counsel with patients, organize group activities, and develop recreation and other leisure-time programs.

A development of the past decade is the **hospice,** a specialized institution for terminal patients who cannot be helped through medical care and who do not need the services of nursing homes, but who require a place to live before they die. Some hospices are integrated into other facilities such as hospitals; others are independent. In all, the focus is on helping dying persons end their lives with serenity and dignity. Although they are not limited to older people, many hospices have, of course, largely aged populations.

One of the key elements in providing satisfactory care to people in residential facilities is maintenance of contact between residents and their families. Frequently, it is the responsibility of the human-service worker to encourage visiting in both directions—from the family homes to the resident and from the residential facility back to the homes of family members.

Increasingly, there are extensions of human-service programs into the home, which make it possible for older adults to maintain their residences. Visiting nurse and visiting homemaker programs provide, respectively, skilled nursing care to older adults who need it and household assistance, such as cleaning and meal preparation.

Community and Foster Care

Among the most modern approaches to caring for physically and mentally disabled older adults are *foster care* and *community care*, through which older people who cannot live in their own homes or with their families can have adequate food, shelter, clothing, and social contacts in the homes of others. Many state mental hospitals, the Veterans Administration, and some public welfare departments pioneered these programs designed to provide living situations outside institutions for older people.

Those who house the older person provide food, including special diets when they are necessary, comfortable living arrangements, some recreation, and some transportation. In the Veterans Administration, the hospital that released the older person remains responsible for providing medical care, prescriptions, and other out-patient services. Social workers in the Veterans Administration recruit the community care homes and visit veterans in them regularly to supervise their situations and to satisfy themselves that the veterans are well cared for. Foster and community care provided by other agencies usually includes money to buy health care, medicines, and other unusual costs of maintaining the older person in the home.

Human-service workers employed in community care need skills in recruiting homes, helping older people decide to enter those homes, and providing supervision to those who live in them.

Some older people live in homes for the aged as couples who are married; others—in fact, a great number of older people—live in small, low-cost hotels in center cities. The task of human-service agencies in those settings is to provide social services to people in their own neighborhoods, occasionally to find them alternative services and alternative housing, and sometimes to assure that they are referred to appropriate health, welfare, and mental-health programs.

Summary

There are a variety of ways in which the physical- and mental-health needs of older people are met. Clearly, the range of needs of older people is great, and the range of services provided to them by human-service workers and human-service agencies is equally wide.

There are probably more opportunities for human-service work aiding older people who face physical and emotional health problems than in any other area.

READING 13.1

Senility Is Not Always What It Seems To Be / Lawrence K. Altman, M.D.
Specialists estimate that approximately 4 million persons are senile. Yet Altman reports that very little can be said about the condition that is definitive.

The brain of a young adult contains about 12 billion neurons, the cells that send nerve impulses through the body's most complex organ, and each day, as part of the aging process, the brain shrinks from the death of 100,000 neurons. After decades of losing these irreplaceable cells in an uneven pattern through the brain, the mind of the older individual may wander and he may no longer be able to care for himself. In a word, he becomes senile.

Lapses of memory are common, and when an older person forgets an appointment or name, he is naturally inclined to ask, "Am I getting senile?" In most cases, the answer is in the negative because humans are fallible at all ages, and most older people are not senile.

Nevertheless, the problem of senility is becoming increasingly important. Sometimes, the problem comes to dramatic public attention as it did last week when a California Supreme Court justice was ordered to retire because of senility. But the case of hundreds of thousands of other senile people who manage to carry out their jobs and daily household activities with varying degrees of success receive far less publicity despite the magnitude of the affliction.

Geriatric specialists estimate that 15 percent of people 65 to 75 years old and 25 percent of those 75 and older are senile, a total of about four million. The National Institutes of Health say that 60 percent of the 950,000 nursing home patients over the age of 65 are senile. No accurate statistics exist to know if a larger percentage of older people are getting senile or if there are more senile people because there are more older people. But some geriatricians express the belief that for unknown reasons senility is truly increasing.

Nor do doctors know the cause of senility. It appears to be more than just the loss of neurons, because many older people who have shrunken brains maintain keen minds, and some senile people do not have unusually small brains. And doctors do not know if senility is a disease or a natural aging condition that would affect everyone who lived long enough.

For unknown reasons, the loss of neurons occurs unevenly in the brain seemingly affecting the frontal and temporal lobes (which among other things play key roles in verbalization and hearing) more than other areas of the organ.

Doctors who have studied senile changes have often found it difficult to pinpoint the exact nature of the anatomical brain changes and even more difficult to correlate such changes with the patient's symptoms.

Senility—the word is derived from the Latin word meaning old—is a condition generally characterized by memory loss, particularly for recent events, loss of ability to do simple arithmetic problems, and disorientation to time and place. It is a diagnosis doctors must make by impression, primarily by a bedside examination, because they have no specific diagnostic laboratory test such as a high blood sugar to confirm diabetes.

The computerized axial tomogram, a new x-ray technique that has revolutionized neurology, has helped diagnose senility in more people by showing a shrunken brain on x-ray. To get the same information in the past, doctors had to inject air into the brain, which involved not only pain but some risk to the patient. Because it is so new, the tomogram technique's usefulness in senility has not been fully explored. At present it can support the doctor's bedside impression, but it is not considered a specific diagnostic test.

Many conditions can produce symptoms that mimic senility, and many people are falsely labelled senile when their symptoms are due to depression, a thyroid gland abnormality, pernicious anemia, effects of drugs like bromides, or a variety of other conditions that can be effectively treated, if not cured by psychotherapy or drugs.

But at most 20 percent of senility cases have a treatable cause. This situation has raised questions in the minds of some budget-conscious officials about the cost-effectiveness of spending up to $500 just for extensive series of diagnostic laboratory tests on all senile patients when they have but a few years to live.

However, the overwhelming majority of physicians would agree with Dr. Leslie Libow, chief of geriatric medicine at the Jewish Institute for Geriatric Care in New Hyde Park, who said:

"Senility is one of the most serious medical diagnoses that can be given to a patient because the prognosis is so serious and the effectiveness of treatment is not clear. If we value our older people, how can anyone seriously argue that every physician should not do the tests to make sure a treatable cause has not been overlooked?"

The older population's growing political influence has led government officials to devote more attention to their medical troubles. Next month, for example, the National Institute of Aging, the newest unit of the Federal National Institutes of Health in Bethesda, Md., will hold one of the larger scientific meetings on senility.

One impetus for the meeting is the recognition from research studies during the last five years that arteriosclerosis, or hardening of the arteries, plays less of a role in senility than doctors previously believed. Senility on the basis of arteriosclerosis tends to produce worsening symptoms on an episodic basis. Now, geriatricians believe the bulk of cases are due to senile dementia, a disease of unknown cause that occurs more commonly in women and that is characterized by the gradual, unrelenting, irreversible deterioration of the mind. The process can occur so slowly and subtly as to escape attention until the affected person shocks his family by wandering away from home, failing to recognize an old friend, or squandering money on a worthless cause.

When senility develops in a 40- or 50-year-old individual—it is then called pre-senile dementia—doctors generally suspect a wide variety of conditions but two in particular, Alzheimer's Disease and Pick's Disease. In Alzheimer's Disease, the shrinkage occurs throughout the brain, whereas in Pick's Disease the changes are more localized. Anatomically, Alzheimer's Disease is indistinguishable from the shrunken, senile brain to the pathologist, raising questions whether Alzheimer's might be the early onset of the more common form of senility.

The main thrust of the meeting will be to explore the various avenues of research through which the mystery of senility might be solved. Among the current areas of focus:

Epidemiology—What clues can be picked up by examining the differences in incidence among various populations that could not be detected by laboratory studies?

Viral—Can viruses that take years to incubate and produce damage be an important cause of senility?

Hereditary—Is there a genetic defect that predisposes some individuals to senility? If so, what is it?

Metabolic—Is there a biochemical abnormality that leads to senility?

The answers to these and other questions could lead to effective therapies and preventions for one of society's more costly troubles.

Questions 13.1

1. Senility presents problems of diagnosis, prognosis, and treatment. Discuss these problems.

2. The lack of conclusive knowledge heightens the conflict between individual rights and the need for protective services. What implications does this have for you as a human-service worker?

3. The facts that senility is primarily an affliction of older people and that its symptoms are often subtle have had an effect on policy decisions at both the national and local institutional levels. Discuss current policy regarding senility. What advocacy stance can you as a human-service worker take?

READING 13.2

Social Needs of the Hospitalized Elderly: A Classification / Barbara Gordon Berkman and Helen Rehr

In this article the authors develop a carefully constructed classification of sociopsychological needs of elderly patients and their families.

Hospitalization may have unanticipated social consequences for some elderly patients and their families.[1] Problems that the patient may have had prior to hospitalization are often exacerbated, and separation from his usual environment may result in a wave of socio-psychological reactions in both the patient and members of his family. These reactions can seriously affect the patient's diagnostic and therapeutic regimen as well as the course of his post-hospital recovery. Therefore, the social worker may be called on to help alleviate the stressful situation.

To understand the hospitalized elderly patient, the social worker tries to understand his previous physical, psychological, and social experiences that may have a special impact on his adjustment to hospitalization.[2] By broadening the dimensions in which the elderly patient is viewed, the worker can help other members of the hospital staff improve the effectiveness of the patient's medical care.

In the traditional system of social work case-finding in most medical settings, social workers seldom select their own clientele directly. Elderly patients make few requests for social service, and thus referrals are usually made by a physician or members of the patient's family.[3]

Because hospital social workers have little influence on their case loads, the question has been raised as to whether physicians understand the function of the medical social worker.[4] For

© 1972 National Association of Social Workers, Inc. Reprinted from *Social Work,* Vol. 17, No. 4 (July 1972), pp. 80–88.

[1] For a complete discussion of social and psychological conditions that are relevant to aging see Richard H. Williams, Clark Tibbits, and Wilma Donahue, eds., *Processes of Aging,* Vols. 1 and 4 (New York, Atherton Press, 1963). See also, National Center for Health Statistics, Acute Condition Series 10, No. 54, and Chronic Conditions Causing Activity Limitations (Washington, D.C., U.S. Department of Health, Education, and Welfare 1967).

[2] Helen Lokshin, "In Memory of William Posner," in Dynamic Factors in the Role of the Caseworker in Work with the Aged (New York Central Bureau for the Jewish Aged, 1962), and "Social Services and the Aging," in Arthur Fink, C. Wilson Anderson, and M. B. Conover, eds., The Field of Social Work (New York: Holt, Rinehart & Winston, 1970), pp. 426–552.

[3] Although nurses and other hospital personnel recognize elderly persons who need social service help, they seldom refer these patients to social service. See Alice Ullman and Gene G. Kassebaum, "Referrals and Services in a Medical Social Work Department," Social Service Review, Vol. 35, No. 3 (September 1961), pp. 258–268; John D. Stoeckle, M.D., Ruth Sitteler, and Gerald E. Davidson, M.D., "Social Work in a Medical Clinic: The Nature and Course of Referrals to the Social Worker," American Journal of Public Health, Vol. 56, No. 9 (September 1966), pp. 1570–1579; Barbara Gordon Berkman and Helen Rehr, "Selectivity Biases in Delivery of Hospital Social Services," Social Service Review, Vol. 43, No 1 (March 1969), pp. 35–41; Berkman and Rehr, "Aging Ward Patients and the Hospital Social Service Department," Journal of the American Geriatrics Society, Vol. 15, No. 12 (December 1967), pp. 1153–1162; and Berkman and Rehr, "Unanticipated Consequences of the Casefinding System in Hospital Social Service," Social Work, Vol. 15, No. 2 (April 1970), pp. 63–70.

[4] See Margaret M. Heyman, "Collaboration Between Doctor and Caseworker in a General Hospital," Social Casework, Vol. 48, No. 5 (May 1967), p. 290; Beatrice Phillips et al., "Studies in the United States and Great Britain Indicate Physicians' Incomplete Understanding of the Function of Social Work Services," Hospitals, Vol. 45, No. 4 (February 16, 1971), pp. 76–78; and Catherine M. Olsen and Marvin E. Olsen, "Role Expectations and Perceptions for Social Workers in Medical Settings," Social Work, Vol. 12, No. 3 (July 1967), pp. 70–78.

example, do the physicians' views of the ways a social worker can be helpful coincide with the caseworker's image of himself as a professional? With these questions in mind, the Social Service Department of Mount Sinai Medical Center, New York City, conducted a study to determine whether the social needs of patients and families referred to social service by other hospital personnel coincided with those identified by social workers themselves.[5]

To collect the necessary data for this project, a reliable and valid classification of social needs had to be developed. Although various classification systems have been used in the past, the one described in this article is a new categorization of social needs that is limited to hospitalized elderly patients who receive hospital social service help. It is not a final classification. Rather, it is a beginning refinement that has proved useful for the purposes of the study. In the following discussion, the instrument and its attributes and problems are described.

Prior Studies

In exploring previous classifications of social needs of patients in medical settings, no consistent definition of social need was found in the social work literature. In fact, the authors first had to decide which concept—"problem" or "need"—was more appropriate. The dictionary defines problem as "any question or matter involving doubt, uncertainty or difficulty." Need is defined as "a case or instance in which some necessity or want exists."[6] After reviewing the Social Service Department's case records and discussing the two concepts with the hospital social workers, it became evident that although workers perceived the problems of patients and families, in their diagnostic formulations, they usually discussed how to resolve them. Therefore, the authors decided to use the word "needs," combined with the word "social," rather than "medical," to describe their classification system.

Another major difficulty was that prior categorizations of social needs or problems often included a combination of variables, frequently not of the same conceptual order. Some items in a single classification were related to the patient's attributes while others described activities related to professional methods, such as the casework process.

The tendency to perceive service functions and needs in the same conceptual frame of reference has been a major obstacle in the development of a useful classification. For example, in 1961, Ullman and Kassebaum tried to determine why patients were referred to the Social Service Department and to assess the services given by medical social workers.[7] Their classification included the reasons for referral and the services provided. There were five categories: Medical casework (e.g., helping the patient adjust to his illness, solving family problems), planning for medical care (e.g., making arrangements for psychiatric care, chronic care, and so on), environmental health (e.g., making arrangements for financial help or homemaker services), facilitating medical care (e.g., arranging for transportation to the clinic or

    [5] Helen Rehr and Barbara Berkman, "Effects of Differential Timing of Social Service Intervention with Aging Patients" (New York: Mount Sinai School of Medicine and Health Research Council of the City of New York, June 1969). (Mimeographed.)

    [6] The American College Dictionary (New York: Random House, 1967), pp. 965 and 812 respectively.

    [7] Ullman and Kassebaum, op. cit.

providing information on resources), and liaison with community agencies. Thus, the reason for referral—or the need, as identified by the worker—was linked with the action taken in the social work process.

The major difficulty with this early formulation was that a family problem, for example, could be associated with a number of categories of service, rather than medical casework alone. Thus, "facilitating medical care," which includes giving information on resources, is a social work activity that may help alleviate a family problem. To clarify this problem further, the following hypothetical case is used to show why this early classification would have been extremely confusing:

Mr. C, age 72, was hospitalized with terminal cancer. Prior to hospitalization, he lived with his son and daughter-in-law in a suburb of New York City. The physician referred the family to social service for discharge-planning because the son and his wife both worked and Mr. C would need care if he returned home. The family wanted Mr. C to come home, but did not know how to manage it. By informing the family about homemaker services and helping them contact an agency in their area, the worker facilitated the patient's return home and reduced family stress.

Where does this case fit into the classification system? Obviously, it is a family problem. Yet it would probably fit into three or more categories of reasons for referral and services. This system does not allow for a choice or mixing of categories. A classification system that combines problem with service function means that the worker has no options to make other possible combinations of service activity and problem. It would be more valid to establish a classification of social needs that is independent of social service activity. This classification could then be used to study whether specific social service activities are actually related to certain identifiable social needs.

In 1968, Goldberg, Neill and Spaak tried to identify which service activities and problems were related by prudently separating requests for a specific type of social service activity from the social problem as perceived by physicians.[8] Physicians' requests for service were conceptualized as "social assessment," "provision of services," or "casework." The problems perceived by the physicians were conceptualized as "physical complaints," "vague symptoms," "psychiatric illness," and "overt social problems only." No one type of social service activity was consistently requested for one type of problem. For example, "casework services" were requested for "physical complaints" as well as "overt social problems only." "Provision of services" was requested for "physical complaints" as well as "overt social problems only" or "psychiatric illness."

However, these classifications of services and problems presented a number of difficulties. Each problem and service activity was considered discrete within its overall classification. The experience of social workers at Mount Sinai indicates that these are not mutually exclusive

[8] See E. M. Goldberg, J. Neill, and B. M. Spaak, "Social Work in General Practice," Lancet, September 7, 1968, pp. 552–555.

categories, and they call for a subjective judgment in choosing the primary problem or service activity. The reliability of these judgments was not tested in the study by Goldberg, Neill, and Spaak, however. In addition, the categories were chosen by the physicians and may have represented their frame of reference. Their conceptualization of problems may have been too gross and not specifically related to social service. For example, although the category "physical complaints" is generally accepted as applicable to the social worker's role with patients, the social components in such a category are unclear.[9]

The Present Study

To develop an initial classification of the social needs of hospitalized elderly patients, the authors analyzed the content of 165 social service case records for patients 65 years or older selected at random from the Mount Sinai hospital files for 1966.[10] The number of items in the classification was then reduced to 30 different statements that represented social needs, as identified by the workers involved in the 165 cases.

To test the "face" validity of the items (i.e., the measuring instrument's apparent relevance) and the "content" validity (i.e., how well the questionaire sampled the subject matter), the statements were pre-tested with three social workers who had a minimum of four years experience in hospital social service. The workers were asked to use the instrument to identify the social needs of all elderly patients known to them during a one-month period (an average of seven cases each). This was done to determine whether the statements on the instrument correspond with the worker's practice experience and could be used on current case loads. Meetings with these workers were held both before and after the pre-test period to discuss and clarify the statements. With the workers' help, the statements of social needs were reduced to 12 descriptive sentences that were assumed to have preliminary validity.

Inherent in this classification (and those that have preceded it) is the fact that the social worker is asked to judge the patient's primary social need as he perceives it. The authors' assumption, based on a reliability study, was that in most cases, different workers would select the same social need in the same case. Although the question of data reliability could have been approached in many ways, the study relied on interobserver reliability, which involved estimates of equivalence.[11] Equivalence was determined by the extent to which consistent results were obtained, using different observers with the same material during the same period.[12]

---

[9] Another study classified the patient's and family's social needs and the methods of meeting these needs and thus differentiated between social need and casework activity. Personal communication from M. C. Goldwyn, Westminster Hospital, London, England, 1968.

[10] A modified critical incident technique was used in this process. See John C. Flanagan, "The Critical Incident Technique," Psychological Abstracts, Vol. 51, No. 4 (July 1954), pp. 327–358.

[11] See Claire Sellitz et al., Research Methods in Social Relations (New York: Holt, Rinehart, & Winston, 1964), pp. 166–186.

[12] A study of 1,348 psychoanalytic clinic records illustrates two types of observer reliability among clinical coders who evaluated the records. See John Weber, Jack Elinson, and Leonard Moss, "The Application of Ego Strength Scales to Psychoanalytic Clinic Records," Proceedings of 20th Anniversary Conference, Columbia Psychoanalytic Clinic for Training and Research (New York: Columbia University, October 1965), pp. 215–273.

The classification's reliability was tested by a content analysis of 84 social service records on elderly patients selected at random from the files for 1966. Six social workers who had a minimum of four years in the medical social service setting acted as judges. The judges were split into groups of two. Each group read 28 randomly selected cases and was asked to select one item from each case as the primary social need dealt with by the worker during the case contact. This selection was based on judgments about material dictated in the record when the worker closed the case.

If the judges did not agree on a specific item, a third judge was called in, and the judgment chosen was the one on which two of the three judges concurred. It was assumed that if the items in the classification were reliable and discrete in definition, at least two judges would agree. If two of the three judges could not agree and the problem was caused by ambiguity among the items in the classification rather than the way the record was written, the item was revised. In all instances, however, agreement was reached, and a third judgment was needed for only 11 of the 84 records.

The final classification instrument does not emphasize needs in specific psychological terms such as depression or hysteria; it is oriented more to socio-environmental factors and emotional stress. (See Table 1.) In the case records used in the study, medical social workers tended to identify social needs from a socio-environmental stress perspective rather than a

Table I   Social Needs of Elderly Patients Referred to Social Service

Categories of Social Needs	Definition
Anxiety reactions to hospitalization	Patient or family member upset, angry, fearful, about diagnostic workup, diagnosis, surgery, hospitalization, and the like.
Anxiety as a hindrance to discharge	Patient or family member too anxious to enter into discharge considerations.
Chronic institutional care	Patient requires chronic institutional care after discharge (e.g., nursing home, home for aged, chronic disease hospital).
Complaints	Patient or family member has complaints related to hospital and medical services (e.g., room, food, personnel, physician).
Concrete aids	Concrete aids have been medically recommended (e.g., appliances, transportation from hospital).
Convalescent care	Patient needs temporary convalescent care away from home following discharge.
Home help	Patient requires assistance at home after hospitalization (e.g., homemaker, nursing services, home aide, domestic).
Housing	Patient's previous housing facilities are unsuitable for his postdischarge needs.
Finances	Patient's anticipated financial situation is inadequate for postdischarge needs.
Potential discharge against medical advice	Patient wants to leave the hospital against medical advice.
"Problem" patient	Patient's reactions to hospital and medical regimen cause problems for the staff (e.g., he will not follow diet, stay in bed); in other words the staff needs help in coping with the patient.
Transitions in role relationships	Social problems as direct result of hospitalization (e.g., new social roles must be assumed by family members).

formal psychological frame of reference. This was also evidenced by the workers who pre-tested the classification. Therefore, one limitation of the instrument may be that it was devised from material previously recorded in case records. In the socio-environmental stress frame of reference, this bias is evident. With a different approach to developing the instrument (e.g., asking social workers to conceptualize social needs), a more psychologically oriented frame of reference might have resulted. However, this classification is based on the assumption that psychological stress is inherent in any social need.

The classification developed by the authors was subsequently used by social workers at Mount Sinai when they entered a case. Because the social needs listed in the classification are not necessarily mutually exclusive, the workers can select the patient's primary social need on the basis of their diagnostic assessment of the situation. Therefore, it is possible that the point at which the worker entered the case would affect her perception of what the patient's primary social need is. But this is a subject for further study.

Sample Categories

Each of the following items used in the classification is defined and then illustrated with a case example:

Anxiety reactions to hospitalization. Following admission, a patient and his family may be anxious about the diagnostic workup, the diagnosis, surgery, or the hospitalization itself. Social workers often must focus on these stress reactions and their effect on the patient's treatment.

Mrs. L., a 72-year-old widow, was admitted to the hospital with a diagnosis of sup-rachiasmal neoplasm with questionable malignancy. Her symptoms included loss of vision and dizziness. Although Mrs. L. was undergoing a series of radiotherapy treatments, she was told only that she had some kind of cranial pressure and that the treatments would help relieve it. A nurse on the floor told the social worker that Mrs. L. seemed upset and cried constantly. The worker found that Mrs. L. was extremely anxious and fearful about her condition. In addition, she was frightened because prior to hospitalization, she had never been physically or emotionally dependent. She wanted to go home as soon as possible.

In speaking to the physician about the patient's anxiety, the worker found Mrs. L. could be treated on an out-patient basis. The physician had assumed she would be unable to travel to the hospital for treatment. Arrangements were made for Mrs. L. to receive radiotherapy treat-ments on an out-patient basis, and she was discharged. Social service intervention helped to alleviate Mrs. L.'s anxiety and supported her in maintaining her treatments. In addition, it helped the physician assess Mrs. L.'s response to treatment, which in turn helped him provide Mrs. L. with sound medical care.

Anxiety as a hindrance to discharge. If the patient and his family do not enter into discharge planning, although the physician has told them the patient is ready to leave the hospital, the social worker's assessment is required to clarify the medical, psychological, or social problems that may be hindering discharge. Psychosocial assessment may also be necessary when alternative post-hospital plans are available to the patient and the choice depends on his social situation. These types of problems are exemplified by questions such as the following: What impact will the patient's needs have on other family members? Is the family ready to cope with his needs? The stress apparent in these situations often deters the patient and his family from making concrete post-hospital plans.

Mr. G., a 65-year-old single man, was hospitalized with the diagnosis of heart block. Surgery was performed to insert a pacemaker. The physician referred the case to social service because Mr. G. was depressed, cried for long periods, and insisted he could not go home. From a medical standpoint, Mr. G. did not need special nursing. But the worker learned that he had no relatives living in the United States and he lived an isolated life. He rented a furnished room in an area where he knew few people.

After talking to Mr. G., the worker concluded that his emotional condition was precarious. He could no longer live alone without extreme anxiety, which could adversely affect his recovery. The worker arranged for Mr. G. to live in a home for the aged after a period of convalescence in a temporary care facility.

Home help. Home help refers to social needs that arise because of inadequate housing or financial difficulties, as well as the need for homemaker service, visiting nurse service, or concrete aids such as appliances.

Mrs. S., a 65-year-old widow, was hospitalized for Parkinson's disease. The physician recommended treatment with a new experimental drug, L-Dopa, but the patient refused.

Subsequently, the worker discovered that it was the patient's daughter who objected to the treatment because the cost of L-Dopa therapy would be $50 a month. Although Medicare and Medicaid covered in-patient use of the drug, there was no insurance to cover the expense on an out-patient basis. L-Dopa was still in the experimental stage and had not been cleared by the Food and Drug Administration. Therefore, it was not available through the usual prescription-filling channels. The patient's daughter and son-in-law supported Mrs. S. financially, but they felt they could not assume the cost of her medication in addition to other expenses related to her illness.

The social worker, in discussing the situation with the doctor, verified that L-Dopa had been quite successful in other cases and that a trial of this therapy was indicated in Mrs. S.'s case. The worker contacted the American Parkinson's disease association, which accepted Mrs. S.'s case for one year, with an option for renewal the following year.

The Association's assistance was enough to ease the financial burden on the patient's family.

Chronic institutional care. The patient who no longer needs closely supervised hospital and medical care, but whose physical condition requires considerable nursing care that cannot be provided in his home environment needs chronic institutional care. Thus the social worker is often called on to facilitate the patient's transfer to an institution such as a permanent nursing home or chronic disease hospital.

Mrs. B., a 72-year-old married woman, was admitted to the hospital with a diagnosis of cerebral neoplasm. After completing a course of Cobalt therapy, she was referred to social service by her physician for assistance in arranging nursing home placement. During the past month, Mrs. B. had had periods of alertness, but generally she did not eat and required intravenous feeding. She was partially paralyzed and showed no improvement in her neurological condition.

The worker's major contact was with Mr. B., age 75, who was alert, obviously devoted to his wife, and able to accept the facts about his wife's condition. With help from the worker, Mr. B. acknowledged how lonely he felt without Mrs. B., but attributed his strength to the fact that they had had a lovely life together. Arrangements were made to transfer Mrs. B. to a nursing home after Mr. B. had visited it and after the situation had been discussed fully with the social worker at the home.

Complaints. Some patients and family members complain about the hospital's social environment or medical services. The social worker usually hears about these situations from the patient or family, but he may observe them himself during rounds. Although the complaints are the presenting problem, they frequently cover underlying anxiety about the patient's hospitalization or illness.

Mr. F., age 72 and married, was hospitalized with a diagnosis of gall bladder disease. The case was opened by the social worker during routine rounds. Both Mr. and Mrs. F. made veiled, as well as somewhat overt complaints about the hospital.

The only concrete request for assistance, however, was made by Mr. F. He wanted to arrange a special visiting pass for his brother, who could not get to the hospital during visiting hours. The social worker obtained the pass for the patient's brother. She then allowed the couple to express their irritation about the hospital. Because the worker acknowledged the inconvenience of hospitalization and allowed them to complain, they began to accept the situation and were more cooperative about necessary procedures.

Convalescent care. After a patient is discharged from the hospital, a temporary convalescent period away from home may be beneficial. An extended care facility can aid the patient's recovery and help him return to independent living.

Mr. P., a 71-year-old married man, was admitted to the hospital with a diagnosis of urinary extravasation, retention, and abscess secondary to urethral rupture. A cystostomy was performed. Mr. P. was referred to social service by the physician, who stated the patient was doing well and the wound was healing, but he would have to take sitz baths three or four times a day for the next three weeks until his genitalia had healed completely.

Convalescent care was recommended, but Mr. P. adamantly refused because he felt he was too ill to leave the hospital. His refusal was based primarily on his lack of understanding of the medical plan and the physician's prognosis, and his self-consciousness about his condition. The worker and the physician interpreted the illness more fully to Mr. P. which enabled him to accept the referral. Mr. P. was discharged to a convalescent after-care facility, where he remained for three weeks. He then returned home.

"Problem" patient. If hospital staff members are to perform their roles effectively, a patient must comply with the socially prescribed role of patient—he must obey the physician's orders.[13] When his reactions to the hospital medical regimen impede his treatment, he is viewed as a problem by staff. A social worker can help such patients adapt to hospitalization.

Mrs. H., a 72-year-old widow, was admitted with severe abdominal pain. The physician prescribed a bland diet in preparation for certain diagnostic tests. Mrs. H. refused to follow his orders; she took food from other patients' plates and asked friends to bring food to her. The nurse on the floor asked the worker to do something about Mrs. H.'s behavior.

The worker found Mrs. H. to be extremely apprehensive and frightened. She thought the physicians knew what was wrong and were hiding it from her. She felt that if she was going to die, staying on a diet was pointless. By focusing on Mrs. H.'s concerns, the worker helped her to partialize her anxiety and understand that by following the diet, she might speed up the diagnosis, as well as her recovery. With the worker's continuous assurance and support and the involvement of the patient's sister, Mrs. H was able to adapt to the requirements of hospitalization.

Potential discharge against medical advice. When a patient is intent on leaving the hospital against medical advice, it may indicate a high level of anxiety about his illness and hospitalization and possibly his home situation.[14]

Mrs. R., age 65, was hospitalized with severe congestive heart failure. She responded to therapy and after two weeks she felt better and insisted on going home. However, she still needed intensive therapy, controlled diet and fluid intake, and bedrest.

The physician referred her to the social worker, who found that she was worried about her invalid husband. Neighbors had been helpful to him, but Mrs. R. did not trust them to care for him properly. The worker arranged for a homemaker for Mr. R., which alleviated Mrs. R's anxiety and she was able to adapt to hospitalization. The worker also arranged to have Mr. R. brought to the hospital twice a week to visit his wife. Thus each was reassured about the other's well-being.

Transitions in role relationships. When a patient is admitted to the hospital, family members are forced to assume new relationships with each other and the patient. Some changes require an inner strength that some individuals do not have. These persons may become emotionally upset, and in turn their reactions may impede the patient's medical treatment.

---

[13] Emily Mumford, "The Patient Role: What Is It? Why? What Can the Doctor Do About It?" Medical Clinics of North America, Vol. 51, No. 6 (November 1967), pp. 1507–1514.

[14] Milton Davis and Robert P. von der Lippe, "Discharge from Hospital Against Medical Advice," Social Science and Medicine, Vol. 1, No. 3, (September 1967), pp. 336–344.

Mrs. K., a 68-year-old married woman, was admitted to the hospital with cancer of the rectum. The physician referred her to social service because he was concerned about how her family would manage when she returned home. It was his impression that Mrs. K. did her own housework, which she would no longer be able to do when she left the hospital. When he suggested to the family that they find a homemaker, Mrs. K. refused, saying she would continue taking care of her home as she always had. The worker contacted Cancer Care and learned that they would be willing to supply a housekeeper. The worker then helped the patient accept her limitations and helped both Mr. and Mrs. K. accept the homemaker into their home.

Implications

In contrast to earlier classification systems, the conceptual categories in the one described in this article are derived from the language of social work and do not rely on the physician's frame of reference. In addition, this system does not mix social needs and social service activities; it is limited to social needs perceived by social workers at the time they enter a case. The authors believe that further research would clarify whether specific social service activities are related to solving specific social needs.

Although the classification system is not considered a final approach, it has proved useful for practical research purposes. For example, it has been possible to compare differences between social workers and other sources of referrals as to the types of social needs identified for social service help.[15] It has also been possible to study whether the social needs identified by the social worker differ, depending on when she enters the case, e.g., shortly after admission, mid hospitalization, or just before discharge.[16] In addition, the classification has proved useful in clarifying with physicians and hospital administrators the types of situations in which social workers can help.

The classification might be adapted for use as a screening mechanism for early identification of patients and families who may need social services. Predictive screening would be potentially beneficial if patients' social needs could be uncovered before they became critical. Early case findings may mean shorter hospitalization for patients who, because of problems in arranging complex post hospital care plans, stay longer than they need to. It is also possible that such a screening mechanism could lead to more appropriate use of professional, as well as non-professional personnel.

Questions 13.2

1. Discuss the purposes of this study.

2. The authors speak of a bias toward a socioenvironmental definition of stress (as opposed to a psychological one). How does this affect the way a human service worker approaches working with a patient?

3. Discuss how the medical social worker can be of service in each of the twelve areas of need.

4. What uses can the human-service worker make of the classification system outlined in this article?

---

[15] Rehr and Berkman, "Effects of Differential Timing of Social Service Intervention with Aging Patients."
[16] Ibid.

chapter 14
meeting the leisure-time needs of the elderly: recreation, volunteer, and self-help programs

When they retire, many older adults find they have leisure time available for the first time in their memories. Their loss of traditional roles as parents, workers, and, in some cases, spouses, which is characteristic of the later stages of life, creates major problems for some. American society has few ways of preparing individuals for the changes in their lifestyles and the increased leisure resulting from retirement. Emotional problems result for many older adults who cannot cope with leisure time, although others thrive on their freedom to try new activities.

This chapter discusses some of the programs, services, and activities available to help older adults use their leisure time. We consider various types of recreation programs and volunteer, self-help, and political programs, which are service-oriented and can aid the older adult in making effective use of free time.

Leisure Time and the Elderly

Leisure time, especially for adults, is one of many issues Americans have failed to handle with skill. Only in relatively recent years have appropriate use of leisure and forms of recreation become subjects of public interest. In fact, only recently have many Americans become sufficiently affluent to be able to afford structured leisure-time activities, so that extensive resources and facilities have developed.

There are many reasons for the American ambivalence toward and lack of attention to leisure-time programs.

First, the nation was founded by followers of self-sacrificing, puritanical religious

groups, and they influenced the lives and philosophies of the nation from its beginnings. More Americans have been inclined to believe that "the devil has work for idle hands" than have believed people need structured and effective leisure-time activities.

Second, for most of the nation's history life has been difficult. Simply earning enough money for food, clothing, shelter, and education has taken all the available time and energy. That was true of the earliest settlers, and it remained true for the later immigrants, most of whom had been poor in their nations of origin and who had little reason to be concerned about the effective use of their leisure time. Today's older people were raised in an atmosphere of scarcity and hard work geared to overcoming that scarcity or to earning sufficient money to survive. Leisure has traditionally been viewed as an evil at worst and a luxury at best. Although the traditions are changing, today's cohort of elderly people grew up in a society that placed low priority on adult leisure-time and recreational activities.

Third, many Americans believe that play is for children; adults are supposed to work. Play is appropriate for the young; as one becomes older, it becomes less and less socially acceptable to engage in organized leisure-time programs. The suggestion of the need for leisure-time services is viewed by some older people as patronizing and insulting.

As is true in many other circumstances, American attitudes toward leisure are contradictory. There is public acceptance and high status accorded to adults using vacation and resort activities. Few question the need for vacations, golf, tennis, bowling, and other commercial activities for employed men and women. However, the conventional view of those activities is that they are releases and relaxations from work. In other words, it is okay to engage in recreational activities if they are designed to make one a more efficient worker. Valuing leisure-time activities for themselves is an idea that has not yet gained wide popular acceptance.

Lack of Models

One of the problems in providing effective leisure-time and recreation services for older people is that most of the models for leisure-time programs come from recreation work with children. Recreation workers may have studied theories of recreation for children and practiced recreational activities with children. At times they may be bound by that experience and, at best, may work to adapt their knowledge of recreational programs for children to the needs of older people. In the worst cases some recreation workers use children's activities as if they were appropriate for groups of older people.

Involving Older People in Planning Leisure-Time Programs

Acceptable and useful programs for older people may arise from careful involvement of the participants in planning their own programs. Involving people in planning for their services makes a difference in every area of human-service work; it makes a crucial difference in the quality of recreation and leisure-time programs for the elderly. Planning *for* older people implies they cannot plan for themselves. However, most who serve older people know that the elderly themselves usually best understand what they want and need, and recreation workers need to develop programs that are planned *with* older adults. That does not imply older adults want no help in developing their own activities. In many cases they very much want assistance in planning programs.

The specific kinds of programs developed are less important than the process used in choosing those programs and the involvement of older people themselves in the selection and planning of their leisure-time activities.

Methods of Planning with Older People in Community Programs

Many recreation and leisure-time activities develop from groups of older people in senior centers and other kinds of community programs. Human-service workers who are staff members in such centers may expedite the planning by organizing meetings with the members. Sometimes a committee of older people elected by the total membership develops recreation and leisure-time activities for the whole center. At other times the staff members meet informally with everyone actively or potentially involved to solicit ideas for activities.

The key to involving members in planning and carrying out their own activities includes knowing how detailed the members want their involvement to be. Some want specific consultation on every element of the activities. Others will want the right to advise and the power to veto plans that staff members develop. It is an error for a worker to force the style of member involvement in planning. The activities belong to the members, and they decide how and to what extent they want to participate.

The more involved the older people are in the program and the more strongly they view it as their own, the more demands they will make for control over the activities. But members come to the point of involvement and control over their programs through several stages of participation. Human-service workers who are effective help their members find levels of involvement that are comfortable and reasonable. Some groups begin with the staff planning most of the activities, using only occasional advice from the older members. After a time those efforts may evolve into elected advisory committees of older members. Ultimately planning might include the members' controlling the group, with only some advice from staff members—a reversal of authority and roles. Pertinent here is Figure 6.2 (Chapter 6), which defines the degree of activity of a worker in line with the social health of a group of members. The process of working with elderly people in planning recreation requires the skills of working with groups that are discussed and delineated in Chapter 6.

The process of involvement and the relative roles of the staff member and the group members are subtle. For example, The Old Timers' Club in a medium-sized community senior center had been operating for five years. It met once each week and chose as its programs a lunch prepared by the members; some remarks from one of the local Protestant ministers; bingo after lunch once each month, with prizes donated by local merchants; a recipe-swapping session once a month; a lecture, frequently on health or social service problems, at another monthly meeting; and group singing at the fourth meeting of each month. The men in the group stayed away from the recipe-swaps and the group singing. The women were inclined to attend every week.

When the recreation worker with the group met with his supervisor, who asked why the group did the same things every month, every year, the worker replied that he was simply letting the group do what they wanted to do. The supervisor suggested that the worker propose something new to the group—an all-day excursion in the spring to a park and museum within easy bus transportation distance, followed by a picnic lunch, a brief hike, and some free time to feed the tame deer that abounded in the park.

When the worker proposed the idea, the members were thrilled with the opportunity to try something different and said that they needed suggestions and encouragement from the worker. The program was held in good weather and led to a series of similar programs as well as other new approaches to their weekly sessions.

Of course, it is also possible to overdo the innovations: The Golden Years Senior Adults Club had been meeting regularly for nearly a year in a metropolitan area community center. A new worker was assigned to the group to help them plan and carry out their program of recreation and leisure-time activities. The worker was full of ideas—an excursion next week, a musicale the following week, attending a movie and discussing it three weeks from now—an idea for every meeting. After six weeks the members approached the worker and said, "We got together after last week's meeting and decided to propose a plan to you. How would it be if you planned the program for the odd weeks of each month and let us decide what we want to do on the even weeks?"

The worker realized his suggestions had been too numerous and that he had been too aggressive with the members, which led to a discussion of how he might help them without taking over their club.

The Worker's Skills

No matter what the level of functioning of the group or its degree of participation, human-service professionals working with the aged need knowledge of potential leisure-time and recreation activities. An effective worker develops lists of possible programs, resource files, guides of places to visit in the community, games, musical activities, dances, and a whole range of educational programs. Workers may find such resources in books, in conversations with other workers carrying on similar activities, from supervisors, and from observing and listening to the members themselves.

**Comprehensive Planning
for Recreation**

Chapter 6 discussed some of the ways in which group services are applied to the recreational interests and needs of older adults through group processes. While the emphasis in working with groups is on helping the members grow and develop through group activities, recreation and leisure-time activities are employed for their inherent value and potential for giving pleasure to the members.

Perhaps the most important principle for human-service workers with older people is that a wide range of activities is needed, because older adults constitute a varied population. For example, some older people will have extensive experience and sophisticated skills in the arts; others may have only limited exposure to such activities. Some older adults may want to participate actively in a wide range of programs—they will be eager to try anything—while others may have no interest in or an aversion to anything new. Older people who consider themselves "clumsy," as well as those who have physical handicaps, may be reluctant to engage in dance. Some older people may associate music with unpleasant experiences from their youth, perhaps unsuccessful school years or association with religious institutions. Therefore, the effective worker will help develop a recreation and leisure-time program that meets needs in many ways.

Some of the principles to follow in organizing and planning recreational programs are the following:

1. *Variety.* There should be a rich and broad opportunity for recreational activity geared to older people. The group's recreation program should not be limited to one kind of activity, for instance, card games, ceramics, or current events discussions, although all three, plus others, might constitute a well-balanced and popular program. A variety of recreational activities ensures each member the opportunity to find something interesting within the group and provides members with new experiences, rather than a repetition of those they have had in the past.

    We do not propose that programs simply permit older adults to carry on their own activities in isolation from one another. Effective recreation programs should enable each older person to find something in which he or she can excel while fostering interaction between the members of the group. Mr. Brown, who may be a fine painter, may take great satisfaction in helping Mrs. Green or Mr. Blue paint a landscape. He has an opportunity to participate in an activity that pleases him and offers him an opportunity to excel while he develops his personal skills in helping others. Mrs. Green may have the same opportunity through organizing a chess tournament, and Mr. Blue may be a gourmet cook who can achieve similar gratification through organizing a cooking lesson.

2. *Development.* Recreational activities should progress. It is usually inadvisable to use the same activities all the time, because they tend to institutionalize the group (see Chapter 6) and because they become monotonous. Activities ought to develop. For example, if a crafts group begins with paper-folding, there ought to be provisions for that activity to grow into other experiences. Perhaps leather work, copper enameling, and other more advanced crafts such as pottery can be introduced to the group and build upon the base that was established with paper work. Participants in recreation programs need to be stimulated and "stretched" through activities. It is often an objective of recreation programs to help people improve skills they already have and to learn new skills. This principle can apply, for example, to dance activities, which might begin with simple movements, similar to calisthenics. Such activities, which are useful in themselves, may provide a base for more complex activities such as ballroom and folk dancing, which have additional physical and social advantages for the members.

3. *Flexibility*. Though members might usefully be "stretched" in their activities, they ought also to be permitted, if they choose, to remain where they are. Some participants in older adult recreation programs may want to spend years playing checkers and never move to backgammon or chess. Of course, that is their right, and one must assume they are benefiting from the activity if it provides them with personal satisfaction. Similarly, a current events group might, under the developmental principle, grow from newspaper discussions to conversations dealing with more advanced theoretical works on political, historical, and social subjects. On the other hand, some members may want to discuss newspapers alone, without any additional growth. Others may want to reminisce about the past and focus on almost personal histories rather than the present or future. There ought to be provisions for people to follow those inclinations, if they choose to do so.

    The principle of flexibility can be established and implemented through such means as having a variety of groups within the program; organizing some recreational activity on an individual rather than a group basis; or providing participants with materials and resources for recreational activities with a minimum of direction.

4. *Degree of Structure*. The concept of flexibility suggests that activities need to be both structured and unstructured. In terms of structure, there ought to be set times and places when activities are provided. For example, a drama club meeting every Saturday from 3– 5 P.M. provides the members with information on when they should come and, in essence, guarantees them compatriots who will join them in dramatic activities. However, a program ought also to have time for relatively unstructured activities, such as "Senior Lounge" from 10– 12, Monday, Wednesday, and Friday, which might be an opportunity for members to join in games, crafts, and other activities they choose at the time. Members should be able to remain affiliated with the program without being involved in structured activity at all times.

5. *Attendance*. Recreation programs for adults have a history of successful participation. However, numbers do not always mean the program is what it ought to be. For example, in one community several senior centers, churches, and other groups sponsor senior recreation programs on different days of the week. On Monday it is the Senior Center; on Tuesday the Presbyterian Church sponsors a drop-in lounge for older people; on Wednesday it's the Roman Catholic Church; on Thursday, the Jewish Community Center; and on Friday, the Kiwanis Club. One day at a community meeting on aging programs, staff from all three programs meet. After they talk for a while, it quickly becomes clear virtually the same people rotate among these programs each week! The programs assumed they were serving a half-dozen special interest groups, but, in fact, they were all serving the same single group.

In many communities older adults are so hungry for leisure-time activities
that they will attend and participate no matter what the quality of the activity or
its sponsorship. Therefore, human-service workers must carefully evaluate programs with their participants to ensure they are genuinely popular and in line
with the needs and interests of the participants. The simple fact that people come
does not mean they are getting what they can and should be able to handle.

6. *Costs.* Workers helping plan leisure-time activities with older adults should ensure that the costs of the activity are within the means of the members. Cost can
   be an important factor for the members of the group, as lack of money is a
   pervasive problem for older Americans. When shortages of funds are the problem,
   costs may be the most significant factor in deciding what to do. It may mean that
   the worker has to help the group choose a program that is relatively inexpensive
   and located, perhaps, within the facilities of the agency sponsoring the group. Or,
   if it is at all possible, the worker may want to find a way to raise funds through
   contributions or grants to support a particularly expensive activity, such as a trip
   to a distant community. Or the agency may have a budget that will provide
   support for more costly programs. In any case, cost is a consideration that cannot
   be overlooked. The evaluation of activities by senior adults may be centered upon
   how much they cost, more than anything else.

7. *Specialists.* Activities also frequently require special skills and special instruction,
   which may be available from part-time specialist staff members within or outside the agency sponsoring the group. Recreational therapists, occupational
   therapists, physical education teachers, dance instructors, and many other
   people may be available to provide the necessary instruction or supervision for
   the members. In all cases the use of outside experts and resource people must be
   taken into consideration when the worker is not equipped to handle the activity
   with the group members.

It is not enough, we stress, for the members to participate in and seem to enjoy
programs. Even more important is that the members reach their maximum level of
functioning in recreation and leisure-time programs through the efforts of the
human-service worker.

As Part One makes clear, older adults have a range of capabilities. They may
move more slowly, respond more slowly, and appear to be less competent than
younger people, but those characteristics are more appearances than reality. With
proper time, help, and resources, most older people can do all or most of the things
younger adults can.

Workers serving groups for recreational purposes should reach beyond the apparent and the simple in developing programs. They should help their members
maximize the level and quality of their participation and the quality of their activities.

**Agencies That Sponsor
Recreation and
Leisure-Time Programs**

There are many organizations that sponsor recreation and leisure-time programs for older adults. Senior centers funded through state, local, and federal funds are best known. In addition, many sectarian human-service organizations provide programs for older citizens. These include the YMCAs and YWCAs, Jewish Community Centers, and church-related settlement houses. These organizations usually receive their funds through voluntary contributions and through allocations from local United Funds and community charitable groups. Although they may be identified with sectarian objectives, they are generally nonsectarian in their programs. That is, participants need not be affiliated with the religious group sponsoring the program in order to participate as a member. Sectarian organizations may be devoted to preserving the heritage of the sponsoring group or to serving members of that group. However, they accept for membership people who want to affiliate with their activities. At times recreational facilities provided by a religious group different from that of the older person may still meet the individual's needs; location may be a more important criterion for the older person than the specific cultural or religious affiliation of the facility. A Roman Catholic older adult may find usefulness in the senior adult program of a nearby Jewish community center. So might an older Jewish person find that a neighborhood Presbyterian settlement house has a good bit to offer.

Public Recreation Programs

City and county recreation programs frequently sponsor leisure-time activities for older adults. These are diverse and vary in quality from community to community. Many will have the whole range of activities for senior adults suggested in Chapter 6; others may be more limited. The majority of recreation and leisure-time programs financed by tax funds include some degree of activity for older people.

Religious Organizations

Churches, synagogues, and other religious organizations frequently sponsor special programs for older adults, particularly their own members. In fact, religious institutions of all kinds probably have the greatest success in attracting and maintaining the interest of older adults.

The programs for older members are not always recreational. Many are based upon religious activity, the degree of which varies from congregation to congregation. Bible study groups, worship services, language instruction (in the cases of Greek Orthodox, Jewish, and other churches that worship in a language other than English), as well as volunteer service activities, such as visiting the sick, preparing meals in order to raise funds, maintaining church facilities, and generally supporting the religious institution, are among the activities that engage the time and efforts of older adults.

Civic Clubs

Some civic clubs serve older adults through recreation and leisure-time programs. Many also involve older adults as local and regional leaders, since they are likely to have extensive experience in the organization as well as sufficient free time to provide it with help. Civic clubs include Kiwanis, Lions, Rotary, Optimists, and various women's organizations either affiliated with these men's groups or independent, such as the American Association of University Women. Fraternal organizations, such as the various Masonic groups, the Elks, Moose, Eagles, and others, also carry on social, recreational, and service activities for older people.

Other civic organizations attract and serve sectarian and ethnically supported groups, including B'nai B'rith, which is primarily for Jewish men and women, the Knights of Columbus, for Roman Catholic men, and various smaller organizations for almost every ethnic group. One of the ways ethnic groups maintain their identity is through such organizations. There are social and civic groups serving blacks, others with a predominantly Chicano membership, and still others for Asian-American men and women.

Veterans Organizations

Veterans organizations are among the most important of those groups serving older adults. The American Legion, Veterans of Foreign Wars, Disabled American Veterans, Jewish War Veterans, and many other smaller organizations are sponsors of leisure-time services for older adults, many of whom may be members of the organizations.

The significance, configuration, and roles and status of these groups will vary from community to community. An effective worker with and for older adults must become aware of the various groups that develop and sponsor programs of recreation and leisure-time activities for older people. Coming to know the range and limits of these activities is an important part of the orientation to the community for workers in older adult programs.

Self-Help Groups

Among the more significant developments in recent years for older adults have
been self-help groups through which older people become engaged in programs designed to help them deal with their problems, interests, or concerns.

The self-help group is an important vehicle for older people in identifying and
dealing with problems. Such groups follow a long American tradition of people organizing themselves to work toward overcoming their problems. The labor union
movement, the ethnic minority groups, the civil rights movement, the National Welfare Rights Organization, neighborhood groups, and thousands of others in American
history have organized themselves to take action that will benefit them.

Perhaps the best known of the self-help groups for older adults is the Gray Panthers, founded and led by Maggie Kuhn, a retired human-service worker. (See Chapter
11.) The core of the membership is older adults, and the group works to define and
overcome problems of the aging in the United States, particularly in the localities of
the various chapters around the country. Although they are nonpartisan, the Gray
Panthers' efforts are to influence local, state, and national governments in ways that
will benefit older people. Members work with legislatures, city governments, law
enforcement organizations, public and private social welfare programs, and many
other organizations whose programs affect the welfare of the elderly.

The Gray Panthers are a prototype of the legislative and governmentally oriented
self-help group. They discovered, as did other groups for older people around the
United States, that modest changes in administrative regulations and legislation
affecting Social Security, Medicare, and other economic aid programs, such as those
described in Chapter 12, could be of major benefit to older people.

Political Action

There is a long tradition of older people's participating in political groups, frequently as individuals but more frequently in recent years as representatives of their
age group.

In addition to groups such as the Gray Panthers, there are local, regional, and
national groups of older people who work for the development of service programs as
well as legislation to benefit their population. In West Virginia there is a state-wide
organization called the Council of Senior West Virginians. It, in turn, has helped
create the Coalition on Legislation for the Aged, which includes a variety of groups
concerned about the problems of the elderly. The Coalition lobbies intensively each
year in the halls of the state legislature.

The extent of such nonpartisan political activity by older people is not known but
it is clearly growing along with the aged population. The American Association of

Retired Persons, with some 5 million members, is an influential voice for older people.

As is discussed later in this chapter, older adults are also active in local, state, and national political committees and campaigns for individual candidates.

In some political jurisdictions, the aged are a crucial voting bloc who can swing an election in one direction or another. The aged in Florida and California are particularly important and aged populations in all states will continue to become active and articulate participants in all political activity.

For a variety of reasons, older people are likely to be effective participants in political campaigns and in efforts to influence government agencies as well as state legislatures. They may function as an active and effective lobbying group in Congress. Some of the reasons are discussed in the section of this chapter dealing with volunteer roles for older people, since political volunteering is one of the main forms of free-time activity engaged in by older citizens.

The self-help group focusing on public policy developments and the needs and rights of older people constitute a significant form of self-help group.

Therapeutic Self-Help Groups

Some older adults are organized into different kinds of self-help groups focused less on changing the larger society than toward helping the individual members overcome specific personal, emotional, or health problems.

The typical personal change-oriented self-help group is Alcoholics Anonymous, which includes many older members. Alcoholics Anonymous accepts no funds from government agencies, foundations, or voluntary human-service campaigns such as United Fund. Rather, they support all of their activities through their own contributions and through the sales of their educational materials. Instead of using professional staff to help them with their problem, alcoholism, the members help themselves and each other through group programs.

There are dozens of similar organizations operated in several problem areas. The Lost Chord group helps those who have had laryngectomies; Synanon is organized for drug abusers. There is a local self-help group for almost every kind of problem in one part of the United States or another.

Such groups require that their members face their problems themselves; they prefer not using professional staff, and they work to be totally self-supporting. One example of a self-help group organized by a human-service worker is the following:

The worker discovered that in her recreation group of 45 older men, some 20 had experienced problems with heart disease or had been warned that they could develop heart disease problems if they failed to care for themselves properly. The worker called these 20 members together and suggested that they might want to organize a self-help group. She offered to help them find an appropriate meeting place, agreed to provide them with some suggestions on how they might organize their program, and offered to provide consultation on a regular basis but also to stay out of the members' activities if they preferred not having her participate.

The men joined together and organized a weekly group meeting, calling themselves "The Powerful Pump Club." They took turns reporting on ways to reduce the risk of heart disease, monitored each other's diets and weight, talked about ways of avoiding anger, and began a program of exercise in the group that could be continued through walking and jogging on their own. When they wanted the worker's help, they asked for it, and they gave her credit for helping them begin. They occasionally called on experts from outside their group, such as physicians, psychologists, and social workers. But it was their group, and they used it well. Over a period of two years, none of the members had any problems with heart disease, and they attributed their good fortune to the activities of The Powerful Pump Club.

Education

Informal and formal education are among the important self-help and self-improvement activities available to older adults. Colleges and universities are frequently open to older adults on the same bases they are available to younger people. Some institutions of higher education cater to older citizens by reducing or waiving tuition for them. Participation by older adults in higher education is of benefit to the institutions as well as the older participants, because the colleges and universities are able to make their classes more heterogeneous through the introduction of people with life experiences to share with younger students and faculty members.

Vocational schools have some classes in auto mechanics and other trades for senior citizens. Continuing education programs sponsored by community centers, YMCAs, YWCAs, and community colleges offer short courses and workshops that may have special interest for older learners on subjects as diverse as creative writing, history, consumer safety, drama, and so on.

Public libraries are important leisure-time resources for some older adults, and occasionally libraries sponsor programs geared to help older adults select and make the best use of books and periodicals.

Of course, the continuing education of older adults is not limited to reading. Some theaters, both live and motion picture, sponsor senior citizen matinees or discount programs to make it easier and financially feasible for older adults to attend.

Miscellaneous Activities

In addition to all the activities already mentioned, there are many others that lie somewhere between simple recreation and creative use of leisure through self-help

programs. These include gardening programs, camping, and the whole range of
sports. Virtually anything pleasurable for people of all ages can be adapted to the
needs of older adults. For instance, many communities have "Master's" long-distance
running groups that include men and women in the senior years. There are national
competitions for older runners. Some of the sturdiest long-distance runners in the
United States are older adults; many are able to outdistance men and women who are
much younger.

Volunteer Programs
for Older Adults

Volunteering to serve others is one of the ways older adults occupy their leisure
time. In recent years, volunteer programs for older adults have been developed by the
federal government as well as by many states and cities. Volunteer programs for the
total population also have attracted many volunteers from the ranks of the American
elderly.

The federal agency Action, which includes the retired senior volunteer program
(RSVP), Senior Companion Program, and Foster Grandparent Program; the Peace
Corps; and Volunteers in Service to America (VISTA) have been a major source of
senior adult recruitment and deployment for voluntary services.

The Peace Corps recruits and trains volunteers to serve in technical and human-
service positions overseas. The cost of their maintenance, travel, and work are borne
by the United States government; the nation that receives the volunteers contributes
some technical assistance and other kinds of help, along with the development of
assignments for them. VISTA does something similar in selected communities in the
United States, usually communities that have high needs for human-service
specialists in fields such as mental health, community development, youth work, and,
of course, services to older adults.

RSVP is a federally funded program that provides for the development of senior
volunteer programs in local communities that apply for and receive grants to develop
and operate such programs. The range of services provided by the senior volunteers is
enormous. Many engage in social service projects, others work on oral histories, and
still others work in hospitals and correctional institutions. Many of the RSVP programs are sponsored by local senior centers that develop plans and programs in
consonance with the needs of the local community and the potential interests of
senior citizens in it.

Volunteers in Human-Service
Agencies

For a variety of reasons, many human-service agencies engage volunteers to carry
out their programs. It is a common practice for departments of public welfare, family

service agencies, community mental-health centers, and many other programs to rely
heavily on volunteers.

Older Adults and Youth Services

Voluntary youth organizations operate almost totally through the efforts of volunteers. This is especially true of the Boy Scouts, Girl Scouts, and Campfire Girls,
which are the three largest voluntary youth organizations. Older people provide an
excellent and frequently untapped resource for volunteer leaders of those youth
groups. Even when they are unable to provide full-time assistance to the program as
scoutmasters, den mothers, or group leaders of other designations, they may be able
to supplement the efforts or other volunteers by assisting them or by providing specialized help with camping, crafts, or educational activities.

There are a number of ways for older adults to be of service in such groups. In one
community center older men played the role of "den grandads" to a Cub Scout den.
The community center decided that the youngsters needed contact with men, particularly with older men, since many of the youngsters did not live in the same city as
their grandfathers. These den grandads fulfilled important functions for youngsters in
their community.

Other Sources for Volunteer Activity

Many communities have volunteer bureaus, voluntary action centers, and other
organizations designed to bring together groups that are seeking voluntary assistance and those who are looking for voluntary activities in which they might be
helpful.

At times volunteers supplement the activities of an agency by extending the
service the agency can provide to its clientele. In other situations volunteers help the
agency develop connections with the larger community. They bring their own knowledge of the community to the agency and provide service to their own special communities on behalf of the agency. Many volunteers serve the functions of relating the
agency to the larger community by serving on the board of directors as policy makers,
helping the agency develop policies that are in line with community norms while
interjecting the interests and concerns of the community they represent. At other
times, they provide help to the agency by soliciting funds in the community. Much of
the fund raising done on behalf of social agencies is carried out through the efforts of

older volunteers. Some people retire from their work with the full intention of devoting all or most of their free time to human-service agencies in the community.

In other cases agencies use older volunteers to help them with new and specialized activities they may not be able to develop on their own. For example, retired music teachers may organize choral groups, artists may develop painting projects or sculptures, and physical educators can introduce sports programs. Retired psychologists and psychiatrists can bolster the mental-health program of counseling agencies. Older adults contribute voluntarily some of the kinds of professional services that the agency might not be able to afford.

Most large hospitals, both psychiatric and general, have large volunteer departments. In some major hospitals, gift shops, visitor food services, information desks, and other crucial parts of the health-care program are directed by volunteers.

Voluntary Political Participation

Among the most significant voluntary activities of older people is political participation. Both of the major U.S. parties and many others use large numbers of older volunteers to help them in their programs. Older people are among the most active workers in local and state political committees and campaigns. There are many reasons why older people can be effective participants in political activity. For one, they are a large and active group. When they are organized, they represent a bloc of voters that is impressive for any political aspirant. When they battle for programs geared to improving their lives, their case tends to be persuasive for members of state legislatures, the U.S. Congress, and administrators at all levels.

Available leisure time, which may seem disadvantageous and problematic for many older people, is a significant advantage in political activity. Older people have the time to prepare and process mailings or to visit with individual voters to convince them to support candidates, and often they are able to help transport voters to the polls. Much of politics involves hours, days, and months of repetitive, difficult work. Older people, more than any other group in American society, have the time for such activity and, for that reason, they are a respected and highly valued resource in many political campaigns.

In addition, older people are often more politically knowledgeable and responsive than the general population. They tend to vote, attend rallies, and, when possible, contribute to campaigns. Moreover, they do not pose a threat to candidates. It is rare for a 70-year-old volunteer to become the candidate's opponent in the next election, but not so rare for a younger supporter to do so.

For all these reasons, voluntary participation in politics is a major opportunity for many older people and one that ought to be considered in the analysis of and development of any leisure-time program for older adults.

The Dual Advantages of
Volunteer Programs

Clearly, older adult volunteers help others of all ages and all situations in many ways. Volunteering is also of value to the older adults themselves. Those who are otherwise unemployed add significance to their lives by helping young people, the handicapped, other older adults, institutionalized people, and others through volunteer programs. Many psychologists would agree that we help ourselves by helping others—that we build our self-esteem when we improve the lives of other people. In addition, people who are occupied with positive activities may improve their mental health through activity.

Summary

The sudden availability of leisure time is one of the obvious results of aging in the United States. This chapter has explored some of the consequences of the increased availability of leisure time for old people and outlined some of the problems and opportunities associated with that change in the lifestyle and patterns of the older person.

Some of the ways in which older people may use leisure time were outlined, including recreation programs, self-help programs, and volunteer programs in many kinds of organizations and institutions.

Increased leisure constitutes one of the more complex problems of older people and from it arise some of the most important needs older adults have and some of the most important contributions human-service workers with the aging may make to their clients. Helping older people find effective ways to use their leisure time that are compatible with their health, interests, and financial resources is one of the most important ways professionals help older clients in the United States.

READING 14.1

Rural Seniors Have Activity Centers, Too / Chuck Yoke
This report offers a brief glimpse of activities at rural senior centers.

Just because your hair's turned gray and you don't live in Morgantown doesn't mean you can't have fun at a Senior Center.

From *The Better Times Weekly*, Morgantown, W. Va., April 11, 1977. Reprinted by permission of the publisher.

There are five senior centers in rural areas of Monongalia County to serve older folks who'd like to enjoy the benefits and camaraderie offered.

Everettville has perhaps the largest program of the five centers. Other centers are in Blacksville, Jakes Run, Wadestown, and Daybrook.

The Everettville group meets daily, enjoying a hot lunch under the federally-funded Senior Nutrition Center program.

But members also enjoy crafts and other activities. Ceramics, Bible study and organized shopping trips are regular features, according to Debbie Poluga, supervisor for the rural senior centers.

Daybrook has the second most active senior Center. It meets every Tuesday. Poluga teaches a ceramics class and holds a covered dish lunch.

Each meets one day a month, Jakes Run on the second Thursday of the month, Blacksville on the fourth, and Wadestown on the third Thursday.

This may change, though.

"Blacksville is in the process of becoming a Senior Nutrition Center," Poluga said, "and if they do become one they will be open every day and serve hot lunches like Morgantown's and Everettville's."

Poluga became supervisor last September. Before that she worked for the state welfare department in Charleston and for the Fairmont Senior Center.

Are these rural senior centers really worthwhile, or are they a waste of time?

"I really like it. It's a wonderful place," said Myrtle White, one of the spirited, eager ladies who frequent the Everettville Center.

At the Daybrook center the activity was similar.

"My goodness, yes, I like it," said Grace DeVine. "I look forward to coming here."

"I see more of my friends," said Eva Williams. "Before the center was open we had a Homemakers Club. But now we have more activities, we have a covered lunch every Tuesday and I get to see more people."

On a recent Tuesday a birthday party was held for one of the members.

The rural senior centers seem to meet the needs of the people who live in outlying areas of the county and can't come to the one in Morgantown.

At each center there is a feeling of closeness and neighborliness. Everybody knows one another and since the members are all from that certain area there is an air of loyalty to each center.

But they are quick to welcome strangers in their midst and make them feel at home.

Even if the stranger is a 22-year-old person with a camera and note pad, within five minutes he felt as if he has known them all for ages and was right at home.

Senior citizens in an outlying part of the county who want to meet some new people, learn a skill or just have a good time should visit their local center.

The Everettville center is housed in the old red brick school building across the street from the old community building.

The Daybrook center is in the third building behind the Daybrook Elementary School in Daybrook.

"It looks like a garage," Debbie Poluga said.

The Jakes Run center meets in the Jakes Run Methodist Church.

The Blacksville group meets at the Blacksville Methodist Church.

The Wadestown seniors meet at the Wadestown Methodist Church.

Questions 14.1

1. What are some special constraints found in rural senior centers that are not as likely to be found in urban senior centers?

2. Nutrition seems to be a central activity of these programs. How can you account for this?

3. Despite the fact that some senior groups seldom meet, the response seems to be uniformly positive. What needs of the elderly are being met?

4. Class project: Conduct an informal survey of your community's volunteer and leisure-time activities for older people. Be sure to include recreation and travel and excursion opportunities as well as church, civic, political, educational, and volunteer activities.

READING 14.2

Teaching Old Folks Is an Art / Robert Coles

This review of Kenneth Koch's I Never Told Anybody . . . Teaching Poetry Writing in a Nursing Home *demonstrates that physical incapacity need not be a hindrance to successful elderly participation in leisure-time activities.*

In a letter to a young admirer, William Carlos Williams once had this to say: "I hear lines of poetry every day from my patients. They sometimes say what they see and feel in interesting ways. In my car, later in the day, I hear their words." Kenneth Koch has had the same willingness to pay close heed to the lyrical possibilities that many ordinary human beings possess, and even demonstrate rather impressively, given any encouragement at all. His book *Wishes, Lies, and Dreams* told of his work with children, who ache at times to use their imaginations and stretch the bounds of language, only to be put down repeatedly by various literal-minded, sadly resttictive adults. The boys and girls he came to know eventually produced strongly worded, suggestive, eye-opening poems. Now he has taken his thoughtful, giving, resourceful and patient spirit to quite elderly and often infirm men and women, in obvious hopes of finding among them a similar responsiveness of mind and heart. If anything, the result is a more poignant and dramatic victory, because many old people have learned only too well that even their prose statements, never mind any written poems they may come up with, are of scant interest to others.

The American Nursing Home (no less) is located on the Lower East Side of Manhattan— not far from the Catholic Workers' St. Joseph House. It was there, with about 25 men and women, that Koch tried to teach poetry. "The students were all incapacitated in some way, by illness or old age," he tells us. He is brief and matter-of-fact with specifics, his purpose being educational and literary, rather than sociological: "Most were in their seventies, eighties and nineties. Most were from the working class and had a limited education. They had worked as dry cleaners, messengers, short-order cooks, domestic servants." To a significant degree they had given up on life; it was enough to stay alive, be fed and cared for. Needless to say, they did not write poems. Yet one day Kenneth Koch and another poet, Kate Farrell, showed up and began to talk about poems, to read them and to suggest that they were not only the creations (or property) of a lucky, privileged few, but also that they could begin to take shape in the thoughts of ordinary people, and be acknowledged, shared, enjoyed by them.

Koch had not romanticized his students. He knew that they were tired, hurt, ailing. Some were blind or hard of hearing. They all had serious complaints, and a number were in constant pain. As he took the measure of his class, he observed the serious initial obstacles of memory loss and rambling speech among many men and women. But he was not there to dwell on negatives. He began by asking the people to think of a sentence or two. He had modest, concrete suggestions: choose a color, say something about it, then something else, then something else again, using the name of the color. He received gratifying responses. Mary Tkalek, for instance, offered this: "I like green; I used to see so many greens on the farm/I used to wear green, and sometimes my mother couldn't find me/Because I was green in the green."

The teacher became bolder. He asked his students to imagine themselves the ocean, or holding a conversation with the moon, the stars. He suggested that they recall especially quiet moments, or make particular comparisons or hark back to one or another time—the end of World War II, for instance. He read to them; he singled out, to start, the verse of Walt Whitman, D. H. Lawrence and William Carlos Williams. He never looked down on his students; he regarded them as quite able to write poetry, given encouragement and provocative hints about what tack they might take. He did not want to blur the difference between the dead poets he cherished (and in a way was calling upon for assistance) and the members of the rather unusual writing class he had chosen to teach. He knew that, finally, he could only count on this from a given student: "The music of ordinary speech and the memories and feelings his long life had given him."

Over the weeks they learned to summon and repeat words joyfully, to exaggerate enthusiastically, to celebrate contrasts, to become immersed in nature, to imagine all sorts of places, to put themselves into many different kinds of shoes. Most of them were wheeled in; some arrived in walkers, and only a few came to class on their own—yet they reached out for the sky, crossed the seas, fashioned their own time-machines and used them gladly, at times wantonly. And their teacher, clearly, loved what happened. He praised them; fed them more and more of his ideas, received back increasingly intricate, dramatic and subtle poems. "Poetry is like being in Inner Space," William Ross decided, early on. "Your leaves sound different," Nadya Catalfano told the season, autumn, one day: "I couldn't understand why/The leaves at that time of year/Had a rustle about them/And they would drop/At the least little thing/And I would listen/And pick up some of them."

The students were encouraged both to speak and write their poems. They were treated to jazz, to readings of Keats as well as more contemporary poets, and as their blood stirred they were asked to talk about their past lives. Their teacher was not, however, interested in becoming yet another of America's flourishing breed of psychological counselors. He makes an important clarification: "I don't think I would like to adjust to a life without imagination or accomplishment, and I don't believe my students wanted to either. It is in that sense, perhaps, that it can best be understood why it is better to teach poetry writing as an art than to teach it—well, not really teach it but use it—as some form of distracting or consoling therapy." And a little later on, referring to one of his students: "We were never contemplating Mary L. Jackson, she and I, but the things she said and wrote." He never expected too little of her—that curious condescension that is masked as compassion: "One trouble with a kind of falsely therapeutic and always reassuring attitude that it is easy to fall into with old people is the tendency to be satisfied with too little."

And so those men and women, nearer death than most of us, worked hard and became in their spirits lively, attentive, dedicated. "I'd like to write the book of my life/I've started it already," Mary L. Jackson observed. Their enthusiasm, their bursts of memory, reflection, fantasy were matched by the evident satisfaction of their teacher. In this book he tells others how they, too, might work with elderly people. He shows us that in Iowa (he spent time at the Lutheran Old Age Home in Cedar Falls), as well as in New York, apparently apathetic, even dazed men and women can suddenly begin to sing with their own words. And with a sentence here and there, he gives us textbooks of psychology and sociology: "Many had spent most of their adult lives at jobs like housework, steam-pressing, being a short-order cook. They had unusual (for poetry) lives and were looking at them now in an unusual time." But he is not one to argue with others or to come up with pompous generalizations: he merely implies with a casual, personal thought the significant difference between his way of regarding people and that of others—with their talk of "cultural disadvantage" and whatever: "I did think sometimes, too, what a marvelous thing it was for someone, for instance, to be writing poetry, and loving it, who had kept through decades of hard domestic work, a fine and delicate sensibility that she could now express with eloquence in words."

Mostly Koch encouraged in his students what he calls "unrhymed, nonmetrical, fairly unliterary poetry"; it was an easier kind for beginning students to approach. But they enjoyed hearing and occasionally trying to write a more formal and intricate language. They would, no doubt, recognize a familiar spirit at play in the pages of "The Duplications." Their teacher has completed a long poem, somewhat arbitrarily divided in half by an autobiographical section. Using mostly rhymed octets, he sets out to abolish space, time and historical experience in order to create exuberant images that entertain, and occasionally (though with a light hand) instruct. The narrator is a rather sensuous, symbol-prone itinerant, at once rhapsodic and skeptical. He clearly sympathizes with those "Students dreaming up some pure Havanas/ Where love would govern all, not francs or dollars"; but he worries that new tyrannies, announced with messianic slogans, keep replacing their predecessors—one of the "duplications" intended by his title, which more broadly refers to the cyclic rhythms of life. He is, always, very much an individual—someone who might not bother Fidel Castro, but who certainly would arouse the suspicions of his bureaucratic henchmen: "O Liberty, you are the only word at/Which the heart of man leaps automatically."

Koch has a delicious sense of ironic detachment running through his rather lyrical, if not ecstatic, celebrations of the flesh. On a Greek island, contemplating the serene beauty of the Aegean, he thinks of the life underneath: ". . . Fish are nice/In being, though we eat them, not revengeful/I think that we would probably be meaner/To those who washed us down with their retsina!" It is an observation utterly worthy of Pueblo or Hopi children, who, like Emerson or Thoreau—speaking of duplications—are not especially inclined to what in the 19th century was called "human vainglory." He is especially wry and touching when he tells of his struggles to write while living in Ireland. He had finished part of the poem, put it aside for other interests (teaching children or the elderly how to write poetry?) and had come back to himself, his mind's (the writer's) self-centeredness. Ought he to go on, "Continue my narration of the fallacy/We find by being born into this galaxy"? His answer is characteristically lacking in egoistic justifications, or sly academic boasting. He simply wants to reach others; maybe make them feel like singing, or smile in recognition of a particular vision, suggestion, anecdote. Of course, he cannot resist, occasionally, tucking into his narrative a bit of philosophical speculation or moral concern.

His is a wanderer's unyielding struggle for life: ". . . Take that, you/Dull insect Death! . . ." His is a naturalist's pantheistic, humorous advocacy: "Now turtles have on Mount Olympus landed/With numerous troops, and pistols, flags, and bells/And hostile mottoes painted on their shells/DOWN WITH OLYMPUS! WHY SHOULD WE ENDURE/AN ALIEN RULE? LET TURTLES REIGN O'ER TURTLES!/AND GODS GO HOME! THE VERY AIR IS PURE/WE TURTLES BREATHE. WE DO NOT NEED MYRTLES,/THE OAK, THE BAY, THE SHINING SINECURE!/GIVE US OUR LIVES TO LIVE IN OUR HARD GIRDLES!" It is a point of view one can imagine the old ones in the American Nursing Home of New York's Lower East Side taking to rather heartily: their good, dear friend Kenneth Koch doing some of his marvelously entertaining and sometimes unnerving acrobatic stunts.

Questions 14.2

1. The poet Koch's way of regarding people does not include "cultural disadvantage." What does this mean? What effects could his point of view have on his program?

2. Koch does not consider himself a psychological counselor, yet his program has therapeutic results. How do you account for this?

What implications does this have for you as a human-service practitioner?

3. Discuss other possible programs for leisure time that would allow successful participation of physically incapacitated senior citizens.

 glossary

Terms as defined here are specifically related to the content of the text and are done in the context of human service work with older people.

Advocate: One who defends or promotes a cause and the subsequent pleading of that cause.

Age-grading: Attributing or classifying types of human behavior as appropriate or inappropriate for specific age groups in society such as the young and old.

Age norms: Socially defined expected behaviors for people at any given age.

Budget: A financial tool, used as part of planning, to allocate available resources to anticipated expenditures.

Confidentiality: Principle that the worker does not reveal information secured from clients.

Demographic: Descriptive information about a population or group based on vital and/or social statistics.

Disengage: To voluntarily disassociate oneself from social contact.

Formed group: A group organized by an outside agent.

Goal: A broad statement of what is to be achieved over time by a program.

Group cohesion: A united group spirit.

Group conflict: Disunited group spirit.

Group process: The stages of dynamic interactions in the development of groups.

Group role: A specific position or set of behaviors assumed by individual group members as part of the interaction of the group as a whole.

Group solidarity: A group's total agreement and presentation of solid front.

Hospice: A facility designed to help people die with as little discomfort and as much serenity as possible.

Impact objectives: Outcomes expected in project participation as a result of project activities.

Later maturity: A phase of the life cycle, including the years 60– 74.

Life cycle: Stages of development in an individual's life span.

Life expectancy: Total number of years an individual can expect to survive at birth.

Middle age: A phase of the life cycle, including the years 40– 59.

Minority elderly: Subgroups within the elderly population who experience difficulties because of their status in society; for example, blacks, Mexican-Americans, native Americans, etc.

Natural group: A group organized by the members.

Needs: Basic requirements; in this context, specifically requirements for elderly people to secure and maintain maximum independence and dignity in a home or home-like environment.

Needs assessment: A means of systematically collecting information about the problems and needs of older people and their service utilization pattern.

Objective: A statement of a precise, measurable outcome to be accomplished by a program within the program year and under the funds requested.

Old age: A phase of the life cycle, including the years 75 to death.

Output objectives: The expected level of service or activities of a project.

Partialization: Breaking down a client's problem into manageable parts.

Physical aging: Physical changes associated with advancing years.

Planning: A process for fully determining a preferred course of future action.

Priority objective: An objective that has been evaluated against all other stated objectives and has been determined to be of greatest relative importance; it therefore will be ranked first in order of execution.

Psychological aging: Changes in adaptive or coping capacities associated with advancing years.

Psychomotor performance: Human behavior having to do with the brain process as it relates to muscular movement.

Reminiscence: Thinking and talking about occurrences of earlier years.

Role: A defined position within a group or in society that is associated with specific defined functions to be performed and expected behaviors as part of the position.

Self-determination: Permitting clients to decide and direct their own lives in a counseling situation.

Self-help group: A group through which older people become engaged in programs designed to help them deal with their problems, interests, or concerns themselves.

Social actions: Human behavior that is exhibited in groups or by classes of people without reference to specific individuals.

Social aging: The habits and roles of aging individuals as they relate to groups or society.

Social problem: A situation affecting a large number of people that they or others believe to be a source of difficulty or unhappiness.

Socialization: Learning of new behaviors and orientation as one moves into new positions in the social structure.

Status: Position in the social order.

Stereotype: Preconceived ideas about individuals or groups, generally not based on fact.

Strategy: The preferred course of action designed to best accomplish stated objectives.

Support services: Supplemental services provided by an agency to facilitate clients' ability to use the primary services of the agency.

Target population: A specific group or subgroup for which a program is intended or who is to benefit from a specific program.

Thanatology: The study of death and dying.

Unmet need: A need for which no service or resource exists, or for which the existing services are inadequate, inappropriate, or inaccessible.

Work plan: A detailed description, including tasks, of what is to be done, who is going to do it, and when it will be done.

ANNOTATEd bibliography

Part One
Chapter 1

Hayflick, Leonard
    1977   "The biology of aging." Natural History 86:22– 30. A discussion of the theories of biological aging and their implication for increasing longevity in later life.

Kessler, Julia Brown
    1976   "Aging in different ways." Human Behavior 5:56– 63. This article demonstrates from an anthropological view the specific patterns of aging in different cultures.

Shanas, Ethel
    1971   "The sociology of aging and the aged." The Sociological Quarterly 12:159–76. An historical literature review of the development of our understanding of the sociology of aging.

Chapter 2

The Graying of America
    1977   Newsweek, February 28, pp. 50– 66. A special report presenting the outcome of the impact of the increased number of older people on the conflict between generations.

Health of the Elderly
    1977   Public Health Report 92:3–64. A special report on the health problems,
             research, and programs for older adults in the United States.

Chapter 3

Haley, Alex
    1977   "Haley's Rx: talk, write, reunite." Time magazine, February 14, p. 72.
             The author of *Roots* depicts the role of elderly blacks as the oral histo-
             rians of the race.

Maldonado, David, Jr.
    1975   "The Chicano aged." Social Work 20:213–16. This article reviews the
             ill-founded views affecting the lifestyles of the Chicano aged and the
             social services they need.

Sommers, Tish
    1975   "Social security: a woman's viewpoint." Industrial Gerontologist,
             2:266–79. The author illustrates how the Social Security program as it
             now stands is highly discriminatory against women, who are penalized
             both as workers and as full-time homemakers.

Wu, Frances Y. T.
    1975   "Mandarin-speaking aged Chinese in the Los Angeles area." The Geron-
             tologist 15:271–75. A discussion of the language, social, and cultural
             barriers of the non-English speaking Chinese and how these barriers
             prevent them from receiving services.

Part Two
Chapter 4

Brody, Stanley, Harvey Finkle, and Carl Hirsch
    1972   "Benefit alert: outreach program for the aged." Social Work 17:14–23.
             The authors discuss the failure of an outreach program intended to
             advocate for the poor.

Sharkey, Harold
    1962   "Sustaining the aged in the community." Social Work 7:18–22. A dis-
             cussion of the important role outreach plans in providing services to the
             community's elderly citizens.

Chapter 5

Burnside, Irene Mortenson
    1973   "Touching is talking." The American Journal of Nursing 73:2060–63. The importance of nonverbal communication in working with older people is discussed in this article.

Pincus, Allen
    1970   "Reminiscence in aging and its implication for social work practice." Social Work 20:47–53. The author offers some new information on the interpersonal significance of reminiscing.

Schmidt, Mary Gwynne
    1975   "Interviewing the 'old, old.'" The Gerontologist 20:544–47. Methods of interviewing the very old are discussed, using illustrative material from studies of two homes for the aged.

Chapter 6

Lowy, Louis
    1962   "The group in social work with the aged." Social Work 7:62. This article suggests how group work can be used to help older people deal with problems of later life.

Mayadas, Nazneen, and Douglas Hink
    1975   "Group work with the aging." The Gerontologist 15:441–44. The authors discuss factors that should be taken into consideration in serving the elderly through groups.

Chapter 7

Milloy, Margaret
    1964   "Casework with the older person and his family." Social Work 45:450–55. The role of the social worker in providing assistance to older clients and their families.

Simos, Bertha G.
    1973   "Adult children and their aging parents." Social Work 18:78–85. A discussion of the involvement of adult children in helping aged parents deal with a wide range of problems.

Chapter 8

Craven, Joan and Florence S. Wald
    1975   "Hospice care for dying patients." American Journal of Nursing
            75:1816–22. Development of the hospice movement in the United States
            and a discussion of care and treatment of the terminal patient and his
            family.

Locker, Rose
    1976   "Elderly couples and the institution." Social Work 21:149–51. The au-
            thor illustrates the effects of separation on couples when one of them
            requires institutionalization due to chronic illness.

Part Three
Chapter 9

Bennett, Louis L.
    1965   "Protective service for the aged." Social Science Review 39:283–93. A
            discussion of the planning of a community protective service program
            for older people.

Caso, Elizabeth and Harry T. Phillips
    1966   "Small-grant project in Massachusetts for the chronically ill and aged."
            Public Health Report 81:471–77.

Kaplan, Jerome, Caroline S. Ford, and Harry Wain, M.D.
    1967   "Assessing the impact of a gerontological counseling service on commu-
            nity health resources." Geriatrics 22:150–54. This article describes a
            referral program that resulted in better use of community agencies in
            planning for the aged and the chronically ill.

Kramer, Elaine and Joyce Unger
    1967   "A survey of need in a public housing project for the aged." The Geron-
            tologist, Part I 7:204–206. Illustration of needs assessment as a base for
            developing community services.

Chapter 10

Sherman, Susan R.
    1975   "Provision of on-site services in retirement housing." International
            Journal of Aging and Human Development 6:229–47. An examination of
            the question of on-site supportive services in retirement housing
            facilities for the elderly.

U.S. Department of Health, Education, and Welfare
  1971   Report of the National Protective Service Project for Older Adults. Washington, D.C.: U.S. Government Printing Office. A comprehensive review of the need for and impact of protective services for older people.

Chapter 11

Kosberg, Jordan
  1975   "Methods of community surveillance on geriatric institutions." Public Health Report 9:144–48. The author presents a scheme for advocating for institutionalized older people.

Shapiro, Harvey
  1977   "Do not go gently . . ." The New York Times Magazine, February 6, pp. 36–41. A discussion of the activity initiated by older people to change the mandatory retirement procedures in this country.

Part Four
Chapter 12

Hulsey, Steve
  1975   "Working seniors prove their mettle." Manpower, June, pp. 23–25. A description of the Seniors at Work Program (SAW) funded by a CETA grant.

Chapter 13

Lamden, Richard S. and Lawrence N. Greenstein
  1975   "Partnership in out-patient day care." Hospital 49:87–89. A description of four hospitals' and two skilled nursing facilities' success in out-patient day-care services.

Merlin, Debrah
  1975   "Home care project for indigent allows dignified care, cuts cost." Hospital 49:77–78. This article describes a social work project that provides oxygen at home for indigent patients, thereby cutting hospitalization time and cost.

Chapter 14

Bross, Dorothy R.
>   1967   "Night college courses for older women." Adult Leadership 15:233–34. Describes a program to help in filling the need of the older woman to communicate.

Parke, James H.
>   1964   "Enlisting retired elderly persons for volunteer services." Hospital 38:66–68. This article discusses the value of older individuals in hospital volunteer services.

Worthington, Gladys
>   1963   "Older persons as community volunteers." Social Work 8:71–75. Describes the experience of an established volunteer bureau with retired people.

REFERENCES

Atchley, Robert C.
1977   The Social Forces in Later Life: An Introduction to Social Gerontology.
        2nd ed. Belmont, Ca.: Wadsworth.

Atchley, Robert C. and Mildred M. Seltzer
1977   The Sociology of Aging: Selected Readings. Belmont, Ca.: Wadsworth.

Auerbach, Arnold
1976   "The elderly in rural areas: differences in urban areas and implications
        for practice." In Leon Ginsberg (ed.), Social Work in Rural Com-
        munities. New York: Council on Social Work Education.

Baltes, P. and K. Warner Schaie
1974   "Aging and I.Q..: the myth of the twilight years." Psychology Today,
        March.

Beauvoir, Simone de
1972   The Coming of Age. New York: Putnam.

Bengston, Vern L.
1972   "A conceptual framework for the analysis of the behavior of aging indi-
        viduals in society." In Delivery and Administration of Services for the
        Elderly. Los Angeles: University of Southern California Press, 1972.
1973   The Social Psychology of Aging. New York: Bobbs-Merrill.

Berne, Eric
1969   Principles of Group Treatment. New York: Oxford University Press.

Birren, James E.
    1974   "Aging: psychological aspects." In Birren and Ruth Weg (eds.), Cur-
              riculum Development in Gerontology. Los Angeles: Ethel Percy Andrus
              Gerontology Center, University of Southern California.

Birren, James E. and Ruth Weg (eds.)
    1974   Curriculum Development in Gerontology. Los Angeles: Ethel Percy An-
              drus Gerontology Center, University of Southern California.

The Black Elderly in Long Term Care Settings.
    1974   Oakland, Ca.: Health Services Administration. Co-sponsored by the
              Ethel Percy Andrus Gerontology Center, University of Southern Califor-
              nia, and the Advisory Committee for Continuing Education: Services to
              the Black Elderly.

Boyd, Rosamond E. and Charles Oakes (eds.)
    1969   Foundations of Practical Gerontology. Columbia, S.C.: University of
              South Carolina Press.

Butler, Robert N.
    1975   Why Survive? Being Old in America. New York: Harper & Row.

Butler, Robert N. and Myrna Lewis
    1973   Aging and Mental Health. St. Louis, Mo.: C.V. Mosby.

Calloway, Nathaniel
    1974   "How We Age" Banquet Address, Symposium 2, Feb. 9–12, 1975, Insti-
              tute of Gerontology, School of Continuing Education, Federal City Col-
              lege, Washington, D.C.

Chen, Yung-Ping
    1970   Income. Background paper for the 1971 White House Conference on
              Aging. Washington, D.C.: U.S. Department of Health, Education, and
              Welfare, Administration on Aging.

Davis, Richard H. (ed.)
    1974   Aging: Perspectives and Issues. Los Angeles: Ethel Percy Andrus Geron-
              tology Center, University of Southern California.

"The elderly: prisoners of fear."
    1976   Time Magazine, November 26, pp. 21–22.

Gutmann, David E.
    1975   "Parenthood: a key to the comparative study of the life cycle." In Leon
              H. Ginsberg and Nancy Datan (eds.), Life-Span Developmental Psychol-
              ogy: Normative Life Crises. New York: Academic Press.

Harrington, Michael
  1960   The Other American. Baltimore, Md.: Penguin.

Jackson, Jacquelyne Johnson
  1973   Proceedings of Black Aged in the Future. Durham, N.C.: Center for the
           Study of Aging and Human Development, Duke University.

Kalish, Richard A.
  1975   Late Adulthood: Perspectives on Human Development. Monterey, Ca.:
           Brooks/Cole.
  1977   (Ed.), The Later Years. Monterey, Ca.: Brooks/Cole.

Kass, Leon R.
  1975   "The pursuit of health." The Public Interest, No. 40, Summer.

Kastenbaum, Robert J. and R. Aisenberg
  1972   The Psychology of Death. New York: Springer.

Kornblum, Seymour and Geraldine Lauter
  1976   "The developmental task of middle age and aging and the implications
           for practice." Conference Papers, New York: Association of Jewish
           Center Workers.

Kübler-Ross, Elizabeth
  1970   On Death and Dying. New York: Macmillan.

Lindsay, Inabel B.
  1971   The Multiple Hazards of Age and Race: The Situation of Aged Black in
           the United States. Senate Report 450, 92nd Congress, first session.
           Washington, D.C.: U.S. Government Printing Office.

Manney, James D., Jr.
  1975   Aging in American Society: An Examination of Concepts and Issues. Ann
           Arbor: The Institute of Gerontology, The University of Michigan-Wayne
           State University.

Morris, Robert
  1970   Facilities, Programs and Services. Background paper for the 1971 White
           House Conference on Aging. Washington, D.C.: U.S. Department of
           Health, Education, and Welfare, Administration on Aging.

Morris, Robert and Robert H. Binstock
  1966   Feasible Planning for Social Change. New York: Columbia University
           Press.

Nader, Ralph
  1977   "The Older American." Morning Reporter, January 3, Morgantown,
           W. Va.

Panitch, Arnold
    1974   "Advocacy in practice." Social Work 19:326.

Philibert, Michel
    1975   "Philosophies of Aging." In James Manney (ed.), Aging in American So-
             ciety: An Examination of Concepts and Issues. Ann Arbor: The Institute
             of Gerontology, The University of Michigan-Wayne State University,
             pp. 9–10.

Revis, Joseph S.
    1970   Transportation. Background paper for the 1971 White House Conference
             on Aging. Washington, D.C.: U.S. Department of Health, Education and
             Welfare, Administration on Aging.

Riley, Matilda W.
    1971   "Social gerontology and the age stratification of society." Geron-
             tologist 2:79–87.

Robbins, Ira S.
    1970   Housing the Elderly. Background paper for the 1971 White House Con-
             ference on Aging. Washington, D.C.: U.S. Department of Health, Educa-
             tion, and Welfare, Administration on Aging.

Schultz, James
    1970   Retirement. Background paper for the 1971 White House Conference on
             Aging. Washington, D.C.: U.S. Department of Health, Education, and
             Welfare, Administration on Aging.

Sobel, Irvin
    1970   Employment. Background paper for the 1971 White House Conference
             on Aging. Washington, D.C.: U.S. Department of Health, Education, and
             Welfare, Administration on Aging.

Stanford, E. Percil (ed.)
    1974   Minority Aging. San Diego, Ca.: San Diego State University Press.

Strauss, Ansel
    1973   "Chronic illness." Society 10:33.

Streib, Gordon F.
    1971   Retirement Roles and Activities. Background paper for the 1971 White
             House Conference on Aging. Washington, D.C.: U.S. Department of
             Health, Education, and Welfare, Administration on Aging.

Sudnow, David
    1967   Passing On: The Social Organization of Dying. Englewood Cliffs, N.J.:
             Prentice-Hall.

U.S. Department of Health, Education, and Welfare, Administration of Aging
    1975   Facts About Older Americans. Washington, D.C.: U.S. Government Printing Office.

Warheit, George, Roger A. Bell, and John J. Schwab
    1974   Planning for Change: Needs Assessment Approach. Washington, D.C.: The National Institute of Mental Health.

Weg, Ruth B.
    1974   "The changing physiology of aging." In James Birren and Ruth Weg (eds.), Curriculum Development in Gerontology. Los Angeles: Ethel Percy Andrus Gerontology Center, University of Southern California.

Wilson, Gertrude and Gladys Ryland
    1949   Social Group Work Practice. New York: Houghton-Mifflin.

Woodruff, Diana S. and James E. Birren
    1975   Aging, Scientific Perspectives and Social Issues. New York: Van Nostrand.

index

Boldface page numbers refer to definitions of terms.